DISCARD

D1250634

"A TOUCH OF GREATNESS"

**AMERICA'S
HISTORICALLY
BLACK COLLEGES
AND UNIVERSITIES**

AMERICA'S HISTORICALLY BLACK COLLEGES AND UNIVERSITIES series examines the varying role of these important institutions throughout the Civil Right struggle and American history as a whole.

"A TOUCH OF GREATNESS"

A History of Tennessee State University

Bobby L. Lovett

Mercer University Press
Macon, Georgia

MUP/ H870

© 2012 Mercer University Press
1400 Coleman Avenue
Macon, Georgia 31207

First Edition

Books published by Mercer University Press are printed on
acid-free paper that meets the requirements of the American
National Standard for Information Sciences—Permanence of
Paper for Printed Library Materials.

Mercer University Press is a member of Green Press
Initiative (greenpressinitiative.org), a nonprofit organization
working to help publishers and printers increase their use of
recycled paper and decrease their use of fiber derived from
endangered forests. This book is printed on recycled paper.

ISBN   978-0-88146-435-1

Cataloging-in-Publication Data is available from the Library
of Congress

With wearied hope we have been waiting the moment of our sacred
freedom.
—Alexander Pushkin

*To the generations of students, faculty, and staff members who have contributed
to the greatness of Tennessee State University, remaining loyal and dedicated to
its principles and traditions throughout the decades. I dedicate this book to
President William J. Hale, President Walter S. Davis, President Andrew P.
Torrence, President Frederick S. Humphries, President Otis F. Floyd, President
James A. Hefner, and President Melvin N. Johnson, and Interim President
Portia Shields. They, along with spouses, fellow administrators, faculty
members, and students, endured the greatest of odds to build a normal school, a
college, and then a university into a nationally and internationally recognized
research level institution of higher education.*

*I also dedicate this book to my five children, my five grandchildren, my two
brothers and my late parents and sister.*

Endowed by
TOM WATSON BROWN
and
THE WATSON-BROWN FOUNDATION, INC.

Contents

Preface

In 1869, Russian-born philosopher, writer, and social activist Leo Tolstoy wrote that, "The subject of history is the life of peoples and of humanity." He explained oppression and freedom in this way: "I sit on a man's back, choking him, and making him carry me, and yet assure myself and others that I am very sorry for him and wish to ease his lot by any means possible, except getting off his back."[1]

In the same vein, *A History of Tennessee State University* is a story about the freedom of an institution and its constituents, the saga of complex economic, political, and social forces that affected the university in a dynamic, multi-racial American society. Tennessee State University offers us a valuable history lesson because the institution reflects a microcosm of America's historically black colleges and universities [HBCUs] as they negotiated the treacherous journey from Jim Crow to the era of racial integration. Just as important, this story fits into the broader history of higher education in Tennessee, the southern United States, and the American nation. This history lesson should help readers understand and appreciate more clearly relationships between African Americans, European Americans, and other Americans regarding issues of public education and the access of American ethnic groups—especially those of African descent—to the nation's socioeconomic opportunities.

There are four persistent themes in this institutional history: First, Tennessee State University's apparent triumphant after intensively fighting against Jim Crow constraints, the insistence of racial discrimination by state officials against the institution, and a protracted mean-spirited battle over the *Geier* desegregation of higher education in Tennessee (1968–2005).

Secondly, the Tennessee State faculty and staff carrying out Herculean tasks while working under adverse conditions, often with low salaries, to usher the institution through its successful stages of history. Even though the state denied the faculty and staff adequate salaries,

---

[1] Lev Nikolayevich Tolstoy, *War and Peace* (New York: The Modern Library, 1977, 1865–69) 1101; and, see Tolstoy, *In Writings on Civil Disobedience and Violence* (1886). Tolstoy (1828–1910) believed in love, freedom, and nonviolence.

equal facilities, and resources, school personnel still carried TSU academic programs forward during difficult and turbulent times.

Thirdly, the students played crucial roles in attacking and dismantling the Jim Crow *de jure* racial segregation system in Tennessee. From 1960 onward, leaders of the student government association fought persistently for their own human and constitutional rights, but the students fought against the maltreatment of Tennessee State by black and white officials. Many leading students devoted their freedom and safety, and jeopardized their careers, to transform wrongs into right. Some of them were visionaries. Indeed between 1984 and 1994, TSU's student leaders saw the struggle to save TSU's HBCU heritage as leading the way in an unfolding national battle to save America's 105 HBCUs from being rendered obsolete and irrelevant.

Fourthly: Though state officials had held the institution by the nape of the neck behind the Jim Crow starting line, TSU student athletes outdid students at other Tennessee institutions that had privilege without restraint. Tennessee State student athletes maintained a touch of greatness in the intercollegiate sports of basketball, boxing, football, golf, swimming, softball, tennis, track and field, and volleyball. They still hold the American record for consecutive national basketball championships under the National Association of Intercollegiate Athletics. TSU student athletes have won half a dozen national titles in football, and 32 gold, silver, and bronze Olympic medals. They have won Ohio Valley Conference championships. These are just a few achievements.

The story begins with an act of the General Assembly that, on 27 April 1909, created the Agricultural and Industrial State Normal School for Negroes, along with three state normal schools for whites in each of the grand geographical divisions: East, West, and Middle Tennessee. The first president, William Jasper Hale supervised the erection of the physical plant, and recruited the faculty, staff, and the first students. They began classes on 19 June 1912. In 1922, Tennessee Agricultural and Industrial State Normal School was raised to the status of a four-year teacher's college and was empowered to grant the bachelor's degree. Eight students constituted the first college graduating class in May 1924. The institution became known as the Tennessee A&I State Normal Teachers College in 1925. The word *Normal* was dropped from the title in 1927, and in 1930, the college discontinued the preparatory and grammar school diplomas.

Tennessee A&I State Teachers College gained initial membership into the American Association of Teachers Colleges (AATC) in 1933. Tennessee A&I administrators organized the National Association of Collegiate Deans and Registrars in 1933 and became a member of the Mid-Western Athletic Conference in 1934. In 1936, the institution adopted the name Tennessee Agricultural and Industrial State College, and was reaffirmed by the AATC in 1939. In 1941, the Tennessee General Assembly authorized graduate programs "equivalent to that at the University of Tennessee for white students." The Tennessee A&I State College graduate school began in June 1942—the year the institution was a member of the Teachers College Extension Association. The institution graduated its first master's degree student in June 1944.

Tennessee A&I State College gained "A" rating from the Southern Association of Colleges and Schools (SACS) in December 1946. The State Board of Education granted university status in August 1951, approved by the General Assembly in September. In August 1958, the SBOE elevated Tennessee A&I State University to *full* land-grant status for extension, research, and teaching functions. In December 1958, SACS granted full (non-Jim Crow) accreditation/membership to Tennessee A&I State University, and so did the National Council for Accreditation of Teacher Education, the successor to the AATC.

When the state authorized the construction of a new UT-Nashville campus a few miles from TSU, a group of citizens, both black and white, filed *Rita Sanders (Geier) v. Governor Ellington* US (1968) to force state higher education to desegregate. On 18 December 1968, the SBOE approved the name Tennessee State University, and the General Assembly enabled it on 8 May 1969. On 1 July 1972, the new State Board of Regents replaced the SBOE as TSU's governing body. UT-Nashville began in 1947 as an extension center that offered two years of resident credit by 1960, three years of resident credit by 1963, and was a four-year, degree-granting evening school by 1974. In January 1977, federal district judge Frank Gray, Jr., in the *Geier* desegregation of higher education case, ordered the merger of the University of Tennessee-Nashville branch and Tennessee State University under governance of the State Board of Regents, effective 1 July 1979. The merger of a traditionally white institution with a historically black college/university caused turmoil during the next generation.

Tennessee State University ranks among the ten largest of 105 surviving HBCUs. The main campus consists of 500 acres, 65 major buildings in a residential setting, the Avon N. Williams, Jr., downtown campus, and an agricultural campus in McMinnville, Tennessee. Starting with 250 students in June 1912, by 2001 Tennessee State served 9,120 students representing 52 countries, most of Tennessee's 95 counties, and 45 of the 50 states. The university housed 3,200 of the students on campus. By 2005, TSU had 434 full-time and 167 part-time faculty members, and a diverse student body that was 75 percent black, 22 percent white, and 3 percent other, had a 45.3 percent graduation rate (1999–2005 freshmen cohort), and awarded 1,633 degrees for the year.

The 26 July 2007 *Statement of Vision, Mission, and Core Values* reads:

Tennessee State University aspires to achieve national and international prominence, building on its heritage and preparing leaders for a global society. Tennessee State University, a Historically Black College/University (HBCU), fosters scholarly inquiry and research, life-long learning, and a commitment to service. Tennessee State, an HBCU and 1890 land-grant institution, is a major state-supported urban and comprehensive university. This unique combination of characteristics differentiates the University from others and shapes its instructional, research, and service programs designed to serve Metropolitan Nashville, Middle Tennessee, the State of Tennessee, the nation, and the global community. The University is committed to maintaining its diverse student body, faculty and staff. Tennessee State University projects itself to its students, faculty, and alumni and to the citizens of the State through the motto, 'Think, Work, Serve.'[2]

By 2009–10,Tennessee State University ranked among America's top ten producers of black college graduates, had research and external funding that ranked in the top three research-level universities in the state of Tennessee, maintained more than one hundred organizations for students, had a library of more than a half million books, digital resources, periodicals, and electronic access to other libraries and archives; the institution's public service and outreach programs were extensive and impressive, and TSU maintained technology-enabled

[2] See http://www.tnstate.edu/about_tsu/ourmission.aspx, 1, a simplified and diminished version [accessed 7 September 2011]; TSU, *Statement of Vision, Mission, and Core Values*, 26 July 2007, 1.

classrooms, computer laboratories, and other core services for students. The institution had earned the label of a Carnegie Level I Doctoral Intensive Research Institution because it offered 42 bachelor's degrees, 24 master's degrees, an EdS, the EdD in three areas, DPT in physical therapy, and PhD in biological and agricultural sciences, psychology, computer and information systems engineering, and public administration. The institution had almost 100 percent of its degree programs approved/accredited by some 20 accrediting agencies. Since 1924, the institution had graduated some 80,000 students. No faculty/staff held doctoral degrees in 1912, but by 2011–12, three of four faculty and staff members held doctorate degrees.[3]

Tennessee State University has had eight presidents and four acting/interim presidents: President William J. Hale (March 1911–August 1943); President Walter S. Davis (September 1943–September 1968); an interim executive committee (December 1967–September 1968), President Andrew P. Torrence (October 1968–June 1974); Acting President Charles B. Fancher (July–December 1974), President Frederick S. Humphries (January 1975–June 1985); Acting President Roy P. Peterson (July 1985–June 1986), Acting President Otis L. Floyd (July 1986–February 1987), President Otis L. Floyd (March 1987–June 1990), Acting President George W. Cox (July 1990–April 1991), President James A. Hefner (April 1991–April 2005); President Melvin N. Johnson (May 2005–Dec. 2010); Acting President Portia Shields (January 2011–December 2012); President Glenda Baskin Glover (January 2013–).

---

[3] TSU, *Fast Facts: All About Us*, http://www.tnstate.edu/about_tsu/fast_facts.aspx [accessed 7 September 2011].

Acknowledgments

"Inasmuch as many have taken in hand to set in order a narrative of those things which have been fulfilled among us, just as those who from the beginning were eyewitnesses and ministers of the word delivered them to us, it seemed good to me also, having had perfect understanding of all things from the very first, to write to you an orderly account, most excellent Theophilus, that you may know the certainty of those things in which you were instructed." -*Luke 1: 1–4*

I started work on this history project in 2001 with encouragement from the president of Tennessee State University, James A. Hefner. The time required for such a project, considering the massive amounts of data to be researched and sifted, is always more than one imagines. Much of the computer work, writing, re-writing, and even research in libraries would have to be done in between classes, on weekends, at my home, and at night. I was able to end my twelve-year-tenure as Dean of the College of Arts and Sciences at TSU with a replacement in August 2000, and thus the stage was set to begin this project. President Hefner, my department heads, the deans of the College of Arts and Sciences, and vice presidents for Academic Affairs up to May 2011, afforded me an environment in which to complete this scholarly work.

I also thank and appreciate Sharon Hull-Smith and Loretta Divens in the Special Collections of the Brown-Daniel Memorial Library at TSU for allowing me use the collections (processed and unprocessed) and even giving me space to work in the library. With limited personnel and resources, these staff members have collected, organized, and maintained the documentation of the institution's precious history. I thank Director of Libraries, Yildez Binkley, for granting permission to use any photographs needed for the book and consistent promotion of my books. I thank the editors of the TSU *Tennessean* yearbook, *The Ayeni*, *The Bulletin*, the *Accent*, and *The Meter*. I am grateful to the Title III Program and a National Endowment for the Humanities grant for funds that also, among other project goals, assisted me in the transition from the dean's office in 2000 to a private professorial office furnished and equipped suitable for my research. I received an HBCU/Educational Testing Service fellowship, including an ETS grant that allowed me to hire a graduate assistant in 2005. And special thanks are in order for people who graciously gave interviews, information, photographs, and anecdotes, although interviews with former TSU personnel and students were minimized in this manuscript. Much of the information gleaned from interviews is corroborated with Special Collections data.

I am deeply appreciative of the following Tennessee State former faculty and staff members: Evelyn P. Fancher, "Tennessee State University (1912–1974): A History of an Institution with Implication for the Future," (PhD diss.), George Peabody College for Teachers, 1975; Raymond G. Lloyd, *Tennessee Agricultural and Industrial State University, 1912–1962* (1962); Lois C. McDougald, *A Time-Line Chronology of the Tennessee A&I State College Campus, 1909–1951: A Salute to Century III* (1981); Samuel H. Shannon, "Agricultural and Industrial Education at Tennessee State University During the Normal Phase, 1912–1922: A Case Study," (PhD diss.), George Peabody College for Teachers, 1978; Carmelia G. Taylor, "A History of Graduate Studies at Tennessee State University from 1935 to 1986," (EdD diss., Tennessee State University, 1993).

President Walter S. Davis and President James A. Hefner promoted special interest in the writing of the history of Tennessee State University. Thanks a million to TSU colleagues Joel Dark (history professor), Gloria Johnson (English and dean of liberal arts), Michelle Viera (director, alumni affairs), and James A. Hefner (president and professor of economics) for reading early versions of the manuscript, and Mercer University Press for helping to finance and perfect this book. I hope students, faculty/staff members, alumni, and the public will find this book, the history of a university, good reading and a valuable resource for local, Tennessee, and national educational history.

1909–22: Born of Jim Crow, Tennessee A&I State Normal School

Before 1904, little public higher education existed for either black or white Tennessee citizens. Since becoming a state in June 1796, Tennessee had had a slow start in funding public education compared to other American states. The 1894 Southwest Territory legislature chartered Blount College in 1794, which was rechartered as East Tennessee College in 1807, and which then evolved into the publicly funded University of Tennessee (UT) in 1904. Between 1869 and 1904, the legislature provided some land-grant funds to UT and appropriations to George Peabody College for Teachers in Nashville. A 1909 state law created Tennessee A&I State Normal School for Negroes and three other teachers' colleges for white citizens. Several of Tennessee's southern neighbors had separate public colleges for black and white citizens before this time.

Therefore, in 1909, when Tennessee A&I State Normal School was born, the state's higher education system was racially separated and slow to develop further. Until 1912, only 7 percent of white and 6 percent of black teachers had professional training, and the state was anxious to improve the quality of teaching given that in 1913, Tennessee had one of the first compulsory school attendance laws in America. Even so, by 1921, one third of Tennessee's 95 counties still did not have a senior high school. To address this shortcoming, the state appointed Perry L. Harned as Commissioner of Education in 1923, and by 1930, Tennessee had 375 four-year high schools—mostly for whites. While Public Act, chapter 43 (1941) finally mandated higher educational opportunities for Negroes equal to those provided for whites, Tennessee officials kept the higher education system *de facto* racially separate and *unequal*.[1]

Black Tennesseans had to struggle constantly for access to education, civil rights and racial equality. Free Negroes and slaves operated clandestine classes

---

[1] "The Tennessee Department of Education: Beginnings, 1835–1873," 2–4, State Department Records 1874–1984, Record Group 273, Tennessee State Library and Archives (TSLA); Cynthia G. Fleming, "A Survey of the Beginnings of Tennessee's Black Colleges and Universities, 1865–1920," *Tennessee Historical Quarterly* 39, no. 2 (Summer 1980): 195–207; US, *Negro Education, A Study of the Private and Higher Schools for Colored People in the United States*, 2 vols. (Washington DC, Bureau of Education, Department of the Interior, 1916); Paul H. Bergeron, Stephen V. Ash, and Jeanette Keith, *Tennesseans and Their History* (Knoxville: University of Tennessee Press, 1999) 38, 75, 222–24.

for their children in the years 1833–56, until white vigilantes closed them down. A handful of Free Negroes attended classes at Franklin College from 1845–62.[2] Maryville College (1831–) admitted a few Negroes, but state officials generally shut the Negro citizens out. Tennessee lacked a deep intellectual tradition relative to public schools and public colleges, and Tennessee remained under the control of two deeply anti-intellectual groups: the slavocracy (slave-owning-class) and the Confederates, until Union army occupation in 1862–63.[3]

Tennessee was allowed back into the Union in July 1866. On 28 February 1867, Congress awarded Morrill Land Grant (1862) funds to the restored state of Tennessee. Negroes enjoyed some protection because of the Thirteenth Amendment to the national Constitution that abolished slavery. There was also the congressional passage of the Civil Rights Act (1866) that granted equal protection of the laws, due process of law, and citizenship to the freedmen. In February 1867, the Republican-controlled Tennessee General Assembly granted Negroes the right to vote. Nashville reopened the public schools in September 1867 and admitted blacks on a segregated basis. But this was not the case in Tennessee's other large cities so soon after the war. On 16 January 1869, the Tennessee General Assembly assigned the federal Morrill Land Grant funds to private East Tennessee University. Tennessee law provided that "no citizens of this state otherwise qualified shall be excluded from the privileges of a land grant university." But Tennessee law in 1867 also imposed racial segregation in public schools.[4]

While on paper Negro citizens seemed to have equal rights, in reality, "black" meant citizens with limited privileges and "white" meant citizens with unlimited rights and privileges. For former slaves especially, the federal Fourteenth Amendment (1868) permanently embodied the Civil Rights Act of 1866—due process, equal protection of laws, and citizenship—and the Fifteenth Amendment (1870) guaranteed and protected Negro citizens' right to vote. However, when the pro-slavery, neo-Confederate Democratic Party regained political control of Tennessee in 1870, they wrote a new state constitution that

---

[2] Bobby L. Lovett, *The African American History of Nashville, Tennessee, 1790–1930: Elites and Dilemmas* (Fayetteville: University of Arkansas Press, 1999) 145.

[3] Bergeron, Ash, and Keith, *Tennesseans and Their History*, 222–24.

[4] Samuel H. Shannon, "Land-Grant College Legislation and Black Tennesseans: A Case Study in the Politics of Education," *History of Education Quarterly* (Summer 1982): 139–57; *Constitution of the State of Tennessee, 1870*, Article XI, Section 12; David C. Mills, "The Desegregation of Public Higher Education in Tennessee," Lovett Papers, Special Collections, TSU (unpublished undergraduate paper, University of Tennessee, n.d.) 1–26; Stanley J. Folmsbee, *Tennessee Establishes a State University: First Years of the University of Tennessee, 1879–1887* (Knoxville: University of Tennessee, 1961) 36.

provided for a poll tax, which would eventually disenfranchise most black voters too poor to pay the tax.

Despite colossal odds, between 1872 and 1896, some fourteen black men gained election to the Tennessee General Assembly.[5] These Negro legislators protested that Tennessee officials continued to provide no money for the higher education of Negro citizens. Some of the Negro legislators pushed the General Assembly to grant at least a few scholarships from Tennessee's share of the federal Morrill land-grant funds to Negro applicants, who could use the money to attend one of the state's private HBCUs. In August 1881, the state finally allowed $30-per-year scholarships for ten "colored youths."[6] In February 1883, black legislator Samuel Allen McElwee said the money spent on thirty Negro student recipients amounted to nothing compared to the $390,000 Morrill funds received by whites. The state received additional funds from the federal Hatch Act (1887) for agricultural experimental stations, but none of the money was spent on black education.[7]

Upon congressional passage of the Morrill Land Grant Amendment (1890), the federal government allowed states to establish and maintain separate colleges for white and colored students. The University of Tennessee gave some of the Morrill funds to Knoxville College—a private HBCU operated by white, Northern Presbyterians. Knoxville College established an agriculture department in the name of the University of Tennessee in 1891. The University of Tennessee received $67,640 in federal land-grant funds and gave $3,526.64 (5.2 percent) to Knoxville College under the pretense of providing access to higher education for Negro citizens, who comprised 26 percent of Tennessee's population. Knoxville College put the Negro Morrill scholarship students into farming and manual labor courses and called this arrangement the Industrial College for Colored Students. Finally, the US Supreme Court in *Plessy v. Ferguson*, 163 U.S.537 (1896) sanctioned "separate but equal" education.[8]

---

[5] Mingo Scott, Jr., *The Negro in Tennessee Politics and Governmental Affairs, 1865–1965* (Nashville: Rich Printing, 1965) 1–352; James C. Napier, "Some Members of the Tennessee General Assembly during the Reconstruction and After," *Journal of Negro History* 5, no. 1 (January 1920): 115–17.

[6] William J. Simmons, "Samuel A. McElwee," *Men of Mark, Eminent, and Rising* (Cleveland OH: Rewell Co., 1887) 498–505; Shannon, "Land-Grant College Legislation," 141; Linda T. Wynn, "Samuel A. McElwee (1857–1914)," Bobby L. Lovett and Linda T. Wynn, eds., *Profiles of African Americans in Tennessee* (Nashville: Local Conference on African American Culture and History, 1996) 85–87.

[7] Shannon, "Land-Grant College Legislation," 141; *Plessy* was overturned by *Brown v. Board of Education*, 347 US 483 (1954).

[8] Mills, "The Desegregation of Public Higher Education in Tennessee," 6–7. Note: the *Plessy* principle of "separate but equal" was declared unconstitutional in May 1954.

Reform and Expansion of Higher Education

Meanwhile, America experienced a movement to reform and expand higher education. Beginning in 1880, the number of high schools across the nation increased from 800 to 5,500, and the number of high school graduates tripled. Because of the Morrill act of 1862, the Morrill amendment of 1890, and the 1896 *Plessy* approval of "separate but equal" for the races, by 1899 most Jim Crow states began establishing the first land-grant Negro public institutions. By 1948, there would be 17 HBCU land-grant institutions, and these institutions generally were not allowed equitable portions of their state's federal land-grant funds. But, in 1900, there were 28,560 Negro teachers and 1.5 million Negro children in America's schools, or one teacher for every 52.5 students. Only about 2,000 Negroes had graduated from institutions of higher learning, and 700 blacks currently were attending colleges.[9]

Around 1900, Northern philanthropists began holding joint education reform conferences with Southern leaders, trying to find ways to move the poverty-stricken region into the twentieth century, especially in regards to public and private elementary, secondary, and higher education. These men were concerned about education for the Southern whites but also for the Negroes that comprised a substantial part of the population in the southern United States. Philanthropic agencies such as the General Education Fund, George Peabody Fund, Julius Rosenwald Fund, Anna T. Jeanes Fund, John Slater Fund, and the Southern Education Board began to finance the reform of Southern education. Northern philanthropists provided much of the funding needed to build Tennessee Agricultural & Industrial State College for black citizens.[10] While helping improve Southern, white education, Northern agencies pushed Southern states to increase Negro access to public schools. This caused Tennessee and other Southern states to begin a Negro division in their state departments of education. Tennessee education agent S.L. Smith wrote "There is not a single four-year high school for Negroes in Tennessee—either in the city or county

---

[9] Shannon, "Land-Grant College Legislation," 145; Note: Alcorn College (1871) was the first among Negro land-grant colleges; Josephine M. Posey, *Against Great Odds: The History of Alcorn State University* (Jackson: University Press of Mississippi, 1994).

[10] "The Tennessee Department of Education: Beginnings, 1835–1873," State Department of Education Records, 1874–1984, Record Group 273, Tennessee State Library and Archives (TSLA), 2–4; Cynthia G. Fleming, "A Survey of the Beginnings of Tennessee's Black Colleges and Universities, 1865–1920," *Tennessee Historical Quarterly* 39, no. 2 (Summer 1980): 195–207; US Bureau of Education, *Negro Education, a Study of the Private and Higher Schools for Colored People in the United States*, 2 vols. (Washington DC: Bureau of Education, Department of the Interior, 1916).

system—and a very limited number of two-year high schools in the cities—none approved or accredited by any rating agency."[11]

University of Tennessee professor Philander P. Claxton, among others, launched an education reform movement in Tennessee in 1902. At that time, some 14 percent of adult whites and 22 percent of blacks still were illiterate in Tennessee. A quarter of Tennessee voters could not read the ballots, even if they could afford to pay the poll tax. Claxton headed the Summer School of the South that invited thousands of teachers from across the region to Knoxville to discuss educational conditions in the South. No blacks were invited, even though the program was funded by the General Education Board of New York and John D. Rockefeller, the wealthy Northern industrialist and oil magnate. But Northern philanthropists were careful not to turn the white, Southern education reformers off by advocating racial equality.[12]

Additionally, by the turn of the twentieth century, Tennessee continued to suffer the socially retrogressive leadership of former Confederates, neo-Confederates and remnants of the old slavocracy. Most of these people opposed any education at all for Negroes. Former slave owner and Confederate Tennessee Governor Isham G. Harris returned from exile in Mexico in 1867, won the Tennessee US Senate seat in 1877, occupied that seat until his death in 1897, and always opposed any state or national legislation that would help former slaves and their descendants. But Nashville, the state capital, called the "Athens of the South," seemed educationally progressive, with several institutions of higher learning including Vanderbilt University and George Peabody Normal College. The two institutions benefited from Northern philanthropic funds, and the city, Davidson County, and the state appropriated money to Peabody College. In 1907, Governor John Isaac Cox (D) approved of such state appropriations and also recommended "at least $300,000 per annum to pension the old soldiers and … at least $60,000 per annum for the purpose of giving pensions to the deserving widows of the old soldiers [who rebelled against the U.S.]."[13] But Governor Cox—even though the state budget had a surplus, did not recommend any

---

[11] Wali Rashash Kharif and William L. Montel, *Reminisces and Reflections: African Americans in the Kentucky-Tennessee Upper Cumberland since the Civil War* (London KY: Janze Publications, 2005) 168.

[12] Robert E. Corlew, *Tennessee: A Short History*, 2nd ed. (Knoxville: University of Tennessee Press, 1981) 526, 527, 533; Paul H. Bergeron, Stephen V. Ash, and Jeanette Keith, *Tennesseans and Their History* (Knoxville: University of Tennessee Press, 1999) 223–24; note: Claxton visited Tennessee A&I to speak to summer session teachers in 1916.

[13] John I. Cox, "Legislative message," 7 January 1907, *Messages of the Governors of Tennessee, 1899–1907*, vol. 8, ed. Robert H. White (Nashville: Tennessee Historical Commission, 1972) 361–62, 367.

money for pensions for ex-slaves or any money to aid the education of the slaves' descendants who, too, were citizens of Tennessee.[14]

Indubitably, Tennessee officials remained steadfast in denying any equal public benefits to former slaves and their descendants. *Berea College v. Kentucky*, 211 US 45 (1908) said states could require racial segregation in private colleges. Berea College then started Lincoln Institute (1909–55) near Louisville, Kentucky, in order to accommodate the displaced black students. Tennessee had a stiff fine since 1901 and because of the *Berea* decision Maryville College had to expel black students. Maryville College used 25 percent of its endowment to sustain her black students at Swift Memorial College—a two-year HBCU.[15]

Quest for Black Public Higher Education in Tennessee

By 1909, fourteen private HBCUs remained in Tennessee: Academy of Athens, Bristol Normal Institute, Howe Bible and Normal Institute (Memphis), LeMoyne Normal Institute (Memphis), Fisk University, Greeneville Industrial College, Knoxville College, Lane College (Jackson), Meharry Medical College, Morristown College, Swift Memorial College (Rogersville), Turner Normal College (Shelbyville), Walden University, and Warner Institute (Jonesborough). These HBCUs enrolled 5,592 students, but only four of them developed a four-year college program.[16]

Finally, in 1907, education reformers introduced a bill in the Tennessee General Assembly to establish public normal (teacher-training) schools in each of Tennessee's three geographical divisions (East, West, and Middle), and that bill,

---

[14] Mary Frances Berry, *My Face is Black is True: Callie House and the Struggle for Ex-Slave Reparations* (New York: Knopf, 2005) 14–19, 42–3; Cox, legislative message, 7 January 1907, 361–62, 367. Note: Governor Cox's mother applied for a Confederate widow's pension in 1909.

[15] Bobby L. Lovett, *America's Historically Black Colleges and Universities: A Narrative History from 1837 to 2010* (Macon GA: Mercer University Press, 2011) 10, 43, 46, 47; Linda T. Wynn, "Swift Memorial College (1883–1955)," *Profiles of African Americans in Tennessee*, 118–119; Carroll Van West, "Maryville College," *The Tennessee Encyclopedia of History and Culture* (Nashville: Rutledge Hill Press, 1998) 576–77. Merl R. Eppse served as dean at Swift Memorial College in 1927–28 before joining the faculty at Tennessee A&I State Teachers College in 1928. Sharon G. Hall, "Merl R. Eppse, 1893–1967: Life and Work based upon an Investigation of Selected Papers" (master's thesis, Tennessee State University, December 1983); "Dr. M.R. Eppse, noted educator, rites Friday," Nashville *Banner*, 23 December 1967.

[16] Lovett, *America's Historically Black Colleges and Universities*, 206; Darlene C. Hine, William C. Hine, and Stanley Harrold, *African Americans: A Concise History*, 2nd ed. (Upper Saddle River NJ: Pearson/Prentice Hall, 2004) 135–36, 139, 140–41, 233–36, 92–93; John H. Franklin and Alfred A. Moss, Jr., *From Slavery to Freedom: A History of Negro Americans*, 6th ed. (New York: Knopf, 1988) 239–44.

too, included nothing for black citizens. The bill failed;[17] however, in 1907, Tennessee adopted its first public college by assuming responsibility for the private University of Tennessee.[18] When the normal school bill was revived in 1909, Negro leaders in Nashville petitioned the General Assembly to include a public Negro state college. The State Superintendent of Public Instruction R.L. Jones called for normal school legislation to include a Negro school but assured Governor Malcolm R. Patterson (D)—a native of Alabama and son of a Confederate veteran—that the Negro school would not be like the existing Negro colleges that prepared Negro students to be no more than "discontented propagators."[19]

Superintendent Jones appeared to be speaking about 1888 Fisk graduate William E.B. Du Bois, a Harvard University PhD and one of two blacks on the Atlanta University faculty. Du Bois had published *The Souls of Black Folk* (1903) that called for Negroes to be treated equally and for black colleges to become real colleges: "The function of the university is not simply to teach bread-winning, or to furnish teachers for the public schools, or to be a centre of polite society; it is, above all, to be the organ of that fine adjustment between real life and the growing knowledge of life, an adjustment which forms the secret of civilization. Such an institution the South of to-day sorely needs."[20] Du Bois co-founded the Niagara Movement that met in 1907 at the HBCU Storer College on the Harper's Ferry, West Virginia, site of John Brown's 1859 raid to free the slaves. Du Bois and the delegates issued a militant manifesto demanding total racial equality.[21]

Tennessee's Negro leaders dared to use militancy to push for a publicly funded state normal school for Negroes. Jim Crow (racial segregation) practices, white mob violence, and changes in voting policies—including the poll tax—had

---

[17] Bergeron, et al., *Tennesseans and Their History*, 223–24.

[18] "Negro education," Nashville *Globe*, 18, 25 January 1907, 1; Cox, legislative message, 7 January 1907, 363; Shannon, "Land-Grant College Legislation," 147; Milton M. Klein, "University of Tennessee," *Tennessee Encyclopedia*, 1010–12.

[19] Tennessee, *Appendix to the Senate and House Journals of the 56th General Assembly* (Nashville: General Assembly, 1909) 1–141; Alrutheus A. Taylor, *The Negro in Tennessee, 1865–1880* (Washington DC: Associated Negro Universities Press, 1941) 298; Raymond Lloyd, *Tennessee Agricultural and Industrial State University, 1912–1962* (Nashville: Tennessee A&I, 1962) 5; *Acts of Tennessee* (Nashville: Tennessee General Assembly, 1909) chapter 264, section 7; Lester C. Lamon, *Black Tennesseans, 1900–1920* (Knoxville: University of Tennessee Press, 1977) 97; "State Normal," Nashville *Globe*, 12 March 1909, 1; correspondence, box 1, Governor Malcolm R. Patterson (1861–1935) 1907–11 Papers, GP35, TSLA, Nashville.

[20] W.E.B. Du Bois, *The Souls of Black Folk* (New York: Penguin, 1903, 1989) 70.

[21] *Acts of Tennessee*, 1909, chapter 264, section 7; Lamon, *Black Tennesseans*, 22, 24, 41, 60, 64, 86, 93, 97; "State Normal," Nashville *Globe*, 12 March 1909, 1; Du Bois, *Souls of Black Folk*, 62–76.

pushed the last of the Negro state representatives out of the General Assembly. Jessie M.H. Graham of Clarksville won election to the General Assembly in 1896, but in January 1897 fellow legislators expelled him and installed a white man.[22] The all-white, male sponsors of the normal school bill confidently inserted the words Agricultural and Industrial into the Negro normal school title without debate. Industrial was a step below the word Mechanical (engineering). They decided the courses of study should be of such practical nature as to fit the conditions and needs of the [Negro] race. The normal school bill passed on 27 April 1909.[23]

Negro leaders in Chattanooga, Memphis, and Nashville intended to bid on the location of the Negro normal school. William Jasper Hale, a Chattanooga school principal, headed a drive to raise $71,000 in pledges to attract the Negro school to Chattanooga. In west Tennessee, where 70 percent of black Tennesseans lived, oppressive politics and black poverty had obstructed efforts to locate the Negro school in Memphis. Whites had rioted against the blacks and had lynched many of them in 1866 and 1892. Private Baptist HBCUs Howe Institute and LeMoyne College existed in Memphis, and Knoxville blacks seemed content with Knoxville College.[24]

The A&I Founders

Nashville-Davidson County had three private HBCUs, but the Negro leaders Henry Allen Boyd, James C. Napier, Richard H. Boyd, Benjamin Carr, Preston Taylor, and others formed the Colored Normal School Association to lobby state officials to locate the state normal school in Nashville. These men were leaders of the Davidson County Negro Republican Club and members of the National Negro Business League Nashville chapter, formed in 1903. They were disciples of Booker T. Washington's conservative racial philosophy and his emphasis on industrial, manual labor education for the black masses. In 1909,

---

[22] Tennessee Caucus of Black State Legislators, *Directory of Tennessee African American Legislators, 1873–1991* (Nashville: General Assembly, 1991) 1–52. Note: Until 1964, no blacks again served in the Tennessee General Assembly. Robert M. McBride and Dan M. Robinson, *Biographical Directory, Tennessee General Assembly, 1861–1901* (Nashville: TSLA and Tennessee Historical Commission, 1979) 239, 676.

[23] Tennessee, *Biennial Report of the State Superintendent of Public Instruction for Tennessee for the Scholastic Year Ending June 30, 1910* (Nashville: SBOE, 1910) 45; *Acts of Tennessee,* 1909, chapter 264, section 7; Lamon, *Black Tennesseans,* 22, 24, 41, 60, 64, 86, 88, 93, 97; "State Normal," Nashville *Globe,* 12 March 1909, 1.

[24] Robert J. Booker, *Two Hundred Years of Black Culture in Knoxville, Tennessee, 1791– 1991* (Virginia Beach VA: Donning, 1993) 1–192; Robert J. Booker, *And There was Light! The 120-year History of Knoxville College, Knoxville, Tennessee 1875–1995* (Virginia Beach VA: Donning, 1994) 27, 72.

they sponsored a statewide railroad tour for Booker T. Washington to speak from Bristol to Memphis. When Nashville's white leaders operated a booster campaign (1890–1915) and a Nashville Board of Trade to improve the city, attract new businesses and be a part of America's Progressive Reform Movement, the local black leaders organized a Negro Board of Trade and supported the white leadership's progressive movement. Black Nashville had two Negro banks, a line of businesses on Cedar and Jefferson streets, the second-largest Negro community in Tennessee, and a prosperous and educated black elite-class.[25]

Henry Allen Boyd (1876–1959) was born in Texas, educated in the local schools and at a freedman's college, and worked as San Antonio's first Negro postal clerk until moving to Nashville around 1900 to assist his father, Richard Henry Boyd (1843–1922). R.H. Boyd was born a slave in Mississippi and raised in Texas. He became a minister in 1869 and attended Bishop College for a short time in the 1880s. R.H. Boyd arrived in Nashville in November 1896 and established the National Baptist Publishing Board. He later helped to establish the National Negro Doll Company, One Cent Savings Bank, National Baptist Church Supply Company, Globe Publishing Company, and the Union Transportation Company. His son, H. Allen Boyd, used the clout of the Nashville *Globe* (1905–60) to advance the cause for a Negro state college. R.H. Boyd and others had formed the Globe Publishing Company to support the Negro streetcar strike and protest against Jim Crow cars in 1905–07. The revenue from their businesses allowed the Boyd family seemingly invulnerability to help lead local black progressive movements.[26]

James C. Napier (1845–1940) was born a slave in Dickson County. Through the will and testament of his grandfather, the white owner of an iron-making plantation, this slave family was freed in 1848 and allowed to relocate to Ohio. In 1850, because of hard times and racial disturbances in Ohio, James Napier's mulatto father, William Carroll Napier (1824–95), brought the family back to Nashville. James attended Wilberforce University (1859–61) finishing school. He later attended Oberlin College for two years, earning his law degree at Howard University in 1872, and won election to the Nashville city council (1878–85). He served on the executive committee of the Tennessee Republican Party, and in

---

[25] "Negro school," Nashville *Globe*, 11, 18, 25 January 1907, and 5 November 1909; Samuel H. Shannon, "Agricultural and Industrial Education at Tennessee State University during the Normal School Phase, 1912–22: a Case Study," (PhD diss., George Peabody College for Teachers, 1974).

[26] Bobby L. Lovett, *How It Came to Be: The Boyd Family's Contribution to African American Religious Publishing from the 19th to the 21st Century* (Nashville: Mega Publishing, 2007) 78, 98; Samuel H. Shannon, "Tennessee," in *The Black Press in the South, 1865–1979*, ed. Henry L. Suggs (Westport CT: Greenwood Press, 1983) 314–54; Larry Elkins, "Richard Henry Boyd: A Portrait, 1843–1922" (master's thesis, Tennessee State University, 1972).

1898 became the first black Tennessean to campaign for a seat in Congress. In March 1911, President William H. Taft (R) and Congress would approve Napier as US Register of the Treasury in charge of printing and distributing currency.[27]

Preston Taylor (1849–1931) was born a slave in Louisiana and served in the US Colored Troops regiments in the Union army during the Civil War. He moved to Kentucky as a contractor and builder of railroad lines. A self-taught man, Taylor moved to Nashville in 1884–85 to pastor the Gay Street Colored Christian (Disciples of Christ) Church. He became owner of Taylor Funeral Home in 1889, the Greenwood Cemetery, the Greenwood Recreational Park in 1905, co-founder of the Union Transportation Company 1907 and chairman of the One Cent Savings Bank (Citizens Bank) in 1904.[28]

Benjamin F. Carr (1862–1930?) became a confidante to Governor Malcolm Patterson (R). Before migrating to Nashville, he demonstrated leadership skills in the Populist Movement's Colored Farmers' Alliance and reportedly persuaded officials to start the first Negro high school in his hometown of Hartsville. Carr was born in 1862 to a slave woman on her master's farm and didn't attend school until age 20. After working for $30 a year, he saved $75, borrowed $25 from a local white man and bought land. He then borrowed two mules and a cow from local whites and made enough to pay his debts and become prosperous. He took off work to attend the local school to learn to read and write. Carr owned a farm of four hundred acres, fine pastures, and good orchards, a two-story seven-room house, two tenant houses, barns, and farm animals. The family spent the winter in their Nashville home so the children could attend Fisk. He briefly attended Roger Williams University. Carr spoke at Washington's National Business League meeting in 1909 in Louisville, where he admitted being handicapped because a lack of the proper literary training, but he believed in further education for himself and his children. Ben Carr gained unbelievable influence and open access to white public officials, Democrats and Republicans, advising them on Negro problems. The whites admired Carr's country demeanor and Booker T. Washington-like conservative attitude on race relations. Local Negroes heard of his power soon after Carr arrived in Nashville. When whites got a bill passed

---

[27] Herbert L. Clark, "The Public Career of James Carroll Napier: Businessman, Politician, and Crusader for Racial Justice, 1845–1940" (PhD diss., Middle Tennessee State University, 1980) 1–91; Bobby L. Lovett, "James Carroll Napier (1845–1940): From Plantation to the City," in *The Southern Elite and Social Change: Essays in Honor of Willard B. Gatewood Jr.*, eds. Randy Finley and Thomas A. DeBlack (Fayetteville: University of Arkansas Press, 2002) 73–94.

[28] Lovett and Wynn, *Profiles of Americans in Tennessee*, 17, 18, 94, 118; Lovett, *How It Came to Be*, 48–50, 63, 64, 77, 78; Bobby L. Lovett, *A Black Man's Dream: The First One Hundred Years, the Story of R.H. Boyd and the National Baptist Publishing Board* (Nashville: Mega Publishing, 1993) 1–25; William J. Simmons, "Preston Taylor," *Men of Mark*, 296–301.

through the General Assembly to shut down any amusement park near a cemetery, Preston Taylor rushed to the governor's office only to be asked if he had talked to Ben Carr. Taylor consulted with Carr. The governor vetoed the anti-Greenwood Park bill.[29]

These influential black men agreed to associate with other local leaders to gain the state normal school for Nashville-Davidson County. The Boyd *Globe* newspaper, with a circulation of about 20,000 subscribers and readers, and the Colored Normal School Association called community meetings in the Odd Fellows Hall on Thursday nights. Ordinary Negro citizens agreed to raise money to match the county bonds. They held meetings in Preston Taylor's offices on Fourth Avenue North. On 18 March 1910, they decided on a house-to-house canvassing campaign to raise more money.[30]

They held a mass meeting at the Ryman Auditorium on Easter Sunday, the same day that the Rev. W.S. Ellington of First Colored Baptist Church of East Nashville held his annual "Prodigal Son" sermon that attracted thousands of persons to the Ryman. Ellington was a Fisk University graduate and editor of Sunday school materials at the Boyd-operated NBPB. Businessman T. Clay Moore, a rare black Democrat, also helped bolster local funding efforts. They raised $20,000 in funds in the door-to-door canvass. Negroes comprised about a quarter of the city of Nashville.[31]

When making the presentation before the Davidson County Quarterly Court to ask for $60,000 in bonds, the Colored Normal School Association representatives assured local officials that the Negro school would be like Booker T. Washington's Tuskegee Institute that emphasized manual labor, industrial arts, domestic science, and other non-threatening subjects. Tuskegee, in Alabama where local whites at first opposed Washington's school, did not offer college degrees until 1921. Tennessee A&I founders did not mention liberal arts curricula that would produce scholars, doctors, lawyers, engineers, and college graduates such as Du Bois. Carr said Tennessee A&I State Normal School would train women who know how to cook and launder; agricultural training and farming would be a paramount focus. Napier said the school would reduce the Negro criminal element and produce better Negro citizens. Henry Boyd said Negro businesses needed mechanics, printers, and persons trained in manual, industrial and clerical work:

> There will be but one Negro state college in Tennessee for the next one hundred years, and if this school is located in the center of the state, there His

---

[29] Lovett, *African American History of Nashville*, 124, 170; Lamon, *Black Tennesseans*, 101–03; "Carr," Nashville *Globe*, 5 June 1912, 9 May 1913, 1; Timothy P. Ezzell, "Malcolm R. Patterson (1861–1935)," *Tennessee Encyclopedia of History and Culture*, 725.

[30] H.A. Boyd, "State Normal," Nashville *Globe*, 31 December 1909, 1.

[31] Lovett, *African American History of Nashville*, 98, 227, 230.

Excellency, the Governor, members of the State Senate, members of the Lower House, the State Education Board, and this County Court can see the property almost any day by just the mere payment of the street car fare. It will be one of the greatest educational institutions in the whole South for Negroes. We constitute nearly one-fourth of the population of the city. We have been deprived of the first [1862] and second [1890] Morrill Fund, the Slater Fund and several other philanthropic foundation assistance that should have come to us ... and now I appeal to you gentlemen to look twenty-five years ahead and make for a worthy people a gift that will go down to the credit of the county, the city and the state in after years. We want to go out in Davidson County and build you a Tuskegee.[32]

The Davidson County government voted 31 to 13 to appropriate $60,000 in 4.5 percent bonds to help establish the Negro state school in Nashville. Carr engineered a meeting with members of the General Assembly. Henry Allen Boyd made the presentation to Governor Patterson, a supporter of the ongoing education reform movement in Tennessee. The mayor of Nashville met with the governor about the proposed school.[33]

During its 9–13 January 1911, meeting, the State Board of Education (SBOE) awarded the Negro normal school to Nashville-Davidson County. The Davidson County government promised another $20,000 in bonds on 10 February 1911, by a vote of 24 to 18, even though the voters of Davidson County did not approve the bond issues for the black school. Elsewhere, the fundraising process was underway for the white schools: Middle Tennessee State Normal School, Murfreesboro (1911–), East Tennessee State Normal School (1911–) in Johnson City, and West Tennessee State Normal School in Memphis (1912–). Students had to be at least age sixteen and have completed elementary school.[34]

W.J. Hale and the Opening of Tennessee A&I

The first task was to select an educator to head Tennessee A&I State Normal School for Negroes, plan the facilities, hire a faculty, develop the curriculum, and recruit the students. The *Globe* reported that William J. Hale, the

---

[32] Shannon, "Land-Grant College Legislation," 148–150; Willard B. Gatewood, *Aristocrats of Color: The Black Elite, 1880–1920* (Fayetteville: University of Arkansas Press, 2000) 90–91, 242, 315.

[33] "Negro school," Nashville *Globe*, 8 April 1910, 1; "Negro school," Nashville *Banner*, 5 April 1910, 2.

[34] Don Good, *East Tennessee State University* (Charleston SC: Arcadia, 2010) 8–9; Frank B. Williams, Jr., "East Tennessee State University," C. Van West, "Middle Tennessee State University," and James R. Chumney, "University of Memphis," *Tennessee Encyclopedia of History and Culture*, 273–74, 621–22, 1009–10; Samuel H. Shannon, "Slow Birth in White and Black: Tennessee's State Colleges in the Formative Years," *Border States*, 4, no. 1 (1983): 28–40.

new president, had been in town the previous weekend. The reporter said that Hale skillfully evaded an interview, but that some of those in the know said he was there to visit with the board that had selected him at the January meeting. The State Superintendent formerly supervised the schools in Hamilton County, where Hale worked, and there were rumors that Hale was the man's relative.[35] State officials sent Hale to visit Hampton Institute and Tuskegee Institute. In March 1911, the board formally announced William Jasper Hale as the school's principal [president].[36]

William Jasper Hale (1873–1944) was born on September 26 in Marion County, and educated in Hamilton County. He was the oldest child in a poor family of four boys and two girls, most of whom were half-siblings, and was named for the town of Jasper. In skin color and facial features he favored his mother, Gene Hale. As a lad, Hale worked many jobs including the coke ovens in Soddy. After working menial jobs in Dayton, Hale earned enough money to attend the biracial Maryville College—a Presbyterian school—for several terms, where he was particularly good in mathematics. Hale taught school in Coulterville for $6 a month, in Retro for $25 a month, and became principal of the St. Elmo School near Chattanooga. He then became the principal of the Fifth Street Grammar School in Chattanooga, Hamilton County.[37]

Carr, Taylor, and Boyd called on the governor about the school's proposed site on a former Civil War fort, a rocky hill that was 33 acres of a farm on the Cumberland River. They suggested several acres of adjoining farmland be purchased to support the school. The *Globe* (31 March 1911) reported Carr as having a great feeling of political triumph, proudly escorting Governor Ben Hooper (R) to the proposed site on rural Centennial Boulevard. The state purchased the land and its three houses by May 5, 1911. Governor Patterson (D) had withdrawn as a third term candidate for governor. Thus with the support of prohibitionist Democrats, Republicans, and black voters, Ben Hooper (R)—a supporter of improved education—became the new governor.[38]

---

[35] Arthur V. Haynes, *Scars of Segregation: An Autobiography* (New York: Vantage Press, 1974) 87. Note: Haynes attended Tennessee A&I State Teachers College.

[36] "State Normal," Nashville *Globe*, 14 February 1911, 1.

[37] Bobby L. Lovett, *The African American History of Nashville, Tennessee, 1780–1930: Elites and Dilemmas* (Fayetteville: University of Arkansas Press, 1999) 101, 169–71, 252; Lovett and Wynn, *Profiles of African Americans in Tennessee*, 57.

[38] Paul E. Isaac, "The Problems of a Republican Governor in a Southern State: Ben Hooper of Tennessee, 1910–1914," *Tennessee Historical Quarterly* 27, no. 1 (January 1968): 229–48; William J. Hale, Tennessee Agricultural and Industrial State Normal School, Nashville, box 3, folder 2, 1911, Governor Ben W. Hooper (1870–1957) Papers, GP 36, TSLA, Nashville.

Carr and other local Negro leaders, who by now were fusing with white politicians regardless of party affiliation to advance the Negro's agenda, convinced another political ally, Nashville's Mayor Hilary Howse (D), to support a city ordinance to buy the remainder of an old plantation property at the end of Jefferson Street (where Centennial Boulevard began) to be made into Hadley Park for Negroes. In the city election of 1911, Howse had promised improved city services, fair police treatment, and convenient polling places for the Negro community. Solomon Parker Harris, a Negro lawyer and employee at Boyd's National Baptist Publishing Board, won election to the city council—the first Negro in the council since James C. Napier had served there in 1886. Nashville was developing a city park system as many other cities were doing in the Progressive Movement. Mayor Howse included Hadley Park in the city's plans.[39]

The site for Tennessee A&I State Normal School was near 35th Avenue North and Centennial Boulevard, just a mile west of Fisk University and near Hadley Park. According to the last slave census (1860), this area below Cockrill Bend was a large fertile plain on the southern banks of the Cumberland River. During the Civil War, Jefferson Street served as the northern boundary of Nashville, and Union army fortification Fort Gillem built partly with black laborers occupied the site of present-day Fisk University. Another gun emplacement on Zollicoffer Hill (the site of today's TSU) protected the bend of the Cumberland. Jefferson Pike (Street) headed west and dead-ended at Mrs. Elizabeth Harding's home, which rested in that Cumberland basin southeast of downtown Nashville. Further up the river, just west of today's Tennessee State campus, W.E. Watkins's place once held dozens of slaves off Charlotte Pike. His mulatto slave daughter Jane Elizabeth Watkins Napier was the mother of James C. Napier.

Thus the area around the future site for the Negro state normal school was historic. The US Census of 1870 for District 13 included 49.6 percent black population. In 1871, Fisk University began building Jubilee Hall in District 13 at Jefferson and Salem Streets (18th Ave. North). In September 1873, Frederick Douglass arrived to speak in Nashville at the Annual Tennessee Colored Agricultural and Industrial Fair. He visited and spoke to the students at the Fisk campus on Church Street before traveling by carriage north to the Jubilee Hall construction site. Douglass and his host, a local white Republican, then turned west down Jefferson Pike to have dinner [site of the future Hadley Park] with a white landowner, who asked Douglass to speak to former slaves. Fisk completed Jubilee Hall in 1874 and moved to there the following January.[40]

---

[39] Nashville *Globe*, 3 February, 29 September 1911, 1.

[40] US Census, 1870 (Washington DC: General Printing Office, 1870) Tennessee tables; plat maps for Davidson County, 1870, Metro Nashville Library, Nashville Room; Bobby L.

With news that State Normal School would be built in this historic area, banks, realtors, and Negro entrepreneurs began buying lots there. Since the advent of electric streetcars in Nashville in 1887, the white middle and upper classes had been creating their streetcar suburbs. The rise in prices of rural land forced the breakup of the large plantations. Thus, impoverished rural Negroes, former slaves and their children moved into cheap inner city rental properties. Nashville's black population rose from 25 percent in 1860 to 40 percent in 1890. Realtors began dividing the area around Jefferson Street in 1890–1910. But the streetcars did not extend westward past Fisk University. Civil District 13 remained heavily black and rural, although many white homes and the old plantation houses—some of them abandoned or rented out—remained scattered in the area. Meharry Medical College moved from its south Nashville campus to a new campus on the west boundary of Fisk University in 1931. As late as 1945, many former slaves resided in the Fisk-Meharry-Tennessee A&I area—the principal black neighborhood.

Meanwhile, in 1911, Henry Allen Boyd and James C. Napier worked on the state officials and the land-grant issue to gain for the infant Tennessee A&I State Normal School for Negroes some of the annual federal appropriation then given entirely to the University of Tennessee. They insulated President Hale from this controversial problem. Again, neither Boyd nor Napier depended on whites for making a living. In 1911, UT received $68,960 in federal Morrill funds through the State of Tennessee and gave Knoxville College $10,350 (15 percent) for Tennessee's 21.7 percent Negro population. On 6 July 1911, the General Assembly approved Tennessee A&I State Normal School to receive funds based upon "the scholastic population of Negro children and the scholastic population of white children, giving each race its just and equitable proportion of the fund received annually by the State of Tennessee."[41]

President William H. Taft (R) in his inauguration speech (4 March 1909) had said, "The Negroes are now Americans. Their ancestors came here years ago against their will, and this is their only country and their only flag.... We should have our profound sympathy and aid in the struggle they are making. We are

---

Lovett, "What's in a Name? Hadley Park" (unpublished paper) Lovett Papers, Special Collections, TSU. Note: Clare Avenue near 28th Avenue North is one block on the south side of today's Hadley Park. Frederick Douglass to the Hon. Gerritt Smith, Washington DC, 25 September 1873, *Frederick Douglass: Selected Speeches and Writings*, ed. Philip S. Foner (Chicago: Lawrence Hill Books, 1975) 615; Lovett, *African American History of Nashville*, 69–70, 126, 231.

[41] Letters, 23 January 1912, Washington, DC, James C. Napier Papers, 1845–1940, Fisk University, Special Collections. Note: State officials did not always follow the guideline.

charged with the sacred duty of making their path as smooth and easy as we can."[42] His words hardly convinced Tennessee officials to be racially equitable.

In a letter to President Taft, James C. Napier, the US Register of the Treasury, protested that Tennessee officials had denied black citizens any benefits from the Hatch Act (1887) federal funds. On 23 January 1912, Napier testified to the Agriculture and Forest Committee of the US House of Representatives that Negro youth had no access to the agricultural experiment stations in Tennessee: "I personally found no Negro at Knoxville College that considered themselves a part of the University of Tennessee ... We [Negroes] never have gotten a full portion of it [the Morrill funds]."[43] Years later when the federal government granted Tennessee federal funds under the Smith-Lever Act for extension activities, the University of Tennessee got $639,496.31 in 1914 and Tennessee A&I State Normal School received $2,000 (0.3 percent).[44]

Hale busied himself with construction projects. Moses McKissack, III, the only Negro architect in Tennessee, placed third in the bidding. White firms intended to construct the buildings at a much cheaper price; indeed, the resulting original facilities lasted only thirty years. Hale carried out one-man tasks: supervising construction, managing a tight budget, ordering supplies and furnishings, and traveling to recruit teachers and students.[45]

At last, in late May 1912, Tennessee A&I State Normal School was almost ready to open its doors to students. The campus, which began at the intersection of Centennial Boulevard and 35th Avenue, was rural, isolated, and rough with rocks and debris from recent construction projects. At the foot of the hill, the Cumberland River rolled silently by the school farm. The campus had just three buildings (boys and girls dormitories and the main building) and soon had a fourth, the president's home. The buildings had large windows to circulate the cool breeze and view the skies filled with stars. The main building was a modern brick and stone structure, three-stories high, with offices, laboratories, recitation rooms, library, reading room, auditorium, dining hall, kitchen and laundry—in all, forty rooms. The auditorium had a gallery and seating for seven hundred persons. Most classrooms were furnished with modern desks and recitation seats. The laboratories waited to be fully equipped with all needed science

---

[42] William A. DeGregorio, "William Howard Taft," *The Complete Book of U.S. Presidents from George Washington to George Bush* (New York: Barricade Books, 1991) 400.

[43] James C. Napier to President William H. Taft, Washington, DC, 18 December 1911, James C. Napier Papers, 1845–1940, box 2, folder 2, Fisk University Library, Special Collections; Lamon, *Black Tennesseans*, 88, 101–02.

[44] Lamon, *Black Tennesseans*, 122, 88.

[45] Lovett, *African American History of Nashville*, 169–71; Linda T. Wynn, "McKissack and McKissack Architects (1905–)," *Profiles of African Americans in Tennessee*, 87; "State Normal School," Nashville *Globe*, 1 September 1912, 1.

apparatus and supplies. The Industrial Training Department occupied commodious quarters. The three-story brick and stone women's dormitory included 33 large bedrooms with closets. All buildings were lighted with electricity, supplied with water service from the city and heated with steam from the central heating plant on the grounds. The 165-acre property soon was valued at $200,000. President Hale later recalled, "We had to solicit outside funds."[46]

Between 19–21 June 1912, the State Normal School for Negroes opened for a two-week summer session. There were 13 instructors and 230 students, mostly schoolteachers from across the state. The students arrived by trains, a few cars, and even some two-horse wagons. Hale arranged for cars, horse-drawn wagons, and trucks to go to the turn-around next to Fisk University and to the train stations to transport new arrivals to State Normal. Hale charged a fee of 15 or 20 cents, placing the money in the reserves. Late arrivals increased summer enrollment to 248, filling the two dormitories to capacity and requiring local residents to board some students for a fee. No one was turned away. The $6 on-campus boarding fee seemed to be insufficient to cover costs. Each room had shades, iron beds, springs, mattresses, dresser, a washstand, center table, straight chair, and a rocker. The reality of having their own state school kept the crowd excited. State Normal with its buildings sitting on a rocky hill near the river was a great contrast to many of Tennessee's one-room Negro schoolhouses made of wood and sometimes roofed with tarpaper.[47]

On Friday, July 4, a traditional Negro holiday since before the Civil War, Tennessee A&I State Normal School held an elaborate closing program. Each county and state representative among the students gave three minutes of presentation on "how we appreciate State Normal." William H. Singleton spoke on Hale's difficulties in opening summer school. Summer faculty consisted of Ben Carr, Singleton, H.R. Merry, Howard H. Robinson, J.B. Hatte, Estizer Watson, Martha Brown, Ms. M.C. Hawes, Edwina Smith, Lillian Dean Allen, Laura Carey, Mrs. B.R. Parmenter, and Hattie Ewing Hodgkins. The students thanked Miss Brown and her dining room staff.[48]

---

[46] W.J. Hale to the Commissioner of the State Board of Education, State Board of Education, Record Group 92, series XI, boxes 93–111, 148, 150, and see Record Group 273, boxes 131, 136, 147, 148, on Tennessee State and "Division of Negro Education"; Bobby L. Lovett, *The Civil Rights Movement in Tennessee: A Narrative History* (Knoxville: University of Tennessee Press, 2005) 7, 57, 236, 338–40, 348, 377, 466; A&I *The Bulletin* 16, no. 15 (16 August 1928): 1.

[47] Lois C. McDougald, *A Time-Line Chronology of the Tennessee A. & I. State College Campus 1909–1951* (Nashville: Tennessee State University, January 1981).

[48] "State Normal School," Nashville *Banner*, 5 July 1912, 1; "State Normal," Nashville *Banner*, 5 July 1912, 2.

The entire school went next door for the dedication of Hadley Park—reportedly the first public park to be set aside exclusively for use by Negroes. The Fisk Jubilee Singers and a band from Murfreesboro provided the music. Standing on the porch of the old plantation house, where Frederick Douglass once stood, were Nashville Mayor Hilary House, three park commissioners, other white officials, Benjamin Carr, black city councilman Solomon Parker Harris, and other Negro speakers. Carr served as the master of ceremonies. He later built a twelve-room home at the back of the park next to whites, but the Carr home burned down.[49]

After the end of the Hadley Park ceremony, chartered electric streetcars transported the entire A&I student body to sightsee and stop at Glendale Park for some amusement. They next went to a picnic at Preston Taylor's Greenwood Park for a picnic. Taylor had constructed horse-drawn wagons with seats running the length of the bed and the passengers facing each other as "Pleasure Cars" that met the customers at the streetcar turn-around and transported them a mile to the park's entrance on Lebanon Road and Spence Lane. At Greenwood's baseball stadium, the State Normal School married men and single men engaged a baseball game to entertain the ladies.[50]

The first fall quarter of the State Normal opened auspiciously on 16 September 1912, and students came from every part of the state. In total, 369 students arrived on campus, and the new school was a regular beehive by Monday afternoon. A few of the students started their program in the grammar school department. There was no tuition for Tennessee residents, and the fee was $2 for each 12-week term and $1 for summer term; meals, room, heat, light, and bath was $9 dollars for 4 weeks; medical fee, $1.50 a year; uniform suit for girls, $13; uniform hat for girls, $2; and every student had to give one hour's work each day. A laundry was available for use by the students and the faculty/staff.[51]

President Hale opened the session with great fanfare and formality. He invited the mayor and state dignitaries to the opening convocation. The State Superintendent of Instruction, J.W. Brister, spoke and reminded the students that the emphasis would focus upon training the head, heart, and hand for a life of usefulness and hard work. Hale wrote to Brister, "Our watchword is 'Think, Work, and Serve'."[52] Taylor admitted the school for free, including transportation on his "pleasure wagons," to the Colored State Fair held at Greenwood Park. Friday was Clean-up Day, with community persons invited to come out to the campus with tools in hand, mules, shovels, hoes, and picks to

---

[49] Ibid; "Hadley," Nashville *Globe*, 4, 5, 12 July 1912, 1; Lovett, *African American History of Nashville*, 126, 231.

[50] Nashville *Globe*, 5, 12 July 1912.

[51] "State Normal," Nashville *Globe*, 1 September 1912, 1; 5 September 1913, 1.

[52] Ibid.

build gravel walks, pull weeds, and trim trees. After the students had spent the day building a coal bin and roadbeds, there was a recreational outing. Faculty and students held a social in the auditorium on Saturday. Classes began on Monday.[53]

The first faculty and staff members included William J. Hale, president and education professor; J.C. Crawley, custodian; Charles G. Smith, engineer; Martha M. Brown (Fisk University), matron; Benjamin F. Carr (Roger Williams University), superintendent of the farm; J. Thomas Caruthers (Roger Williams; Massachusetts Agriculture College), agriculture science; Mae C. Hawes (Atlanta University and Columbia University), mathematics; Hattie Ewing Hodgkins (Fisk, Bryant, and Stratton Business College), business department and secretary to the president; Alonzo M. Meeks (Hampton and Tuskegee institutes), director of industries; Howard N. Robinson (Oberlin College), physical education director and history; Etna R. Rochon (State Normal Ohio), teacher training; Noah W. Ryder (Fisk and Oberlin), teacher and musical director; Lola M. Ruffin (Howard and Western Reserve), English and literature; William H. Singleton, business department (Fisk); Edwina M. Smith (Pratt Institute and Columbia University), home economics; Estizer Watson (Walden University), Model School and matron. By 1912, two Negroes held PhD degrees in America.[54]

All the state normal schools in Tennessee needed more funding. West Tennessee State Normal School still had no men's dormitory. The Middle Tennessee State Normal School had a state appropriation of just $92,558 plus $180,000 in county and city funds. The East Tennessee State Normal School had $92,558 in state funds and $151,875 in county and local funds, while the West Tennessee State Normal School had $92,558 in state funds and $353,891 in county and local funds. These white state normal schools received more state funding than Tennessee A&I for Negroes, but the state gave even more funding to UT— up to $1 million annually by 1917. Samuel H. Thompson was state superintendent of education and was responsible for the growing student population: Middle Tennessee State Normal School had 718 normal school students, 165 high school students and 245 students in observation and practice school; East Tennessee State Normal School for whites had 477 students in normal school, 189 in high school, and 136 in preparatory programs.[55]

---

[53] A&I *The Bulletin* (1912) Special Collections, TSU, 1; W.J. Hale to J.W. Brister, Tennessee A&I State Normal School Report, 1912, *Annual State Report of the Superintendent of Public Instruction for Tennessee for the Scholastic Year Ending June 30, 1911* (Nashville: Williams Printing, 1912) 54, 82–83, 340–343.

[54] Ibid; Lovett, *America's Black Colleges*, x–xvii, 67, n. 87; Lamon, *Black Tennesseans*, 88–109.

[55] Tennessee, *Appendix to Legislative Journals, 58th General Assembly*, January 1913, 1–300; Klein, "University of Tennessee," 1011.

Tennessee A&I served the Negro population across the state. In 1912, only 37 of the 95 counties in Tennessee offered four years of public high school, but most of those schools helped the white state normal schools to enroll a greater number of Normal Department (junior college) students than did Tennessee A&I State Normal. There were no more than four high schools for Negroes. Nashville's Pearl High School (1887–) had eleven grades, whereas the local Fogg High School for whites had 12 grades. In 1896, Pearl High School produced 17 graduates while the white Fogg High School had 74 graduates. Negroes comprised nearly 40 percent of Nashville's population. In 1916, the city spent $130,375 to construct a new Pearl High School and $968,361 to build white schools. Compared to the new white high school, the new Pearl High School for Negroes was so poorly constructed that the local Negro Board of Trade publicly complained about it. In 1920, Pearl High School graduated 45 students. Negro high schools existed in Chattanooga, Knoxville, and Memphis—but without the 12-year curricula equivalent to that of many white high schools. In rural Davidson County, there was no public high school at all for Negro residents unitl 1939.[56]

Twice as many of Tennessee's white, school-age children attended public schools compared to Negro children. Many counties provided elementary through middle school education for Negroes only during months between planting and harvesting time, which totaled about five or six months of instruction per year. Tennessee A&I had to maintain large programs in elementary, middle, and high school grades through 1936.

When Hale made his first report to the State Board of Education (SBOE) for 1912–13, he projected state, county, and private funds totaling about $166,000. Hale said he spent $96,016 for construction, furnishings, and supplies and managed to save the rest for other needs. Hale had about $10,000 remaining to open and operate the school. Unfortunately, some county funds and pledges did not come in. In 1912, Tennessee A&I reported 257 students for summer and 340 for the fall term. Hale requested additional funds to equip the Agriculture and Industrial Normal School for Negroes with tools, machinery, farm equipment, and implements.[57]

Early Curricula and Regulations

Once the students arrived in Nashville, they could take the electric streetcar to the Jefferson Street turn-around at Fisk, and walk fifteen minutes down a dusty road to the campus; or, they could telephone Main 1385 for pick-up by a

---

[56] Lovett, *Civil Rights Movement*, 29–30; Lovett, *The African American History of Nashville*, 74, 138, 139–41.
[57] Ibid.

school farm vehicle for 25 cents. Students had to be at least 15 years of age and of good character to attend the school. *The Bulletin* said, "This is no reform school. When it shall become evident that a student has no settled purpose to study, he will be dismissed." Offending students were given a free ride to the train station or transported to local homes. Students had to have good health, purchase books, bring old textbooks, Bibles for Sunday school, know decimal fractions, and how to read and write. They needed a high school diploma or equivalent scholarship for the Normal and Professional courses, and a minimum of one year of high school classes. Students in grades 1–8 could be admitted to the Training or Model School. Tennessee A&I had three departments: Academic, Agriculture, and Mechanical, and the curriculum was broad and innovative enough to accommodate the needs of a heterogeneous student body of a people only 47 years removed from slavery.[58]

Rules and regulations were designed to give the students discipline. Indeed, in the early twentieth century, black and white juvenile delinquency plagued urban communities. No locked rooms were allowed from 5:30 a.m. until 9:30 p.m., and all rooms were subject to daily inspection. No gambling, card playing, tobacco, liquor, firearms, or overnight absences were allowed. Girls had to be accompanied by a chaperone to leave the campus. Local students could visit their homes in Nashville one night per month. There could be no absences from meals, school, or chapel. No gentleman could call on a lady except by permission of the dormitory matron. Young men could not cross into the "women's campus" (West Campus) without permission. A gravel driveway divided the two sides, and the lack of trees made it difficult for the boys to sneak past Hale's home. He had iron gates installed on Centennial Boulevard to keep students in and outsiders out. Students called these curfew-monitored entrances "Hale's Gates."

Religion became a vital part of A&I's program; students were forced to leave the dormitories to make sure they attended chapel. The Rev. W.S. Ellington served as the first dean of chapel, and half of the A&I founders were ministers of the gospel. The Rev. Henry A. Boyd argued that the Sunday school programs furnished strong men and women who did something for race elevation. Religious services continued on campus every third Sunday at 5:30 in the evening. Local ministers directed the services, and the faculty organized a Young Men's Christian Association (YMCA) chapter on campus.[59]

---

[58] "The first year," A&I *The Bulletin* 1, no. 4 (July 1913): 1–10.

[59] Ibid. Lovett, *A Black Man's Dream*, 164–74; W.J. Hale, *Report on Tennessee A. & I. State Normal School to SBOE*, 15 December 1914; Samuel H. Thompson, *Biennial Report of the State Superintendent of Public Instruction of Tennessee for the Scholastic Year Ending June 30, 1913–1914* (Nashville: Bandon Printing, 1915) 1–211, 225–230.

The Tennessee A&I curriculum included a wide variety of courses to satisfy elementary grades, high school, and two-year college studies. The English curriculum included manual training and remedial work, grammar, composition, inflection, syntax and prosody, sentence analysis courses, composition and rhetoric, English literature, American literature, teacher's grammar, public school literature, and children's literature. Education courses included psychology, pedagogy, methods for teaching grades 1–8, school management, practice teaching, and child study (psychology). To forge the students into good American citizens, the history courses included American, Tennessee, English, industrial, ancient, medieval, and modern history, civil government and history review. The mathematics curriculum included arithmetic, algebra in factoring, fractions, simple equations, high school algebra graphics, theory of exponents, radicals, quadratic equations, inequalities and binomial theorem, and geometry to develop reasoning skills.[60]

The music curriculum was limited to note reading, chorus, piano, and harmony lessons, and students had to pay a $2-per-month music fee for the lessons. The domestic art courses (for grades 4, 5, and 6) included dressmaking, stitching, sewing, and tailoring. In order to accommodate the locals, part-time courses were offered two hours a day, two days a week, over nine months, and the students received a certificate upon completion of the courses. The home economics courses included dietary standards, cooking, sewing supervision, nutrition, food production, canning and preserving food, and practice teaching. The Academic Department accepted grade-school students and prepared them for the academic and normal courses. They could take electives in teaching, agriculture, home economics, trades, and business. The Mechanical Department consisted of carpentry, blacksmithing, wheelwright (building carts, farm wagons, and carriages), painting, bricklaying, plastering, plumbing, shoemaking, cabinetmaking, and mechanical drawing meant to prepare foremen, first-class workers, and teachers of the trades. The Boys' Trades Building included an office, supply room, and a washroom.[61]

The Academic [high school] Course consisted of four years of high school. Year one included advanced arithmetic, elementary algebra, trades, manual training, grammar and composition, American history, agriculture, physical geography, cooking and sewing, spelling, drawing and writing, music, and physical training. Year two consisted of advanced algebra, rhetoric and composition, medieval and modern history, botany and zoology, trades, manual training, cooking and sewing, spelling, drawing and writing, vocal music, and physical training. Year three included geography, English literature and composition, industrial history, physics, drawing and writing, trades, manual

---

[60] "The first year," A&I *The Bulletin*, 1–10.
[61] Ibid.

training, cooking and sewing, spelling, vocal music, and physical training. Year four included geometry, American literature and composition, English history, government, school management, methods and practice teaching, chemistry, history of education, four reading courses, trades, manual training, cooking and sewing, and vocal music.[62]

The Normal Course was the top curriculum. It was designed to be the equivalent of two years of freshman-sophomore college courses. These courses were designed to prepare students with a permanent license to teach high school. They could then continue their studies at a four-year college. During the first year, students enrolled in psychology, agriculture, methods, school management, review of English, trades, manual training, and cooking and sewing. The second year consisted of history of education, child study, practice teaching, public school literature, economics and sociology, reading, trades, manual labor, and cooking and sewing. Students engaged in trades and manual labor in the morning and academic classes in the afternoons or a vice versa course schedule.[63]

Training in the Model School prepared students for teaching grades 1–8. The Model School students engaged in courses in theory, typing lessons, and one year of practice teaching under "an experienced wide awake teacher who will criticize the work of her student teacher and train them into efficiency." The Training School for grades 1–4 included reading, language, art, numbers, geography, reading, language, arithmetic, history, domestic science, geography, art, music, and manual training. Textbooks included rural economics, conservation of the child, public school methods, teaching reading, and teaching poetry, teaching methods, and using library materials.[64]

A physical education teacher supervised the students at recess time in front of the main building as they participated in games and group exercises. The Athletic Association was organized in 1912 and required a fee for membership and equipment. The physical program consisted of activities to promote the physical development and "secure ease and grace of carriage, general development of shoulders, chest and body."[65]

With low fees, the high school department at State Normal attracted some local middle-class high school students who might otherwise have attended Nashville's Pearl High School or the high school departments at one of the local private HBCUs: Walden University, Fisk University, or Roger Williams

---

[62] Ibid.

[63] Ibid.

[64] Ibid; on the library, see the Lois H. Daniel Collection Papers, 1945–, boxes 1–5, Special Collections, TSU.

[65] Ibid.

University. For instance, art teacher Frances E. Thompson transferred from Pearl High School to complete school at Tennessee A&I.[66]

Most of the earliest students attending Tennessee A&I were in the Academic, Grammar, Preparatory, and Special programs. They were admitted into the latter program on a conditional basis, and given remedial work to help them enter the elementary and high school programs. The faculty started some students at the third-grade level, if necessary. The Preparatory Department included 53 students in grades four and five, and 218 pupils in the preparatory C and B classes. The variety of rural schools from whence the students originated made it necessary for the faculty to be creative with levels ("C and B classes"). Only twelve students were qualified to begin in the fourth year of the Academic Department (high school) in 1912–13.[67]

Students and faculty members formed organizations for extracurricular activities and for development of the student's cultural, organizational, leadership, and social skills. These organizations included the Young Men's Council. Gilbert W. Senter headed the campus YMCA chapter. Cassie Cannon headed the YWCA chapter. J. Vaughn headed the Literary and Debating Club. Student O. Holt headed the Willing Workers Club, and L.M. Ruffin was president of the campus Sunday school organization. All these organizations reflected the faculty's philosophy that the whole person must be trained and educated, including learning citizenship and moral values, to be transformed into a new person.[68]

Early Activities and Operations

Tennessee Agricultural and Industrial State Normal School was officially dedicated on 16 January 1913. On stage in the main Academic Building were representatives from the University of Tennessee, East Tennessee State Normal School, Middle Tennessee State Normal School, Davidson County Schools, Fisk University, Meharry Medical College, Pearl High School, Roger Williams University, Hampton Normal Institute, and Shelby County schools. Judge Robert Ewing, George Haynes, Andrew N. Johnson, J.W. Johnson, Preston Taylor, Charles V. Roman, John W. Work, and Chancellor J.H. Kirkland of Vanderbilt University were among special guests. Councilman Solomon P. Harris spoke for

---

[66] See biographical date, box 1, folder 1, personal correspondence, box 1, folder 5, drawing of the school seal, appendix, the Frances Thompson Collection Papers, 1923–, Special Collections, TSU.

[67] Ibid; Hale, *Annual State Report … for the Scholastic Year Ending June 30, 1911*, 36, 49–50; "Advantages of attending State Normal for Negroes," A&I *The Bulletin* 2, no. 2 (May 1914): 1–10.

[68] For the curricula and student information in the above paragraphs, see Tennessee A&I State Normal School *The Bulletin* volumes for 1912–21, Special Collections, TSU.

Negro citizens of Nashville; Governor Ben W. Hooper spoke favorably about State Normal. State superintendent of public instruction J.W. Brister said the industrial phases of education were being emphasized, while S.H. Thomas hoped that the school would be in time for Tennessee what Hampton and Tuskegee were for the nation. Hale claimed a telegraph from Booker T. Washington had praised President Hale for advancing State Normal in so short a time.[69]

Reportedly, on 7 March 1913, Booker T. Washington did stop by Tennessee State Normal School while visiting Fisk University. He was a member of the board of trustees, and his son attended Fisk. Washington spoke to the students: "In the girls dormitory everything is neat but tidy, although a few tooth brushes are missing here and there. A tooth brush shows signs of civilization. I went to a Negro college and saw Greek signs on the walls and grease signs on the floor. I could not get the connection."[70]

In February, the Tennessee General Assembly acknowledged that *a portion* of the federal land-grant funds should go to Tennessee A&I State Normal School.[71] This acknowledgement did not specify anything further. Besides, the federal government would not support black claims. On 4 March 1913, Southern-born Woodrow Wilson (D) became US president. He preferred the segregation of Negro and white employees in federal offices. James C. Napier refused to segregate his Treasury office staff and, instead, resigned and returned to Nashville to manage the One Cent Savings Bank and practice law.[72] Since 1908, the US Supreme Court had allowed states to require segregation, even at private colleges. This had been an issue at Fisk University when then-president George A. Gates resigned after just three years on the job. He was ill and needed to

---

[69] Tennessee A&I State Normal School *The Bulletin* volumes for 1912–21, Special Collections, TSU.

[70] J.W. Hale letter to Gov. Ben W. Hooper, 29 November 1911, Hooper telegram to Hale, 1 December 1911, box 4, folder 9, 1912, Governor Ben W. Hooper (1870–1957) Papers, GP 36, TSLA; Lovett, *Civil Rights Movement*, 29–30; Bergeron, et al., *Tennesseans and Their History*, 194–99; Lovett, *African American History of Nashville*, 169–72; *The Booker T. Washington Papers*, 1912–14, vol. 12, eds. Louis R. Harlan and Raymond W. Smock (Urbana: University of Illinois Press, 1982) 46–48, 113, 302; McDougald, *A Time-Line Chronology*, 5, 7–8.

[71] Editorial Staff, "A Survey of Negro Education," in *Journal of Negro Education* 2, no. 3 (July 1933): 423–25; US Bureau of Education, *Survey of Negro Colleges and Universities, Bulletin No. 7* (Washington DC: Bureau of Education, 1928) 1–120; US Bureau of Education, *Land-Grant College Education, 1910–1920, Bulletin No. 30* (Washington DC: Bureau of Education, 1924); Carter G. Woodson, *The Negro in our History* (Washington DC: Associated Publishers, 1932) 392, 836.

[72] James C. Napier to Booker T. Washington, Washington DC, 3 November 1912, *Booker T. Washington Papers*, vol. 12, 46–48.

return to his home in Vermont. Fisk University alumni had been critical of the way in which Negro visitors were segregated from white visitors on Fisk's campus.[73]

The *Globe* printed rumors that certain Negroes expected to get jobs at State Normal through Gov. Hooper and Republican Party political patronage. Perhaps the editor of the *Globe*, Henry Allen Boyd, printed the story after speaking to President Hale. Tennessee politics was deeply corrupt. As much as Hale tried to prevent the institution from being used for political patronage and graft, a few Negro fusionists (including farm superintendent Benjamin F. Carr), Republicans and prohibitionists received positions at State Normal. William H. Young (lawyer) became farm manager and registrar. M.C. Buford of Giles County became assistant superintendent of farming. Hattie Hale said Carr was no more than "a petty politician.... It was rumored that some members of the state board controlled the A. & I. farm for profit. By stern and diplomatic administrative action and by appointment of very well-qualified faculty members the administration was able to have the farm superintendent replaced by duly selected professors." Carr was dismissed on 3 May 1913. [74]

William J. Hale cultivated good relations with presidents at local HBCUs: Fisk, Meharry, Roger Williams, and Walden. Surprisingly, only the latter two HBCUs had Negro presidents. Hale did the same for the white officials at the traditionally white institutions (TWIs) of George Peabody College and Vanderbilt University. Hale also invited the nation's leading Negroes and others to visit the school in his efforts to gain respect and recognition for state normal school. Hale invited all of them for speaking engagements, seminars, and to grace the Tennessee A&I stage at graduation time. Booker T. Washington's third wife Margaret—a graduate of Fisk, a close friend of J.C. and Nettie (Langston) Napier, and a leader in the Negro Women's Club (1895)—visited Tennessee A&I. Mrs. Washington spoke to the teachers, urging them to hold meetings to help with Save the Negro Children from juvenile delinquency. World-renowned singer Roland W. Hayes of Chattanooga gave a musical recital at Tennessee A&I State Normal School on 31 March 1913.[75]

The first commencement week at Tennessee A&I State Normal School took place during 18–23 May 1913. The Rev. W.T. Ellington gave the Sunday baccalaureate sermon titled, "A Noble Purpose." There were other activities, including presentations by the students. The lower graduation exercise took

[73] Lamon, *Black Tennesseans*, 92, 170, 274–92.

[74] Harriett Ewing Hale to Samuel H. Shannon, Pittsburgh PA, interview letter, 23 April 1971, Samuel. H. Shannon Oral History Collection, Special Collections, TSU, 1–2; H.A. Boyd, "State Normal in Politics," Nashville *Globe*, 15 November 1912, 1–2.

[75] In 1982, the UT-Chattanooga opened the Roland W. Hayes Concert Hall at their fine arts center; McDougald, *A Time-Line Chronology*, 5, 8–9.

place on Wednesday, May 21. Similar programs were held for the Preparatory Department. The fourth-year students had their commencement on Friday, May 23, with Professor H. Beach of Vanderbilt University giving the address. Hale passed the certificates to the graduates with the same pomp and circumstance of a college commencement. Large audiences attended the events. Hazel Thompson (music) played the processional march, while the college chorus sang "All hail you Ye Free," and the Girls Glee Club sang "De Little Pickaninny's Gone to Sleep." Tennessee A&I Young Men's Glee Club rendered three songs after the main address. The following day, the teachers and the students left on the Tennessee Central Railroad for a sightseeing tour of Chattanooga, with Hale guiding them into his city. They attended the Wiley Memorial Methodist Episcopal Church on Sunday morning, where W.H. Young preached the sermon. On Monday evening, after tours of the incline railroad and Lookout Mountain, the Negro citizens of Chattanooga housed and entertained the State Normal party.[76]

The summer session of 1913 was a great success. Students, including ones from Alabama, Kentucky, Georgia, and Mississippi, were so pleased, they formed a State Normal Booster Club (alumni association) to triple the following summer's enrollment. Eighty-nine of the 287 summer school students were from Nashville and St. Elmo (Hale's home). Chattanooga sent forty teachers to the sessions. Summer commencement was held on July 10, and students who passed the state teaching examination received their certificates. Normal Department graduates could teach and organize high schools.[77] The four state normal schools reported 3,000 students. The superintendent asked the governor and General Assembly to appropriate $100,000 for capital projects at each of the white state normal schools and $50,000 (14.2 percent) for buildings and construction at Negro State Normal.[78]

A six-member state education committee visited the Negro school to check on its progress; President Hale and the faculty were expected to develop an institution not quite equal to the other state normal schools. The faculty and staff defined the purpose and aims of the school in Tennessee A&I's *Bulletin* (1913): The purpose was to prepare colored teachers and leaders to meet fully the demands for more efficient and practical service in the public schools and life. The aim was to so impart knowledge, discipline the mind, train the hand, and influence the heart of its students that they should go out of the school fully qualified to discharge every duty faithfully and well. The state visitors approved of Hale and the Negro state normal school.

---

[76] A&I, *The Bulletin* (1913): 1–2.
[77] Ibid.
[78] Hale, *Annual State Report … for the Scholastic Year Ending June 30, 1911*, 1–121.

On 6 October 1913, Hale married Hattie Ewing Hodgkins (1892–1986). Dean C.W. Morrow of Fisk University performed the ceremony. Hattie was born and raised as one of two daughters in Nashville by parents William H. and Joyce Hodgkins. Her father was former dean of the law school at Walden University (Central Tennessee College). She received a BA degree from A&I in 1925 and became the writer of her husband's reports. She was always protective and supportive of her husband against his perceived enemies.

William and Hattie Hale had three children, all born, raised, and educated on the campus of Tennessee A&I. William Jennings ("Will, Jr.") graduated from A&I in 1931, completed the master's in rural education at Columbia University, and taught at Tennessee A&I State College from 1932–38 before teaching at Fort Valley State College in Georgia. Will and his wife, Helene E. Hilyer, had two children: William, III, and Indira. Hale, Jr., became active in the Congress of Racial Equality (CORE) as field office director in New York in the 1950s before moving to Hawaii, where he taught school before retiring in 1979. He married Geraldine Bennett in 1976. She was a 1932 graduate of A&I, served on the home economics faculty for 28 years, and was a member of the First Colored Baptist Church.[79] The president's daughter Gwendolyn Claire Hale completed State Normal in 1939, attended Columbia University and engaged in social work for the American Red Cross School in New York City. Gwendolyn was notable for assisting her mother, Hattie, in entertaining various student groups in the president's home. Edward Harned Hale received his education at A&I, graduating in 1941, then graduated with the MD from Meharry Medical College in 1945—third in a class of 65 students—completed the master's degree in physiology at the University of Illinois (1946–47), served in the Korean War (1953–55), and spent his medical career in Pittsburgh, Pennsylvania, with his

---

[79] Ambrose A. Bennett (1884–1957) Family Papers, 1918–96, ac. no. 1999.100, TSLA, Nashville; "The Hale Alumni Family," *A History of the Alumni Association*, ed. Vallie P. Pursley (Nashville: TSU, August 1990) 25; "Helene H. Hale," *Ebony* 18, no. 6 (1963): 1, 6; Deborah Hale Schexnydre, second-eldest daughter of the late Edward Hale, and her husband attended the TSU 100th anniversary activities in April 2012. Indira, who had been in constant email exchanges with the author, died in April 2012, just before she was scheduled to attend the April 2012 program at TSU. Helene (1922-) was an English teacher at Tennessee A&I before she and Will eloped and got married in Minnesota without W.J. Hale's approval; she became the first black county mayor in Hawaii, where she still resides. Gwen Hale married Melvin R. Bolden (1919–2000); Deborah Schexnydre to Bobby L. Lovett, Pittsburgh, Pennsylvania, email, 2 February, 2012; father Edward Hale was born 15 September 1923 and died 23 July 2006; Indira Hale Tucker, Long Beach, California, to B.L. Lovett, 3 February 2012; James Castro, Nashville, to B.L. Lovett, 24 January 2012; photos of A&I Power Plant, 1928, TSLA, Lovett Papers, Specials Collections, TSU.

wife and four daughters. Harriett Hale lived with Edward until her death on 7 June 1986.[80]

On 17 November 1913, Governor Ben Hooper visited the A&I campus and urged the students to have race pride. They listened politely, applauded him in a gracious manner as they were expected to do, but most likely did not agree with paternalistic attitudes about obedience and service in a Jim Crow society. The education committee of the General Assembly visited the State Normal School for Negroes in March 1914. Students had cards hung about their necks naming their county in order to prompt the legislators to ask questions. The A&I *Bulletin* (May 1914) advertised the advantages of attending State Normal: "Free tuition, superior faculty, industrial and manual subjects, cheerful home life, good students, good environment, hard work, and a prospective, well-equipped library." Students, including those being punished, kept the campus clean, gathering and piling stones to be carried off by a two-mule wagon.[81]

The second annual commencement week was held 31 May–6 June 1914. The activities included the baccalaureate sermon and exercises of the YMCA and YWCA campus chapters on Sunday, the baseball game and exercises of the Industrial Department on Monday, class day, fourth-year Academic exercises on Tuesday, class day and Normal Department exercises on Wednesday, exercises of the Music Department on Thursday, exercises of the Preparatory A Program on Friday, and graduation ceremonies on Saturday. The faculty took their annual group picture. Twenty-four students, including two men, were in the 1914 Normal Department's graduating class.

The 1914 summer session began June 8 with classes starting on June 9. The Colored Farmers' Congress met on campus to instruct Negro farmers in the latest methods of agriculture on small plots of land and to work to improve Negro communities. Speakers for summer term included R.H. Boyd, Josiah T. Settles (jurist), James C. Napier, John Henry Hale (physician), W.S. Ellington, George E. Haynes (Fisk sociologist), J.B. Singleton (dentist), Robert R. Church, Jr., Bert M. Roddy (Memphis businessmen), and Charles N. Langston (manager of One Cent Savings Bank). A total of 904 students enrolled for summer school in 1913 and 1914, with the largest number of students coming from the Knoxville area (275), Nashville (156), and Chattanooga (28). Chattanooga, Johnson City, Maryville, and Morristown supplied representation from East Tennessee. Knoxville (60) and Nashville (59) had the largest enrollments in the Normal Department. Few students came from Memphis and West Tennessee, where nearly 70 percent of

---

[80] W.J. Hale file, Special Collections, TSU; McDougald, *A Time-Line Chronology*, 6.

[81] A&I *The Bulletin* (1913–14): 1–10; Hale, *Annual State Report … for the Scholastic Year Ending June 30, 1911*, 54, 82–83, 340.

black Tennesseans lived. The eight out-of-state students came from Alabama, Arkansas, Kentucky, Ohio, Oklahoma, North Carolina, and Washington, DC.[82]

The General Education Board (GEB) gave Tennessee a grant of $7,000 to hire rural education supervisors. The GEB required that one of the two persons be a Negro hired for the Negro State Normal School. Hale hired S.L. Brown of Clarksville. The Anna T. Jeanes Fund gave $120 to help support the Colored State Institute for Teachers, held in Johnson City and administered by Tennessee A&I. The Anna T. Jeanes Fund began in 1908, the result of a million dollars donated by the wealthy Northern heiress. She trusted Booker T. Washington to establish the first board of trustees including James C. Napier.

President Hale made his 1913–14 report to the SBOE. He carefully measured his words when presenting the curricula to state officials: Students clean dormitories, main buildings, and the grounds. Students build gravel roads and cement walks, erect iron and stone fencing one mile around the campus, work on the farm and raise the vegetables for the cafeteria, make the bread, and do the laundry. The A&I farm has no hogs, cows, and animal shelters, yet. Literary subjects are necessary in making them efficient in their various industries. Religious, literary, musical, and athletic organizations have been established to develop this side of the students. Content courses are growing faster than the agriculture and mechanical programs, because of lack of funds for equipment and facilities.[83] Hale's report also said,

> In the beginning, it was rather a task to incite students to work. Now they force us for more space and equipment and there is not one girl or one boy in school who is not taking some trade willingly. Thus in two years we have been able to impress upon the student body almost adverse to labor, the need and importance of industry. The fact that a school of this kind can thrive in a college city where the prevailing sentiment is against industrialism proves the worth of [A&I].[84]

Students in the Mechanical Department built the shelves for the library, tables for the laboratories, frames for hay, laid bricks and sidewalks, painted and stained furniture, and made plumbing repairs. Students stored tons of hay, clover, and corn, and organized the State Rural Improvement Association to help uplift rural Negro life. Students established corn, tomato, and mother's clubs among rural Negroes. Hale asked for money to build a dormitory with a dining hall, a dairy house and barn, buy livestock, and pay off the balance owed on the

---

[82] Ibid.; 25 percent of Negro farmers owned land in Tennessee.

[83] Ibid., 3.

[84] W.J. Hale, Tennessee A&I State Normal School for Negroes, *Report*, 15 December 1914; Thompson, *Biennial Report … for the Scholastic Year Ending June 30, 1913–1914*, 225–230.

farm. He was afraid to ask for too much, so he said, "By practicing the strictest economy, we can make ends meet with an appropriation of \$50,000."[85]

Enrollment in 1912–13 was 369 in regular term, 441 in summer; for 1913–14, it was 547 in regular term and 594 in summer. By 1914, of 650 students, 258 of them were in the Agriculture Department and 384 in Domestic Art and Domestic Science. The school had produced 21 Normal School graduates, including 15 in teaching, two supervising vocational education, two enrolled in colleges, and two reenrolled at Tennessee A&I. Some 175 students lived in the 66 dormitory rooms. They ate in a dining hall built for 132 persons. Many students had to walk nearly a mile to the streetcar line and reside in private homes. Still, President Hale pumped up the state officials' egos: "You men have surprised the people of other states and your own. You are the talk of the country in school circles because you had the courage to pitch the Negro school on a high plane and keep it there. You must do almost the impossible—please two races."[86] Hale always appeased his bosses.

The US Bureau of Education included site visits to verify the numbers and condition of the HBCUs, institutes, academies, and schools in 1913. Without visits, among hundreds of Negro schools it was difficult to ascertain which ones really were collegiate-level institutions. The report said the 1914–15 budget revenues for Tennessee A&I totaled \$39,319, including \$12,000 from federal sources, and \$4,076 from farm income. They recommended better auditing of the books, an accounting system, and enrolling fewer local students. Instead, the Normal Department found ways to enroll more students in the college program by creating "A and B" levels.[87]

The Tennessee General Education Bill set aside one-third of state revenues for the school fund; the normal schools received 13 percent of the funds. In 1913–14, West Tennessee State Normal School received \$208,309 from the state, \$203,891 from Shelby County, and \$150,000 from the City of Memphis. Middle Tennessee State Normal School received \$293,791 from the state, \$100,000 from Rutherford County, and \$80,000 from Murfreesboro. This school had a 49-acre campus, and a farm equipped with 89 horses, mules, cattle, and hogs. Negro State Normal School received \$47,518 from the state, none from Nashville, and nothing from Davidson County.[88]

In 1914–15, Hale submitted a report to the SBOE claiming enrollment and attendance for the regular term at 401, an increase in the higher grades and a

---

[85] Ibid.

[86] Ibid.

[87] US Bureau of Education, *Negro Education, Bulletin No. 38* (Washington, DC: General Printing Office, 1916) 1–51. Note: Thanks to Fisk University library and Jessie C. Smith for my access to a copy.

[88] *Legislative Journal of Tennessee* (1914–15): 1–121.

decrease in the lower grades; 20 finished the Normal Department course; 50, the 8th grade; 11, plain sewing; 4, dressmaking; 6, domestic science; and, for summer terms: 1912 (248 students), 1913 (287), 1914 (441), and 1915 (980), with 75 counties in attendance. Comparably, the president of Middle State Normal School in Murfreesboro reported for 1913–14 an enrollment of 474 students for regular sessions. He reported 545 for summer 1914, and 544 for fall 1914, with 11 normal and 20 academic graduates in 1915. W.J. Hale continued cultivating good relations with the State Board of Education. His report said, "All the work of the institution—sewing, cooking, laundry (except one hired woman), campus road building, concrete walks, [stone] fence building, farm work—is done by the students under the direction of the teachers. White officials and colored citizens generally have given us unstinted support and co-operation."[89]

Hale Gets into Trouble

For the first two years of Tennessee A&I's existence, the institution lived up to Hale's expectation of educating a growing Negro population; however, 1914–15 proved to be a year when the institution experienced a bitter struggle for survival. W.J. Hale encountered so many problems that fatalists believed officials would find a reason to close the school. It began when the Nashville *Banner* (12 July 1915) announced that an investigation committee would look into charges made by Harry Luck. Luck, a member of the state board and a local judge, was angry about Hale's treatment of the college farm staff and employees who had been appointed to A&I jobs by Luck and others. Luck claimed that Hale assigned and changed the work of the faculty at will, and that the president's wife used a school piano to give lessons for personal fees. Luck said he disagreed with the investigating committee's majority report, in particular the section that commended the administration of President Hale: "In my opinion the earlier his services are dispensed with the better for the good of the school, its patrons and the State." Luck said Hale was "un-business-like and incompetent for the position he holds. I have been able to make it appear to me that the President has for some time past been under the impression that the school was his personal property to manage and do as he chose."[90] One man was resentful that Hale no longer allowed the farm staff to pick up student's trunks at the train depot for fees and sell a few vegetables in town. [Truck delivery—now monopolized by Hale's office—from the train station for incoming students rose to 35 cents from

---

[89] Ibid.

[90] "State Normal School," Nashville *Banner,* 12 July 1915; minutes, state board of education, 1911–14, box 42, Dr. W.J. Hale Investigation, 1922, box 1, folder 1, A&I, 1926, box 2, folder 4, Tennessee A&I Normal School, box 3, folder 9, A&I campus building photographs, box 41, nos. 1681–97, State Board of Education Records, 1815–1958, RG 91, TSLA.

the original 25 cents.] The complainant said Hale changed his assignments because "he just does not like me for some reason." A former dormitory matron who was fired by Hale said the boys played cards, shot craps in the dormitory, and danced "Walking the Dog." And when staff members tried to enforce the regulations, Hale complained the punishment was too harsh. The SBOE's three-man investigating committee concluded, however, "There is nothing tangible that we can get at, and many people feel that this school here is one of the best Negro schools in the country."[91]

Tennessee A&I During the First World War

In August 1914, World War I broke out in Europe, and this military event had some effects on Negroes and race relations. Tennessee A&I students, faculty members, and local Negroes enthusiastically supported America's war effort. America entered the war in 1917, and beginning 5 June 1917, Tennessee men aged 21 through 30 had to register for the military draft. Meharry Medical College became an official training site for the military medical corps, and surplus dormitory space at Fisk and Walden universities housed local army recruits. The Nashville City Federation of Colored Women's Clubs prepared lunches for the recruits, while the local Colored Women's Red Cross Chapter furnished 584 flags, packs of cigarettes, and boxes of matches as the men boarded the trains to travel to the army training camps. Richard H. Boyd loaned the National Baptist Publishing Board's trucks to transport the supplies to the train station. Henry Allen Boyd took his camera and notepad to army training camps in Iowa to publish pictures in the *Globe*. Company K of the U.S. 387th Infantry (formerly Company G, Tennessee National Guard) served in France. They shot down a German plane and sent some parts to the *Globe*. The war continued through November 1918.[92]

During the war, intramural sports replaced intercollegiate athletics at Tennessee A&I that then had six tennis courts, a basketball field, and "spots" for track and ball playing—all built by the student workers. Sunday school was confined to one hour to allow students to attend the local church of their choice. The Sunday School Association held Bible training classes on campus, and the Women's Temperance Christian Union and the YMCA and YWCA campus chapters continued to teach morality. Other campus organizations included: Bowen Literary Debating Club, Phyllis Wheatley Club, Junior Literary Society, Athletic Association, and the Agriculture and Mechanical Association.

In 1917, State Normal had departments of education, English, classics and expression, history, mathematics, music, science, agriculture, and mechanical

---

[91] Investigating Committee Report, SBOE Minutes, 1915–18, 1–20, RG 91.
[92] Lovett, *African American History of Nashville*, 98.

trades. In the academic courses, the faculty often proscribed the textbooks at the college level to challenge the high school students. The Preparatory Department continued to teach students in grades 5–8, including remediation for those children from areas with short school terms and low-grade standards. The Training School taught grades 3 and 4 and served as the Model School for students in the Normal Department. The students observed classes for two terms, and practiced teaching for one term in the junior year and for two more terms in the senior year. The catalog said teacher education majors were trained carefully to prepare and organize clear lessons, teach secondary students to study and act independently, conduct recitations, manage children, and maintain personal health and fitness, and professional attitude. The faculty quietly transformed the Industrial History course into The Negro in History and Literature course, including a textbook by Howard University professor Benjamin Brawley.[93] The Tennessee A&I mathematics curriculum included algebra and geometry. Science courses included zoology, botany, physics, chemistry, geography, and laboratory experiences. Agriculture advanced to horticulture, biology, animal husbandry, veterinary science, agronomy, applied agriculture, agriculture pedagogy, and agriculture research. Meharry Medical College's Victor C. Roman regularly lectured at Tennessee A&I on sanitation and personal health, so woefully neglected in Tennessee.[94]

Tennessee A&I received such favorable press that many education leaders wanted to visit the school. Hale graciously issued invitations everywhere he traveled. He established a system of charging visitors a fee for room and board. So many important personalities boarded in the President's Home, it became known as "Goodwill Manor." The Legislative Educational Investigating Committee visited the campus on 2 February 1917 and gave W.J. Hale and the school good marks. The Negro Press Association, under President Henry A. Boyd, visited the campus on February 9. President Hale, the faculty, and students held a war loyalty rally whose guests included H.A. Boyd; George W. Hubbard, president of Meharry Medical College; Andrew N. Johnson, president of the Negro Board of Trade; W.S. Ellington; Charles N. Langston; Katie L. Boyd, student at Pearl High School and Henry Boyd's daughter; and Captain Charles O. Hadley of Company G, the Negro unit of the Tennessee National Guard. The mayor of the city urged State Normal students to return home and grow food to help the war effort. The A&I band played the *Star-Spangled Banner*, while the

---

[93] Franklin, and Moss Jr., *From Slavery to Freedom*, 332; Benjamin Brawley, *A Social History of the American Negro* (New York: New Publishers, 1921) 1–121, included African origins, civil war and Emancipation, and Negro problems such as disfranchisement, peonage, and lynching.
[94] A&I *The Bulletin* (1914–15): 1–9; Charles V. Roman, *Meharry Medical College, A History* (Nashville: the author, 1934) 1–120.

American flag was being raised outside the Academic Building. Governor Tom C. Rye (D) urged the students to show the same loyalty their ancestors did during the Civil War. Such talk was worrisome because many white Tennessee officials continued to erroneously infer that most slaves supported the bogus Confederacy. Hale responded cleverly and respectfully: "We realize and wish you to realize that this is our flag; we know no other, and we will protect it."[95]

The 600 teachers attending the 1917 summer session held President's Day to honor W.J. Hale. Tennessee counties sent representatives, and Ellington, Roman, and F.S. Smith (principal of Pearl H.S.) served as speakers. By 1917, total enrollment of 1,246 included students from 66 of Tennessee's 95 counties. Many graduates returned for normal studies; others went to Fisk and other HBCUs.

In February 1918, a large group of state legislators visited the campus. They, however, said nothing about the federal Smith-Lever Act, 1915–22, that allotted $639,496.31 to Tennessee for higher education. The state gave State Normal School for Negroes a mere $2,000 (0.3 percent) of the money.[96] During the visit, one official commented on how Negroes were appreciated because the slaves supported the South during the Civil War. He was apparently ignorant of the 20,133 Negro men who served in the Union army in Tennessee and who helped administer a humiliating final defeat to the Confederate army of Tennessee during the Battle of Nashville.[97]

To support the American war effort, the Tennessee A&I choir participated in local fundraisers. The school also shipped packages to the Negro troops stationed near Chattanooga. Hale and Andrew N. Johnson headed the War Thrift Stamp campaign in the Negro community, and Hale also headed the executive committee for the Negro Liberty Bond Drive. A student military training unit was established at A&I on 25 October 1918. In November 1918, word of the armistice arrived, and Negroes mingled freely with whites celebrating in Nashville's downtown streets. Blacks held their own celebration at Andrew N. Johnson's Bijou Theater. The *Globe* (27 December 1918) reminded people, "Democracy does not mean the unrestricted rule of the majority." A local Negro soldier wrote to the *Globe* saying the black soldiers had helped the allies push the "Huns" back into Germany and "Hopes America appreciates it."[98]

---

[95] A&I *The Bulletin* (1917–18): 1–10; William J. Hale (2) President, Tennessee Agricultural and Industrial State Normal School, box 11, folder 2, 1916, lynching in Tennessee, 1917–18, folder 9, Governor Tom C. Rye Papers, 1915–19, GP 37, TSLA.

[96] McDougald, *A Time-Line Chronology*, 18–24; A&I *Calendar 1918–19*, Special Collections, TSU.

[97] Lynching in Tennessee, 1917–18, folder 9, Governor Tom C. Rye Papers, 1915–19, GP 37; James W. Johnson, "The Lynching at Memphis," *The Crisis* 13, no. 1 (1917): 285.

[98] "The war," Nashville *Globe*, 27 December 1918, 1; Nashville *Globe*, 27 December 1918, 1; A&I *The Bulletin* 7, no. 1 (1918): 1–2.

On 25 January 1919, ninety students and faculty members were listed on the Tennessee A&I State Normal School Honor Roll in Military Service; ninety-five Negro soldiers from Tennessee died in the war. A&I accepted a Student Auxiliary Training Corps (SATC) unit on campus, under the command of Lt. Grant Steward, who conducted the first military drills on campus on January 22. Some 200 veterans at Tennessee A&I studied for six months in the trades under the federal rehabilitation of disabilities program.[99]

Despite the Negro contribution to the war, President Woodrow Wilson (D) refused to speak against radical white supremacists and lynching, which was experiencing a horrifying uptick. Instead, Wilson tried to censor Negro newspapers for reporting on American race relations. Thousands of Southern Negroes began to flee during the great Northern migration. William Crosse, in his poem "The Land of Hope" said,

> Yes, we are going to the north!
> I don't care to what state,
> Just so I cross the Dixon Line,
> From this southern land of Hate,
> Lynched and burned and shot and hung.
> And not a word is said.[100]

In a particularly brutal incident, ten uniformed Negro soldiers were lynched and burned in Mississippi. In January 1919, James C. Napier and 92 others formed the Nashville branch of the National Association for the Advancement of Colored People (NAACP) and marched on the governor's office to protest racial lynching. Governor Albert H. Roberts (D) wrote to W.J. Hale "I want to encourage the colored youth of Tennessee to rally to this school and help us make it the greatest school of its kind in the South. I want also to encourage your faculty in your work, and to assure you that it is our pleasure to assist in every possible way in building up this school."[101] But the governor's office gave no relief to the NAACP complaint. Thus, racial tensions continued to be inflamed, culminating in the Knoxville race riot, which occurred in August

---

[99] A&I *The Bulletin* (1917–19).

[100] Arna Bontemps and Jack Conroy, *Anyplace but Here* (Columbia: University of Missouri Press, 1945, 1966) 162–63.

[101] Ibid., 25; Gov. Albert H. Roberts to W.J. Hale, Nashville, August 1919, A&I *The Bulletin* 8, no. 1 (August 1919): 1; McDougald, *A Time-Line Chronology*, 25; petitions—inviting the governor to visit to Tennessee A&I Normal School, series 8, box 43, folder 14, box 18, folder 6, incoming correspondence, Napier, Gov. Albert H. Roberts Papers, 1918–21, GP, 38, TSLA.

1919.[102] Tennessee A&I constituents supported such activities that documented the Negro's demand for equal treatment in the US.

A&I Progresses Toward Four-Year College Status

On 22 February 1920, Noah W. Williams, a chaplain, and Negro members of the Henry A. Cameron Post No. 5 American Legion held a Colored Soldiers' memorial in Nashville. They issued certificates for each deceased local World War I Negro soldier.[103]

In late 1921, federal officials accused W.J. Hale of profiting off the veteran soldiers on campus, charging fees for everything in the SATC, and making high-interest loans to the veterans. Hale said he made no money off the loans; he simply tried to help the men who ran out of their government checks each month. Some people claimed Hale was being held for extortion. Hale said that when the SATC was quartered on the campus, it was one of the most hectic and trying periods in the school's history:

> Charges and counter charges were hurled about the heads of the administration of the college by both informed and uninformed. President Hale was the storm center and at risk of his future dared stand for the ideals of the institution and to defy the most powerful interests that were bent on using the school as a political football. The SBOE sustained President Hale. They gave him a vote of confidence. The Board replied to the War Department that the soldiers had to leave A. & I. if their remaining was to be held at the expense of the resignation of President Hale. When the last soldiers left the campus, peace came in which to continue the work of building an educational institution—free from the desecrating hands of petty politicians and jealous enemies. We can never fully repay the State Board for its justice and honor.[104]

Once the soldiers had departed and Tennessee A&I was back on an even keel, two distinct courses of study began to emerge: Academic and Normal. The academic certificate was awarded after four years of preparation to teach elementary schools. The graduates then could enter the Normal Department that required two years of thirty-six weeks each in freshman and sophomore level college courses. Students took four to seven courses in fall, winter, and spring terms, and upon completion were awarded a teaching diploma for the high

---

[102] Robert J. Booker, *Race Mixing, Race Rioting in 1919 Knoxville* (Knoxville: Rutledge Books, 2001); Lester C. Lamon, "Tennessee Race Relations and the Knoxville Riot of 1919," *East Tennessee Historical Society Papers* 41, no. 1 (1969): 67–85.

[103] Lovett, *African American History of Nashville*, 98, 99–102, 125, 165, 253.

[104] "Hale for extortion," Nashville *Tennessean*, 10, 15, 16, 17 February 1922, 26 March 1922, 1; Nashville *Banner*, 27 February 1922; Hale's explanation in Hale Papers, 1935; A&I *The Bulletin* 10, no. 11–12 (1922); McDougald, *A Time-Line Chronology*, 36; Dr. W. J. Hale Investigation, Feb. 10, 1922, box 1, folder 1, SBOE Records, 1815–1958, RG 91, TSLA.

school level. Tennessee A&I continued the Preparatory Department and the issuance of three- to four-year special certificates for industrial training.

From 1912 to 1920, 703 students received diplomas and certificates at Tennessee A&I. Eleven states were represented in the student body and alumni. By this time, the campus had expanded to thirty-five acres and the adjacent 165-acre farm.[105]

The faculty steadily tightens the rules and regulations, sending letters to parents about students coming late and leaving early. Some of the families needed the children for planting and harvesting crops, but the A&I *Bulletin* (July 1919) warned them to "plan for nine months at State Normal. We have no vacation." Christmas vacation had been suspended during the war to save expenses, which had risen from $96 to $114 a year. The institution consisted of 42 faculty/staff members, four extension workers—including ones working out of Jackson and Knoxville—and a few staff members to help President Hale with the work. The out-of-state enrollment had grown to 41, out-numbering the students from Memphis. The faculty increased its list of weekly speakers, including a dean at Howard University, a professor of geography at George Peabody College, a Rosenwald Fund supervisor, the governor of Tennessee, seven local ministers, and the Rabbi for Nashville's Vine Street Jewish Temple. Meharry physician Charles V. Roman continued to give lectures on "Sex Hygiene." Meharry meant to counter the spread of venereal diseases brought back from the European war theater. The Legislative Education Investigating Committee visited the A&I campus on 14 March 1919, followed by the SBOE visit on May 7. Sais honorary society with 37 members with a B+ average was initiated on 27 March 1919. Students had to take special classes in writing and spelling if "below the standard in penmanship and spelling." Analytic chemistry, advanced physics, trigonometry, advanced expression in English, and French joined the curriculum. Napier and Hale joined the Commission on Interracial Cooperation (CIC) founded in 1919 to improve race relations. Hale became chair of the colored section of the Tennessee Interracial League that held weeklong sessions on the A&I campus.[106] The state visits approved operations at A&I.

By 1920, Tennessee's four state normal schools, including A&I, began to move toward offering college degrees. The A&I *Bulletin* (1919) already listed "Junior College and Normal Departments" with 33 courses in the junior year and 31 courses for the senior year. The *Bulletin* (1920–22) listed a College and Normal Course that aimed to:

> meet the needs of those who plan to pursue professional work. The two concentrations consisted of science and classics. The student must have

---

[105] A&I *The Bulletin* (1919–21): 1–10.
[106] McDougald, *A Time-Line Chronology*, 30–37.

completed the Academic Course [high school] or have a high school diploma. Students are admitted to the College Department who show aptitude for that work and who give evidence of a desire to pursue that work with profit to themselves. Students will be given a try-out in the department for which their credentials call but the school reserves the right to re-classify all students if the best interests of the school make it necessary.[107]

In his inaugural address, 15 January 1921, Governor Alf A. Taylor (R) said: "There can be no real and enduring civilization without universal popular education." However, worldwide post-World War I economic depression in 1921 left the state treasury in dire shape. According to *Financial Condition Reports* (1921) made to Governor Taylor, the state of Tennessee owed $34,080.75 to the "Colored Normal Fund," with another $17,488.09 in federal funds due to the same fund, but lesser amounts due to the white schools. Monies were being withheld from all state agencies. Taylor's "Veto Message of February 7, 1921," said the average term for rural elementary schools was only 104 days—ten days fewer than a decade earlier—and only 75 percent of Tennessee's total school population enrolled in the public schools; 34 percent of the students were lost by irregularity of attendance. Only 5 percent of the school enrollment in Tennessee was in high schools, compared to 9.3 percent in the US. "It is shown that during the late [world] war in one of the leading counties in the State 2,600 out of the 2,900 men drafted had not attended school beyond the third grade," said Taylor. In his Special Message of 8 March 1921, Taylor said, "There are now in Tennessee, approximately 50,000 rural school children out of school for the want of teachers. The educational situation in Tennessee, particularly as relates to our rural schools, is such that it ought to arouse within the soul of every citizen of the State a crushing sense of humiliation."[108] The state owed the Negro normal school $51,568.66 by 15 January 1921.[109]

Nevertheless, A&I continue to make progress using other financial sources. Robert E. Clay became the rural building agent for the Rosenwald Fund in Tennessee. By 1919, Clay was headquartered at A&I to help raise matching

---

[107] "College and Normal Courses," *The Bulletin* 8, no. 10–11 (June 1920): 1–10; W.J. Hale, "Report to the State," 58th General Assembly, 6 January 1913, 59th General Assembly, 4 January 1915, 60th General Assembly, 1 January 1917, essay by TSU Special Collections staff, Special Collections, TSU, 1–4.

[108] Alfred A. Taylor, "Messages to the General Assembly," *Messages of the Governors of Tennessee 1921–1933*, vol. 10, ed. Steven V. Ash (Nashville: Tennessee Historical Commission, 1990) 17–60; general correspondence, box 1, Gov. Alfred A. Taylor Papers, 1921–23, GP 39, TSLA.

[109] Ibid., *Report of the Financial Condition of State*, 15 January 1921, Taylor's messages, 38–39; state normal schools, local and state funds, 1917–19 files, box 29, folder 2, SBOE, RG 273.

money for the erection of schoolhouses. The number of extension workers working out of Tennessee A&I State Normal School increased due to Smith-Hughes federal funds[110]

The institution now had a small home economics building for domestic art and domestic science programs and new dining rooms for teachers and students. The school expanded the Boys Trade Building (1914) with anticipation of a director being hired shortly. They added an auto shop, as well as a small gymnasium with the students doing the work under the supervision of the teachers on the second-floor. The changes in the facility allowed the industrial department to offer automobile mechanics, blacksmithing, carpentry, masonry, printing, electrical, mechanical, steam, wood and iron repair, and plumbing. The agriculture department received a poultry division and colony houses to supply the campus with meat and eggs. They received dairy cows with a veterinarian.

Tennessee State Normal School Becomes a Four-Year College

The General Assembly and the SBOE authorized A&I, and the other three state normal schools, to proceed to collegiate status. From 7 June–14 July 1922, the bachelor's degree was advertised. Hale appointed a dean and department heads for the college program. Walter Denny, Aeolian Lockert, Lillian Oliver, Hattie Rose, Birdie Stanley, and Mable Welch constituted the junior class.[111] Martha M. Brown expanded the library in two rooms of Old Main. She was born in Nashville and attended Fisk, studied library science at Hampton Institute, and taught in the Nashville School for the Blind; she also directed music and managed a dormitory.[112]

Elementary school teachers could get permanent certificates after two years of teaching, six weeks of summer school, and passing tests in English, grammar, and arithmetic. Students could receive diplomas in commerce, dressmaking, sewing, domestic science, mechanical engineering, blacksmithing, auto mechanics, license for chauffeurs, millinery, first-aid, broom-making, handicrafts, and penmanship, and certificates for the short summer courses. Daily recitation was required.[113]

Many normal school students helped to distinguish the institution. Meredith G. Ferguson started as a painter when A&I was constructed, becoming a painting instructor in 1912–16, and fulltime faculty member under Calvin McKissack and the mechanical department 1916–17. Ferguson served in World

---

[110] McDougald, *A Time-Line Chronology*, 34–36.

[111] Ibid., 34.

[112] Biographical data and information on the library, correspondence, Harriett E. Hale, box 1, folder 3, Lois H. Daniel Collection Papers, 1945–, Special Collections, TSU.

[113] Ibid. Note: *The Teacher's Bulletin* became *The Broadcaster* (a quarterly) published at Tennessee A&I from 1927–67.

War I and returned to work at Citizens Bank, becoming assistant president of the bank after being there for 25 years. He later became president of Citizens Bank. Alfred Galloway became a tradesman under his uncle Emmett C. Campbell, who taught heating, plumbing, electrical, and automotive courses at A&I. Alfred attended the college and later became founding president of Community Federal Savings and Loan Association Bank. Albert Howell attended the Fifth Street School in Chattanooga and State Normal School from 1912–15; he served as Hale's chauffeur and then a as teacher in Dyersburg in 1916.[114]

By 1922, Tennessee A&I State Normal School included Goodwill Manor, Women's Dormitory, Men's Dormitory, Main Academic Building, and Boys' Trades Building. Old Main had 22 rooms, and the large auditorium (the Chapel) was expanded to a thousand seats, including a balcony, stage curtains, movie screen, and footlights. The campus farm, dairy barn, farmhouses, greenhouses, and outbuildings were valued at $16,000. Two teachers' cottages were built in 1921 on the east campus facing south on Centennial.[115] William J. Hale recalled, "The year 1922 marks the beginning of the institution as a senior college."[116]

---

[114] A&I *The Bulletin* (1919–22) 1–10.

[115] Ibid.

[116] W.J. Hale, "The History," 1935, W.J. Hale Papers, incomplete manuscript, Special Collections, TSU.

2

1922–36: Transformation From Normal School
to Four-Year College

Tennessee A&I State Normal School started its transformation from a normal school to a four-year college during a time of great socioeconomic change. Negro writer and NAACP officer James Weldon Johnson characterized 1919 as "the red summer" when blood spilled across the country in urban race riots, including the one at Knoxville. Black Tennesseans, including Negroes in Nashville remained loyal to the Republican Party. Women gained the right to vote through the Nineteenth Amendment (1920), and Negro women outvoted Negro men. The Negro Renaissance or Harlem Renaissance began with Alain Locke, *The New Negro* (1925):

> There is ample evidence of a New Negro in the last phases of social change and progress, but still more in the internal world of the Negro mind and spirit. America seeking a new spiritual expansion and artistic maturity, trying to found an American literature, a national art, and a national music implies a Negro-American culture seeking the same satisfactions and objectives.[1]

James Weldon Johnson the "father of the Harlem Renaissance"[2] showed other Americans that the Negro, too, made creative contributions to American civilization. Also in New York, Marcus Garvey, an immigrant from Jamaica, organized his Universal Negro Improvement Association (UNIA) that promoted a black Christ, the Negro's right to bear arms, black pride, and racial separatism. There were half-dozen UNIA chapters in Tennessee by 1927. This New Negro movement affected Fisk University, whose students rebelled against the white administration, forcing the president to resign in 1925. The HBCU became the cultural center of the New Negro Renaissance. Tennessee A&I State Teachers

---

[1] Alain Locke, *The New Negro: An Interpretation* (New York: Albert & Charles Boni, 1925) ix; Eugene Levy, *James Weldon Johnson: Black Leader, Black Voice* (Chicago: University of Chicago Press, 1973) 1–380.

[2] James W. Johnson, who, in admiration of Frederick Douglass and Paul Lawrence Dunbar, published dozens of poems during his student life at Atlanta University. He composed, along with his brother Rosamond, *Lift Every Voice and Sing* to commemorate Abraham Lincoln's birthday in 1900. They put the poem to music in 1905, and it became known as the "National Negro Anthem." The anthem graced many programs at Tennessee A&I. J. Weldon assumed a chair in creative writing at Fisk University by 1931.

College quietly joined the movement in 1928, hiring Merl R. Eppse to direct the history program with an "emphasis on the Negro."[3]

Northern philanthropists bought into the New Negro awakening, significantly increasing their investments in the HBCUs, including Tennessee A&I. They invested money to whittle the HBCUs from about 240 institutions down to those that could become accredited four-year colleges. Meharry Medical College gained medical association approval in 1921. Howard University (1921), Lincoln University, Pennsylvania (1922), and Morgan State College (1925) achieved accreditation from the Middle States Association of Colleges and Schools. West Virginia State College (1927) earned accreditation from the North Central Association of Colleges and Schools. In 1930, Fisk University gained "A" approval from the Southern Association of Colleges and Schools. According to Jim Crow practices, SACS awarded the HBCUs an "A" or "B" approval rating instead of equal membership as enjoyed by traditional white institutions (TWIs). The *Journal of Negro Education* protested that "This classification is not only confusing to examining-officials in higher education, but it is misleading to students." Tennessee A&I gained approval of the American Association of Teachers Colleges by 1933.[4]

The dire racial situation in Tennessee and this Jim Crow barrier slowed the growth of Tennessee A&I State Normal School and hindered its potential. Mrs. Harriett E. Hale recalled,

Tennessee A. & I. State College was born in an atmosphere where its acceptance by both whites and Negroes was dubious…. The campus as a whole was not beautiful in sharp contrast to those of older, well-established colleges and universities. So, the school was created where the adverse sentiment for its mere presence made for an attitude of intense struggle just to survive. A positive justification for its existence brought forth strong arguments in favor of all kinds of vocational education to lift the masses of economically poor and uneducated Negroes…. All students were required to pursue some vocational education along with academic requirements. Tennessee A. & I. modeled its philosophy and curricula after Hampton and Tuskegee … with a connotation of a lower level of offerings and training….

---

[3] Raymond Walters, *The Negro on Campus: Black College Rebellions of the 1920s* (Princeton NJ: Princeton University Press, 1975) 1–121.

[4] Bobby L. Lovett, *America's Historically Black Colleges and Universities: A Narrative History from 1837 to 2010* (Macon GA: Mercer University Press, 2011) 102–03; "Editorial Comment: Why a Class 'B' Negro College?" *Journal of Negro Education* 2, no. 4 (October 1933): 427–31.

The state appropriation to A. & I. was very small; so the growth of the school was definitely hampered.[5]

President W. J. Hale, too, recalled,

The name Agricultural and Industrial was forbidding and incongruous to many of the educated local [Negro elite] group. Many of the prophets of the time expected an early demise of the institution due to [externally imposed] low standards, lack of [equal state] support and the problems incident to a politically controlled institution of higher education. The student was compelled to carry chairs from classroom to classroom and even to the dining hall, had to get his own water from a spring, sleep in crowded rooms, in halls, or in stairway landings.[6]

The First Bachelor's Graduation

In 1922, the state of Tennessee authorized public normal schools to move toward collegiate status. President W.J. Hale, the faculty and staff members organized Tennessee A&I State Normal School into the Academic (high school, grades 9–12), Normal (junior college), and College Division including departments of agriculture, vocational, teaching, English, and science. The Normal Department enrolled 62 students in a two-year program, granting diplomas and certificates for teaching high school. Students no longer had to meet the manual arts and manual labor requirements. Some 43 students were in the college program.

The Eleventh Commencement Exercise took place on 29 May 1923 with the usual festivities, including senior class day, May Festival, alumni reception, drama and music programs, and the President's Reception for alumni, parents, and graduating students. The Alumni Association was reorganized during commencement week, with Christopher C. Purdy (Normal, 1922) elected as president and an office on campus under advisor and corresponding secretary R.B.J. Campbell. Henry Allen Boyd gave the invocation. Guy E. Hoffman gave an oration, "The Negro in History," and J.L. Kessler, professor of education at Vanderbilt University, served as speaker. Hale presented the graduates, and Commissioner of Education Perry L. Harned handed out certificates and diplomas. The program listed 31 Normal diplomas, 19 juniors receiving academic certificates, and 36 Academic diplomas. College seniors Walter D.

---

[5] Harriett E. Hale to Samuel H. Shannon, Pittsburgh PA, interview letter, 23 April 1971, Samuel. H. Shannon Oral History Collection, Special Collections, TSU, 1–3; Bobby L. Lovett, *The Civil Rights Movement in Tennessee: A Narrative History* (Knoxville: University of Tennessee Press, 2005) 93–94, 134, 338–42.

[6] W.J. Hale, "The History," 1935, W.J. Hale Papers, incomplete manuscript, Special Collections, TSU, 1–20.

Denney, Aeolian Lockert, William McKinley Lowe, Lora Meyers, Reginald Neblett, Christopher C. Purdy, and Thudman A. Ramsey received special recognition.[7]

During summer school, 1923, a record 1,200 people attended the sessions and workshops. Special trains brought teachers from across Tennessee along with delegates for the Smith-Hughes summer session.[8] The summer students participated in the home economic teachers' workshops, a forum for education supervisors, the high school principals' association, and Hale's Annual Conference of the Tennessee Interracial League. The latter organization brought leading whites and blacks to the campus to discuss race relations, and allowed W.J. Hale to show off progress made on the campus. Shelby County and Memphis sent the largest contingent of teachers and principals. They held Shelby County Day on July 12 and presented the college with twenty-four chairs and a speaker's stand to relieve teachers and students of transporting chairs back and forth from one classroom to another room. W.S. Ellington preached the baccalaureate sermon on July 8. Wilbur F. Tillett of Vanderbilt University gave the commencement address on July 13 for 5 Normal and 24 Academic graduates.[9]

In 1923–24, Tennessee A&I completed the Girls' Trades Building (home economics) with seating for 600 people in the dining hall on the upper floor that allowed development of a room and board office—one of the first among HBCUs—and a modern serving line for faculty and students, classrooms for sewing, dressmaking, design, tailoring, handicrafts, domestic science, millinery, and housekeeping. At each table, an appointed student served as the host, refilled bowls of food and drink at the serving line, and brought the items to the individual table.[10]

Tennessee A&I was supposed to phase out the high school program and stop granting the Normal School diploma as other normal schools were doing, but the faculty opposed this plan because "the State had relatively few high schools for Negroes which did anything like first-class secondary [SACS-accredited] work to prepare students for more advanced courses."[11] Tennessee had five public high schools for Negroes: Austin H.S. (Knoxville), Kortrecht H.S. (Memphis), Howard H.S. (Chattanooga), rural Hyde Park H.S., and Pearl H.S.

---

[7] Lois C. McDougald, *A Time-Line Chronology of the Tennessee A. & I. State College Campus 1909–1951* (Nashville: Tennessee State University, January 1981) 25–39; A&I *The Bulletin*, 21, no. 12 (1923): 58, 59, 62, 65, 68.

[8] Congress passed the Smith-Hughes Act (1917) to provide subsidies to the states to underwrite vocational and industrial education.

[9] McDougald, *A Time-Line Chronology*, 37–38; A&I *The Bulletin*, 21, no. 12 (1923): 1–3.

[10] McDougald, *A Time-Line Chronology*, 25–39.

[11] McDougald, *A Time-Line Chronology*, 43–44.

(Nashville) in 1910. By 1928, some 5.8 percent of Southern Negroes attended high schools compared to 17.7 percent of Southern whites. Twenty-one black high schools existed in Tennessee by 1930, but some of them (i.e., Hardeman County) did not have a twelfth grade.[12] Arthur V. Haynes, a native of Nashville wrote,

> There were no high schools for Negroes operated by the public school system in Davidson County until the late 30's. There was one high school in Nashville [Pearl H.S.] which was attended by the city kids. A tuition charge was made for any county students who were admitted. Roger Williams University, located only about a half-mile from us [in east Nashville], operated a high school department like many other colleges....[13]

In 1930, America had 11.9 million Negroes (9.4 million in the South). Tennessee had 477,646 (18.3 percent) blacks, but fewer than 100 of them graduated annually from high schools.[14] Not until the Rosenwald Fund of Chicago came south in 1913 and began to infuse funds and national building standards did several Tennessee counties began to erect more schools for blacks and whites. Union H.S. in Gallatin, Sumner County, was built in 1922 for $17,875; black citizens raised $5,825; Rosenwald contributed $2,100, and public money covered $9,950.[15]

For 1923–24, Tennessee A&I enrolled 457 students for fall quarter, 460 for winter, 535 for spring, 905 for summer, and had a $97,908.75 budget including $49,709.81 in state funds. President Hale's report to the SBOE also said A&I had enrolled 14,510 students since 1912, including 5,414 in the regular quarters and 9,096 in the summer sessions. Students originated from 81 of Tennessee's 95 counties. Several teacher vacancies were unfilled, but the staff remained effective. The institution had 38 faculty members including Laura Averitte

---

[12] J.Q. Johnson, "Negro Schools and Universities of Nashville," "World Largest Negro Publishing House," and "Fisk University," Nashville *Banner*, 13, 25 May 1924, 4, 5, 8, 18; "Roger Williams University," Nashville *Tennessean*, 4 June 1924, 17. The college graduates are not mentioned in Hale's reports to the SBOE until 6 November 1924, report, box 138, folders 1–5, RG 273, Tennessee State Library and Archives (TSLA); Juan Williams and Dwayne Ashley "Tennessee State University," *I'll Find a Way or Make One: A Tribute to Historically Black Colleges and Universities* (New York: HarperCollins, 2004) 407.

[13] Arthur V. Haynes, *Scars of Segregation: An Autobiography* (New York: Vantage Press, 1974) 23.

[14] Ina C. Brown, *National Survey of Higher Education of Negroes: Socio-Economic Approach to Educational Problems* (Washington DC: US Office of Education, 1942) 556; Ambrose Caliver, *Secondary Education for Negroes*, US Bureau of Education, *Bulletin No. 17* (Washington DC: US Bureau of Education, 1932) 7, 11, 25, 29, 77, table 11.

[15] Velma H. Brinkley and Mary H. Malone, *Images of America: African American Life in Sumner County* (Dover NH: Arcadia Publishing, 1998) 33. Note: Nashville had 123,424 people—Nashville *Banner*, 17 July 1924, 1.

(English), Martha M. Brown (library and music), Harriet E. Hale, John H. Hale (physician), C. Victor Roman (biology-sex education), Frances E. Thompson (art), Mary L. Wilson (dean of women), fifteen Smith-Hughes workers, and twelve extension workers, including two men as paid Rosenwald agents. Claude Hezekiah Harper (University of Michigan and Howard University) became head of education, organizer and advisor of the Sais Honorary Scholastic Society, and dean of the College. Harper was studying for his doctorate at Cornell University. No public HBCU offered graduate studies until 1921, and only three HBCUs did so by 1935.[16]

On 27 May 1924, Tennessee Agricultural & Industrial State Normal School for Negroes graduated the first recipients of the A.B. degree: Walter Daniel Denney (Lebanon), Aeolian Lockert (Clarksville), William M. Lowe (Mobile, Alabama), Lora A. Myers (Nashville), Reginald C. Neblett (Clarksville), Walter V. Potter (Smithville), Christopher C. Purdy (Tiptonville), and Thudman A. Ramsey (Nashville). Lockert became A&I's Smith-Hughes agent in Whiteville, gained a degree from Michigan State College, and joined the A&I faculty in agriculture. Lora Meyers became home demonstration agent in Robertson County. Reginald Neblet and Walter D. Denny completed programs at Meharry Medical College. Other graduates included 113 Normal and 48 Academic diplomas, and 41 certificates in sewing, chauffeur skills, penmanship, dressmaking, "mechanical engineering" (steam engines), and auto mechanics. The SBOE now required the separation of secondary school work from college studies.[17]

Alma Mater, Buildings, and Symbols Fit for a College

Tennessee A&I State Normal School needed facilities fit for a college. On 6 February 1924, Hale wrote to Commissioner Harned that "I suggest a representative of the General Education Board be invited to visit the school, and that our Commissioner or representative of our State Board of Education go to

---

[16] A&I *The Bulletin* (1922–30), for data on faculty, graduates, curricula, buildings, and students; Charles Victor Roman, *History of Meharry Medical College* (Nashville: author, 1934) 1–51; W.J. Hale, *Report to SBOE*, 6 February 1924, box 138, folders 1–5, SBOE Records, RG 273, TSLA.

[17] McDougald, *A Time-Line Chronology*, 43–44; J.Q. Johnson, "Negro Schools and Universities of Nashville," "World Largest Negro Publishing House," and "Fisk University," Nashville *Banner*, 13, 25 May 1924, 4, 5, 8, 18; "Roger Williams University," Nashville *Tennessean*, 4 June 1924, 17. The college graduates are not mentioned in Hale's reports to the SBOE until 6 November 1924, report, box 138, folders 1–5, RG 273, TSLA; Juan Williams and Dwayne Ashley "Tennessee State University," *I'll Find a Way or Make One: A Tribute to Historically Black Colleges and Universities* (New York: HarperCollins, 2004) 407; "Negro State Normal," Nashville *Banner*, 22, 27 May 1924, 7, 17.

New York, if necessary, to put our needs before the General Education Board." Hale presented his requests to the SBOE meeting on February 7, and the motion was approved. On April 28, Hale reported to Harned on the equipping of "our beautiful dining room with an up-to-date cafeteria, by which we are able to serve three hot meals a day to our students and teachers. Through this means we also teach lessons in the collection of foods to meet proper bodily needs. The cafeteria, therefore, is our education asset." And "Music has been a vital part of our activities." He claimed the institution served 13,511 students since 1912. He asked for the construction of a library, science building, teachers' home, a practice school, and equipment for science, a gym, and band instruments. On May 8, the SBOE agreed to ask the legislature for matching capital funds. On the June 12 report to SBOE, Hale reported a total of 1,440 students including 535 for the regular three quarters and 905 for the summer session.[18]

Tennessee A&I became the state's Negro civic and social center, including the Du Bois Literary and Debating Society, Sigma Phi Psi, Alpha Gamma Sigma (women), Memphis-Shelby County Club, Chattanooga Club, Book Lovers Club, Do Society, Epsilon Sigma Chi Honor Society, YMCA, YWCA, and the College Chorus; the Sais Society (1919), the Billy Hale Junior Club (1915), organized by David Anderson and others, and the Supreme Circle Club (1919).[19]

Tennessee A&I reportedly had the largest summer program in Tennessee. But rumors circulated that people flocked to A&I's summer school to have a good time "on the hill." Harned sent a letter to Hale: "Teachers must attend classes a minimum of 24 days during an entire six weeks of summer, with no more than six days absent for sickness. The purpose of the summer school work is to improve the efficiency of the teachers and not to help them mark time for the purpose of having their certificates renewed. Let's all strive for higher standards."[20]

On 30 September 1924, Harned enlisted the help of the director of extension at the University of Tennessee (UT) to help lay out plans for locating A&I's new buildings. Hale then submitted "A Building Program Plan." He requested

---

[18] A&I *The Bulletin* (1922–30); A&I *The Bulletin* (1933–41); W.J. Hale to P.L. Harned, 8 May 1924, Presidential Papers, 1912–, W.J. Hale Papers, Special Collections, TSU; Hale to Harned, 6 February 1924, box 138, folders 1–5, Tennessee Department of Education Records, 1874–1984, RG 273; series 6, box 384, folder 26, and box 8, 1928–30, Board Chair P.L. Harned, mf 9, box 4, Enrollment in Teachers' Colleges, 1928, Commissioner of Education Records, 1913–70, RG 92, TSLA. Note: Hale counted the fall, winter, and spring quarter enrollments as a total figure, which inflated his figures, but the SBOE later disallowed this accounting of enrollment on the quarterly and annual reports.

[19] Ibid. Note: the Tennessee Department of Education and the Commissioner of Education were created by the Legislature in 1923.

[20] Education Commissioner P.L. Harned to W.J. Hale, Nashville, 27 May 1924, Tennessee A&I, SBOE Minutes, 1907–83, RG 245, TSLA, 1–270, 1–128, 1–236, 1–124, 1–221.

ownership of 80 acres of land across Centennial Boulevard (south side) to safeguard the institution against any undesirable development. Hale wrote to Harned: "In view of the growing needs of the physical equipment for the State Agriculture and Industrial School for Negroes and the very considerable cost of buildings and equipment at this time—feeling that the State might obtain aid from the General Education Board, I went to New York last July for a conference with this board. The purpose of the trip was to interest the board in the development of the institution."[21]

Harned received a letter from the GEB, suggesting that the state submit a building plan and a funding request for Tennessee A&I. Hale quickly appointed three faculty members to form a committee for facilities planning. They expanded Hale's list and recommended a full-service library to replace the two-classroom library in Old Main, an additional dormitory for girls, more teachers' cottages, and a science building. Harned and the SBOE agreed to send the need for $325,000 to the legislature: "It is the desire of the Board to develop this institution so that it will be the outstanding Negro institution in the South."[22]

In the fall of 1924–25, the newly equipped gym opened on the top floor of the Boys' Trades Building (industrial arts). The renovation included installation of a new water line to increase pressure for fire fighting and a vacuum steam line to replace stoves. They expanded the library in old Main. Hale's 6 November 1924, report to the SBOE counted 498 in the fall enrollment and 8 college graduates for 1924. On the same day, Frank Bachman of the GEB sent a telegram to Harned to say that the state had approved Tennessee A&I's request.[23]

In 1924, the staff began to define Tennessee State's collegiate symbols. W.J. Hale refined the school's motto: "Enter to Learn, Work; Go Forth to Serve." "One must raise oneself to the highest potential of efficiency and then employ oneself with the highest actually efficiency," he said. The school had a yearbook, *The Radio* (1925). Shortly after, *The Ayeni* [pronounced A and I] replaced *The Radio* and gained membership in the National Scholastic Press Association. Hayden Wilson (1920 graduate) directed the band and orchestra from 1926–29, traveled and studied in Europe, became a teacher in St. Louis. Wilson co-authored the *Alma Mater* with Laura Averitte (English and drama):

---

[21] Correspondence between Hale and Harned, P.L. Harned files, 1924–29, box 242, folder 1, box 242, folder 2, 1930–36, Commissioner of Education Records 1913–70, RG 92, TSLA; Tennessee A&I Normal College, 1924–25, box 1, folder 7, A&I, 1928, box 3, folder 9, State Board of Education Records, 1815–1958, RG 91, TSLA.

[22] Ibid; SBOE Minutes, 6 August 1924, SBOE to GEB, 6 November 1924, box 138, RG 273.

[23] Ibid, Hale, *Report to SBOE*, 6 November 1924, telegram from F.J. Bachman, General Education Board, New York, to P.L. Harned, box 138, folders 1–5, RG 273.

In the land of gold-en sun-shine,
By the Cumb'r-land's fer-tile shore.
Stands a school for great-est ser-vice
One that we a-dore.
Al-ma Ma-ter, how we love thee,
Love thy white and blue
May we strive to meet Thy Man-dates
With faith that's true.

Man-y come to Thee for know-ledge,
Come from East, North, South and West.
For they know that Thou dost of-fer
Such a rich be-quest.
Al-ma Ma-ter, all Thy chil-dren
Wor-ship at Thy shrine;
May the God of na-tions bless thee
With gifts di-vine

Send forth sons both strong and val-iant,
Send forth daughters wise and true.
Filled with hope and daunt-less courage
Mo-tives sane and true.
Al-ma Ma-ter, kind-ly moth-er
Smile on Ten-nes-see
May she lift her head toward heav-en
Honor Country, God and Thee.[24]

Averitte graduated from Tennessee A&I in 1918, joined the English faculty, and gained graduate degrees from Columbia University. President Hale asked art teacher Frances E. Thompson to design a seal for the college in place of the usual State of Tennessee seal. The Tennessee A&I State Normal Teacher's College seal was similar to the state seal, but had a lamp and rays of light symbolizing the spread of learning, a plowshare and a sheaf of wheat to symbolize the school's agriculture mission, and a mechanical wheel to symbolize the industrial, business, and commerce curricula; an open book denoted the liberal arts education mission. Thompson used the circle and the shield divided into three parts: Agriculture in the upper left, industry in the upper right, and education in the lower center—the larger part of the shield, because education was the important thing. She placed the slogan—Think, Work, Serve—beneath the symbol. "To emphasize learning I placed a hand holding a lamp, extending rays

[24] TSU, "Composers of the 'Alma Mater'," *The Tennessean: Diamond Jubilee, 75th Anniversary Edition* (1987) 23. Wilson and Averitte were honored by the Alumni Association at Homecoming in 1949.

of light above the symbol." [25] Thompson completed the lettering. The college catalog evolved into a separate document, allowing *The Bulletin* to become the newsletter for training journalism students.

On 10 November 1924, Hale and his faculty committee sent the campus master plan drawings to Commissioner P.L. Harned. The SBOE then sent a three-man team to inspect A&I's administration, finances, and buildings, and after a week, they submitted a report. On November 24, Hale asked Commissioner Harned for a formal letter and a SBOE resolution to be sent to the GEB. Harned, the SBOE, and the governor approved the request. On December 2, the Tennessee A&I faculty committee further suggested some landscaping plants in order to beautify the rocky campus that only had some dirt roads and walkways.[26]

Tennessee State now existed in a crowded, highly competitive Athens of the South: Fisk University announced the successful campaign to raise a one-million-dollar endowment for paying faculty salaries and to attract some top professors in the upcoming five years. Pearl High School graduated 65 students in June 1924, and Walden College, Meharry Medical College, and Roger Williams University announced dozens of graduates that year.

Changing the Name to Tennessee A&I State Normal Teachers College

Beginning 1925–26, Tennessee A&I State Normal School for Negroes changed its name to Tennessee A&I State Normal Teachers College. State law said the function of the agricultural and industrial normal college for Negroes "shall be to train Negro students in agriculture, home economics, trades, and industry, and prepare teachers for elementary and high school for Negroes in the state. All curricula of said college shall conform to the federal statue providing for land-grant colleges." Tennessee A&I charged no tuition for persons with a high school diploma, admitted persons over 21 as special students, and ensured that nonresidents of the state paid tuition rates as prescribed by the SBOE. Students needed 90 quarter hour credits for the Normal School diploma and 180 quarter hours (120 semester hours) for a college degree. Entering students had to have good moral character, attend an orientation session during College Week, and have 15 high school units to enter the college curricula. There were minors in chemistry, pre-medicine, and economics, and major areas in agricultural and biological sciences, education and teacher training, languages, literature and fine

---

[25] See Frances E. Thompson digital file, Special Collections, TSU, "Laura M. Averitte" in History Makers at TSU, Frances E. Thompson, *Art in the Elementary Schools* (Nashville: SBOE, Negro Division, 1943) 1–21; Note: Thompson, a graduate of Radcliffe College, served at A&I from 1923 until 1969.

[26] W.J. Hale files, Special Collections, TSU; A&I, box 199, folder 8, 1923–25, SBOE Record Group 245, TSLA.

arts, physical education and mathematics, social studies, and secretarial commerce.[27]

Some reorganization of the curriculum resulted from constructive criticism from the University of Chicago in August 1924 after a Tennessee A&I student enrolled at the university without the proper credentials. The university admitted the student into a study program for two months with the intent of admitting her to full college work the following quarter. In the meantime, the adviser wrote to Commissioner Harned saying that Tennessee A&I State Normal needed to separate college and high school work on a clear transcript and revise the catalog to show just what curricula were being offered and what credit hours were assigned in subjects to complete any curriculum: "The whole system of recording and transcribing credits needs to be studied and perhaps revised."[28] Harned asked Hale to begin to submit transcripts with applications for diplomas before the SBOE would approve the graduates. Since there had recently been problems with diplomas at West Tennessee State Normal School, Harned ordered system-wide uniform admission and graduation requirements.

In the summer of 1925, Hale visited Columbia University, Ohio University, Oberlin College, University of Chicago, and Western Reserve University to recruit new faculty, find graduate study opportunities for faculty members, and learn more about college organization. In the meantime, the 1925 summer school students agreed to help raise $65,000 for the college building fund. One hundred and sixty thousand dollars was solicited from the GEB and a matching amount came from the state. The fall enrollment included 161 men and 288 women. From 1912 to 1925, A&I serviced 16,321 students and had eight college graduates.[29]

The 1925–26 college graduates totaled 16 students, including Edith E. Foster, Leon D. Foster, and Broughton Jones. Edith and Leon Foster were the children of the janitor, while Jones was one of the first students from Memphis to complete A&I College.[30]

Students at Tennessee A&I came from all walks of life and often returned to their home towns, spreading black college graduates throughout Tennessee's rural counties. The Bate family, in particular, exemplified the importance of Tennessee A&I in this mission. Ola Mae Bate was the first Negro woman in

---

[27] A&I *The Bulletin* (1925–26): 1–10.

[28] A&I *The Bulletin* 15 no. 1 (1925–26): 1–2. Correspondence between Hale and Harned, P.L. Harned files, 1924–29, box 242, folder 1, box 242, folder 2, 1930–36, Commissioner of Education Records 1913–70, RG 92, TSLA

[29] Ibid.; McDougald, *A Time-Line Chronology*, 42–45; Hale's reports to the SBOE, 7 May, 6 November 1925, box 1, folder 7, SBOE, RG 91; "Tenn. State College Breaks Enrollment Record," *The Bulletin* 16, nos. 2–3 (October–November 1927).

[30] *The Radio* 2, the yearbook, 1926, Special Collections, TSU; McDougald, *A Time-Line Chronology*, 43–46.

Sumner County to graduate from college. Born in Sumner County in 1902, Ola attended high school at Roger Williams University in Nashville, where her mother and father had completed the normal school program prior to becoming teachers. Ola Bate recalled that her mother and father were picking blackberries in the fields in 1923 when she called to tell the good news of being admitted to Tennessee A&I State Normal School's four-year college program. She recalled the good times when they cleaned out the coal truck to haul the students to the Ryman Auditorium in downtown Nashville to hear the Rev. Ellington preach his annual "Prodigal Son" sermon—they would do almost anything just to get off the rural A&I campus. Bate remembered how President Hale was liked but feared by students. They saw him two or three times a week, froze in their actions, spoke cordially to him, and then talked about him when he walked away. Bate also remembered the annual visits by the legislators and all the cleaning the students had to do to get ready for the visit. The white men visited the classes, looking as if they knew what was going on, asking the students a few questions—mostly what county they were from. The students dined well on that day, though the food at A&I was pretty good anyway. On May Day, the students had breakfast at 9 a.m., festivities through the day, and drama at night. The matron sometimes allowed the boys to come over to the girls' [west] side of the campus. Ola Bate was sent over to a couple on the swing set to tell the boy he was too close to the girl. A chaperone was required for a couple to go off campus. Ola Mae taught in the public schools for 41 years before retiring in Sumner County. She received the Mary C. Strobel Award at age 82 for forty years of unselfish public service. She attended TSU's 89th summer commencement before she died in 2005.

Her two brothers, Charles and Wilbur, completed college degrees at Tennessee A&I. Charles B. Bate became a medical doctor, and Wilbur a college professor. Their mother Nora O. Bate rode the Trailways bus back and forth between her rural teaching job to complete additional studies at Tennessee A&I. Nora was born in the hills of northern Trousdale County to Pleasant and Caroline Turner, enrolled in high school at Fisk University, and graduated from Roger Williams University normal school in 1900. In June 1901, she married Charles B. Bate, the first Negro man in Sumner County to earn a college degree. Nora Bate began teaching in a one-room Sumner County public school with fifty-one students. When teachers were required by the county to pass a certification examination in 1922, she was the only Negro to pass. She was selected to teach English, Latin, and library science at the ten-teacher Union High School. She entered Tennessee A&I in 1924 in the summers, and graduated in 1943 at age 63. Union High School graduated 22 students including seven males in 1944.[31]

---

[31] "Ola Bate Roberson showered with roses during 75-year anniversary," *TSU Alumni Life* 1, no. 1 (Spring 2002): 8; the author's interview with Ola Bate Roberson,

Rheba I. Palmer (class of 1926) was editor-in-chief of *The Radio* (1926), which she and the staff dedicated to "our honorable President, W.J. Hale." *The Radio* included photographs of the faculty, staff, and students. One local business, Terry's Pharmacy, gave the students an advertisement for *The Radio,* which included views of the institution's sports teams and the best of student writings. Nathaniel D. Williams, who would become a famous Memphis journalist and Tennessee's first black radio personality, wrote one of his first essays titled "The Collegian" in *The Radio* (1926), explaining what college life was like at A&I.[32]

In 1926, James C. Napier used his influence to get the electric streetcar line extended to the 190-acre campus. Napier and Hale persuaded the Tennessee Interracial League to help raise some private capital funds, and Henry A. Boyd advertised this capital campaign in the Nashville *Globe.* The Colored Division formed a Funding Committee, and recommended the name W.J. Hale for the new women's dormitory. The schoolteachers, who attended summer classes and the League's meetings, heartily supported this recommendation. They, and other Negro citizens, donated $65,000 for the proposed facilities. The governor instructed the SBOE to request that Hale "deposit all collections of money with the state funds and make report of same."[33]

Governor Austin Peay (1923-1927) attempted further reform of Tennessee's antiquated education system. His most important accomplishment was the General Education Act (1925) that set standards for teacher licenses, the codification of state education laws, and conversion of the state normal schools into four-year teachers' colleges. Peay also focused on building professional programs to serve rural Tennessee communities and the equalization of funds to permit all the counties to have eight-month terms and pay teachers according to a state salary schedule. In his 1927 message to the General Assembly, Peay recommended $600,000 for new buildings and improvements at the teachers' colleges and set the University of Tennessee as the capstone of the whole educational system. He asked for not less than $500,000 a year to go to UT for the following five years. Peay also chastised the legislature for providing so little money to expand health care: "And then what about the Negroes? No provision is made for them. So the big problem is what to do with our tubercular Negroes.

Gallatin, Tennessee, spring 2002, Lovett Papers, Special Collections, TSU. Paul Oldham, "This family loved Gov. Bate, Dr. Bate," Nashville *Tennessean,* 1 January 1992, 1G, 3G.

[32] *The Radio,* 2, the yearbook, 1926, Special Collections, TSU; Ernestine Jenkins, "The Voice of Memphis, WDIA, Nat D. Williams, and Black Radio Culture in the Early Civil Rights Era," *Tennessee Historical Quarterly* 65 (Fall 2006): 254–67; McDougald, *A Time-Line Chronology,* 43–46.

[33] Austin Peay to the SBOE, 26 November 1926, SBOE Papers; *Messages of the Governors of Tennessee 1921–1933,* vol. 10, ed. Steven V. Ash (Nashville: Tennessee Historical Commission, 1990); McDougald, *A Time-Line Chronology,* 46.

You are doing nothing for them."[34] Some 273 Negroes per 100,000 of the population, compared to 104 whites per 100,000 of the population, died of tuberculosis in Tennessee. A Certificate of Health was now required for A&I students.[35] Governor Peay protested spending public funds to pay Confederate pensions: "The Lost Cause is sacred to the South, and let us continue to hold its heroes in everlasting affection … but I solemnly protest against our pension rolls bestowing unearned gratuities or becoming the medium for a promiscuous waste of public funds."[36] Nevertheless, Governor Peay requested no specific funds for black citizens.

With the help of Northern philanthropists, state, and private funds, Tennessee A&I State Normal Teachers College began construction of a science building, a women's dormitory, and a library. By enclosing the south end of the Old Campus with these three new facilities, the Old Campus then had a quadrangle design with a center plaza. Students, alumni, and teachers donated stone benches and money to construct a large fountain in front (north) of the new library. The Delta Tau Iota Club donated the water fountain. The Alba Rosa Club donated the stone benches. After planting of trees, the fountain and benches made an inviting place to gather and relax in front of the library. It lit up beautifully at night through arched panes of glass windows.[37]

Hale saved the opening of the three buildings for the summer session of 1927. They turned on the lights in the Memorial Library during the evening of 22 June 1927. Hale Hall Women's Dormitory opened on 25 June 1927, three stories high, with 128 rooms, constructed with fireproof materials at an initial cost of $70,000 and later valued at $136,000. Harned Science Hall was opened on June 27 for the 7:30 morning classes, at a cost of $96,000, with 13 recital rooms and laboratories to house departments of commercial business, physics, chemistry,

---

[34] Elbridge Sibley, *Differential Mortality in Tennessee, 1917–1928* (Washington DC: Negro Universities Press, 1930, 1969) 1–20. Negroes were twice as likely as whites to die of pneumonia, typhoid, pellagra, and tuberculosis, partly because there were not enough black doctors.

[35] Austin Peay, "Message to the General Assembly, 6 January 1927," *Messages of the Governors of Tennessee 1921–1933*, 197–220; Joseph T. Macpherson, "Democratic Progressivism in Tennessee: the Administrations of Governor Austin Peay 1923–1927," *East Tennessee Historical Society Papers* 40, no. 1 (1968): 50–61; Paul H. Bergeron, Stephen V. Ash, and Jeanette Keith, *Tennesseans and Their History* (Knoxville: University of Tennessee Press, 1999) 236–41; Tennessee Senate and House Journals, 1909–1920: SBOE reports, normal school presidents' reports, and W.J. Hale reports on Tennessee A&I.

[36] "Inaugural Address of January 18, 1927," *Messages of the Governors of Tennessee 1921–1933*, 225.

[37] McDougald, *A Time-Line Chronology*, 46–54; Harned was commissioner, 1923–1932; A&I construction, vault, box 2, folders 104–06, 1928, A. & I construction, box 234, 1928, RG 92, TSLA.

biology, agriculture, and private studies for the teachers. In 1927–28, regular session students voted to name the new science building for Perry L. Harned, "a Christian gentleman." This building had attractive trimmings in white marble. The new library had Greek columns on its north side. Hale moved the administrative offices from the renovated A-Building (Old Main) and across the quadrangle to the first floor of the new library. The old Training School moved from the Girls' Trades Building to Old Main.[38]

Carter G. Woodson, a history professor at Howard University in Washington and head of the Association for the Study of Negro Life and History, Inc. (ASNLH) (1916–), was the A&I Chapel speaker on "'The Negro in American History" in May 1927. Woodson and the ASNLH initiated Negro History Week in 1926. Woodson, and later his colleague Lorenzo Greene, began visits to Negro college campuses in efforts to get the students to write more about their people's history. Woodson, who earned a PhD from Harvard University, returned to the A&I campus on 24 June 1927, when they inaugurated the local branch of the ASNLH in A&I's brand new Memorial Library. They elected Nashville native George W. Gore Jr. as chapter president.[39]

The mayor of Nashville gave the welcoming speech at the opening summer school convocation. The Negro State Teachers' Association convened on campus on 2 July 1927. A field agent for the General Education Board (GEB) was the main speaker. Also on campus were the National Association of Teachers in Colored Schools (NATCS), Supervisors and Principals Conference, and the Tennessee Interracial League. NATCS elected Hale as their first president.[40]

Becoming Tennessee A&I State Teachers College

In fall 1927, the institution dropped the word Normal and became Tennessee A&I State Teachers College. It began phasing out the two-year program. Tennessee A&I State Teachers College had 700 students representing all Tennessee counties, several other states, and some foreign countries. About 100 active schoolteachers entered the last six weeks of spring quarter—when often there was a planting season break for many rural Negro schools. The institution began to offer late evening classes, including extension work for teachers, nurses, commercial workers, social workers, ministers, and others in towns with a critical mass of students. Teacher education students had to take 9 hours of physical education. Expenses increased to $62.80 plus $39 for board per quarter, $201 total cost with a $4.20 discount for advance payment. Hale started

---

[38] McDougald, *A Time-Line Chronology*, 43–55.
[39] Gore was dean at Tennessee A&I by 1928 and a native of Nashville who graduated from Pearl High School.
[40] McDougald, *A Time-Line Chronology*, 45–54.

scholarships in piano and voice. He also became vice president of the National Negro Business League during the St. Louis meeting in August 1927.[41]

Commissioner Harned asked President Hale to submit enrollment reports and to describe other new buildings that the institution needed. The faculty and staff envisioned a new administration building with a large auditorium to hold 1,200 people. They needed a gymnasium, a swimming pool (three swimming courses had to be created), industrial arts buildings to replace the Boys' and Girls' trades buildings, and more dormitories. Old Main had suffered a fire in the picture show booth. Enrollment increased 56 percent in the years 1922–27.[42]

President Hale reported to the SBOE that George W. Gore Jr. *and* Dean Claude H. Harper vacated their positions. Hale persuaded Gore to change his mind and assume Harper's position. Dean-elect Gore had completed DePauw University and began his tenure at State Normal in the fall of 1923. He became executive secretary of the Tennessee teachers association and co-founder of Alpha Kappa Mu Honor Society. Gore became adviser to the yearbook staff, editor and adviser to the *Bulletin*, and taught classes in English and journalism. Students and faculty members considered him a scholar. He used a GEB fellowship to continue his graduate studies.[43] Dean Gore organized Tennessee A&I State Teachers College into departments of agriculture, art, biology, education, English, foreign languages, geography, health, history and political science, home economics, industrial education, library science, mathematics, music, physical education, physical science, secretarial commerce, sociology and economics, speech, and the Practice School Department. John W. Riley became the acting principal of the Tennessee A&I High School Department. College-level students could be admitted with 16 high school credits or on the basis of an entrance examination from an unaccredited high school program and on a temporary basis until inaccessible credits could be confirmed. A&I accepted no students below age 14 except by special permission. Laura Averitte supervised the Kindergarten class of 11 students and 5 practice teachers. Each boarding student was required to write a letter home each Sunday. "The courses are so planned as to make the Negroes useful citizens," said Hale.[44]

In January 1928, philanthropist Julius Rosenwald gave $2,000 to the library book fund. After visiting the campus, he said, "Service and standing entitles the

---

[41] Ibid.; Cordell H. Williams, "The Life of James Carroll Napier from 1845–1940," (master's thesis, Tennessee A&I State University, 1955).

[42] P.L. Harned to W.J. Hale, Nashville, 10 October 1927, SBOE RG 273.

[43] Ibid.; Hale to Harned, Nashville, 1 November 1927; McDougald, *A Time-Line Chronology*, 47.

[44] A&I *The Bulletin* 13, no. 12 (1927); *The Bulletin* 15, no. 1 (1928–29); *The Bulletin of the Tennessee State Association of Colored Teachers* 1, no. 1 (1927); McDougald, *A Time-Line Chronology*, 47, 48, 50–56.

institution to recognition." By 1928, the Rosenwald Fund had built 296 school buildings for Negroes in Tennessee at a cost of $1,424,434, including $245,348 (matching funds) raised by Negroes. Tennessee received money to help build schools for 42,075 students, both black and white. The Fund eventually erected 366 Rosenwald schools—including 26 in predominantly black Haywood County. Rosenwald schoolhouses housed a majority of rural Negro children attending Tennessee public schools. Throughout the South, Rosenwald built 4,119 Negro schools at a cost of $18.9 million including $3.7 million contributed by Negroes and $830,073 by other contributors. When the Rosenwald Fund closed in 1947–48, some 5,334 Rosenwald schools existed in Southern states.[45]

Tennessee A&I State Teachers College enrolled 1,049 students in 1927–28. Women outnumbered men, but most women were in the home economics programs. In the 1928 study of Negro education, and following a visit to the campus, the US Bureau of Education team praised Tennessee A&I State Teachers College for its statewide involvement in the training of teachers and the quality of instruction. Faculty salaries ranged from $1,260 to $1,960 a year. The visiting team said more faculty members needed graduate degrees even though many of them already were working on graduate degrees in Northern universities. The state required each faculty member to have a four-year college degree and at least one year of graduate school. President Hale himself had no four-year college degree and no graduate studies; he no longer was listed as a faculty member and did not teach courses. The team visitors said the teaching loads of the faculty were burdensome in a number of instances, particularly with regard to student clock hours, and ultimately could impair the quality of student education and the morale of the teaching body. At least six teachers engaged 600 to 800 student clock hours per term—meaning they taught 200 to 265 students per quarter. Of 46 classes taught in the college, class size could reach 50 students. The team praised the construction of the new library, science building, and women's dormitory as a quality too little seen in college buildings.[46] They praised Gore's leadership, but said that A&I faculty and staff salaries were too low. Tennessee A&I was not ready to apply for SACS accreditation.

The *National Survey of the Higher Education of Negroes* (1928) provided new expectations for Negro institutions of higher education. The proliferation of

---

[45] Mary S. Hoffschwelle, *The Rosenwald Schools in the American South* (Gainesville: University Press of Florida, 2006); Peter M. Ascoli, *Julius Rosenwald: The Man Who Built Sears, Roebuck and Advanced the Cause of Black Education in the American South* (Bloomington: Indiana University Press, 2006); Rosenwald building agents, 1926–27, box 20–21, box 36, Rosenwald Fund, S.L. Smith, and R.E. Clay files, 14–18, 1933–35, and R.E. Clay, box 142, 1933–43, RG 92.

[46] US Office of Education, *National Survey of the Higher Education of Negroes* (Washington DC: Bureau of Education, 1928) 1–141.

institutions called black "colleges" still numbered more than 200. Overall, US institutions produced 83,065 bachelor's degrees in 1928, including 1,512 held by Negroes. The collegiate-level HBCUs enrolled 13,860 students in two- and four-year programs and granted 165 BA degrees in 1926–27. The SBOE ordered copies of the *U.S. Survey of Negro Colleges* for all its members.[47]

Philanthropic agencies pushed the Commission on Interracial Cooperation (CIC) and the US Bureau of Education to pressure Jim Crow officials to continue to improve Negro access to quality education. Even so, while Tennessee A&I received a small increase in funds in 1927–28, the state of Tennessee approved $750,000 for the construction of new facilities at four of the white public colleges. On 8 October 1928, the SBOE met to distribute a $110,000 equalization fund, and after considerable debate, the commissioners gave the HBCU slightly more than the smallest white school. They gave 18 percent to Tennessee A&I, which had 20.4 percent of the enrollment in SBOE colleges. In a 6 July 1929 meeting, the SBOE approved an equitable division of federal agricultural vocational: 80 percent for whites, 20 percent for the blacks. A&I now included 650 college students (416 boarders) and 227 high school students (96 boarders) for summer. The regular session included 607 college students (121 male and 200 female boarders), 283 high school pupils (106 boarders), and 46 grammar school children (5 boarders). For 1928–29, A&I serviced altogether 1,813 students but without enough dormitories.[48]

The governor, President Hale, and three SBOE members met with a Rosenwald Fund agent in March 1930 to discuss further building and equipment needs for Tennessee A&I. The SBOE approved Hale's request to ask the Andrew Carnegie Corporation for funds to improve the A&I library: Carnegie Corporation and the Spelman Fund had already built and stocked a new library at Fisk University. Hale still was proposing a practice school building and a new building for men's vocational programs and space for the 164 students in agricultural, trades, and industry. There were also 144 students in home economics needing new equipment, and A&I needed an administration building with offices, classrooms, a gymnasium, and restrooms. Hale told the philanthropists that Tennessee A&I State Teachers College needed another $525,000. Rosenwald gave money to proceed with bids to build four teachers' cottages totaling $25,000. The SBOE approved land purchases from the Normal View Land Company, and in February 1928, bids for the new heating plant were

---

[47] Ibid.; correspondence, appropriations for Teachers Colleges, 1927–28, box 136, folder 2, RG 273.

[48] A&I, *1928–29 Enrollment Report to the SBOE*, Special Collections, TSU.

accepted for construction, for a total of $70,000. The campus now consisted of twelve structures and 231 acres including a large farm.[49]

On 9 November 1928, Hale wrote to Harned, requesting that landscape architect D.A. Williston be hired to prepare plans for the campus and grounds. Williston already had answered on November 3 Hale's October 31 requests for services. Williston would grow the plants in the campus nursery and buy local shrubbery. He wanted to hire greenhouse caretaker and gardener E.Z. Nesbit at $65 a month. It would take two years to transform the rocky hill into a presentable campus, including asphalt roads, concrete walkways and general landscaping. They intended to use A&I student labor.[50]

In the fall of 1929, there was a 22.9 percent enrollment increase, and for the year 1929–30, A&I graduated 28 persons with bachelor's degrees. Howard L. Thurman—a premier Negro theologian—addressed the Chapel on 2 October 1929, speaking on "Deep River: Life is a process changing like a River."[51]

Meanwhile, on 24 October 1929 the stock market crashed, signaling the beginning of the Great Depression. President Herbert G. Hoover (R) tried some conservative remedies to restart the American economy, but things got worse. Unemployment reached 25 percent overall, and 50 percent of black Americans had no job because the agricultural sector, in particular, suffered greatly. Negro and white tenant farmers went on strike and organized the Southern Tenants Farmers Union. Many landowners banded together and expelled them from the farms; an estimated half a million poor Negroes migrated out of the Mississippi Delta into Memphis and other towns. In urban areas, Jim Crow rules allowed white workers to take jobs from Negroes. Many Negro children went malnourished; shantytowns for whites sprung up around Knoxville. Private charities tried to give relief, and Negro churches kept many people alive. Hale dipped into his reserves and depended more heavily on the Northern philanthropic agencies. A&I's Student Employment Bureau gave a limited amount of work to needy students to meet their expenses. The state of Tennessee budget suffered, but funding of education continued, partly due to the effective organization of white and black teachers' associations in the 1930s.[52]

Negro families in West Tennessee, especially those dependent on cotton crops, suffered the most from the Great Depression, and a great Negro migration from rural West Tennessee and the nearby Mississippi Delta counties inundated

---

[49] Rosenwald building agents, 1926–27, box 20–21, box 36, Rosenwald Fund, S.L. Smith, and R.E. Clay files, 14–18, 1933–35, and R.E. Clay, box 142, 1933–43, RG 92; note: Heating plant completed 6 June 1928, TSLA photo files.

[50] W.J. Hale to W.A. Williston, Nashville, 8 November 1928, Hale Papers, Special Collections, TSU.

[51] See A&I *The Bulletin* (1927–28).

[52] Lovett, *America's Black Colleges*, 99–141.

Memphis. However, Tennessee A&I student enrollment was not so dependent on West Tennessee students prior to 1929–39. Also, because of the poll tax and poverty, a third of all eligible voters did not vote in Tennessee state elections. However, in Memphis, Democratic Party machine boss Edward H. Crump paid the poll taxes, and blacks in that constituency voted heavily and maintained reasonable levels of employment, even with low wages, during the Great Depression. Federal New Deal funds kept employment projects alive in cities that were dominated by the Democrats, and Negroes found work, though not at the higher-paying levels of white workers. Memphis and similar Tennessee cities also included some middle-class, professional, and working-class blacks who could still afford to send their children to A&I State. In the mid-1940s, Tennessee A&I State College would use its football teams, choirs, and bands to recruit heavily in Memphis, Knoxville, Chattanooga (which had no black college), and Nashville.[53]

In November 1929, Hale became president of the Negro Land Grant Colleges Association. Webster L. Porter, editor of *The East Tennessee News* often visited the campus, reporting Negro progress. State officials visited the campus on 12 December 1929, and faculty members served as hosts and used personal cars to transport the guests from Capitol Hill. Governor Henry L. Horton (D) praised Hale and Tennessee A&I's progress. Students gave band and choral musical presentations and exhibited manual arts in Memorial Library.[54]

On 28 January 1930, President James H. Dillard of the Jeanes-Slater Fund addressed the student body. W.J. Hale received the Harmon Gold Medal for Distinguished Achievement in Education, including a $400 honorarium. Dean William Russell of Teachers College at Columbia University presented the award in the Tennessee A&I auditorium on February 18.

Hale still struggled with the limited resources from the state, and the budget for Tennessee A&I in 1929–30 of $394,466.34 came mostly from capital and non-state funds. State officials continued to deny adequate funding for the education of black citizens. The total state budget for education was $7,420,242.31, 30 percent of which was earmarked for colleges; the state debt included $2,915,000 for improvements at the University of Tennessee. Tennessee's teacher training institutions enrolled 8,881; the high schools 67,437; and the elementary schools included 558,056 students. Dean Gore complained that 122,586 [82 percent] of a 150,200 Negro scholastic-age population were

---

[53] Robert E. Corlew, *Tennessee A Short History* (Knoxville: University of Tennessee Press, 1979) 527; Bergeron, Ash, and Keith, *Tennesseans and Their History*, 273–79; B.L. Lovett, *The Civil Rights Movement in Tennessee: A Narrative History* (Knoxville: University of Tennessee Press, 2005) index.

[54] See A&I *The Bulletin* (1929).

attending schools, but that per-pupil daily attendance reached only 85,790 by 1929.[55]

Fortunately, Hale continued to win funds from Northern agencies. Negro schoolteachers and students on campus helped out, too. Hale was forever busy trying to make Tennessee A&I State Teachers College a showcase. In his diary, historian Lorenzo J. Greene wrote on 31 August 1930, "Such travesties on the name of colleges like Morris Brown [GA], Knoxville College, and even Bishop College [TX] would do well to merge or close down altogether. Baptist College at Little Rock is a disgrace, a misnomer, and an eternal mark of shame upon the Baptist denomination." Greene described Samuel Huston College in Texas, as "A fairly nice school," but noted that it "Can't compare with Tennessee State or Arkansas A.M.& N."[56] Admission into Tennessee A&I State Teachers College was becoming more rigorous and now required 16 high school units: 4 units of English, 1 unit of history, 1 unit of algebra, 1 unit of laboratory science, 1 unit of plane geometry, and 8 electives, in line with Carnegie and state standards. College students had to take a comprehensive senior final examination. Summer school allowed students to complete the bachelor's degree or high school certification.

In January 1931, the state distributed $1,225,000 for buildings at the teacher-training institutions. Governor Horton in his message to the General Assembly said, "Under the General Education Act of 1909 the Legislature endeavored to set up and establish in Tennessee the first broad, comprehensive and uniform system of public education." This system conceived by the legislature should "meet the needs of a growing and progressive state, should embrace first, and of primary importance, the elementary schools, then high schools, next the Teacher Training Colleges and, finally, as a capstone of the system, the University of the State." Horton called for a school of engineering at UT to serve the state's [white] citizens, a better way to govern the state institutions of higher education, and an effort to address duplication at institutions of higher learning: "It has not been many years since we had only a three-month term in our elementary schools and we had no county high schools. Today, we have in every county of the State one or more county high schools and elementary schools being conducted for a

---

[55] George W. Gore, "A Brief Survey of Public Education in Tennessee," *Broadcaster* (1931): 1.

[56] Lorenzo Green, *Selling Black History for Carter G. Woodson: 1930–1933*, ed. Arvarh E. Strickland (Colombia: University of Missouri Press, 1996) 1–121, 79–83, 110, 111, 118, 133, 164; A&I construction, vault, box 2, folder 104–06, 1928, and Tennessee A&I construction, box 234, 1928, RG 92, TSLA. Note: Greene worked at Lincoln University (MO) and Howard.

period of eight months a year to which any and all children of school age may go."[57]

On 7 May 1931, the SBOE received a report that $260,000 in funds was available for Tennessee A&I, including $100,000 in local funds and $125,000 from Rosenwald. Tennessee asked the GEB for another $175,000. By 1931, A&I had 1,635 students and a combined capital and operating budget of $579,452.60. Hale set aside some funds (salary savings) and donations into a secret reserve fund. On Rosenwald Day on campus, *The Broadcaster* said,

> For over a score of years he [Rosenwald] has been the backbone of Negro education in the South. [He established] rural schools for Negroes, industrial museums, YMCAs and YWCAs for Negroes, the University of Chicago, Negro housing enterprises, Jewish Theological Seminary, American Jewish Agriculture Corporation, scholarships for Negro teachers, and funds for libraries and buildings and equipment for Negro colleges. Tennessee schools received generously from his hands. A. & I. State College has received and even at this movement is enjoying the fruits of Julius Rosenwald's philanthropy in the present building program.[58]

On 31 August, the SBOE gave authority for Tennessee A&I to proceed with other construction projects, including the construction of walls of stone along Centennial Boulevard. Albert Everett, a notable Negro stonemason living on Cedar (Charlotte) Street, won the bid for the stone fence, and quarried the stone from the A&I campus as Hale wished. Two more teachers' cottages opened in 1931, bringing the total to two five-room bungalows and two eight-room apartment type residences. These cottages (demolished in 1989) housed many different faculty families over the years. They lived within the close-knit A&I community that helped define the institution's character and furnished audiences for activities on campus.[59]

In January 1932 when Julius Rosenwald died, Tennessee State held a memorial service, and the faculty adopted a "Resolution of Thanks to Julius Rosenwald." They also praised another white friend: "The colored people of the Southland could not have reached the present educational and civic status of achievements had it not been for the sane, wise and efficient cooperation and

---

[57] Governor Henry Horton, messages, 8, 21, 27 January 1931, *Messages of the Governors of Tennessee, 1921–1933*, vol. 10, ed. Stephen V. Ash (Nashville: Tennessee Historical Society) 377.

[58] "Julius Rosenwald," *The Broadcaster* (1 January 1931): 1–2.

[59] A&I, 31 August 1931, SBOE Minutes, RG 245; A&I construction, vault, box 2, folders 104–06, 1928, and Tennessee A. & I construction, box 234, 1928, RG 92, TSLA; McDougald, *A Time-Line Chronology*, 67, 76–80.

judgment of Dr. S.L. Smith concerning the best elements of both races, who has brought better standards or racial adjustment to all."[60]

Robert E. Clay, the rural building agent for the Rosenwald Fund in Tennessee, had toiled in this effort to extend schools to black Tennesseans. Clay was operating a small business in Bristol when he joined the Booker T. Washington grand tour from Bristol to Memphis in fall of 1909. Clay came to Tennessee A&I State Normal School around 1917–19 to help direct the Rosenwald schoolhouses program, and he worked with S.L. Smith in the state division of Negro education. Clay teamed with A&I professors to go to Negro schools and help staff with their curriculum development based on state and Carnegie Foundation guidelines. Clay completed his college degree at Tennessee A&I in 1932 and got married on campus. When the Rosenwald Fund began phasing out in 1948, the state converted him to the college payroll, and Hale put "Daddy Clay" in charge of "student discipline."[61]

In May 1932, Rosenwald officials visited the campus and saw that the "Cafeteria and Women's Building is in the process of being erected on the present campus just west of the library, and it will house the departments of home economics and sectional commerce" (*Bulletin,* 13 January 1932). Mars and Holman served as the architects. They designed the boys' Industrial Arts Building, being erected across the Boulevard from the present campus to house the departments of agriculture and industrial education. That same month, the GEB donated $70,000 to convert Old Main into a Practice School. In 1931–32, a GEB-sponsored delegation of black college presidents and state education officials visited the campus. Tennessee A&I now had 34 percent of the 1,976 college students enrolled in Tennessee's HBCUs.[62]

Phi Beta Tau, an honor society patterned after Phi Beta Kappa, began on campus in 1931. The entire faculty, along with students, staff members, and others posed for photographs. Twelve faculty members received graduate degrees from Columbia University, or were currently enrolled there. The History Club held its annual banquet in the cafeteria on May 28. The campus was often crowded because many groups, including the Annual State High school Symposium for Teachers, held their annual gatherings, conventions and meetings at Tennessee A&I.

---

[60] "Julius Rosenwald Dies in Chicago," A&I *The Bulletin* 20, no. 1 (January 1932): 1.

[61] A&I *The Bulletin* (1940–41); photographs of P.L. Harned, W.J. Hale, George W. Gore, Jr., R.B.J. Campbelle, Martha M. Brown, R.E. Clay, Alger V. Boswell, Wilifred W. Lawson, Mary L. Wilson, *Ayeni Yearbook of Tennessee Agricultural and Industrial State College* (Nashville, 1931) 13–22; S.L. Smith to P.L. Harned, Nashville, 7 May 1927, P.L. Harned to R.E. Clay, Nashville, 23 September 1926, box 13, folder 1, 20, RG 92, TSLA.

[62] "Survey of Negro Education," *Journal of Negro Education* 2, no. 1 (Howard University, January 1933): 1–40.

Tennessee A&I State Teacher's College helped greatly to level the Southern education playing field for Negro citizens. Families such as the Lewises exemplified the importance of HBCUs in the state. At the age of eleven, Hattie Lucille Fitzpatrick Lewis moved from the McKenzie community in Marshall County to the Tennessee A&I State Teachers College campus with her family in 1930. Her grandfather, T.H. Fitzpatrick, was hired to help run the college farm in 1929. She attended the Practice School along with Hale's children and the children of Charles S. Johnson (future Fisk president). Hattie spent the last two years of school at Pearl High School. She recalled the college was closed for six weeks after summer school—the lonely times in the college farmhouse, where she lived until getting married in 1940. In that year, she met her husband Robert Lewis during a Fourth of July celebration in Hadley Park (next to the farm). Hattie graduated from Tennessee A&I State College in 1941 and had her first child in 1944. Robert operated a "seven cents jitney," transporting riders to jobs and homes between the streetcar lines. After the decline of the cab business, the family entered the funeral business in 1948 and lived in the Andrew Jackson Housing Project next to Fisk University. After Robert died of kidney failure in July 1959, Hattie was forced to take over the business. The president of Tennessee A&I hired her as a counselor in Hankal Hall and Wilson Hall dormitories until 1968, and all four of her children completed college, including at Tennessee State, and enjoyed careers as teacher, airline pilot, funeral home director, banker, a member of the Tennessee Board of Regents, and health administrator.[63]

In November 1932, former governor of New York Franklin D. Roosevelt (D) defeated President Herbert G. Hoover (R) in the presidential election. The new president and the New Deal Democrats included a host of white liberals and several Southern progressives such as Lyndon B. Johnson of Texas and Estes Kefauver of Tennessee. The New Deal Democrats began to focus on the economic rehabilitation of the Southern United States—the worst off of America's sectors. President Franklin D. Roosevelt celebrated his inauguration on 4 March 1933 and immediately closed all the banks. They reopened a week later with new federal guidelines that closed the bad banks and strengthened the good ones. Congress then passed New Deal legislation that created programs for relief, recovery, and reform. President Hale became involved in the welcoming of President Roosevelt to Nashville on 17 November 1934. The 84-year-old James C. Napier, the leading local black Republican, gave the welcoming speech on behalf of the Negro community, and Roosevelt received several gifts, including the

---

[63] McDougald, *A Time-Line Chronology*, 59–71; Ronald Weathersby, "TSU Alumni Profile: Richard A. Lewis, Sr.—Class of '66," *Tennessee Tribune*, 27 September–3 October 2012, 1B.

Tennessee A&I Book of Views. The New Deal administration included 43 Negroes in assistant and advisory positions, called the black cabinet.[64]

At a Minneapolis meeting in February 1933, Tennessee A&I State Teachers College became one of three out of a total of 18 Negro teachers' college applicants admitted into the American Association of Teachers Colleges. The AATC was the accrediting body for teacher preparation programs that dated back to the 1830s when Horace Mann and others sought to improve teaching in the nation's normal schools.[65] The *Broadcaster* (March 1933) featured photographs of the newest buildings on the campus, and the *Globe* (October 6, 1933) featured a full-page photograph of the South's largest state school for Negroes. About 23,038 Negroes attended colleges, and nearly 1,000 of them attended Tennessee A&I State Teachers College.[66]

During the spring quarter of 1933, nearly a third of the state's Negro teachers attended the annual meeting of the Negro Teachers' Association on campus. Carter G. Woodson of the Association of Negro Life and History spoke on his new book *The Mis-Education of the Negro* (1933). He said all Negro colleges needed to do more to include Negro culture and history in the curriculum.[67] Faculty members presented other topics at the meeting, including "The Project Method in the Teaching of English," by Selma Redmond, who had joined the A&I faculty in 1927. The Negro state teachers association elected Hale to represent them at the World Federation of Education Association in Dublin, Ireland, the next August. At the *Program for Visit of the Governor and the 68th General Assembly, April 13, 1933,* the audience sang *Lift Every Voice and Sing,* promoted by the ASNLH as the Negro National Anthem.[68]

During the 1930s, Tennessee A&I State Teachers College welcomed chapters of sororities and fraternities. Sigma Pi Phi fraternity was the first Greek-letter fraternity for Negro professional men; it began on the east coast in 1905 and spread across the country, inaugurating the Chi chapter in Nashville on 1 May 1939. It consisted of twelve charter members of Chi chapter Boulé who were professional men from Fisk, Meharry, and Tennessee A&I State College,

---

[64] Lovett, *America's Black Colleges*, 88, 98–137.

[65] "History" of the AACTE, http://www.aacte.org/index.php?/About-Us/History/history-aacte.html [accessed 9 September 2011].

[66] "Negro Colleges," *Crisis* (August 1933): 1; "Largest school," Nashville *Globe*, 6 August 1933, 1–2; *Broadcaster* (March 1933): 1–2; McDougald, *A Time-Line Chronology*, 70.

[67] Carter G. Woodson, *The Mis-Education of the Negro* (Washington DC: Associated Universities Press, 1933).

[68] *Program for Visit of the Governor and the 68th General Assembly, April 13, 1933,* Special Collections, TSU; McDougald, *A Time-Line Chronology*, 68–72; Woodson, *Mis-Education*; W.E.B. Du Bois, "Does the Negro Need Separate Schools?" *Journal of Negro Education* 4, no. 3 (July 1935): 328–29; Monroe Work, *Negro Yearbook: An Annual Encyclopedia of the Negro, 1931–1932* (Tuskegee AL: Negro Year Book Co., 1931).

including George W. Gore, Jr., and W.J. Hale (honorary LLD, Wilberforce University).[69] Robert E. Clay, Walter S. Davis, and Forrest Strange advised the Omega Psi Phi fraternity (Rho Psi chapter), which began on the Tennessee A&I State College campus on 30 April 1930. The Phi Beta Sigma (Zeta Alpha chapter) began on 1 May 1931 with Alger V. Boswell as the faculty adviser. Kappa Alpha Psi fraternity established the Alpha Theta chapter on campus on 23 May 1931; Kappa chapter had been established on the Meharry Medical College campus on 19 February 1919, and they organized the Nashville Alumni chapter on 24 April 1926. History professor Merl R. Eppse, who was a charter member of Omega chapter (1925) at Drake University, became one of the faculty advisers for Kappa Alpha Psi (Alpha Theta chapter). Sigma Gamma Rho sorority (Alpha Beta chapter) was chartered in March 1932, and Alpha Kappa Alpha sorority came to the campus on 13 May 1932 as the Alpha Psi chapter. The Ivy Leaf Club began on 18 November 1932, with Lois H. Daniels as president. Zeta Phi Beta (Epsilon Alpha chapter) started on 19 February 1933. The Beta Omicron chapter of Alpha Phi Alpha fraternity began on 11 May 1933, with Dean Gore as adviser. Delta Sigma Theta sorority (Alpha Chi chapter) began on May 9 with six pledges and chartered on 13 May 1936 under the advisership of Emma T. Burt, E. Walcott Gordon, and Shirley Graham.[70]

Shirley Graham a graduate of Oberlin College was destined to become the third wife of W.E.B. Du Bois. Her father had pastored a church in Spokane, Washington, where Graham grew up, and the family had entertained Du Bois in 1920, allowing him to take Shirley's bedroom. He noticed her again in the summer of 1932, when Shirley Graham put on a play in Cleveland, Ohio. Du Bois allowed Shirley Graham to publish "Black Man's Music" in *Crisis* magazine (August 1933). After disputes with executive director Walter White in 1934, Du Bois left the NAACP after 24 years of service as editor of *Crisis* magazine and resumed his professorship at Atlanta University. In 1936, after Shirley Graham contacted him about a research secretary during his trip through Nashville to Kentucky, the 68-year-old Du Bois arranged for a friend of the Graham family to allow him to pick up the 29-year-old Shirley Graham at the friends' Nashville

---

[69] Charles H. Wesley, *History of Sigma Pi Phi: First of the Negro-American Greek-Letter Fraternities* (New York: Sigma Pi Phi Fraternity, Fred Weidner & Son Printers, 1954, 1969, 1992) 237–38.

[70] Sharon G. Hall, "Merl R. Eppse, 1893–1967: Life and Work Based upon an Investigation of Selected Papers," (master's thesis, Tennessee State University, December 1983); "Dr. M. R. Eppse, Noted Educator, Rites Friday," *Nashville Banner*, 23 December, 1967; McDougald, *A Time-Line Chronology*, 67; William L. Crump and C. Rodger Wilson, *The Story of Kappa Alpha Psi* (Philadelphia: Grand Chapter of the Kappa Alpha Psi Fraternity, 1972) 74, 107, 229, 237, 250, 318, 342, 438, 443, 494; "Tau Lambda History," http://www.taulambda.org/chapter/history.html [accessed 20 February 2012].

home. The two-day affair included a picnic on the way back to her quarters in the A&I faculty apartments. Graham recreated the romantic meeting in *His Day is Marching On* (1971). Shirley Graham felt confined on the small A&I campus, so, she moved to the Chicago Writers Project, managed the Prince Theater by 1939, and continued her relationship with Du Bois. He recommended her for a Rosenwald Fellowship to study drama at Yale University.[71]

Hale and the faculty next tackled the construction of an administration building, a physical education-health building, the practice school renovations, and stock and dairy barns. However, state authorities did not want to build two separate buildings. Instead, they approved a make-do gymnasium in the new administration building. The State Attorney General deferred construction until sufficient funds were in the hands of the SBOE. Hale suggested use of local funds to proceed with construction. State officials agreed. The state selected Tidsdale and Pinson as architects for the administration building; R.H. Wollwine for the health building; Granberry Jackson, Jr., for the stock and dairy barn; and Hart, Freeland, and Roberts for the practice school building. Wollwine agreed to combine his plans with those of Tidsdale and Pinson to develop the unique floor plans for the new Administration, Physical Education, and Health Building. This complex, constructed by U.L. Nicholson Builders, contained facilities for administration, auditorium, classrooms, academic department programs, offices, a swimming pool in the basement, and an auditorium with a gymnasium on the stage.

By 1934, Tennessee A&I State Teacher's College campus had 14 major buildings. These included the old buildings, 1912–24: Old Main—now the Practice School, Old Wilson Hall for Women—called West Hall, Men's Hall—East Hall; Goodwill Manor—President's Home, Boys' Trades Building—old gymnasium built by the students, old steam plant, and former trades shops; and the old Girls' Trades Building—built as the women's and home economics building and cafeteria (1923) and later converted to Recreation Hall and teachers apartments. There existed the newest collegiate buildings (1927–34): Hale Hall for Women; Harned Science Hall; Memorial Library; Heating Plant; Women's

---

[71] David L. Lewis, *W.E.B. Du Bois: the Fight for Equality and the American Century, 1919–1963* (New York: Holt, 2000) 384, 495, 498, 538, 545, 540, 550, 554. Note: When Atlanta University forced the 78-year-old Du Bois to retire in 1944, Graham secured him a one-bedroom apartment on prestigious Sugar Hill in Harlem. There he resumed his work with the NAACP. Graham resigned her work with the NAACP and signed on with a notable communist writer, becoming a writer herself and publishing *Paul Robeson: Citizen of the World* (1946). Graham became a member of the American Communist Party, and influenced Du Bois to join. She and Du Bois wed in 1951. He died at age 95, in Ghana, West Africa, 1963; Shirley Graham, *His Day is Marching On: Memoirs of W.E.B. Du bois* (New York: Lippincott, 1971).

Building with the new cafeteria and rooms for home economics; the men's Industrial Arts Building; and the "I" shaped Administration and Health Building under construction. Tennessee gave A&I $147,000 toward the cost of construction.[72] The wide concrete sidewalks in front of the Women's Building next door to the girls' dormitory became another gathering place for students in lieu of a student union or campus center. Students also used the stone retaining wall along Centennial Boulevard as a favorite perch when President Hale was not in sight. Former student Arthur V. Haynes recalled,

> On this beautiful day, when the chapel bell rang, there were students sitting on the fence which separated a part of the campus, boy and girl together, couples lined up almost as far as you see along this highway. The president came out of his home. He decided to go down the fence with his cane and with no uncertain tone of voice demanded that each one go into the chapel. He talked harshly to students sitting on the wall, saying he did not want state authorities to think they had nothing else to do at Tennessee State.[73]

In March 1934, the college spent an extra $22,530 to design and build broad steps and sidewalks to align the Memorial Library with the new A-Building on opposite sides of Centennial Boulevard. The walkways formed a beautiful promenade for the formation of the graduation march in front of Memorial Library. They marched across Centennial Boulevard, up the limestone stairs, through the arched portico and double doors, and into the A-Building auditorium for the 1934 graduation exercises. The back (south side) of Memorial Library thus became the front entrance facing south toward Centennial Boulevard and the A-Building. The college also built concrete walkways connecting the library, Women's Building, and Harned Science Hall. When growing grass on the rocky campus proved nearly impossible, the SBOE approved grass sod for the A-Building site. A faculty committee recommended a public address system, motion picture equipment, pipe organ ($10,000), post office equipment, stage curtains, gym equipment, pianos, file cabinets for the offices, shades for the glass doors, 312 tablet armchairs, 856 opera chairs, knock-down bleachers [for the gym on the stage], and lecterns for a total of $19,500 to make the A-Building "first-class."[74] The campus was impressive.

In 1934, the SBOE approved Hale's application for New Deal federal funds to build agriculture facilities including a dairy barn and repair of the dormitories.

---

[72] Tennessee A&I Normal College, 1924–25, box 1, folder 7, 1926, box 2, folder 4, 1928, box 3, folder 9, 1932, box 4, folder 3, 1933, box 4, folder 11, 1938, box 6, folder 3, GEB budget and teacher requirements—A&I, 1932–34, GEB state agent for Negro schools, 1934–35, box 236, folder 3, GEB correspondence, 1925–40, box 235, folders 1–5, box 236, folders 1–12, SBOE Records, 1815–1958, RG 91, TSLA.

[73] Haynes, *Scars of Segregation,* 91.

[74] Ibid.; Hale Papers, 1934.

The Works Progress Administration (WPA) granted $148,183 in return for quarrying stone on the hill. The WPA was putting the unemployed to work building things in Davidson County, including a new country courthouse and restoration of Civil War Union Fort Negley. The WPA employed 222 workers to build an athletic field, bleachers, grandstand, field house, stables, barns, tennis courts, add a two-story annex and new stairs to the men's dormitory, build a lake and rock garden, extend the stone walls, and remodel the Recreation Hall (old Girls' Trades Building). The southwest campus included three lakes, ten tennis courts, canoeing, swimming, and picnic sites.[75]

The Name Changes to Tennessee A&I State College

The State Board of Education (SBOE) pressured Hale to move toward SACS approval. In 1934, Hale submitted to the SBOE a self-study titled *Personnel Study of the Agricultural and Industrial State College, 1928–1935*. Gore, Harriett Hale, and Martha Brown (librarian) comprised the study committee. Between 86 and 94 percent of A&I's students had high school certification while the remainder of the students gained admission on examination or as special and conditional students. Sixty-one percent were on work-aid, 12 percent on credit, 36 percent had no radio at home, 38 percent had no electricity at home, 60 percent took no daily newspapers at home, 79 percent had no telephone at home, and 83 percent had no family automobile. The largest in-state groups came from Shelby County-Memphis and Davidson County-Nashville, and Alabama students represented the largest out-of-state enrollment. Campus salaries remained low. Hale earned $3,000, his wife $1,800, and Dean Gore earned $2,500 a year. SBOE required each institution not to exceed 18 hours of teaching per week, or 16 hours per week average, and its officers of administration should not be included in computing this average. Twenty-seven staff members had no bachelor's degree and 40 percent of the faculty consisted of grossly underpaid women. At one time, Frank J. Perry (education) was the only full-time faculty member holding a doctorate degree. By 1934, E.F. Dupree (chemistry and health) held a PhD from University of Edinburgh, Samuel Moss Carter (social science) held a PhD from Yale University, and George E. Loder (sociology) held a PhD from Cornell University. Eight faculty members enrolled at Columbia in summers. Z. Alexander Looby (doctorate in law) and physician C.V. Roman (MD) continued to teach part-time. The turnover rate for A&I was 7 percent—not a high figure, but still an indication that salary levels and working conditions perhaps could affect

---

[75] Ibid., Hale Papers, 1935; McDougald, *A Time-Line Chronology*, 82–89; Works Progress Administration files, 1934, 1936–37, box 135, folders 17–19, federal relief administration files, 1933–34, box 133, folder 5, reports of the GEB, 1934–1935, box 133, folder 6, SBOE, RG 273; P.L. Harned files, 1924–29, 1930–36, box 242, folders 1–2, Commissioner of Education Records, 1913–70, RG 92, TSLA.

stability of faculty in some critical content areas. The institution did not apply to SACS.[76]

In 1935–36, Tennessee A&I State Teachers College became Tennessee A&I State College. From 15–21 April, Hale, the faculty, staff, and students held a formal dedication for the old and new campus facilities. Hale said, "The Rosenwald Fund and the GEB generously lent their experts as advisors to the curriculum."[77] In November, there was a more elaborate program to dedicate and name new facilities, to celebrate the Silver Anniversary, and to announce the official new name of Tennessee A&I State College. The institution now required 69 quarter hours of general education requirements, including 18 quarter hours of English, 12 hours of history, 6 hours of mathematics, 9 hours of health and physical education, 18 hours of social studies, and 6 hours in special subjects, plus 36 hours in the major subject, two minors for a total of 36 hours, 6 hours of vocational education, and 15 hours of electives. The last three quarters of work in any department had to be done in residence. The student had to complete at least 48 quarter hours of college work [meaning, upper-level] to be recommended for graduation (162 quarter hours). Courses above 499 were for advanced students [graduate].

Nineteen thirty-five was also the year in which President Hale celebrated his 25th anniversary, and he was honored on February 22 with a dinner for 500 people hosted by the History Study Club and held in the cafeteria. Merl Eppse wrote a letter to President Franklin D. Roosevelt (D) asking him to send a letter of congratulations to be read at the dinner. Eppse reminded Roosevelt that Tennessee A&I State Teachers College's choir had provided music for Roosevelt's 1934 visit to Nashville.[78]

The 16th annual meeting of the Tennessee Interracial League (CIC) took place on 4 February 1936, with T.C. Barr as state chair; Hale headed the colored division. The CIC had been organized in 1920 in response to white lynch mobs roaming the South and taking Negro lives. The Tennessee chapter intended to facilitate meetings between sympathetic whites and moderate Negro leaders willing to cooperate in building better communities and securing justice and

---

[76] A&I The Bulletin (1935–36); Southern Association of Colleges and Schools, Commission on Approval of Negro Schools, Enrollments in Negro Colleges, 1934–35 (Atlanta: SACS, 1935) 1–10; "A.&.I State Teachers College," Nashville Globe, 16 March 1934, 1, 4.

[77] Tennessee, Souvenir Bulletin: Dedication of Six New Buildings, April 19, 1935, Special Collections, TSU.

[78] Ibid.; M.R. Eppse to President F.D. Roosevelt, Nashville, 5 February 1936; Hall, "Merl R. Eppse," appendices; Eppse correspondence with W.J. Hale, mf 7, box 38, folders 12–14, Merl Raymond Eppse (1893–1967) Papers, 1927–61, ac no. 89–120, TSLA; McDougald, A Time-Line Chronology, 80; "A. & I. to Celebrate Twenty-fifth Anniversary," A&I The Bulletin 25, no. 12, 1–2 September 1937.

opportunity for all citizens in Tennessee. It should be noted that the CIC did not promote racial integration, but still supported the "separate but equal" principle.

After the death of Julius Rosenwald, the Rosenwald Fund continued to award scholarships up to $1,500 each to 18 whites and 34 Negroes. The fellows agreed to return to the South to teach. The Jeanes Fund continued to sponsor Negro supervisors, including A&I alumni and faculty members, to attend Columbia University. Will Ed Turner, the white director of Negro Education for Tennessee, made arrangements for A&I alumnus Shellie T. Northcutt (Jeanes supervisor for Chester and Henderson Counties), A&I's Laura M. Averitte, and James H. White (Hardeman County) to attend Columbia University.[79]

James Herbert White completed public grammar school in Gallatin, Tennessee, and at fourteen headed to work in a factory in Indiana, later enrolling at Tennessee A&I in the elementary and high school departments. He organized a quartet called the National Harmony Four on campus, traveled with the A&I Glee Club, played trumpet, served as assistant band director, and earned his normal school diploma from A&I in 1924. He worked in the Gallatin public schools for two years, becoming assistant principal of Union High School before marrying fellow A&I graduate Augusta Charter in November 1926. The couple separately engaged in teaching in various Tennessee towns until they settled together in Lexington.

In 1928, White became principal of Hardeman County Training School at Whiteville after the county had contacted Hale to recommend someone. The previous Negro principal had not been able to raise the money needed to match the Rosenwald Funds for the new seven-room brick schoolhouse. White raised the money, completed the bachelor's degree at A&I, and turned Allen-White High School into a showcase. The faculty increased to seven persons by 1929. This was a great advance, seeing as in 1893 Hardeman County had had 2,394 Negro children enrolled in 47 mostly one-room public schools with 49 teachers. White recalled that by 1929, "The community was hostile, race relations were poor, the country was on the brink of the great depression and the concern for education was at low ebb."[80] White said Allen-White had a two-year program by 1930, advancing to four years of high school by 1934. He also organized a high school band and had the English faculty publish *The Allen-White Voice* monthly. He was talented at getting support from Northern philanthropists, and was able to expand the facility to include a vocational building, and a frame building as a dormitory for girls and teachers. He got the Parent-Teacher Association to

---

[79] Will Ed Turner, letter to the Jeanes supervisor at Columbia University, 19 August 1936, Nashville, "A. & I.," SBOE Minutes, RG 245; Commissioner Duggan, 1939–42, box 50, folder 9, RG 92.

[80] James H. White, *Up from a Cotton Patch: The Development of Mississippi Valley College* (Itta Bena MS: the author, 1979) 12.

finance a gymnasium, a sandwich shop, and a boy's dormitory. National Youth Administration camp for 45 boys was on campus. White completed his master's degree at Columbia University in 1943, became president of Lane College in 1947, and gained SACS "A" rating approval in 1949. A week later, White became the founding president of a Mississippi public HBCU.[81]

NAACP Begins Attack on Jim Crow Graduate Education

About the time that the NAACP began suing the Jim Crow states over unequal graduate education for blacks, the Negro schoolteachers and the Tennessee Negro Teachers Association pressured Hale to offer graduate courses. The 1935–36 Tennessee A&I *Bulletin* read, "Courses above 499 were for "advanced students" and included English (5), vocational education (1), mathematics (3), history (3), economics (1), and secretarial commerce (7). The summer *Bulletin* said these courses could be used toward a graduate degree "once A. & I. received approval from the state." The Nashville *Tennessean* (4 August 1935) announced a General Assembly bill granted to A&I that afforded the right to award master's degree in education; "only Eastern and Northern colleges are now available to the Negro for the higher degrees."[82]

However, as the NAACP began to argue, blacks needed expanded access to graduate work, and should not be forced to travel to the North to get such degrees. Tennessee barred even the private, integrated TWI Maryville College from admitting Negro students. In the trade and industrial courses, many of the teachers had no college degree, and even at the HBCUs, only 41 percent of the teachers had college degrees. Only five HBCUs—including Fisk and Howard—had graduate programs by 1939. Only Atlanta University, Howard, Meharry, and Xavier (New Orleans) had professional programs in medicine, dentistry, law, and pharmacy. Negroes had earned 43,821 college degrees since 1828. By 1936, blacks held 153 PhD degrees and 1,555 master's degrees, with Northern colleges accounting for almost all graduate degrees. Northern philanthropic agencies financed a study through Fisk University to find out what a Negro with a college degree could actually do within a racially segregated society. Northern white institutions had hired only two black PhD holders, and almost all other Negro doctorates worked at HBCUs.[83]

Tennessee's Jim Crow officials were nervous about the graduate school issue because in 1936 the NAACP was beginning to attack Jim Crow states for

---

[81] Ibid., 17.

[82] "A. & I. granted right to award master's degree in education," Nashville *Tennessean*, 4 August 1935, 11.

[83] Ina C. Brown, "The National Survey of Negro Higher Education and Post-War Reconstruction: The Place of the Negro College in Negro Life," *Journal of Negro Education* 11, no. 3 (July 1942) 375–81.

not respecting the *Plessy v. Ferguson* 163 US 537 (1896) "separate but equal" requirement. Tennessee became a part of the NAACP's five-state strategy to attack the Jim Crow system through the US federal courts. In 1936, William B. Redmond of Franklin filed for admission to the University of Tennessee School of Pharmacy, but his application was not acted upon. After Redmond contacted the NAACP in April 1936, Charles Hamilton Houston, the chief legal counsel for the NAACP, filed *State of Tennessee Ex. Rel. William B. Redmond, II v. O. W. Hyman, et al. of the University of Tennessee* in Chancery Court, Shelby County, Tennessee. In June the judge claimed NAACP attorneys were outside agitators that enlisted Redmond as a troublemaker. The judge issued an opinion against Redmond on 16 April 1937, saying his suit was prematurely filed and Redmond should have waited for UT to answer his appeal before suing the university. Roy Wilkins of the NAACP wrote to the Memphis *World*, saying the NAACP "simply stand ready to assist any eligible candidate who exhausts the ordinary means of entering these schools in the event he wishes to go forward with a court fight."[84] The NAACP's fight continued for twenty-three years.

On 7 August 1936, the self-study showed that among A&I graduates for 1927–36, 54 percent had become teachers, 5 percent were the state's farm agents, 3.3 percent were secretaries, 3.3 percent were in insurance, and 6.1 percent were in industry. There were also nine physicians and three dentists among the graduates. *The Report of the Survey of the Agricultural and Industrial State College* (1936) said they could find no officer except the president who could speak with finality on any activity or phase of the college program. They suggested that Hale appoint a director of instruction (dean), with department heads reporting directly to him. They also recommended a business manager be in charge of financial affairs, with a budget, prepared by the dean, department heads, and business manager, to be sent to the president to make sure all academic programs and equipment needs were accounted for. In particular, they criticized the accounting system at the institution—although records showed some 59.1 percent of the income went toward instruction—but commended the institution for operating auxiliary enterprises at a profit despite suggesting that this money should not be relied upon to any great extent as a source of income.[85]

The biggest concern, however, was that salaries were still too low. The average A&I salary for full professors was $1,493, compared to $1,754 for Negro land-grant colleges, and $2,150 in some private HBCUs. They recommended

---

[84] David C. Mills, "The Desegregation of Public Higher Education in Tennessee," Lovett Papers, Special Collections, TSU (unpublished undergraduate paper, University of Tennessee, n.d.) 1–26; Mark V. Tushnet, *The NAACP's Legal Strategy Against Segregated Education, 1925–1950* (Chapel Hill: University of North Carolina Press, 1987) 54–56.

[85] By 2010, less than 51 percent of Tennessee State University's budget was directly assigned for instruction.

decrease of charges to faculty for room, board, and services—a move that would increase their real take-home pay. They suggested written contracts for faculty, closer state control of the budget and salaries actually paid to faculty members and other employees. The report strongly recommended that all appearance of nepotism be avoided in the institution. Some faculty complained that the president's family drove cars registered to A&I State College. In addition, Hale, Jr., had a faculty position but was frequently absent from campus. The secretary for the president had a salary of $1,800—higher than a full professor—Mrs. Hale $2,400, Bursar R.B.J. Campbelle $2,400, Alger V. Boswell $2,400, and Merl R. Eppse $2,400, even though none of these persons had a doctorate. George Loder with a PhD degree earned $2,000; other faculty members earned as low as $900 a year. Gore earned $3,000 on a twelve-month basis.

Controversy developed over the manner in which Hale paid the faculty members: he used verbal contracts; he approached a faculty member on payday, asking, how much you need, Hon?; he counted cash from his pocket. The staff/faculty member signed a check face down on a clipboard. Reportedly, Hale filled in a higher amount for SBOE records, placing the difference in the reserves. An instructor took the matter to the SBOE, and Hale explained away the discrepancies to the board. The board, however, established more uniform standards for presidential salaries, including raising President W. J. Hale's salary.[86] He was still one of the most powerful college presidents in Tennessee, but over the next six years, Hale's tenure would come to a crashing end.

In the meantime, the study criticized campus and state authorities for allowing the 1912 buildings to be neglected and subject to being torn down. The Old Administration Building [used for sewing projects for the federal Works Progress Administration] was entirely too good a plant to abandon, and there was no long-range plan for the plant in relation to educational needs. The physical plant was okay—thanks to philanthropy—but growing faster than current faculty and staff could service an expanding educational program. The college farm needed to become a real part of the agriculture curriculum instead of operating as the equivalent of a farm being rented to a sharecropper. The big question now was, were public officials gouging the A&I farm for personal profit? The report recommended a new Training School to enroll 300 students from local and nearby communities. This school could be placed in the Industrial Arts Building that was not being fully used for anything other than some manual

---

[86] Tennessee A&I, box 4, folder 3, folder 11; box 6, folder 3, State Board of Education Records, 1815–1958, RG 92; Hale case, 1938, box 150, folder 2, SBOE RG 273; McDougald, *A Time-Line Chronology*, 81, 82–83; See *The Bulletin* (1936–40).

labor and industrial trade shops. The team noted that only one floor of three-story Harned Hall (1927) was in use.[87]

The report said the faculty needed to be expanded to 32 full-time equivalents as the workload was too heavy and should be confined to 16 hours per week, with a maximum of 480 student credit hours; the out-of-state population of students needed to be contained by raising fees; the curriculum should be refined further; fourteen courses, including an orientation course, should be added. The visitors also found 27 high school students still enrolled in college classes.

They recommended that no graduate programs be offered until the current program was improved. In the case of Negro citizens who desired graduate studies not offered at the Agricultural and Industrial College, the report argued that the state should recognize its obligations and suggested that Tennessee might follow the example of Maryland, which had recently created out-of-state scholarships for Negroes. Nine other Jim Crow states eventually used this method to counter the NAACP.[88]

On 29 October 1936, the supervisor for the Department of Negro Education sent a letter to his counterpart in Georgia asking him to inquire at Atlanta University about taking Negro graduate students from Tennessee. AU said it would be happy to do so at $500 per year for each student. Spelman College offered the prerequisite courses for such students. On 1 July 1937, Tennessee out-of-state graduate fellowships for Negroes went into effect, projecting a cost of $3,709 per annum for "bona fide residents who possess qualifications, health, character, ability and preparatory education required for admission to the UT."[89] Ultimately, the Jim Crow out-of-state scholarships helped keep Tennessee A&I State College from being upgraded for SACS approval and prevented this public HBCU from developing a graduate program.

Tennessee A&I expanded and prospered during the years 1922–36. The institution navigated the difficulties of a growing institution, but managed well within the confines of a Jim Crow higher education society. A&I survived the worst years of the Great Depression, hardly with ease, but with a touch of greatness. The state of Tennessee treated the institution equally, relative to policy in 1922, when the state normal colleges were authorized to proceed to four-year college status. By then, however, the former Blount College—now the University of Tennessee—was receiving more than a million dollars a year in state support, had been coeducational since 1892, and was adding professional schools and colleges. In this comparison, higher education for black Tennesseans was hardly

---

[87] *The Report of the Survey of the Agricultural and Industrial State College* (1936), Special Collections, TSU, 1–45.

[88] Ibid.

[89] *Tennessee Laws*, 1937, chapter 256, section 1.

equal, and Tennessee A&I State Teachers College was the only institution of higher education that would admit black students. However, A&I had none of the professional and graduate programs that were available to whites at UT. The University of Tennessee was championed as a flagship institution by state officials, while the state normal schools were struggling to realize their identities. Fortunately, the State Normal School for Negroes had not lost ground to its white sister institutions and grew to become, in 1925, Tennessee A&I State Normal Teachers College. It became the nationally approved Tennessee A&I State Teachers College in 1933. Despite the state treating Tennessee A&I unfairly in regard to public funding, the Negro institution effectively solicited and used Northern philanthropic resources to equal, and in some ways outdistance, its white sister state teachers' colleges. However, in 1935, as black Americans, led by the NAACP, began to challenge Jim Crow education, Tennessee A&I would find itself part of the civil rights movement, and the years 1937–43 would be quite dramatic for both Tennessee A&I and President W.J. Hale.

3

1937–43: William J. Hale and the Great Battle

From 1937–43, when Tennessee A&I State College seemed to have made great progress, the quiet battle between Jim Crow officials and the NACCP, with its black plaintiffs, exploded. William J. Hale and Tennessee A&I State College were caught between those horrific forces.

By fall 1937, Tennessee Agricultural and Industrial State College was continuing its feverish pace toward building a campus fit for a four-year collegiate institution. The federal New Deal Works Progress Administration (WPA) campus projects included farm buildings ($54,035), remodeled Recreational Hall ($13,852), men's dormitory addition ($16,073), additions and repairs to Goodwill Manor ($19,955), field house and facilities ($37,520) and bleachers for the athletic field and stadium ($59,250). In 1938, WPA workers tore down the crumbling Boys' Trades Building. In 1939, Tennessee A&I requested WPA funds to build a three-story faculty apartment building and a play area for faculty children. In 1941, the new residence hall for faculty opened with a parlor and guest rooms. The federal funds helped construct two faculty residences, tennis courts, build stables and a tool house, erect seats for the baseball field, equip the main lake, and construct an outside swimming pool.[1]

Tennessee A&I continued to exist in a racially dissolute milieu in the years 1936–43. President Franklin Roosevelt could not afford to alienate the Southern Democrats, despite their insistence on maintaining Jim Crow. Eleanor Roosevelt toured the American South and was saddened by the ragged, unhealthy children (both white and black) who flocked to her. The New Deal administration gave Tennessee more than its share of federal funds, yet most leaders in the solid-Democratic South continued to use the poll tax, other undemocratic measures, and Jim Crow laws to rule over the white masses and the Negroes. In Memphis, the Youth Chapter of the NAACP at LeMoyne College entered a war of words with Edward H. Crump, the boss of the local Democratic Party machine because they were angry about racist Memphis police officers who killed a black US mail carrier for no reason other than the Negro man made more money than the

---

[1] Arthur V. Haynes, *Scars of Segregation: An Autobiography* (New York: Vantage Press, 1974) 94–98. Tennessee A&I correspondence, 1937–41, box 100, folders 57–60, Tennessee Department of Education Records, 1874–1984, RG 92, Tennessee State Library and Archives.

police did. Crump spoke racial epithets on the radio, and his political machine forced two of the city's leading Negro leaders to relocate to Chicago.[2]

But slowly and surely the civil rights movement began to make progress. In 1936 in Berlin, Germany, Jessie Owens a Negro college student born in an Alabama sharecropping family became the first man to win four gold medals in the Olympics. On the night of 22 June 1937, Joe Louis knocked out the white champion James Braddock and became the first Negro heavyweight boxing champion since Jack Johnson. Negroes danced in the streets because Joe Louis and Jessie Owens proved that blacks could equal whites in achievement.[3]

After giving a radio speech in November 1936 on the subject of Negro education in the South, Bruce R. Payne of George of Peabody College for Teachers sent a copy to Will Ed Turner, the state supervisor of Negro education.[4] Payne argued that education improved Negroes as citizens, improved the economic prosperity of the US, and taught Negro parents to save something for the future education of their children. Payne sympathized with the South, but he argued the South, as an impoverished area, was less able to carry two sections of education than any other region of the US. He said, "We cannot have a region, part of whose population is educated and the other part is not." Will Ed Turner the white director of the Tennessee Department of Negro Education responded blandly: "Those of us in the South who are especially interested in the promotion of Negro education are not unmindful of the many things which you have done and said to promote this cause."[5]

In response to *The Report on Economic Conditions of the South* (1938) that illustrated how far the South was behind the rest of the United States in terms of academic achievement, Southern progressives and civil rights leaders, including

---

[2] Bobby L. Lovett, *The Civil Rights Movement in Tennessee: A Narrative History* (Knoxville: University of Tennessee Press, 2005) 242–46. G. Wayne Dowdy, *Crusades for Freedom: Memphis and the Political Transformation of the American South* (Jackson: University Press of Mississippi, 2010).

[3] Darlene Clark Hine, William C. Hine, and Stanley Harrold, "Jessie Owens and Joe Louis," in *African Americans: A Concise History*, 2nd ed. (Upper Saddle River NJ: Pearson/Prentice Hall, 2006) 424–25.

[4] Note: The Division of Negro Education served as an agent for the GEB, the Southern Foundation, the Rosenwald Fund, other philanthropic agencies, and as coordinator between the state department of education and institutes of education in Tennessee. The Division was overseer of the Jeanes Fund in Tennessee, and supervised classroom instruction, promoted community education activities, and cooperated with the Division of Schoolhouse Planning and Transportation pertaining to buildings, grounds and equipment for Negro citizens; "Divisions in the Department of Education, 1873–1980," Tennessee Department of Education Records, 1874–1984, RG 273, 5–7.

[5] Payne's 15 November 1936 radio speech sent to W.E. Turner, Nashville, 5 January 1937, correspondence, Tennessee A&I, 1937–38, box 100, folder 58, RG 273.

Eleanor Roosevelt, met in Birmingham, Alabama, to form the Southern Conference on Human Welfare (SCHW) to fight poverty, Jim Crow, and poll taxes. Sociologist Charles S. Johnson of Fisk University and a few HBCU presidents were at the meeting. W.J. Hale was not there, perhaps because Negro public officials such as Hale had to be careful. Tennessee historian Robert E. Corlew said it was "turbulent times, 1937–1953." The authors of *Tennesseans and Their History* wrote that, "Blacks well remembered that whites had used violence to reaffirm white supremacy after World War I." [6] White liberal Myles Horton had opened the Highlander Folk School in Grundy County in impoverished east Tennessee in 1932, and Highlander officials attended the meeting in Birmingham.[7] NAACP lawyers out of New York City, Knoxville, and Nashville already had begun their attack on Tennessee Jim Crow higher education. In 1937, they filed for a *writ of mandamus* to force the officials to admit William B. Redmond, a graduate of Tennessee A&I, to the University of Tennessee pharmacy program. The state judge ruled against Redmond. *The Broadcaster* of the Tennessee Negro Teachers Association agitated, "When will graduate work be started at A. & I.?" Editor George W. Gore, the dean of Tennessee A&I State College, wrote, "The executive committee of the Negro Teachers Association met with the Commissioner and members of the State Board of Education. Promises were made but to date there has been no definitive action."[8]

In fall 1937, the new class of students began arriving on a Sunday. They marveled at the campus near the Cumberland. They held the traditional candle-lighting ceremony on the lawn of Memorial Library. The 1937–38 graduating class of Tennessee A&I, with 129 students, was 40 percent male. Howard University had 196 graduates in 1937–38; Lane College had 30 graduates; Fisk University had 44 graduates. Alma Dunn-Rhodes (English), who came to campus in 1933 after serving as an education supervisor in South Carolina, received a GEB fellowship to study in New York at Columbia Teachers College. Columbia University in New York cooperated with the philanthropic agencies to help produce more blacks with graduate degrees, enrolling 246 Negroes including 57 Southern blacks by 1939. University of Cincinnati, Illinois, Kansas,

---

[6] Paul H. Bergeron, Stephen V. Ash, and Jeanette Keith, *Tennesseans and Their History* (Knoxville: University of Tennessee Press, 1999) 285; Robert E. Corlew, *Tennessee: A Short History*, 2nd ed. (Knoxville: University of Tennessee Press, 1981) 480–99.

[7] *The Report on Economic Conditions of the South* (Washington, DC: General Printing Office, 1938) 1–21.

[8] See *The Broadcaster* (1937), Special Collections, TSU, 1–3; correspondence, attorney general's office, 1939, box 123, folder 1, Negro scholarship applications, 1937, box 149, folder 26, Negro scholarships issued, 1938–39, box 149, folder 28, RG 273. Note: the NAACP lost the Redmond case in November 1939. Redmond became a store proprietor in Franklin, and never realized his dream to become a pharmacist because of Jim Crow laws.

Ohio State University, University of Chicago, and New York University also enrolled black graduate students.[9]

Graduate Programs and Land-Grant Funding

Many of the existing 118 HBCUs were intent on upgrading to graduate programs, but they were under pressure from the US Bureau of Education and accreditation agencies to engage the faculty in more research and writing. Professor W.E.B. Du Bois at Atlanta University helped with the call for Negroes to publish more research and literature, convincing AU to finance the *Phylon* journal about race and Negro culture. Carter G. Woodson and others expanded the quarterly *Journal of Negro History* (1916–) and the monthly *Negro History Bulletin* (1933–). Charles H. Thompson and others at Howard University began publishing the quarterly *Journal of Negro Education* (1931–). In 1935, Ralph Bunche organized a conference to look into the Negro's economic position during the Great Depression. Johnson C. Smith College sponsored the *Quarterly Review of Higher Education Among Negroes.* In 1935, Theophilus McKinney, Sr., dean and registrar at Johnson C. Smith, and other HBCU social scientists organized the Association of Social Science Teachers (Association of Social and Behavioral Scientists). The group published conference proceedings in the *Quarterly Review of Higher Education Among Negroes,* and later the *Journal of Social Science Teachers* (today's *Journal of Social and Behavioral Sciences).* In April 1937, a group of English teachers founded the Association of Teachers of English in Negro Colleges during a meeting at LeMoyne College and began publishing the *News-Bulletin.* Wilberforce University in Ohio issued the *Negro College Quarterly,* while Lincoln University in Pennsylvania published the *Research Journal (The Midwest Journal,* 1947–56). Florida A&M University published a *Quarterly Journal.* Tuskegee Institute published the annual *Negro Yearbook,* edited by Monroe Work. Tennessee A&I faculty formed a research club and published papers in *The Newsletter (Faculty Research Journal).* Merl R. Eppse published three textbooks and George Gore published articles in the *Quarterly Review of Higher Education among Negroes* (1941).[10]

---

[9] Bobby L. Lovett, *America's Historically Black Colleges and Universities: A Narrative History from 1837 to 2010* (Macon GA: Mercer University Press, 2011) 110, 117, 118, 120, 125, 130; graduates, colleges and universities, 1937, box 149, folder 10, RG 273; Commission on Interracial Cooperation, *A Summary of the Provisions being Made in Certain States for the Professional and Graduate Education of Negroes* (Atlanta: Commission on Interracial Cooperation, 7 September 1940) 1–21; Henry W. Greene, "Recent Negro College Graduates," *Nashville World,* 10 May 1932, 1.

[10] Ibid.; Merl R. Eppse (1893–1967) Papers, 1927–1961, speeches and writings, boxes 77–83, Tennessee State Library and Archives (TSLA); Merl R. Eppse, *An Elementary History of America including the Contributions of Negro Americans* (Nashville: National Publication

Dean Gore headed Phi Beta Tau beginning in 1931, the successor to Sais Society (1919). Gore and others spread the society to other HBCUs through the National Federation of Honor Societies in Negro Colleges and held the first meeting at A&I on 26 November 1937. In 1939, they adopted the name Alpha Kappa Nu. The A&I chapter retained the name Phi Beta Tau and sponsored the annual Spring Fine Arts and Lecture Series, a Dinner and Dance on campus.[11]

The Annual Conference of Presidents of Negro Land-Grant Colleges met at Howard University, allowing the HBCU presidents to petition federal officials for a redress of grievances. They made a special connection with US Interior Secretary, Harold Ickes. He made a radio speech, "In Spite of the Obstacles" (1933), saying that the progress through education of the Negro population furnished proof that could be cited of the value of education to a nation. He urged all Americans to give the Negro the fullest possible education opportunities. Hale and other HBCU land-grant presidents discussed agriculture, domestic arts, HBCU needs in mechanical arts, and more guidance programs to help the students. They felt recent students were better prepared academically and more independent, but many of them had an indifference to learning. They visited with Secretary Ickes, trying to get more federal help with the reorganization of the HBCU curriculum in a rapidly changing society with new demands on its citizens. By 1937, because of the Northern migration, Negroes made up only 23 percent of the Southern population instead of the 34 percent that it did in 1890. But Southern Negroes still comprised the majority of all blacks in the US. White Southerners comprised 34 percent of the nation's whites and outnumbered blacks two-to-one in the South, where most HBCUs were located. Since 1929, enrollment in land-grant HBCUs had grown from 3,691 to 6,031 students. Tennessee A&I State College had the largest enrollment among land-grant HBCUs.[12]

Co., 1949); Merl R. Eppse, *The Negro, Too, in American History* (Nashville: National Publication Co., 1943); Merl R. Eppse, *A Guide to the Study of the Negro in American History* (Nashville: National Pub. Co., 1943); "Tennessee State Professor Writes *A Guide to the Study of the Negro in American History,*" *The Bulletin* 25, no. 12 (September 1937): 1; Lovett, *America's Black Colleges*, 112–13.

[11] See A&I *The Bulletin* (1931–37).

[12] Annual Conference of Presidents of the Association of Negro Land-Grant Colleges Reports, 1933–39, Special Collections, TSU; John W. Davis, "The Participation of Negro Land-Grant Colleges in Permanent Federal Education Funds," *Journal of Negro Education* 7, no. 3 (July 1938): 282–91; *Leadership and Learning: An Interpretive History of Historically Black Land-Grant Colleges and Universities—a Centennial Study*, ed. James W. Smith (Washington DC: National Association of State Universities and Land-Grant Colleges, 1993); Herman B. Long, "The Negro Public College in Tennessee," *Journal of Negro Education* 31, no. 3 (Summer 1962): 341–48; Charles W. Dabney, *Universal Education in the South* (Chapel Hill:

Hale and other HBCU land-grant presidents sent letters to Ickes, asking for the equitable division between the races of all federal funds and matching state funds in states that maintained racially separate educational systems. In 1937, white land-grant colleges in Southern states expended $13,360,598 of federal funds, but the HBCU land-grant institutions received only $504,767 (3.7 percent). The National Coordinating Committee for Equitable Distribution of Federal Aid to Education (1938) said the appropriations for Southern states grew to $16,846,274, and federal money for HBCUs and black education increased to 9 percent. Tennessee received $839,353 in federal land-grant funds for fiscal year ending 30 June 1937, and shared $30,217 (3.6 percent) with Tennessee A&I State College. Negroes comprised more than 18 percent of Tennessee's population. White Tennesseans kept the Hatch-Adams funds ($30,000), the Smith-Lever funds ($839,353), military training funds ($37,950), Clarke McNary Funds ($1,620), Purnell Fund ($60,000), Capper-Ketcham Funds ($35,917), Bankhead-Jones Funds ($375,883), and extra US agricultural funds ($22,000). None of the land-grant HBCUs had professional programs in medicine, dentistry, law, pharmacy, engineering, social work, or any other graduate program, and Southern, white, land-grant institutions excluded black citizens.[13]

At the meeting in Washington DC, Hale turned attention away from such racially intense issues and invited his fellow land-grant presidents to attend "our Silver Jubilee to illustrate we have succeeded in the land-grant college program with teachers, students, and recently purchased land." Mordecai W. Johnson, the first Negro president of Howard University, was the speaker for Tennessee A&I's Silver Jubilee Program on Thanksgiving Day in the Chapel. Johnson arranged for Howard University to award an honorary doctorate to Hale, which took away the stigma that Hale had no four-year college degree.[14]

Issues of race, fairness, and equality continued to influence practices at Tennessee A&I. Carter G. Woodson of the Association for the Study of Negro Life and History (ASNLH) asked Will Ed Turner to place Negro history in the

University of North Carolina Press, 1936); Martin D. Jenkins, "Enrollment in Negro Colleges and Universities, 1937–38," *Journal of Negro Education* 7, no. 2 (April 1938): 118–23.

[13] Ibid.; Tennessee A&I files, 1936–39, box 151, folders 6–8, RG 273; see Martin D. Jenkins, "Enrollment in Negro Colleges and Universities, 1937–38," *Journal of Negro Education* 7, no. 2 (April 1938): 118–23; D.O. Holmes, "The Future Possibilities of Graduate Work in Negro Colleges and Universities," *Journal of Negro Education* 7, no.1 (January 1933): 5–19; *Proceedings of the Conference of Presidents of Negro Land Grant Colleges*, 1936, 1937, 1939, 1944, 1945, 1949, 1950 (Washington DC: US Office of Education), and "Ten Years of the Presidents' Conference, 1923–1933," 1936 volume, 10–11 November, Special Collections, TSU.

[14] "1912–1937: Twenty-fifth Anniversary Celebration of Tennessee A. & I. State College," *The Bulletin* (1937): 1–10; "Roster of College Graduates, 1924–1937," *The Bulletin* (1937).

Tennessee secondary curriculum by using the monthly *Negro History Bulletin* and celebrating Negro History Week. The Tennessee department of education published *The Negro: Selected List for School Libraries of Books by or about the Negro in Africa and America* (1941).[15]

The NAACP continued the pressure on Tennessee officials. Charles Hamilton Houston and other NAACP lawyers won *Missouri ex rel. Gaines v. Canada, Registrar of the University of Missouri et al.,* 305 US 337 (1937) on 12 December 1938, when the court said that to deny Lloyd Gaines admission at the white public university and force him to accept an out-of-state scholarship was a violation of the Fourteenth Amendment. The University of Missouri admitted Gaines; but, to keep other Negroes out, the state established a law school for three Negro plaintiffs in St. Louis. The NAACP opposed the bogus law school as no more than a Jim Crow diversion.

Negro schoolteachers again pressured Tennessee A&I State College to offer graduate courses. On 11 June 1938, the Commissioner wrote to Hale: "I am asking you to inform those students who are expecting credit for graduate work, that such an arrangement has not been approved by the State Board of Education." While Hale replied he did not know of the source of such reports about graduate work being offered at A&I State College, it is likely he did know.[16]

Black leaders often spoke on *Wings over Jordan*, a black radio program out of Cleveland Ohio, picked up by Columbia Broadcasting System (CBS) from 1938 to 1947. Many leaders used this radio program to expound a Bookerite racial philosophy and to reassure the audience that the HBCU educated and trained students to be good citizens, loyal Americans, and not revolutionaries. One man said the HBCU must provide more general education curricula to better educate the students, stop trying to imitate the liberal arts colleges, and get into the vanguard of American educational progression, including the training of workers as extension workers, home economics, and health education to serve the general Negro population. Other Negro speakers talked about morals, ethics,

---

[15] C.G. Woodson to W.E. Turner, Washington, DC, 17 December 1937, "A. & I.," SBOE Papers; State Department of Education, *The Negro: Selected List for School Libraries of Books by or about the Negro in Africa and America* (Nashville: SDOE, 1941).

[16] A&I Graduate work, 1942–45, box 199, folder 8; UT report on Tennessee A&I, 1941–42, box 266, folder 10; A&I reorganization and audit, 1941–43, box 200, folder 8; Commissioner of Education Records, 1913–70, RG 92, TSLA; Commissioner to W.J. Hale, Nashville, 11 June 1938, and W.J. Hale to Commissioner, Nashville, 15 June 1938; correspondence A&I, 1936–41, box 100, folders 58–60; correspondence A&I, 1942–44, box 136, folders 27–29; W.J. Hale case, 1938, 1942–43, box 150, folders 2–3; A&I subject files, 1941–49, box 151, folders 9–10, Tennessee Department of Education Records, 1874–1984, RG 273.

and religion needed by young Negroes, but they did not speak against Jim Crow. On 4 December 1938, A&I's President W.J. Hale spoke:

> The Negro is being called upon to take on the stature of citizenship. He is beginning to realize that America is his America, that the Stars and Stripes truly wave for him, that the Statue of Liberty is his statue, that all of the capitols of the United States are his, that he must stand up as a man and assume civic responsibility, that if there is anything wrong with the World, it is his duty to help make it right. The challenge of the white man is to encourage Negro leadership, Negro participation in civic life, and Negro cooperation in working out the common problems, to make the Negro feel a sense of ownership of his city, county, and nation. With such attitude, the Negro and the white man can work together toward the creation of a better day for the sons and daughters of all the people of the nation. The time to sing the blues and play Uncle Tom is passed. Real men of both racial groups want sincerity and the truth. [17]

Some criticized Hale's *Wings over Jordan* speech because it seemed to gloss over the problem of American racism. Recent NAACP federal court victories had advanced the movement against Jim Crow, and the Nashville *Globe* (20 January 1939) announced "Eight Negroes applying to the University of North Carolina." Instead, North Carolina was forced to establish law and graduate programs at two HBCUs. [18]

Some of W. J. Hale's detractors also criticized him for having a large student payroll. Hale had to explain to the SBOE that students got *credit* for work but no checks. Then some campus dissidents complained that Hale was trying to prepare Will, Jr., as a successor. Hale said the Smith-Hughes officials suggested Hale, Jr., to replace Walter S. Davis, who was on academic leave: "I am not trying to slip anything over on the [state] board." [19] The SBOE denied Hale's son becoming the presidential assistant, but Hale skillfully mended his relations with the officials by hosting a knockout reception for them. A Joint House and Senate Resolution, *Public Acts of the State of Tennessee*, 71st General Assembly, thanked President Hale, the faculty and students for the "transportation, entertainment, and a bounteous dinner. [It] was never surpassed by any institution of this state provided to this body and to our great Governor last February 9, 1939." [20]

---

[17] W.J. Hale, *Wings over Jordan* speech, 4 December 1939, TSU Presidential Records, 1912–, speeches, Hale Papers, 1912–44, Special Collections, TSU.

[18] Lovett, *America's Black Colleges*, 217–20.

[19] W.J. Hale to the SBOE, Nashville, 10 February 1939, A&I, RG 273; correspondence, TSU Presidential Records, 1912–, Hale Papers, 1912–44, Special Collections, TSU.

[20] Joint House and Senate Resolution, *Public Acts of the State of Tennessee*, 71st General Assembly, 14 February 1939, Hale Papers.

At the 1939 Conference for the Association of Land Grant Colleges, President Hale had several of his faculty members to give presentations on business education. Hale became vice president of the National Negro Business League. His friend J. E. Walker of Memphis, a chief officer in the National Negro Business League, also addressed the conference. Walker spoke about the need to continue to inspire our people to fight for jobs despite racial discrimination. Harriett Hale, the driving influence behind the business education movement at Tennessee A&I spoke on "The Place of Secretarial Training in Business Education." In 1929, Harriett Hale had written, "I consider the successful training of [Negro] youth in the business field, as most essential so as to place our future business on a solid and firm foundation." She also wrote, in 1934, that, "the object of the Secretarial Commerce Department at the A. & I. State College is primarily to make the words Negro and Business synonymous. The Negro's place in this world will be, to a large degree, made possible along economical lines." Comparing the Negro to the Jews, she said, "Why cannot we [Negroes] do something for ourselves?" Harriett Hale published "The Place of Secretarial Training in Business Education" in *The Broadcaster* (1940).[21]

For his A&I master's thesis, Henry T. Boyd wrote, "A follow-up Study of the Graduates of the Department of Business Education at Tennessee A. & I. State College with Implications for Evaluating the Curriculum and Guidance Program" (1951). He pointed out that the business program at Tennessee A&I State College began in 1912 with one typewriter and one teacher and had made great progress since Harriett Hale had become the program director in 1918. Since 1922, there had been a college program to prepare secretaries, office assistants, clerks, semi-executives, teachers, and students for the federal civil service examinations. By 1930, the business education program had graduated 450 students, and 56 percent of them worked in Tennessee. An orientation course became part of the curriculum in 1943–44, and the Division of Business became a distinct unit by 1949–50, offering extended education to businesspersons in sales, advertising, purchasing, and management. The Pi Omega Pi business fraternity began in 1950—the first at HBCUs.[22]

The white University of Tennessee was also steadily growing as a state institution. Charles Dabney, president (1887–1904), had started a law school that admitted women, and the state of Tennessee had given UT the first million-

---

[21] 1939 Conference for the Association of Land Grant Colleges, 1–21; Harriett Hale, "Negro Business Education," *The Broadcaster* (February 1934): 1, and *The Bulletin* (December 1929): 1. Note: Bethune-Cookman College granted an honorary doctorate degree (1952) to Harriett E. Hale.

[22] Henry T. Boyd, "A Follow-up Study of the Graduates of the Department of Business Education at Tennessee A. & I. State College with Implications for Evaluating the Curriculum and Guidance Program," (master's thesis, Tennessee A&I State College, 1951).

dollar allocation by 1917. UT had schools of medicine, dentistry, nursing, pharmacy, and programs in agriculture, architecture and planning, arts and sciences, business, communications, education, engineering, human ecology, social work, veterinary medicine, and more.[23]

Despite losing the *Redmond* appeal in 1939, the NAACP and the Legal Defense Educational Fund (LDEF) continued their attack on UT. Thurgood Marshall replaced Charles H. Houston as chief NAACP legal counsel. NAACP-affiliated lawyers Carl A. Cowan of Chattanooga, Z.A. Looby of Nashville, and Leon Ransom from Ohio found half a dozen qualified applicants willing to file another court challenge to UT's admissions policies.[24]

In September 1939, the NAACP lawyers in New York launched their attack on Jim Crow pay for public school teachers in Norfolk, Virginia, where a white teacher was paid 53 percent more than a black teacher with the same teaching experience and credentials. The evidence was glaring. NAACP researchers estimated an annual loss of $25,000,000 by Negro teachers because of salary discrimination. Southern schools spent on average $38.87 educating each white pupil and $13.09 educating each Negro pupil. NAACP lawyers and plaintiffs won salary cases in Maryland. Tennessee Negro teachers earned 69 percent of the salary paid to white teachers[25]— although most of them were Tennessee A&I graduates who sometimes had better credentials than many white teachers. Tennessee A&I had also earned national accreditation from the American Association of Teachers Colleges (AATC). The NAACP filed a case in Tennessee.

NAACP Intensifies the Battles Against Jim Crow

By now, Tennessee A&I College was quite self-sufficient, with 320 acres: 60 in corn, 30 in oats, 12 in truck gardening, 10 in barley and rye, and pastureland.

---

[23] Milton M. Klein, "University of Tennessee," ed. C. Van West, *The Tennessee Encyclopedia of History and Culture* (Nashville: Rutledge Hill Press, 1998) 1010–12; Note: C. W. Dabney, first UT president with a PhD (University of Gottingen, Germany), believed the Negro was in the South to stay and that the Southern people must educate him, too, or the Negro would drag the whites down. His son Robert was an active neo-Confederate who utterly opposed any improvements for the region's Negro people; this attitude characterized many of the officials and faculty at UT by the 1930s. "Charles W. Dabney: Eleventh President, 1887–1904," http://web.utk.edu/`mklein/dabney.html, 1–4 [accessed 10 September 2011].

[24] Note: Marshall's first cousin Avon N. Williams, Jr., of Knoxville was headed to Johnson C. Smith College and destined to become a top civil rights lawyer in 1951. He became a great supporter of Tennessee State.

[25] NAACP, *Teachers' Salaries in Black and White* (New York: NAACP-LDEF, 1941) 1–31; R.A. Margo, "Teacher Salaries in Black and White: Pay Discrimination in the Southern Classroom," in Robert A. Margo, *Race and Schooling in the South, 1880–1950: An Economic History* (Chicago: University of Chicago Press, 1990) 52–67.

The students in the industrial arts department and the home economics program manufactured and renovated campus furniture. Filmmakers scheduled a film on A&I's progress and facilities for showing at the University of Toronto. The passing of James C. Napier on April 21 closed the college for a day in his honor. Napier personally had presented the awards for scholastic achievement on Commencement Day. There were 166 graduates in 1940, making Tennessee A&I one of the largest producers of Negro college graduates. Charles C. Spaulding spoke on "Efficient Work is the Law of Life." Spaulding was the first Negro on the John F. Slater Fund board and had ties to the National Negro Business League and to Will W. Alexander, who presided over the Commission on Interracial Cooperation (CIC). Marie Brooks-Strange and the A&I Concert Choir performed at graduation and in Memphis, Chicago, Minneapolis, and New York.[26]

Hale, Will Ed Turner, and the SBOE Commissioner addressed the opening convocation on September 10. Dormitories and classrooms were renovated, new draperies hung in the auditorium, and a new outdoor pool and some additions to photography and cinema courses were ready. The faculty expanded offerings in education, health and physical education, music and fine arts, business education and home economics. The Nashville Coach Company discontinued the electric streetcars and extended motorbuses to the campus gates. *The Bulletin* (January 1941) said, "The 10 to 15 minutes between the two modes of transportation means much in the busy life of the college students."[27]

In February 1941, Fisk University, Meharry Medical College, and Tennessee A&I State College jointly sponsored Christian Mission week. Walter S. Davis was poised to receive a PhD in agriculture from Cornell, becoming the first A&I graduate to receive a doctorate degree. His wife, Ivanetta Davis, another A&I graduate, earned the master's from Cornell in the summer session of 1941. Faculty member Forrest Strange received his LLB degree from Kent School of Law operated by Z.A. Looby. Gwendolyn Claire Hale received the MA degree in romance languages and arts from Columbia. J.C. Blaine received the master's degree from Drake University. Ray L. Ferguson received the law degree from Drake University. L.W. Lee obtained the MS. degree from Fisk. D.H. Turpin and W.M. Springer became dentists and National Dental Association officers. Since

---

[26] See A&I *The Bulletin* (1939–April 1940); A&I files, 1938–49, box 151, folders 8–11, RG 273; W.J. Hale, Report on Federal WPA Projects at Tennessee A&I State College, 30 October 1942, m-104, box 138, folder 18, RG 273: photos of faculty, students, buildings, teachers' cottages, and WPA expenditures on each building, total valued at $1,460,500; and Dedication Program, 5 November 1942.

[27] Ibid.; TSU Presidential Records, 1912–, Hale Papers, speeches, 1912–44; report committee on A&I Audit, September 1943, SBOE minutes, August 1943, box 12, folders 1–4, RG 91.

1912, Tennessee A&I had enrolled 24,287 students in regular sessions, 22,580 in summer sessions, and had issued 1,456 diplomas.[28]

On 18 October 1939, six Negro graduates of Knoxville College applied for admission to the University of Tennessee—four to the graduate department and two to the law college. Being denied admission, they and the NAACP filed separate petitions for *writ of mandamus* on behalf of all Negro citizens in the Chancery Court of Knox County. White officials were using the police powers of the state to protect Jim Crow and to violate the Fourteenth Amendment that guaranteed equal protection of the law to all American citizens. However, while the case was pending, the Tennessee General Assembly quickly enacted sec. 2403.3 of the Tennessee Code titled "Educational Facilities for Negro Citizens equivalent to those provided for white citizens":

> The state board of education and the commissioner of education are hereby authorized and directed to provide educational training and instruction for [Negro] citizens of Tennessee equivalent to that provided at the University of Tennessee by the State of Tennessee for white citizens of Tennessee. Such training and instruction shall be made available in the manner to be prescribed by the state board of education and the commissioner of education; provided, that members of the [Negro] race and white race shall not attend the same institution or place of learning. The facilities of the Agricultural and Industrial State College, and other institutions located in Tennessee, may be used when deemed advisable by the state board of education and the commissioner of education, insofar as the facilities of same are adequate.[29]

The judge disposed of the case on the grounds that it was moot. An appeal *State of Tennessee Ex. Rel., Michael et al. v. Witham et al.*165, SW 2d 378 was taken to the Supreme Court of Tennessee. On 7 November 1942, the Tennessee Supreme Court justices affirmed the lower court:

> The manner of providing educational training and instruction for Negro citizens, equivalent to that provided for white citizens at the University of Tennessee is for the Board of Education to determine in its sound discretion, but the furnishing of such equivalent instruction is mandatory. Upon the demand of a Negro upon the State Board of Education for training and instruction in any branch of learning taught in the University of Tennessee, it is the duty of the Board to provide such Negro with equal facilities of instruction in such subjects as that enjoyed by the students of the University of

---

[28] Ibid.

[29] "Gray v. UT," *Gray et al. v. UT et al.*, 20 April 1951, US District Court, Eastern District of Tennessee, ND, http://tn.findacase.com/research/wfrmDocViewer.aspx/xq/fac.%CFDCT%5CETN%C19, 1–4 [accessed 10 September 2011]; Tennessee Public Acts, Chapter No. 43, SB No. 379, HB No. 509, 1941, Tennessee Department of Education, 1874–1984, RG 273, R-104, box 136, folder 18, TSLA

Tennessee. The SBOE is entitled to reasonable notice of the intention of a Negro student to require such facilities. The legislation of 1941 took no rights away from appellants; on the contrary, the right to equality in education with white students was specifically recognized and the method by which those rights would be satisfied was set forth in the legislation. Appellants will pay the costs incident to the appeal.[30]

Again, Tennessee law outlawed integrated classrooms, and the *Berea* (1908) US Supreme Court case affirmed Tennessee and Kentucky in this regard. The NAACP still argued that Jim Crow states violated the Fourteenth Amendment and failed to respect *Plessy* (1896).

But it seemed that the Tennessee General Assembly act "Educational Facilities for Negro Citizens equivalent to those provided for white citizens" (1941) would finally make Tennessee A&I State College the equivalent of the University of Tennessee in academic programming and facilities. On 13 February 1941, Education Commissioner B.O. Duggan sent a letter to the president of UT asking him to appoint sub-committees "to work out procedures for installing graduate work at the A. & I. College for Negroes.... [And] We believe we can establish a Law School on the Tennessee Agricultural and Industrial College campus as economically and efficiently as could be established at any standard college in the state."[31] But Duggan also wrote that he was continuing negotiations with Meharry Medical College administrators for a more formal agreement to admit Negro residents at state expense to study medicine, dentistry, pharmacy, and nursing.[32]

Northern education reformers were watching how Tennessee's Jim Crow officials would deal with the HBCU Tennessee A&I State College. When Duggan was attending a national conference in New York, a GEB official suggested Duggan employ an outside agency to study Tennessee A&I and include a Negro

---

[30] *Tennessee Laws*, 1941, chapter 43, section 2, 136; A&I files, 1941–48, box 151, folder 9; Negro scholarships issued, 1938–39, box 149, folder 27; audits, Tennessee A&I, 1938–57, box 147, folder 2; correspondence, Tennessee A&I, 1940–41, box 100, folder 60, RG 273; Carmelia G. Taylor, "A History of Graduate Studies at Tennessee State University from 1935 to 1986," (PhD diss., TSU, 1995); US District Court, Eastern District of Tennessee, ND, http://tn.findacase.com/research/wfrmDocViewer.aspx/xq/fac.%CFDCT%5CETN%C19, 1–4 [accessed 10 September 2011].

[31] Ibid., B.O. Duggan to UT president, Nashville, 13 February 1941, A&I files; A&I file, 1940–41, box 84, folder 4, Tennessee Office of Attorney General and Reporter, 1906–69, RG 241, TSLA, Nashville.

[32] Commissioner Duggan exchange of letters with GEB officials in New York, Nashville, 1941, A&I files, correspondence, 1940–41, box 100, folder 60; Will E. Turner, 1940–41, box 101, folder 73, RG 273; A&I graduate work, 1942–45, box 199, folder 8; A&I college reorganization and audit, 1941–43, box 200, folder 8; UT report on Tennessee A&I, 1941–42, box 26, folder 10, RG 92.

college president on the team. On May 9, Duggan appointed Will Ed Turner as SBOE coordinator between UT planning committees for implementing graduate study at A&I. The SBOE directed Turner to help A&I achieve SACS approval. Turner established a second office on the campus in the Industrial Arts Building. Duggan traveled to Knoxville to meet with the UT faculty/staff to discuss all these issues, as they apparently did not trust Hale, a black man, with these important white supremacy tasks.[33]

In 1941, Tennessee had 17,729 elementary schoolteachers, 4,935 high school teachers, 650,000 children in schools, and 653 college teachers. The $71.3 million dollars state budget included $12.9 million of federal funds. On 5 January 1943, Governor Prentice Cooper (D) said, "I am glad to report that progress is being made toward providing higher education for the Negro citizens of the State equal to that provided for the white citizens, as provided by Chapter 43 of the *Public Acts of 1941*. I am glad to report … for the first time there has been provided an 8-month school term for all Negro schools."[34]

The UT visiting teams received copies of the 1936 study on Tennessee A&I. They concluded that Hale needed to push for more faculty scholarship and for SACS approval, reorganize the college, improve the library, and consider discontinuing engineering courses. They recommended that A&I publish the next college catalog to reflect the UT format. The UT dean of the law school feared more NAACP lawsuits.[35]

On 14 July 1941, Duggan called a meeting, including Will Ed Turner, Robert E. Clay, and a Negro consultant who had recently set up the HBCU Lincoln University Law School for Negroes in St. Louis, Missouri.[36] Duggan and his colleagues spoke boldly in front of Turner's Negro assistant, Robert Clay. The UT representative said the NAACP was a good organization but "bad leaders dominated the agency; and, the NAACP officials were not thinking either of the

---

[33] Will E. Turner, 1940–41, box 101, folder 73, RG 273; A&I graduate work, 1942–45, box 199, folder 8; A&I college reorganization and audit, 1941–43, box 200, folder 8; UT report on Tennessee A&I, 1941–42, box 26, folder 10, RG 92.

[34] A&I files, 1941–43, RG 92; index to minutes, 1940–44, Tennessee Board of Education Minutes, 1907–83, RG 245; Gov. Prentice Cooper, message to the Tennessee General Assembly, 5 January 1941, 1–9, TSLA; *Messages of the Governors of the Tennessee General Assembly* 3, ed. Wayne C. Moore (Nashville: Tennessee Historical Commission, 1988); photographs, A&I College, 1944, box 253, folder 29, Gov. Prentice Cooper Papers, 1939–45, GP 44, TSLA.

[35] W.J. Hale files, 1942–43, box 150, folders 1–3, A&I files, 1941–48, box 151, folder 9, 10, correspondence, Tennessee A&I, 1942–44, box 136, folder 28, 29, RG 273.

[36] Lincoln University, "52 Steps, the Journey of Lincoln University of Missouri," six photos of the LU School of Law students and the facility at St. Louis, 1942–55, 1, http://contentdm.auctr.edu/cdm/landingpage/collection/lumo [accessed 21 November 2011].

best interests of this country nor of the [Negro] race." Will Ed Turner said there was no need to consult the NAACP or the colored race as a whole, but deal with those Negro plaintiffs that were responsible for filing the UT lawsuits. Turner bragged that the Negro Division had dealt with many colored people and never through any NAACP. One man said the law school could be set up in Memorial Library, but Turner said he did not know if Hale would be in accord with this because they needed more library books; the library that had been built in 1927 still had an entire empty floor. Clay had no recorded comments.[37]

Turner seemed to be building a case to avoid establishment of a law school at Tennessee A&I. The Negro consultant also urged him to forget the whole law school idea, increase the amount of the out-of-state scholarships to the six Negro plaintiffs, and remove the requirement that the recipient had to attend the nearest institution. Duggan and Turner agreed. On September 18, Duggan called Hale, Gore, R.B.J. Campbelle, Clay, and Turner to his office. Hale said A&I had set the catalog according to the UT format. Then Hale made a mistake: He suggested that Tennessee A&I State College should offer certain graduate curricula and UT should not offer certain curricula. Duggan hit the ceiling. He told Hale he would *not* present *any* ideas to the SBOE or any plans not first approved by the Commissioner. Turner and Clay sat silently.[38]

The UT people seemed so desperate to resolve the NAACP crisis that they would make A&I into a University of Tennessee Negro division, much like the Jim Crow arrangement with Knoxville College from 1891–1912. But Duggan stood firm, convinced that SBOE was the *sole* authority for Tennessee A&I, that UT was acting in an advisory capacity only, and that Will Turner was the clearinghouse. Some UT members complained that Hale was not working cooperatively with them, and a few disgruntled A&I faculty members took advantage of Hale's predicament and fed the UT visitors rumors about hidden accounts and the unorthodox management style of W. J. Hale.[39] President Hale appointed the graduate committee of W.S. Davis, Merl Eppse, T.H. Hughes,

[37] A&I State College graduate work, 1942–45, box 199, folder 11; A&I State Normal—Practice Teaching, 1942, box 199, folder 6; A&I State College, 1943–46, box 200, folder 1; A&I State College—funds deposited with treasurer, 1941, box 200, folder 5, A&I State College, Committees' visits—expense accounts, 1941, box 200, folder 6; report—UT report on Tennessee A&I, 1941–42, box 266, folder 10; Commissioner of Education Records, 1913–1970, RG 92, W.J. Hale case files, 1942–43, box 150, folder 3, RG 273, TSLA.

[38] A&I State College graduate work, 1942–45, box 199, folder 11; A&I State Normal—Practice Teaching, 1942, box 199, folder 6; A&I State College, 1943–46, box 200, folder 1; A&I State College—funds deposited with treasurer, 1941, box 200, folder 5; A&I State College, Committees' visits—expense accounts, 1941, box 200, folder 6; report—UT report on Tennessee A&I, 1941–42, box 266, folder 10; Commissioner of Education Records, 1913–1970, RG 92, W.J. Hale case files, 1942–43, box 150, folder 3, RG 273, TSLA.

[39] Ibid.

Gore, Harriett Hale, W.J. Hale (chair), and Corrine E. Springer, but then made another mistake. He returned $100,000 of the 1941 state appropriation to the public treasury, perhaps trying to gain favor with Duggan.[40] State auditors arrived on the campus and found that Hale had placed at least $317,000 in reserve accounts in various banks. The reform-minded Memphis evening daily *Press Scimitar* said, "What a refreshing bit of news comes out of Nashville: that the State Agricultural and Industrial College for Negroes has a—no, not a deficit—a surplus of $317,000. It is that much less money out of Tennessee taxpayers' pockets." *The Bulletin* defended Hale and printed summaries of the budgets since 1911, showing the state gave the least amount of support to Tennessee A&I for Negroes. Hale had raised money from philanthropic agencies and other donors, from federal grants, $509,540 from the WPA, and $1,288,270 from institutional income. Over the years, Tennessee A&I had lost $234,203 in state funds that "lapsed," were "impounded," or were withheld by Tennessee. *The Bulletin* listed Tennessee A&I's achievements and all universities that accepted the school's graduates. Some observers feared that Hale could be charged with attempted embezzlement. President Hale said, "I have no comment. The audit will speak for itself when completed and I feel that our record will be excellent." [41]

NAACP lawyers filed a salary equity case in Chattanooga. The chief plaintiff was Clarence B. Robinson a graduate of Tennessee A&I State Teachers College (1934). Robinson headed the Chattanooga Negro teachers union. On 20 September 1941, *Clarence B. Robinson and the Mountain City Teachers Association v. the Board of the City of Chattanooga, Tennessee* US (1941) was retired without going to trial because the school board offered 62 percent of new money for salary increases for equalization of salaries. Thurgood Marshall advised the plaintiffs *not* to accept the promise, but Robinson agreed to it to maintain local racial harmony. The white teachers union did not object to the equalization pay plan, and salary adjustments began the next year. Chattanooga instituted a uniform pay scale and graduate degree requirements for certain pay.[42]

---

[40] W.J. Hale case files, 1942–43, box 150, folder 3, Hale to SBOE, Nashville, 8 May 1942, SBOE minutes, Nashville, 7 February 1941, box 136, folder 1, RG 273.

[41] "Refreshing news," Memphis *Press Scimitar*, 24 September 1941; A&I *The Bulletin* (September–November 1941); "A. & I. creates $316,000 Reserve Fund; Turns back Appropriation," Nashville *Tennessean* (2 September 1941): 1, 4. Note: Walter C. Robinson, editor and publisher of the Chattanooga *Observer* (1927–62) supported Hale in this battle. His daughters attended Tennessee State, taught there, and donated the W.C. Robinson Collection, 1924–68, to Special Collections, TSU; William M. Springfield, dentist and A&I alumnus, Cincinnati, Ohio, to Duggan, 3 November 1942, R-104, box 136, folder 18, RG 273.

[42] Mark V. Tushnet, *The NAACP's Legal Strategy Against Segregated Education, 1925–1950* (Chapel Hill: University of North Carolina Press, 1987) 53–54, 65–67; C.B. Robinson earned a master's at Atlanta University, was a school principal, and head of the Tennessee

In 1941, public focus changed when the Japanese bombed Pearl Harbor, Hawaii, on December 7. America entered World War II. One million Negroes—including Tennessee A&I faculty and students—served with 17 million other Americans. Besides bringing a pillow, three sheets, two pillowcases, two spreads, two pairs of curtains, towels, dresser cover, table runner, and so on, students now had to bring their war sugar ration book. The faculty began listing the required senior thesis titles in the *Bulletin*. Raymond Chiles, history/political science major, wrote his senior thesis on "Negro Suffrage and White Politics in the South" (1941). Raymond G. Lloyd (1939) completed the master's at Columbia University. He joined the A&I staff and later wrote the fifty-year history of Tennessee State. The war nearly depleted the men on campus.[43]

Back at Tennessee A&I, state auditors complained to Duggan that they believed the bursar, R.B.J. Campbelle, was carrying out Hale's orders to obstruct the audit. On 6 February 1942, the SBOE met in executive session to receive a report that $3,300 of A&I petty cash funds were missing. Two of the three auditors recommended immediate dismissal of the bursar. Duggan called Governor Prentiss Cooper, who apparently told Duggan to comply with the audit report. By a vote of 6-1, the commissioners dismissed Campbelle. Duggan directed Hale to deliver the letter to Campbelle and collect the bursar's keys. On March 13, the auditors took over financial functions. They said the student accounts were in a mess. Dean Gore had to report to Duggan a list of students whose accounts showed debits for as little as $6. The state comptroller insisted that the newly discovered reserve funds be placed in the state treasury and credited to Tennessee A&I State College. The state attorney General Roy H. Beeler said in a letter to the state comptroller,

> It seems to me there is more feeling [emotion] than anything else in connection with this audit. President Hale has agreed to turn over all records. Be reminded we are making an effort to give the Negro equal access to graduate work to relieve the University of Tennessee of the embarrassing question made by an application of Negroes for admission to the University of Tennessee. If there isn't anything wrong with the management of this institution, and I am constrained to believe there is not anything radically wrong from the records before me, it would be a shame to besmirch the

---

chapter of the A&I Alumni Association, served in the Tennessee General Assembly, and chaired the Tennessee Caucus of Black State Legislators.

[43] See A&I *The Bulletin* (1940–41); photographs of P.L. Harned, W.J. Hale, George W. Gore, Jr., R.B.J. Campbelle, Martha M. Brown, R.E. Clay, Alger V. Boswell, Mary L. Wilson, Wilifred W. Lawson, and other staff/faculty, the *Ayeni Yearbook* of Tennessee Agricultural and Industrial State College, Nashville, 1931, 13–22; Raymond Lloyd, *Tennessee Agricultural and Industrial State University, 1912–1962* (Nashville: Tennessee A&I, 1962).

institution and do it irreparable damage by an ill-advised, ill-considered, and inaccurate audit.[44]

Campbelle turned against Hale. Campbelle had an ally in Goldie G. Bruce, who formerly managed one of the dormitories and who now lived in St. Louis. Bruce told all she knew in a letter (2 November 1942) to Duggan. Bruce claimed she had deposited $1,075 in the Arcade US Post Office Bank in Nashville from funds collected from transient guests who were placed in student rooms or guest rooms that were available when needed. Duggan sent a request for Hale to produce the records for visitors, but Hale said the records burned in a fire that hit Old Main. Duggan searched SBOE minutes to find that a storm blew the roof completely off Old Main on 11 May 1933 and that small fires had damaged Harned Hall (1934). A teacher's cottage caught fire in 1937, and a recent fire had done damage to the Women's Building but Duggan could find no report about a fire in Old Main.[45]

Campbelle called Duggan to request a meeting on December 1. The commissioner agreed to the meeting as long as there was a stenographer present. Campbelle complained that the auditors had taken the matter personally because Campbelle had refused to open the vaults after 5 p.m. to allow them to check cash on hand because he had closed the books. Upon his return, Campbelle found his letter of dismissal. Campbelle blamed Hale for the mess and said that Hale owned land on the south side of Centennial Boulevard. As Hale's attorney, Campbelle had completed the paperwork for the transactions. Hale said he intended to place the lots in the school's name. Campbelle pleaded he could clear up some of these matters if the state would only allow him to access his files in the bursar's office. But other state officials had bought lots in the A&I area, and Duggan refused to open this can of worms.[46] In a statement notarized by Z.A. Looby, Campbelle said, "His tenure covers more than thirty years, and he has in a way peculiar to himself 'run the show' in his own way, himself having no formal college or training, he disregards all orthodox methods of college organization."[47]

---

[44] A&I State College—funds deposited with treasurer, 1941, box 200, folder 5, RG 92; W.J. Hale case files, 1942–43, box 150, folder 3, RG 273; note: Duggan hired Mrs. E.P. Johnson to replace Campbelle. She and Gore now reported to the SBOE; James N. Hardin, secretary to Gov. Cooper to Duggan, 17 April 1943, Duggan to Hale, Nashville, 1 January, 19 April 1943, RG 273, R-104, box 136, folder 18, TSLA.

[45] Ibid., G.G. Bruce to B.O. Duggan, St. Louis, Missouri, 2 November 1942, A&I State College, 1943–46, box 200, folder 17, RG 92, W.J. Hale case files, 1942–43, box 150, folder 3, RG 273, TSLA.

[46] Ibid.

[47] Ibid.

Campbelle said Hale acted as if he were above the law and even kept the department heads fighting with the faculty to keep them divided. Gore, Eppse, Boswell, and Clay answered the president's every command and acted as his henchmen, claimed Campbelle. On the praising of Hale's 1938 radio address, Campbelle said Hale had sent letters and telegrams in the names of other leading Negro men and women without their knowledge, until their names appeared in a black newspaper and one man demanded a retraction. Harriett Hale allegedly made up the college's payroll, and Hale wrote the checks and personally paid each employee. Various offices kept cash funds, which the president would draw from without receipts, and Hale personally retained all payroll and bank account books at home. Campbelle accused Hale of "payroll high-jacking." Hale loaned money to faculty and students for a fee, and even cashed teachers' checks (who were supposed to be on the summer payroll) without their knowledge. He would tell a teacher he did not need her for the summer but since she did such a fine job, he was giving the teacher a bonus and asked her to sign a check (face down). Campbelle expressed resentment that Hale did not let him use the rank of associate professor after the SBOE granted tenure to faculty members at the state normal schools in May 1927. He also resented that Boswell was the man listed in the catalogs as treasurer at A&I State College. Campbelle said, "President Hale ... alone is responsible for the conditions and deficits at the College."[48]

Despite ongoing controversy with the auditors, A&I maintained their extensive program of activities for the students. One of the few places in Nashville that allowed for racial integration was Ryman Auditorium, and it was to here that the Third Biennial Meeting of the Southern Conference of Human Welfare (SCHW) was moved after last meeting in Chattanooga. Mary McLeod Bethune, the president of Bethune-Cookman College, head of the New Deal's Negro Youth programs and a chief fundraiser for the SCHW was attending the meeting, and was invited to speak on the Tennessee A&I campus on 19 April 1942 by Delta Sigma Theta. The SCHW moved its headquarters to Nashville and continued its fight against Jim Crow and poll taxes. Bethune said, "The double battle, which the Negro is facing, is one at home: the battle of racial prejudice, discrimination, and injustice, and the one abroad the battle with courage and spirit to rise economically, educationally, and spiritually as a people equal in the eyes of all Americans."[49]

Bethune's friend Eleanor Roosevelt had impressed many Negroes with her strong commitment to racial justice and peace. In 1939, when the Daughters of the American Revolution barred Marian Anderson, the world famous Negro

---

[48] Ibid. Note: the SBOE reinstated Campbelle, giving him the opportunity to resign. He resigned.

[49] Lovett, *Civil Rights Movement*, 6, 13, 16, 41, 164, 206, 237, 250, 416, 425.

contralto, from holding a Howard University concert in Constitution Hall, Eleanor Roosevelt, Secretary Ickes, and the NAACP arranged the concert at the Lincoln Memorial before 75,000 people. Anderson began the concert with "My Country, 'Tis of Thee." She later performed at Tennessee A&I State College.[50]

In April 1942, after the Nashville city council and the school board did not adequately respond to his friendly petition for them to remedy the racial inequities in teacher pay, attorney Z.A. Looby found plaintiff Harold E. Thomas, a teacher in his sixth year at Pearl High School who had a master's degree in chemistry from Fisk but was paid only $110 a month compared to $170 a month for an equally qualified white teacher. On July 28, the federal judge ended *Harold E. Thomas v. Louis Hibbits et al.* US (1942) by asking defense counselor, "Can a Negro teacher go to the store and buy a bottle of milk cheaper than a white teacher can?" Judge Elmer A. Davies ruled that Nashville was in violation of the equal protection clause of the Fourteenth Amendment. The Nashville chapter NAACP held an appreciation banquet for Thomas and Looby. Tennessee A&I graduates that were teachers benefited greatly from the *Thomas* case.[51]

On 31 May 1942, Tennessee A&I State College finally implemented the graduate program. Sixty-six students among approximately 700 in the summer school enrolled in the program. There were six full-time graduate students among the fall 1942–43 enrollment of 1,518 students.[52] Related to the UT graduate school case of *State ex Rel, Joseph M. Michael, Complainant and Appellant, Knox County*, on 4 November 1942, the SBOE dissolved the 1937 Negro

---

[50] See A&I, *The Bulletin* (1942–43, 1956); Hine, et al., *African Americans*, 396. Note: Marian Anderson, a supporter of the ongoing black civil rights movement, gave a concert in the Tennessee A&I State University auditorium in 1955; Eleanor Roosevelt was received at Tennessee A&I by President Hale, faculty, and students. Indira Hale Tucker, Hale's granddaughter, shared a copy of the photograph of Mrs. Roosevelt in the A-Auditorium with the author on 23 February 2012, and shared a citation of the Marcus O. Tucker and Indira Hale Tucker, Special Projects and Black Women's History Collection at the Burnett Public Library, Long Beach, California, Lovett Papers, Special Collections, TSU.

[51] Lovett, *Civil Rights Movement*, 12, 14; note: the school board did not renew Thomas's contract. He ended his career as business proprietor on Jefferson Street just blocks from the Tennessee A&I. His wife, Lillian Dunn (1935–), affectionately called "Ootsie," served TSU as a homecoming honoree; "Thomas v. Hibbits et al.: Equal Pay for Black Teachers," http://www.pbs.org/wgbh/amexx/partners/early/e_segregation_law-suit.html, 1–3 [accessed 10 September, 2011].

[52] A&I catalog/*The Bulletin* (1942, 1942–43), Special Collections, TSU; Lois C. McDougald, *A Time-Line Chronology of the Tennessee A. & I. State College Campus 1909–1951* (Nashville: Tennessee State University, January 1981) 125–26.

Scholarship Committee and formed a committee "on the whole question of Negro education in Tennessee."[53]

Tennessee A&I During World War II

On 5 November 1942, Tennessee A&I State College held dedication ceremonies for the Faculty Women's Residence Hall, Faculty Men's Residence Hall, faculty cottages, garages, poultry houses, athletic field and field house, outside swimming pool, golf course, tennis courts, pipe organs, hog pens, and the farmhouse. The horseshoe driveway that entered and exited the Old Campus through the iron gates connected to Centennial Boulevard and allowed automobiles to parade past the buildings. Hale ordered these iron gates closed after the night curfew. Old Main had recently succumbed to the wrecking ball, and only three major buildings remained from the earliest days of A&I. Hale and the staff scheduled the 39th Founders Day during the Homecoming Week of November 27–29. Festivities included a football game, dance, and reception. The regular 1942–43 session ended with commencement on 31 May 1943. There were six full-time graduate students. George R. White (Nashville) was the only male graduate student on campus.[54]

Two-third of the students on campus were women. Instructors Forrest Strange and Thomas G. Laster had left campus to serve in the US army. Despite the University of Tennessee visiting team's opposition, Tennessee A&I continued to work toward offering engineering courses and afternoon and evening classes for defense workers. Tennessee A&I established the US Enlisted Reserve Corps, the Management Defense Program, and adapted all departmental practices to war emergency procedures. On October 9, Henry A. Boyd and Citizens Bank held "A&I Day" that raised $3,000 for war bonds. Hale headed the Negro state War Bond Drive with a rally on campus on November 6. The campus hosted the mother of heavyweight boxing champion Joe Louis to help raise $40,000 in war bonds.[55] Former students Benton Adams and Grady Sherrill were in the navy. John L. Wilson, Sgt. Gerald Howell, Frank Cox, and William Holden visited the campus in their military uniforms. Robert J. Hudson was a technical corporal stationed at Camp Butler, North Carolina as part of the 925th Air Base Security Battalion. Shirley Shockley and Hazel E. Scott were among A&I women serving

---

[53] A&I State College graduate work, 1942–45, box 199, folder 11, A&I State Normal—Practice Teaching, 1942, box 199, folder 6, A&I State College, 1943–46, box 200, folder 1, A&I State College—funds deposited with treasurer, 1941, box 200, folder 5, A&I State College, Committees' visits—expense accounts, 1941, box 200, folder 6, Report—UT report on Tennessee A&I, 1941–42, box 266, folder 10, RG 92, W.J. Hale case files, 1942–43, box 150, folder 3, RG 273, TSLA.
[54] A&I *The Bulletin* (1942–43): 1–10.
[55] Ibid.

in the military. The Memorial Library was one of 140 War Information Centers. Gwendolyn C. Hale worked with the Red Cross. James Arthur Jackson (1941) became a trainee at the Army Air Corps at Tuskegee. Ollie Stewart became European war correspondent for the *Baltimore Afro-American*. AKA Sorority presented the campus with a flag of 150 stars to denote A&I members serving in the military.[56]

In the fall of 1942, Carl Thomas Rowan traveled from rural McMinnville County with $20 in his pocket to Nashville to attend Tennessee A&I State College. McMinnville was a farm-industrial community of about 5,000 close to the Cumberland Mountains. Rowan had been given several secondhand suits by the local doctor, which made him one of the best-dressed freshmen on the Tennessee A&I campus. Attending Tennessee A&I and living in Nashville changed Rowan forever. He was fortunate to get out of McMinnville, where a young Negro man had no chance of advancing to a good life, and even though he finished only one year of schooling before going off to the war, Rowan felt that those nine months at A&I helped him outgrow his hometown. Professor Merl R. Eppse kept a keen eye in his history classes for the brightest students. Eppse approached Rowan about taking a test for the US Navy Officers Training School; Rowan passed the test. In October 1943, Rowan boarded a Jim Crow train and completed his training at the US Naval Reserve Midshipmen's School. He became one of the first Negroes commissioned in the US Navy. Rowan visited the campus in April 1945 and spoke to the students at Chapel, recalling how a country boy who arrived from McMinnville feared competing with the students of big cities. In June 1946, Rowan returned to McMinnville, before moving north for better opportunities. He graduated from Oberlin College in mathematics (1947), receiving a master's in journalism from the University of Minnesota (1948) and becoming a reporter for two Minneapolis newspapers. The Minneapolis *Tribune* sent him south in 1951 to write a series of articles on how the Jim Crow South had or had not changed, resulting in Rowan's first book, *South of Freedom* (1952), based on his newspaper articles "How Far from slavery?" Rowan served as assistant secretary of public affairs with the US State Department in 1961, Ambassador to Finland (1963), director of the US Information Agency (1965), and as the first black on the National Security Council. As a radio commentator, he even called for the racially prejudiced FBI Director J. Edgar Hoover to resign. Rowan, a syndicated newspaper journalist, wrote at least sixteen books. He frequently revisited Tennessee State. Rowan recalled that art A&I teacher Frances Elizabeth Thompson "gave me precisely

---

[56] Ibid.

what a green country kid from a little red-clay town needed: a little bit more self-esteem, a little bit more belief in myself."[57]

The 1942 US Bureau of Education report said the typical HBCU senior in the forty-nine institutions surveyed was 22.6 years of age, had low family income, and needed financial aid. Females represented 57 percent of undergraduate enrollment by 1940. Fathers could be found in most Negro families, but typically had few skilled or professional jobs. Negro freshmen and seniors scored below white college students on standardized tests, but many HBCU students scored above the national median and sometimes at the very highest levels. Students in Southern institutions for white persons did not, as a group, attain the level of students in Northern colleges and universities on standardized examinations. Negro test takers did not score well on Negro history.[58]

The year 1942–43 was a good one at Tennessee A&I. The Players Guild presented three one-act plays: "Two Crooks and a Lady," "Deceivers," and "Thirst," with Laura M. Averitte, advisor/director, William D. Cox set designer, and Robert Twiggs, president. In February 1943, A&I celebrated the 78th Anniversary of the Thirteenth Amendment and Negro History Week. Lewis R. Holland (business), Alma T. Watkins (Spanish), and Christine Alexander (home economics) joined the faculty. Race Relations Sunday took place on February 14. Student reservists reported for active military duty on March 29. Junior-Senor Prom, Senior Day, Senior Class Night, and the President's Reception for Graduates at Goodwill Manor comprised the 31st commencement week (1943), where Henry A. Boyd gave the baccalaureate sermon, "God's Gift to Man," for 128 graduates from 18 states.[59]

W.J. Hale's Final Months at Tennessee A&I

On 7 May 1943, Commissioner Duggan reported to the SBOE that he had asked President Hale to submit a graduate school budget approved under recommendations made by the University of Tennessee, but Hale said he did not have enough funds for such a budget. A frustrated Duggan said, "If the A. & I. State College is not brought up to a standard that will satisfy UT, [desegregation] lawsuits will start over again. The question now before the board is, what can be done about it." A member asked, "What if the same action which had been taken on the other colleges should be taken on the A. & I. College budget and

---

[57] Ibid; "Rowan," A&I, *The Bulletin* (May 1945): 1–10; Carl T. Rowan, *South of Freedom* (Baton Rouge: Louisiana State University Press, 1997); Carl T. Rowan, *Just Between Us Blacks* (New York: Random House, 1974).

[58] Lovett, *Civil Rights Movement,* 126, 124, 130–34. A&I *The Bulletin* (May 1945) 1–10; A&I files 1941–48, box 151, folder 10, RG 273.

[59] See A&I *The Bulletin* (1942–43): 1–10.

recommendations?" One SBOE member attributed the situation to "mismanagement or poor management of the institution." Another member said Hale had been given too much liberty over the years, but that "the suits were not sufficient to justify the action that has generally been whispered around, and there might be criminal action there." One member said, "Ever since that institution was started way back in its infancy it was turned over to President Hale to run. The board ignored it—past boards—and would say 'that's good enough for the Negroes and let it go'."[60] Duggan refused to recommend approval of the A&I budget.

In an audit response letter, Hale explained he had a mere $80,638.60 to build the original facilities; he raised more money, often putting aside some of that money to expand the college:

> We had a very small income, $10,000, with which to open the school, and we had to solicit outside funds ... I have never transferred a record, nor written a receipt, nor made out a transcript in the 32 years, nor had charge of any of these records. You would not expect a president of the bank to take charge personally of the details of the bank deposits.... There are many inconsistencies, honest mistakes, and if I have approved anything as far as I am concerned you do not approve of, I am willing to abide by any decision you proud Tennesseans make ... There is Divinity that shapes our ends.[61]

Hale enclosed a personal check for $3,225.19 to cover the deficit in petty cash funds.[62]

But the commissioners felt that W.J. Hale had to go. Indeed, as well, he could not help them ward off NAACP attacks. It seemed that George W. Gore, Jr., with a PhD and dean of the college since the 1920s would succeed Hale. But Commissioner Duggan contacted A&I graduate Walter S. Davis, who had recently completed his PhD in agriculture at Cornell. Davis had spoken for the New Farmers of America organization on *Wings over Jordan* radio broadcast (CBS) in April 1942 and had praised Booker T. Washington's conservative racial philosophy. Ivanetta Davis recalled that her husband was out in the nearby woods doing a little hunting when she took the call, agreeing to have Davis call Duggan right away. Davis reportedly had gained support from some influential

[60] Report—UT report on Tennessee A&I, 1941–42, box 266, folder 10; Commissioner of Education Records, 1913–70, RG 92, TSLA.

[61] Minutes and letters regarding W.J. Hale and SBOE, Nashville, box 200, folder 5, 2, 4, 6, 7, 10, 1941–43, 8 August 1943, RG 92; W. J. Hale case files, 1942–43, box 150, folder 3, RG 273, TSLA.

[62] Hale to Harned, Nashville, 9 January 1926, showed A&I had $50,921.74 deposited in three local white banks, according to a Harned directive to normal school presidents; Hale Quarterly Report to the SBOE, 23 January 1943, Duggan to Gov. Cooper, 22 June 1943, Duggan to Hale, 19 April 1943, R-104, box 136, folder 18, RG 273, TSLA.

middle Tennessee white men but kept it quiet. W.S. Davis accepted the offer to be president of Tennessee A&I. Commissioner Duggan then sent a letter to President William J. Hale:

> At the called meeting of the State Board of Education on August 27, 1943, the Board adopted a resolution relieving you of your duties as president of the Agricultural and Industrial State College, effective as of September 1, 1943, to accept other work with the State. Dr. W. S. Davis, Professor of Agricultural Education, has been appointed Acting President of the Agricultural and Industrial State College, pending the selection of a permanent President. Dr. Davis' remuneration will include his residence in the President's home on the college campus. You will, therefore, vacate this residency and the campus not later than September 15, 1943.[63]

President Hale was hurt deeply, but he respectfully sent a letter of reply to Duggan:

> This is to acknowledge receipt of your letter of August 28, 1943, advising me of being relieved as president of the Agricultural and Industrial State College, to be transferred to other duties in the State. P.S.: Residence was turned over to President W. S. Davis on Monday, August 30, 1943. As announced by you, my first assignment is writing the history of A. & I. College. This I have started.[64]

Duggan paid Hale for the month of September and cancelled Hale's $10,000 bond policy. State auditors returned to the campus to check Hale's accounts, check Davis into the office, and complete an inventory of supplies. Davis acknowledged this with a signed receipt. Hale and his wife moved from Goodwill Manor to the Teachers Apartment quarters. The couple then headed to Mexico to see their daughter, who was interning down there. Some of Hale's enemies informed Duggan that former President W.J. Hale intended to continue to reside on the campus, while Mrs. Hale operated the business education program. Duggan wrote to Governor Cooper:

> I had not intended to disturb Mrs. Hale as head of the Business Education Department, but if she lives in an apartment on the campus ... the husband would want to live with her. I think it would be embarrassing to the [new] president ... to have Dr. Hale and his wife on the campus. The family should be required to move off the campus.[65]

Duggan then wrote to Hale:

---

[63] B.O. Duggan to W. J. Hale, Nashville, 28 August 1943, final letter of instruction to W.J. Hale, box 200, folder 4, RG 92.

[64] Hale to Duggan, Nashville, 6 September 1943, RG 92; Hale case files, 1941–1943, box 150, folder 3, RG 273.

[65] Duggan to Gov. Prentiss Cooper, Nashville, 1 September 1943, RG 92.

I received your airmail letter of September 6, 1943, from Mexico City and mailed on September 14, 1943, from San Antonio, Texas, by September 16, 1943. When the State Board of Education relieved you of all connection with the Agricultural and Industrial State College, its responsibility ended as far as you are concerned. You did turn over the President's residence to Dr. Davis but you <u>did not</u> vacate the campus as directed. You merely transferred your household effects to another building on the campus. To 'Vacate the College campus' means: that you and your family with your belongings establish your residence outside the College campus.[66]

After eviction from the campus that had been his home for 32 years, Hale did not complete the school's history despite more than 32 years (March 1911–August 1943) of knowledge. Hale collected his dignity, self-respect, wife, records, and personal papers and left Nashville for New York to work for the US Treasury Department to promote war bonds.[67] Duggan sent a letter to 38-year-old Davis to "appoint persons to assist in the administration of the college program."[68]

On 18 November 1943, Duggan wrote a letter to the state attorney general: "It strikes me that there be a faint ray of hope that the Supreme Court of the United States will reverse their [pro-Negro] attitude and divest themselves of what might be called their present Ethiophobia [fear of the Negro]."[69] Duggan said he was unable to get Fisk University to agree to establish a Negro law school. Duggan suggested to SBOE members that the Southern states could form a regional Negro law school. Tennessee attorney general Roy H. Beeler said the federal court probably would not accept the regional law school idea, and he advised them that "if the U.S. Supreme Court dismisses the UT lawsuit is moot; new NAACP lawsuits will be filed immediately."[70]

---

[66] Duggan to Hale, 25 September 1943, SOBEP.

[67] Ibid.; H.A. Boyd, "W. J. Hale," Nashville *Globe*, September 1943, 1.

[68] B.O. Duggan to W.S. Davis, Nashville, 15 September 1943, RG 92; W.J. Hale case files, 1942–43, folder 3, RG 273.

[69] Duggan to the Tennessee State Attorney General, Nashville, 18 November 1943, RG 92, RG 273. "New College Head, Davis Acting A. & I. President, Hale Shifted," Nashville *Banner*, 4 November 1942, 10.

[70] Ibid., Attorney General Beeler to Duggan, Nashville, 13 October 1943, Duggan to UT Dean Henry B. Witham, Nashville, 2 November 1943, Duggan to Nat Tipton, Asst. Attorney General, Nashville, 18 November 1943, UT Dean Witham to Duggan, 18 November 1943, SBOE meeting minutes, Nashville, 18 November 1943, 1940–43, box 230, folders 1–12, state board of education minutes, 9 May 1941, 6 February, 4 November 1942, 3 February 1943, 1944, RG 92, RG 273; mf R-70, folder 3, and subject files on Tennessee Agricultural and Industrial State College, 1939–44, box 232, folders 1–10, photographs on Tennessee A&I College, Nashville, 1944, box 253, folder 29, Gov. Prentice Cooper Papers, 1939–45, GP 44, TSLA. Note: Roy H. Beeler, a graduate of Maryville College and the

W.J. Hale had tried to use the NAACP vs. University of Tennessee situation—without outright challenges to Jim Crow—to gain more funding for Tennessee A&I State College, but near the end of his tenure, he seemed unable to make the right decisions. Nor did he have it in him to tell white, Southern officials what needed to be said. Hale also could not team up with the NAACP and the Negro plaintiffs in their lawsuits against the University of Tennessee. Nonetheless, Tennessee officials pounced on Hale, humiliated him, took $337,000 in reserves from Tennessee A&I State College and in the process—whether Hale was guilty of anything or not—further impeded the progress of the state's only public HBCU and damaged the future of black Tennessee citizens.

Even so, time was running out for Jim Crow. The president of the Carnegie Corporation, Frederick P. Keppel, had hired Swedish scholar Gunnar Myrdal to do a study on race relations in America. Myrdal toured the South, attended the 1938 SCHW organizational meeting, and reported he was mortified by what he saw in the Southern states. White and Negro scholars on the Myrdal team, including Fisk University sociologist Charles S. Johnson, poured out studies on race relations. Myrdal published the main, two-volume study that convinced more whites to join the civil rights movement.[71] Walter S. Davis and Tennessee A&I State College were about to enter even more turbulent waters while trying to become equal to the University of Tennessee.

University of Chicago law school, served as Tennessee attorney general and reporter from 1932–54.

[71] Lovett, *Civil Rights Movement*, 112, 113, 115; Gunnar Myrdal, *An American Dilemma: The Negro Problem and Modern Democracy*, 2 vols. (New York: Harper, 1944) vol. 1, 438, 550, 906.

4

1943–51: Walter S. Davis:
Transforming a College into a University

Tennessee A&I State College entered its third phase of history under the leadership of Walter Strother Davis, who began an institutional journey to make this Negro College into a competitive university. He began as Acting President on 1 September 1943. Negro college education was still in its infancy: Among the HBCUs rated by SACS only 29 of the 764 faculty members had PhDs and 383 had master's degrees. The income of all these institutions together was just $4,614,776.18. Very little was budgeted for libraries and laboratories.[1]

Walter S. Davis was born in 1905 in Canton, Mississippi, growing up on a cotton plantation and receiving his early education in a two-room school. His parents, who grew to be self-supportive landowners unlike most Negroes in Mississippi, sent him to Tougaloo College, a freedmen's school (1869–) near Jackson. There he completed grades 5–8 and attended Cameron Street High School in Canton. In 1926, Davis attended the pre-college program at Alcorn A&M State College (1871–) in Claiborne County. He headed to Tennessee A&I State Normal Teachers College in 1927. He was captain of the football team in 1931, the year he graduated. Davis remained at A&I to coach the team and teach vocational education in the high school department. He attended Cornell to complete his master's degree by 1935.[2] In 1936, Davis married Ivanetta Hughes of French Lick, Indiana. She was a graduate of Tennessee A&I, and received her MS degree from Cornell University. She became a member of AKA sorority and other civic and social organizations in Nashville. By attending school in the summers and taking leaves of absence, Davis completed the requirements for a PhD degree in agricultural science at Cornell University. He became a deacon at First Colored Baptist Church, a member of the Meharry board of trustees, member of the Agora Assembly, hunter and fisherman, weekend farmer, and a

---

[1] Jackson Davis, "The Outlook for the Professional and Higher Education of Negroes," and Fred McCustion, "The Present Status of Higher Education of the Negro," *Journal of Negro Education* 2, no. 3 (Summer 1933): 1–3, 379–96. Note: Morristown Normal and Industrial College merged with Knoxville College in the 1980s, Roger Williams University merged with LeMoyne by 1930–31; Swift Memorial College closed in 1955.

[2] TSU, "Davis background," 1, Walter S. Davis Papers, 1943–68, Special Collections, TSU; Lois C. McDougald, *A Time-Line Chronology of the Tennessee A. & I. State College Campus 1909–1951* (Nashville: Tennessee State University, January 1981) 119–92.

civic leader. He was known as a practical man with the ability to analyze situations and effectively meet them with ability, adaptability, energy, and resourcefulness.[3]

Watching Davis's presidency every step of the way was Will Ed Turner, the fourth in a succession of white men who headed up the SBOE Negro Education Department. Turner had an office downtown and another in A&I's Industrial Arts Building next door to the A-Building that housed Davis's presidential suite. Turner wielded influence among professional Negroes because he administered the out-of-state scholarship program (1937–62) for Negroes desiring graduate or professional studies that Tennessee A&I did not offer. Robert E. Clay and two secretaries assisted Turner's operations on campus.[4] Northern agencies had funded the office.

In his 4 February 1944, weekly report to Commissioner Duggan, Will Ed Turner said he conferred with Robert E. Clay every Monday and met at least twice a week with W.S. Davis. Turner and Davis were in charge of overseeing Tennessee A&I's final moves toward SACS accreditation. On April 27–29, Ed Turner and President Davis met with the Southern Association of Colleges and Schools representative to discuss what more had to be done to gain approval.[5] The graduate credentials of the A&I faculty members needed improving—only Gore and Davis had doctorate degrees in 1942. Soon there was the arrival of other PhDs: Hubert B. Crouch (graduate studies), Oscar J. Chapman (education), Carl M. Hill (chemistry), Earl L. Sasser (English), Jessie J. Mark (agronomy), Thomas E. Poag (speech and theater), Virginia S. Nyabongo (foreign languages), and John Milton Smith (social science). Tennessee A&I State College claimed ten faculty members with doctorates by 1944–45, and hired sixteen part-time faculty members with doctorates in law, medicine, and other fields to help meet SACS accreditation standards. Davis and Gore continued pushing more research and

---

[3] Ibid., Davis Papers. Note: Dr. and Mrs. Davis had one child, Ivan R. Davis, who completed Tennessee A&I State University, completed Meharry Medical College, and became a physician in Nashville and director of the Tennessee State University medical services as well. Ivan married Elizabeth Prudent of Memphis, a Tennessee A&I State University graduate, and they had one son, one daughter, and a grandson by 2011. Mrs. Ivanetta Davis was approaching one hundred years old by then, but was still in regular attendance at First Baptist Church, Capitol Hill. "Ivanetta Hughes Davis," *A History of the Alumni Association*, ed. Vallie P. Pursley (Nashville: TSU, August 1990) appendix 11; "Ivanetta Hughes Davis, 100th Birthday Celebration," 7 July 2012, Tennessee State University.

[4] R.E. Clay files, folder 27, box, 144, folder 2, Division of Negro Education, 1938–39, Rosenwald Fund, S. L. Smith, Clay, folders 14–18, Commissioner of Education Records, 1913–70, RG 92, TSLA.

[5] McDougald, *A Time-Line Chronology*, 149; *The Broadcaster* (March 1944): 1–5, Special Collections, TSU.

scholarship. *The Broadcaster* featured articles written by A&I faculty members, including Francis Thompson, Eppse, Raleigh Wilson (history), and others. Thompson's "The Negro in Tennessee—His Contributions in Art" highlighted Negro architects James Averitte of Trousdale County, James Nichols of Cheatham County, Moses McKissack in Giles and Maury counties, and Negro painters and designers. Turner and Davis also reported to the Commissioner of Education and SACS that the University of Tennessee faculty gave consultation on remodeling the science laboratories to meet SACS approval.[6]

In responding to a Young People's class at First Christian Church in Maryville that had inquired about the moral implications of Jim Crow education, Will Ed Turner said, "Opportunities for Negro youth on the higher level are being made equal to those for white youth. [We] are organizing graduate work in all seven divisions at Tennessee A. & I. State College."[7] The seven divisions included: Agriculture, Business Administration and Business Education, Engineering, Home Economics, Liberal Arts, Education, and Graduate Studies. A&I's divisional heads included: Lewis R. Holland (business), Merl R. Eppse (liberal arts), Thomas E. Gould (engineering), and Neal McAlpin (agriculture). They set goals and objectives. The agriculture division expected to become more productive, increase the involvement of students, and mesh more with the overall A&I college curriculum. McAlpin said the college farm had established "Animals for Food—Food for [WWII] Victory": 200 pigs, 6,000 dozen eggs, 3,000 broilers and fryers, 250 turkeys, 450 ducks, 5,000 pounds of beef, and 3,000 gallons of milk. The farm realized $9,000 in profits from revenues of $25,000. Holland expected majors "To meet the demands of the business world and pass the acid test ... [and] possess the following traits upon graduation: good character, mental alertness, efficiency, thoroughness, emotional stability, and the right attitude." Gould said, "It is intended to meet the needs of the Negro youth

---

[6] Herman B. Long, "The Negro Public College in Tennessee," *Journal of Negro Education* 31, no. 3 (Summer 1962): 341–48; Bobby L. Lovett, *America's Historically Black Colleges and Universities: A Narrative History from 1837 to 2010* (Macon GA: Mercer University Press, 2011) 130; Martin D. Jenkins, "Graduate Work in Negro Institutions of Higher Education," *Journal of Higher Education* 18, no. 6 (June 1947): 300–06; E. Franklin Frazier, "Graduate Education in Negro Colleges and Universities," *Journal of Negro Education* 2, no. 2 (July 1933): 329–41; Commission on Interracial Cooperation, "A Summary of the Provisions being made in Certain States for the Professional and Graduate Education of Negroes," 7 September 1940, CIC Papers 1919–1944, R. W. Woodruff Library, Atlanta University, Atlanta; Mark V. Tushnet, *The NAACP's Legal Strategy Against Segregated Education, 1925–1950* (Chapel Hill: University of North Carolina Press) 55–56.

[7] W.E. Turner to Young People's Class at First Christian Church in Maryville, Nashville, 18 May 1944, A&I State Normal, box 199, folder 8, box 200, folder 1–9, Commissioner of Education Records 1913–1970, RG 92, Tennessee State Library and Archives (TSLA), cited hereafter as RG 92.

that they may take their places in the post-war world as trained engineers and skilled workers. We are working to have one of the best divisions on the campus and to introduce one- and two-year courses in the vocations."[8]

Tennessee A&I's third building phase began under President Davis. He was responsible for paying off state bonds for constructing facilities fit for a college equivalent to the University of Tennessee. All buildings needed repair. The old intramural gymnasium above the Men's Trades Building was no longer in use; the rest of the building housed an auto repair shop. The gymnasium on the stage of the A-Building could not accommodate A&I's phenomenal expansion in collegiate sports. Tennessee State had to move some of its games to nearby Pearl High School. The power plant's boilers wore out, and A&I had to install three used boilers. The Industrial Arts needed remodeling and better equipment. The livestock barn needed enlargement, the campus needed more dormitories, and Harned Science Hall (1927–) needed minor repairs.

After years of work to install a graduate program, Tennessee A&I State College conferred its first master's degree on 5 June 1944 to Martha W. Wheeler (BA, Shaw University) of Raleigh, North Carolina, who also earned an MS in business education. She was related to leaders of the North Carolina Mutual Life Insurance Company. Some 117 undergraduates, including 15 men and 42 persons from Nashville, graduated. President William R. Banks of Prairie View A&M State College in Texas gave the baccalaureate sermon.[9] However, controversy developed after President John W. Davis of West Virginia State College delivered the commencement address titled "Race Matters from a Negro Point of View." The speech was in line with the New Negro and his expectations resulting from America's engagement in World War II, but some dignitaries on stage believed the man's remarks were a veiled threat to white supremacy. Students and alumni revered John W. Davis at West Virginia State College, which had an atmosphere of confidence since gaining accreditation in 1927. WVSC had a Civilian Pilot Training Program, an airfield and a ROTC Artillery Unit—the only one among HBCUs—by 1941. In 1943, WVSC became a site for the Army Specialized Training Program (ASTP) along with Howard, Prairie View, Wilberforce, North Carolina A&T, and Meharry.[10] At the A&I graduation

---

[8] McDougald, *A Time-Line Chronology*, 147–51; "Negro Colleges Unite in Drive to Raise Funds," Nashville *Globe*, 10 March 1944, 1.

[9] Walter B. Weare, *Black Business in the New South: A Social History of the North Carolina Mutual Life Insurance Company* (Durham NC: Duke University Press, 1993) 246–253. Note: John H. Wheeler and his father John L. Wheeler, Sr., were connected to the company's leadership. Charles C. Spaulding, key founder of the company, spoke at Tennessee A&I, and he, like W.J. Hale, was a leader in the Commission on Interracial Cooperation (CIC).

[10] Lovett, *America's Black Colleges*, 311; McDougald, *A Time-Line Chronology*, 129.

ceremonies, it was announced that Carlton M. Goodlett, Richard M. Haskins, and Hiram B. Moore had completed studies at Meharry Medical College. This was a significant A&I contribution seeing as Negroes comprised just 2 percent of America's 158,000 doctors. After graduation, Davis sent Duggan a letter to apologize for the speaker's remarks and promised "this would not happen again at Tennessee A. & I."[11]

From 19 June–25 August 1944, sixty-five graduate students enrolled in classes. An A&I student could enroll in 15 quarter hours of graduate work in the twelve weeks of summer school. Undergraduates could enroll in a maximum of 18 quarter hours. Professor Holland and the business faculty cooperated with Fisk University and the Negro Business League to plan a study of local Negro business conditions. The 41st Annual Convention of the American Teachers Association (ATA) met on the campus on August 15–17. Dean Gore reminded the delegates that ATA began in Nashville in 1910 as the National Association of Teachers in Colored Schools.[12]

Hubert B. Crouch became head of the Division of Graduate Studies, which enrolled 176 students. Including Tennessee A&I, a dozen HBCUs enrolled 1,864 graduate students by 1944. A&I's graduate division included nearly thirty fields of study leading to master's degrees. On 22–23 November 1946, the graduate division held its first research seminars. By 1952, the graduate offerings included Saturday and evening courses to accommodate teachers and out-of-school adults. The institution offered the MEd, MA, MS, and MAEd degrees. By 1968, Tennessee A&I State granted 1,743 master's degrees in the 24 years since 1944, significantly contributing to the national effort to expand the number of blacks holding graduate and professional degrees. In 1955, Howard University was the first HBCU to award a PhD degree.[13]

In 1944, Henry Allen Boyd, editor of the *Globe*, chairman of Nashville's Citizens Bank, and a leading founder of Tennessee A&I State Normal School was doing all he could to keep the memory of his friend W.J. Hale alive. The *Globe*

---

[11] "A. & I. Commencement," Nashville *Globe*, 2, 7 June, 25 August 1944, 1–2. Note: Hiram B. Moore (class of 1939) was born in South Pittsburgh, Tennessee. After the death of his mother, he dropped out of school and joined his older brother in picking tobacco, corn, and cotton for 50 cents a day. He left his father's home and joined a traveling circus at age fifteen, but soon returned to the family farm. Moore got sick and ended up at Hubbard Hospital, where he decided he wanted to be a doctor. Some Meharry faculty got him in touch with a doctor in Pittsburgh who would help him. He moved to the ninth grade, walking three miles a day to classes, wearing muddy overalls. He attended Tennessee A&I State College, washing pots and pans to help pay his expenses. Moore became the only doctor in South Pittsburgh. A white hospital official accompanied Moore into racially hostile towns. They trusted him to deliver their babies, but ignored the Negro doctor as he walked by, holding his daughter's hand, to find a seat in the back of the bus.

[12] See A&I *The Bulletin* (1943–47).

[13] Ibid.

announced the birth of daughter Indira to Will, Jr., and his wife, "with the distinction of being the first grandchild of Dr. and Mrs. W.J. Hale—the first president and for 32 years the guiding star in the A. and I. State College."[14] The *Globe* announced that Citizens Bank had reelected W.J. Hale as First Vice President and that he was in California and New York working for the Fifth War Loan Drive.[15] Then campus residents heard that Hale had died of a heart attack in New York City on 5 October 1944. It was, however, October 27 before the *Globe* reported the death. Boyd said he had just received a letter from his friend and had returned a reply, which apparently arrived after Hale's death. Boyd expressed disappointment that Harriett Hale had chosen to keep the death so quiet. Boyd wrote:

> What deeply grieves the many friends is that he died a brokenhearted man. His record of achievement in building the [A. & I.] college, despite only 'chicken feed' support from the state treasury, won him the name of the best business manager of a college that the state has in either race. Dr. Hale's removal on September 1, 1943, did not come [because] of anything the board was able to prove concerning his handling of the institution's funds. The State demanded and took over some $300,000 that [he] saved over a long period of years, which sum President Hale contended was to be used in the expansion of the college. Hale gave a personal check to replace any deficiencies found by auditors on the part of trusted employees at A. & I. College.[16]

The West Tennessee Educational Congress held memorial services for Hale at Lane College, where Boyd gave the address. The Negro Teachers Association regretted that some painted President Hale as autocratic and too overbearing to join other Negro citizens in racial and civic movements, as a mediocre educator but possessing political pull enough to keep him head of the Negro state institution. The teachers association said these perceptions were false. The main memorial services took place in the Chapel at 10 a.m. on November 14, with W.S. Ellington giving the message. President Davis gave Hale's biographical sketch.[17]

---

[14] "W. J. Hale," Nashville *Globe*, 7 January 1944, 1.

[15] "W. J. Hale," Nashville *Globe*, 21 January, 7 July 1944, 1.

[16] "W. J. Hale," Nashville *Globe*, 27 October, 3 November 1944, 23 February 1945, 1–2.

[17] McDougald, *A Time-Line Chronology*, 131–35; "Tennessee A. & I. Holds Memorial Service for Dr. W. J. Hale," *The Bulletin* 33, no. 2 (1944): 1; Tennessee A&I State College, *Memorial Service for Dr. William Jasper Hale, First President*, 14 November 1944, Chapel Services, Special Collections, TSU; H.A. Boyd, "Legislature Puts $317,000 Saved by School," Nashville *Globe*, 23 February 1945, 1. Note: Harriett Hale sends certain documents to the state on 2 February 1946 saying W.J. Hale's will and testament was prepared on 28 April 1944, signed by Hale on 19 June 1944, and probated on 30 January 1945. The four survivors got a quarter each of W.J. Hale's assets. Seventeen lots near the campus were deeded to the state, and the state bought 12 lots from the late W.J. Hale's estate for $6,500; Harriett and

Walter S. Davis Becomes President

SBOE members had already visited the campus on November 9. At the next board meeting they approved Walter S. Davis as permanent president. The inauguration took place on Thursday, November 30, during Homecoming Week. His former adviser at Cornell came down and spent many days at Goodwill Manor. President F.D. Patterson of Tuskegee Institute gave the inaugural address. Patterson was the principal founder of the United Negro College Fund (1944–) and had attended the initial SCHW meeting in 1938. W.S. Ellington gave the invocation, and Gore served as master of ceremonies. Duggan, Turner, and other college presidents and college representatives (including Harvard) offered encouragement. President Davis said,

> I am more convinced than ever that serving as president of Tennessee A. & I. State College represents an unusual task. To develop and maintain the right kind of educational program … is a tremendous challenge to me. I accept that challenge: To improve the total civilization of this state and nation is the job that confronts us. We must develop a strong university system with instruction on both the undergraduate and graduate levels. Nothing less will do the job. With the backing of Commissioner B.O. Duggan and other SBOE members, Mr. W.E. Turner, State Coordinator of Higher Education for Negroes, and the University of Tennessee, we have begun to do the job.

Davis said the state budget for Tennessee A&I State College had doubled in the previous year, and the number of faculty members had increased from 32 to 57. Thomas E. Poag gave acknowledgements for the faculty. Taz David Upshaw, Jr., (president of the class of 1928) represented the Alumni Association (1944–47), and Edward Mullins gave greetings on behalf of students. The Rev. Walter M. Davis, Sr., the president's father gave the benediction. The Nashville Negro Board of Trade held a banquet in President Davis's honor.[18]

State officials seemed to get serious about the 1941 General Assembly mandate to upgrade the state Negro college. In a 5 January 1945 legislative message, Governor Prentice Cooper said,

> There exists a fund of $317,000 which belongs to the Agricultural and Industrial State College for Negroes in the hands of the State Treasurer who must hold the same for your deposition. In view of needed improvements at

---

Edward were the administrators without bond, Davidson County, Will Book 60, 171, Metro Archives, Nashville.

[18] *A History of the Alumni Association*, ed. Vallie P. Pursley (Special Collections, TSU, August 1990) 10; "A. & I.," Nashville *Globe*, 12 December 1944, 1; "Tennessee A. & I. State College, Inauguration of Dr. Walter S. Davis as President of the College, 30 November 1944, College Auditorium," *The Bulletin* 32 (1944): 1–4; McDougald, *A Time-Line Chronology*, 135–37; "Negro Colleges Unite in Drive," Nashville *Globe*, 10 March 1944.

the school and the need to add 200 acres to the small school farm, I recommend that this sum be used solely for the benefit of the school to which it rightfully belongs and for the above purpose.

Duggan, too, believed Negro leaders [i.e., Henry Boyd], Tennessee A&I faculty, and the state's black citizens would be upset if the money remained in the state's general fund:

It might ... hamper the present reorganization of the College in offering comparable work to that offered at the UT. I believe the re-allocation of the entire $462,985.93 will prevent such complaints in the future from leaders and others of the Negro race.

The SBOE affirmed that since September 1943 Tennessee A&I State College had a mission to offer training in agriculture, engineering, home economics, business administration, and liberal arts.[19]

Were Tennessee's Jim Crow officials serious about making black Tennessee A&I State College programs and facilities equal to those at the white University of Tennessee? Not likely. On 18 April 1945, Governor Cooper signed an agreement to renew the Jim Crow scholarship contract with Meharry. Cooper said his priority was keeping University of Tennessee as the keystone of the education system of the state. Cooper recommended an increase of $325,000 for UT's budget and $500,000 for the Tennessee Polytechnic Institute to build a library, health building, and additional dormitories for men at Cookeville. Henry Allen Boyd spoke out:

Legislature Puts $317,000 Saved by the School in State Treasury. Tennessee grabbed this money, as much money as the State of Tennessee has spent from its treasury in 30-odd years for buildings at A. & I. State College. Where the colored citizens have a legitimate kick over the apparent ruthlessness of the state in taking the trust fund is that practically none of it is money the state, itself, put into the fund; the state could use the money as a retirement fund for teachers.[20]

Boyd castigated Negroes for being silent and for allowing white officials to take advantage of black citizens. State officials did not return the money to Tennessee A&I. They left Davis struggling with mountains of debt, state bonds, and deficits as he tried to build up the institution.

---

[19] Prentice Cooper, *Message to the General Assembly*, 5 January 1945; Duggan to Beeler, 10 February 1945, Tennessee A&I State College, 1941, box 135, folders 4–6, and W.J. Hale Dismissal, 1942, 1943, box 236, folders 1–2 in Gov. Prentice Cooper Papers, 1935–45, GP 44, TSLA.

[20] Boyd, "Legislature Puts $317,000 Saved by the School in State Treasury," 1; Prentice Cooper, *Message to the General Assembly*, 5 January 1945, and W. J. Hale Dismissal, 1942, 1943, box 236, folders 1–2 Prentice Cooper Papers, 1935–45, GP 44.

Davis was hoping to gain acceptance as A&I's leader after the 32-year reign of W.J. Hale. Twenty-one of the 57 faculty members had served under Hale, and in 1946, twenty-eight students sent a petition to the SBOE, protesting the "unfortunate and embarrassing circumstances which led to the resignation of our instructor." President Davis formed a committee to investigate the problem, which involved Merl Eppse head of the division of liberal arts and some of the new doctorate holders. Hugh B. Smythe was upset because Eppse had taken over his class after Smythe was a few minutes tardy. This caused a confrontation in front of the students. Eppse also took over the class of a tardy female doctorate in a history class and she resigned in protest. The protestors said Eppse was jealous of those faculty members who had doctorates and subjected them to petty bickering. Davis and his Administrative Council, including Gore, Crouch, and Boswell, sent their report to the board, and the matter closed. Eppse had some clout among state officials, and even had the state textbook committee approve one of his Negro history books for use in colored schools. Eppse was conservative and paternalistic, believing that Negroes were being exploited by religious leadership, and that blacks felt insecure.[21]

Post-World War II Civil Rights Movement

After Franklin D. Roosevelt died in office in April 1945, the new president Harry S. Truman (D) presided over the end of World War II, from May through August 1945. Thereafter, the post-war civil rights movement caught fire, and Tennessee officials began to tighten up the defenses of the whites' Jim Crow system. Davis asked permission to send Dean Gore and others to the American Association of Teacher Colleges (AATC) meeting, but the commissioner denied approval: "You surpass all the other colleges in the State with these requests. Your institution has gained a reputation of a spendthrift one, as I tried to emphasize to you in person when I last talked with you. This is to remind you to watch all expenditures closely."[22] Gore and Davis had to report on the telephone bills. The SBOE commissioner seemed to have forgotten that Tennessee was supposed to be making Tennessee A&I State College "equivalent to UT for white students." [23]

The 33rd commencement took place on 4 June 1945, and Davis chose the commencement speaker carefully, not wishing a repeat of the previous year's

---

[21] M.R. Eppse to Samuel E. James, Jr., Nashville, 31 March 1943, Sharon G. Hall, "Merl R. Eppse, 1893–1967: Life and Work Based upon an Investigation of Selected Papers," (master's thesis, Tennessee State University, December 1983) 72.

[22] State Education Commission Burgin E. Dossett to W.S. Davis, Nashville, 24 April 1946, Davis Papers, Special Collections, TSU, and see A&I State College—W.S. Davis, President, box 200, folder 3, 1946–47, Commissioner of Education Records, RG 92.

[23] Ibid., Davis Papers.

incident. This time, President Karl M. Downs of Sam Houston Junior College spoke on "Frontiers Are Calling." Roy B.J. Campbelle, Jr., Pauline W. Gould, and Rachel Johnson Patillo received the only master's degrees. Enrollment in 1944–45 was 1,005, including 177 men and 828 women. Some 864 students enrolled in summer 1945.[24] Due to lack of housing, Tennessee A&I could not accommodate all students that applied for admission. A&I had a budget of $476,508 including $224,625 (47 percent) provided by the state. As of 30 June 1946, UT received $1,215,827 in federal land-grant funds, while A&I received $17,105 (1.4 percent).[25] Tennessee officials had no intent of giving Negroes equal higher education.

On 6 August 1945, the same day the US dropped an atomic bomb on Hiroshima, Japan, forty civil rights leaders met with President Truman to request that he protest lynching and racial discrimination. Dean Gore represented Tennessee A&I State College on 22 October 1946, when a group of HBCU leaders met with President Truman, asking for help against Jim Crow land-grant funding and apprising him of the importance of HBCUs to the progress of the American nation. Truman was willing to appease the NAACP and other black leaders if they would support his foreign policies and anti-communist Cold War campaign. On December 5, Truman created the President's Committee on Civil Rights that produced *To Secure These Rights* (October 1947). Based on the report, President Truman issued an executive order forbidding racial discrimination on the federal level. The NAACP reconsidered a prepared *Statement on the Denial of Human Rights to Minorities in the Case of Citizens of Negro Descent in the U.S.A. and an Appeal to the UN for Address* (1947). But the Youth Chapter NAACP in Houston continued to protest, "The South is Poor. Segregation will make it poorer; Not Communism; But Democracy."[26] This was embarrassing to the US, particularly during the Cold War against the Soviet Union. In 1948, President Truman appointed the Committee on Equality of Treatment and Opportunity in the Armed Forces to study racial discrimination in the military. After accepting the report *Freedom to Serve* (1948), he issued *Executive Order 9981* on July 26 against discrimination and segregation in the armed forces.[27] The US Supreme Court also began to help dismantle Jim Crow. In *Morgan v. Virginia*, 328 US (1946) the

---

[24] McDougald, *A Time-Line Chronology*, 143–46; Vicke J. Shaw, "Dr. Burley: Five decades in the pharmacy business," *Nashville Pride*, 24 May 2002, 14.

[25] "Summer School students," photograph, *The Bulletin* (September 1941): 5; July 1943, 2; "Carl T. Rowan," *The Bulletin* (May 1945): 1; *The Bulletin*, (August, November 1945): 1–10.

[26] Bobby L. Lovett, *The Civil Rights Movement in Tennessee: A Narrative History* (Knoxville: University of Tennessee Press, 2005) 22, 132, 133–34, 174, 352.

[27] John H. Franklin and Alfred A. Moss, Jr., *From Slavery to Freedom: A History of Negro Americans*, 6th ed. (New York: Knopf, 1988) 412.

court ruled against segregation on interstate buses. Most Southern officials ignored the ruling; therefore, in 1947, the Congress of Racial Equality (CORE) instituted a freedom rides project called the Journey of Reconciliation. In *Shelley v. Kraemer*, 334 US (1948) the Supreme Court ruled against restrictive housing covenants based on race.[28] Indeed, a new racial environment would engulf Tennessee A&I.

In 1946, one of America's first post-World War II race riots broke out at Columbia, Tennessee, just south of Nashville. Columbia had 8,000 citizens, including 3,000 (38 percent) Negroes. Negro veterans and others refused to allow the lynching of a fellow veteran for standing up to a local white merchant when the storeowner and his son slapped the veteran's mother after she disputed the proper repair of her radio on February 26. After several police died in the gun battle, Governor Nance McCord (D) sent state troopers into the town. Negro citizens were barred from employment in the Tennessee state troopers. The all-white troopers joined with local whites in destroying the prosperous Negro business district. They arrested 25 Negro men and accused them of murder. Two Negroes died in the jail and no whites were indicted, though local Negroes believed the two black men were murdered in revenge for the deaths of the white policemen. The state moved the trial to Lawrenceburg. In turn, local Negroes contacted the NAACP. From the nearest NAACP branch in Nashville, Z. Alexander Looby and a battery of lawyers hired by the New York headquarters and the Legal Defense Fund including Thurgood Marshall, Leon Ransom, and Maurice Weaver (a white labor lawyer from Chattanooga) traveled to Lawrenceburg. This high-powered defense team overwhelmed the less experienced local prosecutors and gained the freedom for 23 of the 25 accused Negro men. The other two blacks received light sentences. Many of Tennessee's near-illiterate white law officers disliked educated, prosperous Negroes, like that tall, smart "yellow boy" Thurgood Marshall. One of the Southern white lawyers was so mad that he proposed to fistfight Looby, but Looby said in a cool voice that he was there to practice law and not to fight in the street. That night, Thurgood Marshall almost lost his life when local law officers intercepted his and Looby's car as it headed back to Nashville. Looby refused to leave when the whites tried to drive toward the river with Marshall in the back seat under drawn guns. Instead, the men took Marshall back to town where the justice of peace—reportedly a heavy drinker—dismissed the trumped up charges of drinking and driving. Marshall ran back to the black community to find Looby. Local blacks loaned them a car, and a local black man agreed to drive Looby's car as a decoy. The NAACP lawyers escaped to Nashville.

The Columbia race riot exposed Jim Crow Tennessee and made national news. It also made the NAACP attractive to the Negro masses, and NAACP

---

[28] Lovett, *Civil Rights Movement*, 138, 159–79.

membership in Tennessee and elsewhere skyrocketed. Truman's US Department of Justice became involved but concluded no federal laws were broken. The Southern Conference on Human Welfare (SCHW), labor unions, and others became involved. They printed thousands of copies of flyers that advertised the post-war Columbia race riot. Governor McCord tried to save face by claiming that outside agitation and Communist influence had caused the racial trouble, which was untrue. When former Tennessee A&I student and journalist for the Minneapolis *Tribune* Carl T. Rowan later interviewed people in Columbia, one black man assured him that after the race riot, the local whites understood there would be "no more lynching down here."[29]

The Tennessee A&I campus stayed quiet but busy. The residence halls held meetings on etiquette and student behavior. The Southern Association of Dramatic and Speech Arts held the 10th annual conference on campus, April 10–12. Faculty members Virginia Nyabongo and Alger V. Boswell represented the college at the 17th annual conference of the National Association of Personnel Deans and Advisers, April 18–19, at Dillard University in New Orleans. The 24th session of the Tennessee Negro Education Association was meeting on campus, April 18–20. The third annual meeting of the National Institute of Science met on the campus on May 1–3. Merl Eppse and a group of faculty and students headed to the annual meeting of the Association of Social Science Teachers in Negro schools for May 3–4, in Atlanta.[30] During 1946–47, the state appropriation for Tennessee A&I State College was $328,607.86. Davis estimated that a total of 21,516 students (32 percent from Davidson County, 12 percent from Shelby County) had enrolled at the institution between 1912 and 1946. A&I. had issued 2,288 college degrees since 1924. Fall enrollment in 1946 increased by 54 percent over 1945 to 2,146 upon the return of the veterans.[31]

A&I Campus After the War

The GI Veterans Benefits Bill (1942) and the Veterans' Readjustment Assistance Act (1952) aided hundreds of students attending Tennessee State and other HBCUs. HBCU enrollment totaled some 44,000 students in 1940. For fall 1945, 118 HBCUs reported to the US Bureau of Education that enrollment increased by 26 percent. Negro veterans comprised 31 percent of the 58,842 students at the public and private HBCUs in 1946. This figure climbed to 35 percent of the 74,173 enrolled in those institutions in 1947. Veterans at the TWIs

---

[29] Lovett, *Civil Rights Movement*, 18–21; Paul H. Bergeron, Stephen V. Ash, and Jeanette Keith, *Tennesseans and Their History* (Knoxville: University of Tennessee Press, 1999) 285; John Egerton, *Speak Now Against the Day: The Generation before the Civil Rights Movement in the South* (Chapel Hill: University of North Carolina Press, 1994) 363–65, 393.

[30] McDougald, *A Time-Line Chronology*, 143–45.

[31] McDougald, *A Time-Line Chronology*, 145–47.

comprised 50 percent of enrolled students among America's 2.5 million enrolled college students. HBCU land-grant presidents intensified their efforts to develop departments of business, engineering, and vocational rehabilitation training for veterans.[32]

But the environment for Tennessee A&I State College was quite different after the war. Racial economic disparities between black and white income and wealth and American racial discriminatory practices in real estate, mortgage, and banking industries limited the participation of Negro citizens in the nation's prosperous post-war economy. Some 45,000 former slaves still lived in America, and many of them died destitute without the slave pensions that Mrs. Callie House of Nashville had fought for. Since the Great Depression (1929–39), the number of Negro banks had declined by half, while the white banks accepted few black veterans' mortgages that the GI Bill guaranteed. Jim Crow housing practices prevailed *de jure* (by law and custom) in the South and *de facto* (in fact by practice) in the North. Nashville built a federally funded, low-income housing project for whites and the Andrew Jackson Homes (1937–) for blacks, built next to Fisk University. In the 1950s, Nashville built more federal housing projects for Negroes, including Preston Taylor Homes next to the Tennessee A&I State University campus. The city opened McKissack Elementary Public School under Principal Ivanetta Davis to service this growing middle-class black neighborhood. However, Nashville's post-war urban renewal projects had wiped out three downtown black neighborhoods, forcing the poor and working-class residents to crowd into north Nashville around Fisk, Meharry, and Tennessee A&I. Working-class and poor families began to overwhelm middle- and professional-class blacks. All classes of blacks were barred from moving to new housing in white, post-World War II neighborhoods. Upper-, professional-, and middle-class Negroes began moving north of the river into suburban developments built by black bankers and contractors. Around Jefferson Street, the property values declined; poverty and crime increased; white flight and state and federal highway projects further disrupted the business sector and economic growth in that part of north Nashville.

Tennessee A&I State College housed the overflow of 700 veterans in 1947, using bunk beds on the stage of the auditorium in the A-Building. They acquired some wooden barracks donated by the military, placed on the site of today's library. Whereas the black veterans had been accustomed to hearing Negro music piped to them in some military camps, they were disappointed that Nashville had no radio stations that played blues and jazz. In the late 1920s, Nashville's WLAC Radio had featured the Tennessee A&I music ensembles, but by the 1940s, American radio stations had no programming featuring Negro music. As if on a secret combat mission, late one night in 1946, a few Tennessee

---

[32] Lovett, *America's Black Colleges*, 132–34, 310–14.

A&I State College students sneaked past the guard in a downtown Nashville building, and rode the elevator up to the WLAC Radio Station suites. They politely handed the startled announcer a stack of records to play on the air. The man complied, at a time when the station was barely making it with current programming. The response from the audience was surprisingly without racial protests. WLAC became the first radio station to regularly include black music. One could hear WLAC throughout the Mid-South, down in the Mississippi Delta and in the Border States late at night. The station began selling Negro recordings, jazz, blues, and gospel via mail order. In 1948, Memphis WDIA radio station hired Nat D. Williams (A&I class of 1928) as the country's first regular Negro radio announcer.[33]

In December 1946, Tennessee A&I State College gained approval ("A" rating) by the Southern Association of Colleges and Schools (SACS). The report cited a modern facilities plan, a faculty of 107 full-time persons including 18 with doctorate degrees, a student enrollment of 1,445 with 737 veterans, and a university-type organization with a $328,608 state budget. SACS approved another 16 HBCUs in 1941–46, but most HBCUs still awaited approval.[34]

The Division of Schoolhouse Planning and Transportation in the Office of the State Board of Education (SBOE) began to refine plans for new facilities at Tennessee A&I State College. Architect Granberry Jackson, Jr., designed the plans for barns and agricultural facilities. Hart, Freeland, and Roberts got the bid for the practice school, and Annus and Clark won the library additions. Negro architectural firm, McKissack and McKissack gained contracts for the president's residence, the cannery, renovation of an old two-story farmhouse, addition to the dairy barn, rehabilitation of the old trade school into a warehouse, and renovation of Harned Science Hall. Tidsdale and Pinson won the new gymnasium. Marr and Holman gained contracts for the men and women's facilities. On 6 May 1946, SBOE and the governor approved $6,500 for acquisition of land in the W.J. Hale estate. The Hale heirs agreed to sell some of the 27 lots

[33] Lovett, *Civil Rights Movement*, 248, 252, 263.

[34] Lovett, *America's Black Colleges*, 58, 77, 78, 86, 96, 102–04, 131, 136, 144, 150, 170, 179, 211, 219, 293, 333; McDougald, *A Time-Line Chronology*, 149; "Institution Details, Tennessee State University, Accredited 1946," http://www.sacscoc.org/details.asp?instid=72240, 1 [accessed 23 July 2011]. Note: Many HBCUs that could not achieve accreditation or approval merged with other HBCUs, downgraded to high schools or junior colleges, or closed down. The number of HBCUs fell from 269 in 1909 to 240 by 1920, to 119 by 1939, and to 105 by 2010.

and sign over 17 of the lots that had been improved with state and federal funds.[35]

President Davis Promotes Art, Music, and Theater

Walter S. Davis began to use sports and the arts to bring attention to Tennessee A. & I. on the regional and national levels. Student demands near the end of the war had caused Davis to reinstitute the football program, and the Tennessee State sports program really took off with the return of military veterans. Many of these young men had played sports in military camps. In November 1944, the football team resumed the playing of a game in Memphis. The Tennessee A&I State College Tigers won the Vulcan Bowl in football among black colleges.

Davis noticed at the games that Tuskegee and Florida A&M had flashy marching bands. The pure form of ragtime music made Americans dance to a black man's tune, Scott Joplin was the father of ragtime, which had all but died soon after World War I. Ragtime, however, transformed into jazz—a popular black music that some parents and teachers opposed. But President Hale, though he did not like blues music, allowed the student bands to play jazz and big band music. Davis particularly encouraged big band music, and students formed, managed, and composed the music for their jazz bands and dance orchestras at dozens of the HBCUs.[36]

In 1944, Davis hired doctorate holder H.F. Mells to head the music program. They recruited J.D. Chavis to form the Tennessee State Collegians dance band and create a dynamic marching band—like the high-stepping bands at Ohio State and Michigan State football games. The A&I marching band was ready to play at HBCU football games in September 1946. The Tennessee A&I State College Collegians began touring the country in their own bus, playing in Washington, DC, in 1947 and in New York's Carnegie Hall in 1949. They met tragedy on June 14, when student Paul Kidd and the band's business manager James Welch died after a truck hit the bus in Mississippi. This tragedy did not put a damper on the A&I music scene for long, however. Commercial bands by Duke Ellington, Count Basie, Ray Charles, Louis Armstrong, and others recruited new band members from HBCU campuses. William C. Handy, known as the father of the blues, was the featured speaker in the A-Auditorium on 25 April 1947. After the president of Alabama A&M State College criticized Handy for playing ragtime music at the convocation, Handy settled in Memphis and formed his own band of eight pieces. He composed the Memphis Blues (*St. Louis*

---

[35] A&I State College, purchase and donation of W.J. Hale estate, box 200, folder 10, RG 92, TSLA. Note: Then living at 572 Nicolas Avenue in New York City, Hale had signed his will on 19 June 1944. His estate included rental houses he owned in Chattanooga.

[36] Lovett, *America's Black Colleges*, 343–48.

Blues) around 1909. He later established his music publishing business in New York City. The History Study Club sponsored Duke Ellington's band at the downtown Ryman Auditorium in 1949.[37]

Frank T. Greer became the marching band director at Tennessee A&I in 1951. He organized the nationally famed Aristocrat of Bands. Greer had played with several dance and show bands, and his assistant Anceo M. Francisco had some experience with the University of Michigan marching band. Greer turned the A&I band into a marching show band. They played for the Chicago Bears football team on national television (NBC) in 1955. The 110-ten-piece A&I State band also played at the Cleveland Browns-New York Giants football game on 14 October 1956, on CBS-TV. They made ten other national appearances, including at the Rice Bowl for four years. Greer's "The Marching 100" had to appeal to the public to help send the band to the Southern University football game on 7 November 1959. In 1960, they played for the Baltimore Colts football game on NBC-TV before 50,000 fans and millions of viewers. They stopped and played in Knoxville and Bristol on the way to Baltimore. In order that Negro youngsters could come to Tennessee A&I and learn real music, Davis created twenty music scholarships to recruit top quality band members from the major cities. The band produced students who became directors for bands at Alabama State, Morris Brown, Kentucky State, Compton College in California, Texas Southern, Michigan State, and various high schools. Clarence Hayden Wilson became president of the National Association of Negro Musicians and a teacher in the St. Louis public schools. The Aristocrat of Bands became one of the first HBCU bands to participate in the Presidential Inauguration Parade in 1961. Until Frank Greer retired in 1972, the marching band made many national appearances and won citations, plaques, and awards. Edward Graves, who would become the next longtime director of the university bands, often had his mentor Greer come to the band room to speak to the students. Greer's presence seemed to bring a sense of awe and legacy to the students in Graves's band. Under the direction of Graves, the Aristocrat of Bands participated in presidential inaugurations in 1993 and 1997. Charles Dungey, who had experiences with the great dance bands in America, resurrected TSU jazz bands in 1998. HBCU marching bands and football reached high levels of popularity. Graves directed the bands until 2012.[38]

---

[37] Ibid.; Darlene Clark Hine, William C. Hine, and Stanley Harrold, *African Americans: A Concise History*, 2nd ed. (Upper Saddle River NJ: Pearson/Prentice Hall, 2006) 320; Arna Bontemps, *Father of the Blues: An Autobiography, William Christopher Handy* (New York: Macmillan, 1941) 1–317.

[38] "TSU Band," videos and essays, Special Collections, TSU; Craig Havighurst, "Brain hemorrhage kills Charles Dungey, 68, one of city's top jazz musicians," Nashville *Tennessean*, 25 September 2003, 4.

In the 1940s and 1950s, whatever was at hand—whether it be religion, lectures, jazz bands as preferred by the veterans, marching bands, concert music, or athletics—President Davis, the faculty and students used that medium to engage Tennessee State in the Negro's quest to become a vital part of American cultural life. Davis used Negro arts, religion, speech, and theater programs to attract students from across the nation and to instill in the student body a deep sense of appreciation for the arts and humanities. Both presidents Hale and Davis believed these subjects instilled in the students a greater sense of discipline, morality, learning, work, and service.

Francis Thompson and her art students used paint to depict peculiar aspects of Negro life. Thompson's beautiful murals depicted a black Christ, and she even adorned a church's baptismal walls in Gallatin. Thompson and the famous Harlem Renaissance painter Aaron Douglass of Fisk University became close friends. Merl Eppse re-published his books on Negro history, and maintained a campus chapter of the Study of Negro Life and History (ASNLH). February Negro History Week became a campus-wide celebration. Like Fisk University's famous Spring Festival of Arts, Tennessee State held its celebration of the arts, spirituals, gospel, blues, jazz, dance, and drama, and created the W.S. Davis Lecture Series with Ina C. Brown of Scarritt College giving the first lecture, "Backgrounds of Race Relations in the South," on 7 February 1947. Rayford Logan, a noted historian at Howard University and expert on black international affairs spoke at the Davis Lecture Series on 3 February 1949.[39]

Tennessee A&I State College also became a leader in the development of the theater program among HBCUs. Upon becoming a 1918 normal school graduate Laura M. Averitte joined the faculty and immediately began organizing the students into drama work, and teaching technique and presentation. In response to the national Little Theater movement, in 1925 Averitte organized the Dramatics Club, which became a member of the National Dramatics Association. By 1938, the Little Theater and the Dramatics Club were the first permanent theater organizations at an HBCU. The Children's Theatre presented programs for the summer including children in the neighborhood and ones belonging to the faculty members. They called it, "Ms. Averitte's Little Theater." Averitte remained on the Tennessee A&I faculty until 1966. The name Dramatics Club changed to Tennessee State Players Guild in 1939 when Thomas E. Poag joined the faculty. The institution introduced a course in play production in winter quarter 1940 and had a full array of drama courses by 1944. Tennessee A&I State College organized the first degree-granting Department of Speech and Drama

---

[39] McDougald, *A Time-Line Chronology*, 140–80; Lovett, *America's Black Colleges*, 25, 308–59; see the Frances E. Thompson Collection Papers, Special Collections, TSU; Rayford Logan, *The Betrayal of the Negro: from Rutherford B. Hayes to Woodrow Wilson* (London: Collier Books, 1954, 1965).

among HBCUs. The Tennessee State Players Guild presented three one-act plays for summer school, including "Flight of the Natives"—a Negro historical play. Thomas Poag also organized the Humanities Club on 9 January 1947, with Guild leaders Singer A. Buchanan as president and Granville Sawyer the publicity manager. Buchanan received his PhD degree at Michigan State University, became head of speech and drama at Kentucky State University, and then headed the TSU Department of Communications in the 1990s. Granville Sawyer, an assistant to President Davis, earned a PhD degree, became head of speech and drama at Sam Houston College, and later the president of Texas Southern University. Alphonso Sherman became chair of the department of speech and drama at Southern University. Moses Gunn became a famous actor for television, film and Broadway.[40]

The Tennessee State Players Guild (T. E. Poag Players Guild) won the highest honors in acting in 1948 at the Theatre Festival of the Southern Association of Dramatic and Speech Arts. In 1948, more than 2,700 persons saw Macbeth by the Players Guild. Poag and the students took "See How They Run" to US service members in Newfoundland, Greenland, Labrador, and the Azores in 1960. The Guild performed "Wake Up and Live," a variety show, in France and Germany in 1965. Poag received the US Department of Defense award for his drama services. In 1967, the debating team continued building on the foundation left by Laura Averitte in the English department and A&I's Du Bois Debating Society. The Guild performed 37 plays from 1959 to 1968, making Tennessee A&I one of the most productive HBCU theatre programs. Poag, who titled his dissertation "The Negro in Drama" (Cornell University, 1943), became one of the first Negroes to earn a doctorate in the field, president of the Southeastern Association of Dramatic and Speech Arts and president of the renamed National Association of Dramatic and Speech Arts, which held its 10th Annual Convention on the A&I campus 10–12 April 1946.[41]

A&I Begins the Drive Toward University Status

President Davis told the 1947 summer students that Tennessee A&I State College was traveling at a terrific rate of speed towards building a university that would be second to none. Davis prided himself for reorganizing the college on a democratic university plan and establishing one of the best salary scales among Negro colleges with provisions for tenure and retirement. But also he complained about the loss of three excellent faculty members to other state colleges because the maximum salary at Tennessee A&I State College was

---

[40] McDougald, *A Time-Line Chronology*, 128–81.

[41] Ibid.; "The Negro in the American Theater from 1925 to 1950," 1–24, box 1, Thomas. E. Poag Collection Papers, 1939–73, correspondence, photographs, and scrapbooks, Special Collections, TSU.

several hundred dollars less than the maximum at peer HBCUs. The engineering and industrial education program offered sheet metal work, welding, drafting, radio repair, electricity, aircraft and auto mechanics, aviation flight training, brick masonry, carpentry, and cabinet making, refrigeration, and pipes trade. Teaching loads observed SACS standards. Per capita cost was low. Books cost $25 per semester; non-state residents paid $75 tuition fee and state residents paid $29 and a boarding fee of $119. Summer 1947 enrollment reached 1,400 students. Davis reported 2,149 students including 934 women (43 percent) and 1,215 men (57 percent), 770 veterans (36 percent), and 713 boarders (33 percent) for fall 1947. And Walter Davis said he was outlining steps to transform the college into university status.[42]

From 1947–48, the HBCUs graduated more than 8,000 students. The Northern colleges and universities that accepted Negro students reportedly granted Negroes eight of 3,775 doctorate degrees awarded to American students in 1947. HBCUs produced 481 master's degrees. Less than 1 percent of the PhD degrees granted in the 1940s were given to blacks.[43]

Under the leadership of Tennessee Governor Jim Nance McCord in February 1948, several Jim Crow states formed the Southern Regional Education Board (SREB)—a written regional compact to provide medical education for their Negro citizens. Tennessee had been experimenting with such arrangements since 1937 in efforts to preserve the Jim Crow system while pretending to provide equal graduate/professional opportunities for its black citizens. McCord argued that Southerners could not afford to let the federal government take over higher education and force racial integration. However, McCord claimed, "This compact [is] not intended as a subterfuge designed to perpetuate segregation, or to avoid the civil obligations of the States in the field of education as the professional leaders of the NAACP whom reside in the North would have you believe…. As it is related to Meharry it was, and now is, an honest and sincere effort to preserve for the Negro boy and girl, both in the South and elsewhere, their only real opportunity for an education in medicine, dentistry, and nursing."[44]

---

[42] McDougald, *A Time-Line Chronology*, 153–54, 157, 158; "President Davis and A. & I.," Nashville *Globe*, 31 October 1947, 1;TSU Presidential Records, 1912–; W.S. Davis Papers, 1943–1968, Special Collections, TSU.

[43] Lovett, *America's Black Colleges*, 266–307.

[44] Governor J.N. McCord, message to the Tennessee General Assembly, January 1949, Southern governors' conference, 1945–48, box 8, folders 8–9 and box 19, folder 1, A&I State College, 1947–48, box 10 correspondence, folder 2; McCord speeches-education, 1947–48, box 17, folder 4, Gov. Jim Nance McCord (1879–1968) Papers, 1945–1949, GP 45; minutes, SBOE, 1946–50, box 141, folders 1–6, box 142, folders 1–7, Tennessee Department of Education Records, 1874–1984, RG 273, TSLA; Lovett, *America's Black Colleges*, 326.

Kappa Alpha Psi Fraternity made a dedication to "Daddy [R. E.] Clay" in September 1947. Ollie Steward, staff member of the Baltimore *Afro-American* newspaper, a former A&I journalism student, visited the campus in November 1947. Carl M. Hill, head of chemistry, received a $3,000 grant to provide student fellowships and assistantships and purchase of research equipment. Hill had a Tennessee Valley Authority contract to study the freshness of foods produced in Tennessee. Davis expanded the engineering program. The recent Conference of Presidents of Negro Land Grant Colleges set such a goal. Among 100 students on the 1948 winter-quarter honor roll, many of them later distinguished themselves. Pearl Gore earned a PhD and became head of psychology at TSU. Callie M. Lentz (Stevens) later became a member of the State Board of Education, a teacher, and an administrator in the Memphis Public Schools. Helen D. Smith (Cotton) completed graduate school, joined the faculty with her husband (Jimmuir Cotton, geography), and later earned a PhD in English from Vanderbilt University. Hazo W. Carter, Sr., became professor of agriculture at Tennessee State. His son later became president of Philander Smith College and currently serves as president of West Virginia State University. In April, the General Assembly appropriated capital outlay funds of $800,000, but the state attorney general impounded the money, until McCord reminded him the acts of 1945 and 1947 authorized $7.8 million in capital outlays, including $1,666,149 for Tennessee A&I. The man released the funds on August 27, but said any residue would revert to the state's general fund.[45]

McKissack and McKissack received the state contract to design the three-story engineering building. On 26 November 1948, Calvin McKissack notified Foster and Creighton Company to proceed with construction of 29,904 square feet (479,600 cubic feet of space). Davis would name the building for Governor McCord. McKissack designed the Library Annex for $39,748 to house another 120,000 volumes, and designed the Heating Plant expansion. State authorization included $150,000 for additional farmland, an annex to Wilson Hall, and other projects. Sanitary sewer lines extended to the cafeteria, Hale Hall, Wilson Hall, Recreation Hall, and the Men's Dormitory or East Hall. This construction stage brought the outlay of state capital funds to $667,189. The federal government gave demountable army barracks for use as the infirmary and temporary classrooms. On June 8, fire destroyed the barn annex that had been built during WWII at a cost of $48,000. The state attorney general delayed the SBOE proposal to purchase an additional 120 acres of land for the A&I farm. But President Davis

---

[45] McCord to state attorney general, Nashville, 16 September 1948, Davis correspondence the governor and the attorney general, Davis Papers; and see box 10 correspondence, A&I State College, 1947–48, McCord Papers, GP45, TSLA.

wrote pleas to the governor and the attorney general that Tennessee A&I State College only had 50 of 125 acres worth cultivating and needed land.[46]

At the fall convocation on September 27, the faculty notified the undergraduates that the senior project had to be filed in the dean's office as a general graduation regulation. The student could receive a maximum credit of 3 hours in a course numbered 450 preceded by the name of the department in which it is written, and no one teacher could be assigned to or agree to sponsor more than a total of ten projects a year. *The Bulletin* began carrying senior project abstracts in summer of 1949, including David Hamilton, "A Proposed Farm Training Program for Negro Veterans of Fayette County." Hamilton later completed a PhD in agriculture, joined the A&I faculty and retired as Dean of the School of Agriculture and Home Economics. In his *Annual Report* (1949), Davis reminded the SBOE that of the 3,000 Negro teachers in Tennessee more than 1,500 had been enrolled at Tennessee State. Negro teachers worked hard; some 35 Negro schools still operated in church buildings.[47] Davis sent his report to the SBOE, copied to McCord, saying A&I. had advanced to "A" rating with SACS, five A&I graduates had received PhDs, and A&I had produced two college presidents. Davis again pleaded for higher salaries to retain A&I's doctorate holders. For now, state officials defended Davis against the state auditors, saying he was not responsible for audit exceptions left from the W.J. Hale administration.[48]

After World War II, hundreds of Tuskegee pilots and other Negro aviation personnel wanted to work at HBCUs and spread aviation education and training among the Negro population. The Tennessee A&I State College engineering program had no building but it began training students in aviation. The pilot for the Tennessee A&I aerospace mechanics program Elliot Gray used his two-seater to take students on short flights at Nashville's Cumberland Airfield. Robert Tucker had Gray take him into the air to drop student government association (SGA) campaign leaflets on the campus; Tucker won election as SGA president (1951–52). George B. Turman, formerly with Capitol Airways, taught aeronautics at Tennessee State under Cecil J. Ryan, a former fighter pilot. George Turman was instructor and airplane mechanic. The post-war aviation programs soon lost

---

[46] Davis correspondence the governor and the attorney general, Davis Papers; and see box 10 correspondence, attorney general's office, 1944–49, box 2, folder 4, 5, A&I State College, 1947–48, box 10, folder 2, McCord Papers, GP45.

[47] Roberta Greenfield, "A History of the Development of County Public Schools for Negroes in Giles County, from 1938 through 1949," (senior thesis, education, Tennessee A&I State College, 1949); W.S. Davis, *President's Annual Report*, Tennessee A&I State College, 1949, 1–21; A&I, *Souvenir Bulletin: Dedicatory Exercises and Ground Breaking Ceremonies*, 23 November 1949, 1–13.

[48] W.S. Davis, report to the SBOE, (22 January 1948), 6 February 1948, Davis Papers.

their zeal, but 55 years later, the Tennessee State University Aeronautical and Industrial Technology program had 110 students.[49]

President Davis promoted the development of the Tennessee A&I State College Alumni Association. The program had been conceptualized in the summer of 1913 when summer school students pledged to do more to get more students to attend the institution. In June 1915, eleven members of the 1914 class formed an alumni association. President Hale graciously provided an office for the Alumni Association in 1923. C.D. Purdy (class of 1924) served as president until 1928, followed by Meredith G. Ferguson. Tennessee A&I alumni chapters then existed across the state. Ferguson completed A&I's high school course in 1915, entered the US army in October 1917, and was one of fifteen Negroes in the 368th Infantry to attend the 79th Division Army War School in Washington, DC. There, he received the commission of Lieutenant on 1 June 1918. He returned to Nashville to work as an insurance man, bookkeeper at Citizens Bank, and eventually president of the bank upon the death of Henry A. Boyd in 1959. During Homecoming 1944, the association was reorganized and the alumni office began to preserve information on graduates. The *Alumni News* started in 1947 with Taz D. Upshaw as the first national A&I alumni president. The Nashville chapter was organized on 20 March 1949.[50]

Alumni, guests, and organizations loved to visit the areas near Tennessee A&I, as Jefferson Street was to Nashville what Beale Street was to Memphis: a black enclave for nice homes, hotels, restaurants, nightclubs, and shops. The Kappa Alpha Psi fraternity brought its 39th National Conclave to Nashville in January 1949, holding most of the meetings on the A&I campus and in Jefferson Street clubs and restaurants. Robert Churchwell a reporter for the Negro weekly Nashville *Commentator* recalled that coal smoke floated so thick on Jefferson Street and much of Nashville by 1948 that it seemed like fog. Some homes burned a poorer grade of coal. Visitors frequented Annie's Place on Claiborne Street with its "Pig's Feet Specialty and Bar-B-Q" and beer and Fat Man's Club at 12th and Jefferson. There was Lucy's Dinner Club at 1013 South Street, James Lamb's Auto Wash at 815 Rear Broad, Roy's Barbecue Pit at 1126 Jefferson, Chicken Shack at 12th Avenue, Blue Room Morocco at 2417 Jefferson, Capitol

---

[49] McDougald, *A Time-Line Chronology*, 163–87; "Student Government Presidents," TSU Countdown to 100: A Centennial Celebration, 1912–2012, http://www.tnstate.edu /alumni/centennial/history/sga.aspx, 2 [accessed 24 January 2012].

[50] *History of the TSU Alumni Association*, ed. ed. Vallie P. Pursley, 1–65; McDougald, *A Time-Line Chronology*, 172; *Tennessee State University Alumni Directory 2006* (Chesapeake VA: Harris Connect, 2006). Michelle Viera served as director of the Alumni Affairs Office at TSU.

Café on Jo Johnston, and Johnson's Rhythm Café on Ewing. There were five Negro cab companies.[51]

On 15 February 1949, Davis wrote to the commissioner that the University of Tennessee was offering statewide programs in agriculture and extension, law, medicine, and PhD degrees. He said Tennessee A&I needed:

a school of education, school of agriculture, school of liberal arts and fine arts, school of home economics, school of law, school of engineering, and new buildings for fine arts, agriculture, health and physical education, home economics, law, new steam lines, and upgrading other facilities for a total of $3,975,000. Our Next Steps: The School of Engineering, School of Agriculture and Home Economics, School of Education, School of Liberal and Fine Arts, School of Law, and Medical School; erection of a chemistry and chemical engineering building.[52]

In 1949, McKissack and McKissack Architects showed the plans for the Health and Physical Education Building including archery, hydro- and physiotherapy, handball, arts and crafts, dance, health, audio visual aids, bowling, boxing, wrestling, a basketball arena, tennis, volleyball, badminton, shuffleboard, classrooms, offices, conference rooms, lockers, showers, and storage rooms. The physical therapy section included whirlpool, heat and x-ray therapy, and baths. A fourth floor (attic) dormitory housed visiting students. The new arena had 4,500 seats for basketball. Harlan Construction Company was building the facility at a cost of $1.5 million.

Homecoming 1949 featured the official naming of buildings that Davis had announced the previous December: "[We will] officially name ... the Martha M. Brown Memorial Library; Cafeteria and Women's Building, Jane E. Elliott Building; and the R.E. Clay Sunday School. Each of these honorees had been connected with the College for more than 23 years. The expansion is in keeping with the policy of the College administration and State Board of Education to develop the Tennessee A. & I. College to a point comparable to that of the UT."[53] Indeed, by 1947–49, Tennessee A&I's facilities were less than those at UT.

---

[51] See Nashville city directories, 1912–60, Nashville Room, Nashville Public Library.

[52] Davis to the Commissioner, 15 February 1949, RG 92, and Davis Papers; McDougald, *A Time-Line Chronology*, 170, 174; note: no strong indication of Browning support appears in division of Negro education, 1949, box 134, correspondence, folder 4, correspondence file, A&I, 1949–52, box 94, folder 1, Governor Gordon W. Browning (1895–1976) Papers (second term) 1949–1952, GP 46, TSLA.

[53] McDougald, *A Time-Line Chronology*, 179; *The Broadcaster* 23, no. 2 (November 1950): 30, and 23, no. 3 (December 1950): 43; note: By 1949–50, seven land-grant HBCUs, including A&I State College offered engineering courses or programs in architectural, civil, electrical, mechanical, and general industrial engineering. Howard University had the most extensive program among HBCUs; aerial view of A&I campus, 28 March 1941, photo no.

On 20 March 1950, the campus honored Dean George W. Gore, who had led the academic program at A&I for 23 years. He and his family were preparing to leave for Florida A&M State College, where Gore would assume the presidency on April 1. Henry A. Boyd spoke at Gore's testimonial dinner; Gore had trained some outstanding journalist students at Tennessee A&I. [54]

Growth of Student Programs

One outstanding journalism student was Samuel F. Yette, born in Rockwood, Tennessee, in 1929. He entered Tennessee A&I State College in 1948 as a transfer from HBCU Morristown Junior College. Yette got elected to the student government association, became head of a once defunct student publications board, and went to President Davis and requested a student newspaper. Davis was a little nervous about the idea, but told Yette to present a proposal. In 1950, *The Meter* became the measure of student opinion, sentiment, and campus highlights. William L. Crump and Robert J. Hudson became faculty advisers. In March 1951, after elections by the publication board, graduating senior, Yette engaged a ceremony to hand over *The Meter* to the new editor, Henry H. Lindsay. [55]

Yette finished officers' candidate school as a second lieutenant in 1953, and served in Korea in the US Air Force. He served as a high school teacher in Rockwood, and then taught English at Chattanooga's Howard High School. He completed a BS in English at Indiana University in 1956 and an MA in journalism and political science there in 1959. He was director of information at Tuskegee from 1959–62, when he became a journalism professor at Howard University. By 1968, he was a popular speaker about civil rights. While a journalist for *Time* magazine, Yette authored the award-winning *The Choice: the Issue of Black Survival in America* (1971) that illustrated blacks as a colonized community in a racist society. Yette wrote about starvation and birth control as the ultimate weapons to get rid of America's unwanted blacks. He considered the black soldier fighting in Vietnam as a mercenary suicide, a man expendable in war and obsolete in peace. He called President Richard Nixon's White House Conference on Food and Nutrition of 2–4 December 1969 worse than a farce. *Time* magazine

---

4351, box 18, file no. 12, aerial view of UT-Knoxville campus, 19 November 1949, photo no. 5723, box 18, file no. 21, and aerial view of A&I, 7 February 1962, photo no. 9842, box 18, file no. 37, Photographs Series—colleges and universities, TSLA.

[54] George W. Gore, "Negro Journalism—An Essay on the History and President Conditions of the Negro Press," 1922, biographical data, box 1, folders 1, 5, Alpha Kappa Mu Honor Society papers, box 2, George W. Gore Collection Papers, 1922–82, Special Collections, TSU.

[55] McDougald, *A Time-Line Chronology*, 175–76; "The Meter," *The Meter*, 21 April 1950, 1.

fired him; Yette sued, but lost his case in the courts. Yette served as a commentator on television by 1991. His book, *The Choice*, is considered an American classic, and activists worldwide consider Yette a pioneer in calling for liberation of the black Americans— citizens who are despised and considered no longer needed by white America. Samuel Yette visited TSU on several occasions and was the keynote speaker for Tennessee State University's 85th Anniversary on 21 March 1997.[56]

Theodore Roosevelt A. Poston (class of 1928) was another notable journalism graduate. He played basketball at Tennessee A&I State Normal Teachers College. Poston moved to New York to perform odd jobs before writing for the Pittsburgh *Courier*, the *Amsterdam News* in Harlem and as a nationally celebrated journalist at the New York *Post*. He won journalism awards in 1949 and received a nomination for the Pulitzer Prize.[57]

On 16 March 1950, Charles S. Johnson, the president at Fisk University, spoke at the Alpha Kappa Mu annual observance at Tennessee A&I State College. Morehouse College Glee Club performed on campus. For the Davis lecture series, Julius A. Thomas, an official for the National Urban League, spoke in the A-Auditorium on "Opportunities for Jobs after Graduation." Fifty faculty and staff members met in the library to begin application for the Tennessee State Federal Credit Union in April 1950. There were 254 graduates at the 38th commencement on 28 May 1950. Horace Mann Bond, the first Negro president of Lincoln University in Pennsylvania, spoke on "A Half Century of Heroes." In July 1950, the noted black theologian Howard Thurman returned to A&I to speak on "The Objective Basis for Hope and Optimism." President Davis said, "We believe in religious education and genuine inspiration. We want students to acquire as much learning and knowledge in the skills as possible; but we...want them to develop desirable attitudes and have faith in themselves. Through organized and informal activities we seek to inspire them, and set religious standards to guide them."[58]

---

[56] Samuel F. Yette, *The Choice: The Issue of Black Survival in America* (Silver Springs MD: Cottage Books, 1982, 1971); "Samuel Yette Biography," http://www.thehistory-makers.com/biography.asp?bioindex+800&category=med, 1 [accessed 23 July 2011]; "Celebrating 85 years of thinking, working and serving," TSU *Blue Notes* 3, no. 4 (May 1997): 1–4; Samuel F. Yette, "How and Why I started the Meter," *TSU Today* 2 (April 1994): 3. Yette passed in 2011.

[57] Lovett, *Civil Rights Movement*, 169, 248, 252, 263, 275–76; Tennessee A&I State Teachers College, *1928 Commencement Program*, 5, 7, Special Collections, TSU; Kathleen A. Hauke, *Ted Poston: Pioneer American Journalist* (Athens: University of Georgia Press, 1998).

[58] McDougald, *A Time-Line Chronology*, 178, 179; Davis Papers, 1950; Matthews F. Allen, "Howard Thurman: Paradoxical Savior," *Journal of Negro History* 77, no. 2 (Spring 1992): 84–96.

By now, there were fifty campus organizations for student membership. The dormitory staff members held meetings on etiquette, make-up for young ladies, and tips for the modern man, while the faculty presented a list of must-read books such as, *Behave Yourself, Manners for Moderns,* and *The Correct Thing to do, to Say, to Wear.* A&I. graduates teaching in the schools both across the region and up North also instituted assemblies to train their students to be educated persons. There were 178 graduates at the August 1950 commencement, and 23 persons joined the faculty for the following fall.

By May 1951, the US Air Force and school officials were making plans for establishing Detachment 790 of the Air Force ROTC at Tennessee A&I. State College—one of two Negro colleges granted an AFROTC unit in 1951. In 1955, the AFROTC named Clay, Davis, and Frances E. Thompson as honorary officers. President Davis said the AFROTC at A&I and three other units at the black colleges trained a majority of the African-American officers in the US Air Force. Vance H. Marchbanks, Jr., would become the first Negro to attain the rank of full colonel in the Air Force Medical Service as a staff surgeon in 1955. The number of veterans on campus declined after the Korean War, and by 1956 there were plans by the Air Force to close the AFROTC programs at several colleges; Tennessee State survived the cuts. Detachment 790 graduates became commercial pilots and Air Force officers. Four-star general Lloyd W. Newton was the highest-ranking officer to graduate from this AFROTC unit.[59]

Meanwhile, the civil rights movement continued in post-WWII years. Avon N. Williams, Jr., of Knoxville completed Johnson C. Smith College, served in the US army, and received two degrees in law from Boston University by 1948, when Z.A. Looby accepted him as a law intern. In 1950, Williams filed two federal court lawsuits: desegregation of public schools in Anderson County and *Eugene Gray et al. v. University of Tennessee.*[60]

Tennessee A&I Achieves University Status

The state audit report said, "I find the A. & I. State College is still growing and will become a university with the fall term." In August 1951, the SBOE approved university status, and the name was changed to Tennessee Agricultural and Industrial State University on 23 September 1951. Davis directed art director Frances E. Thompson to complete the sculptural medallions

---

[59] McDougald, *Time-Line Chronology,* 183; "Dept. of Air Force and A&I," Chattanooga *Observer,* 11 May 1951, 4; Mozel Avery, "Newton urges commitment to excellence," *The Meter,* 13 April 1994, 5.

[60] Lovett, *Civil Rights Movement,* 335–70; "Gray v. University of Tennessee," http://tn.findacase.com/research/wfrmDoeViewer.aspx/sq/fac.%5CFDCT%=5CETN%5 Ci9, 1–4, 9/10/11.

to decorate the façade of the Memorial Library.[61] The campus included East Dormitory for Men, Wilson Hall Dormitory for Women, President's Home, Martha M. Brown Memorial Library, Hale Hall Dormitory for Women, Harned Science Hall, Men's Vocational Shops Building, Women's Vocational Building or Women's Building, Faculty Cottages, Industrial Arts Building, and the Administration and Health Building; the Alumni Building for faculty and guests, the three-story Faculty Women's Residence Hall, a temporary General Classroom Building, "Trailer City" for married war veterans, two temporary barracks for single veterans, and Veteran Teachers Apartments. Additionally, there was the Engineering Building (1950), Mechanical Engineering Building or Steam Plant (1950), the cafeteria and annex to Elliott Hall (1950), and the new Physical Education and Recreation Building (1951).

From 20–22 November 1951, an inaugural program formally recognized university status. It started with a processional in academic regalia from the Memorial Library into the A-Auditorium. President Davis lit a low candle, symbolizing the old institutional history, and then used that candle to light a taller one, which represented the new university. Governor Gordon Browning (D) was one of the speakers. Kelly Miller Smith, Dean of Chapel, assisted Davis in the ceremonies. Davis said Tennessee A&I State University aimed to provide training in intellectual and technical services and produce education services to the people of Tennessee as well as to develop leadership and serve all states.[62] Benjamin E. Mays the president of Morehouse College served as major speaker.[63] The 1951–52 graduating class consisted of 206 persons, and there were 235 faculty/staff members and 2,082 students.[64]

Between 1951 and 1968, A&I would be buffeted by the turbulence of the civil rights movement, the Vietnam War, and white backlash against both events, while Walter S. Davis tried to focus on continuing to expand A&I's facilities in order to meet the 1941General Assembly mandate to make "Tennessee A. & I.

---

[61] Biographical data, general papers, Frances E. Thompson Collection, 1923–92, Special Collections, TSU; Louise Davis, "A. & I. Appoints 4 Chairmen to head schools in new university," "The Birth of a University," Nashville *Tennessean*, 8, 19 August, 16 September 1951, 4.

[62] McDougald, *A Time-Line Chronology*, 187; *The Broadcaster* 24, no. 1 (September 1951): 8–9, 15.

[63] Lovett, *America's Black Colleges*, 114, 147–48, 155, 163–64; Benjamin E. Mays, *Born to Rebel: An Autobiography* (New York: Charles Scribner's Sons, 1971); Clarence A. Bacote, *The Story of Atlanta University: A Century of Service, 1865–1965* (Atlanta: Atlanta University, 1969).

[64] Tennessee A&I State University, Bureau of Public Relations, *The Stage is Set at Tennessee Agricultural and Industrial State University* (1953), Special Collections, TSU; A&I audit, 1 July 1945–30 June 1950; 26 September 1951 auditor, mf 117, box 155, folder 28, Dept. of Education Records, 1874–1985, RG 273.

equivalent to the UT for white students." Already under governors Cooper and McCord, Tennessee officials had begun to ignore the mandate. Instead, they continued to fight against NAACP desegregation efforts. They granted to Tennessee A&I only enough resources to keep up the appearance of meeting the "separate but equal" principle of *Plessy v. Ferguson* (1896). Tennessee officials concentrated on defending the maintenance of Jim Crow. This state policy caused neglect of Tennessee A&I State University and hindered the education progress of the state's black children for the next three generations. Though state officials had granted university status, Tennessee A&I was not nearly equivalent to the University of Tennessee for white students as promised by the legislative mandate of 1941. Tennessee officials continued to impress "separate but unequal" upon its Negro citizens.

William Hale, president, March 1911–August 1943

Walter S. Davis, president, September 1943–September 1968

Andrew P. Torrence, president, November 1968–June 1974

Frederick S. Humphries, president, January 1975–June 1985

Otis L. Floyd, president, July 1986–June 1990

James A. Hefner, president, April 1991–June 2005

Melvin N. Johnson, president, June 2005–December 2010

Henry Allen Boyd, a founder

James Carroll Napier, a founder

Julius Rosenwald, philanthropist, 1929,
helped finance Tennessee A. & I. facilities

John D. Rockefeller, philanthropist, 1928,
helped finance Tennessee A. & I. facilities

Above, President Hale and the first faculty and staff members, 1912;
pictured below, the first A. & I. College graduating class, 1924

Above, the main building, Tennessee Agricultural & Industrial State
Normal School, 1919; pictured below, commencement ceremony
in 1950, A-Auditorium

Above, Muhammad Ali visits A. & I. campus, 1965;
pictured below, Martin Luther King Jr. speaks in A. & I. chapel

Above, world renowned contralto, Marian Anderson (seated left)
at A. & I. Goodwill Manor, 1955; pictured below, President Hale and
George N. Core (center) flanked by two BOE members

Tennessee A. & I. State University represents U.S. in 1960 Olympics.
(front row, left to right) Jo Ann Terry, Shirley Crowder, Lucinda
Williams, and Martha Brown; (back row, left to right) Anna Lois Smith,
Wilma Rudolph, and Coach Edward S. Temple, Barbara Jones,
and Ralph Boston

State Senator Avon N. Williams Jr. (1922–1994)

Above, Oprah Winfrey, commencement speaker and graduate, 1987;
pictured below, the Tennessee State University Choir, 1990s
(courtesy of B. L. Lovett)

TSU students march on Federal Courthouse in protest of the Geier Case

Above, TSU students march on state legislature to protest campus conditions, 1980s; pictured below, " A touch of greatness," Tennessee State University, students marching on downtown Nashville

Tennessee A. & I. State University wins NAIA national
basketball championship, 1957

Above, TSU Aristocrat of Band Members, 1978; pictured middle, the 1930 Tennessee State College football team; picture below, TSU volleyball team, 2007 Ohio Valley Conference champions

Members of Delta Sigma Theta and President Hale present Certificate
of Appreciation to Eleanor Roosevelt, A. &. I A-Auditorium, 1942
(courtesy of Indira Hale Tucker)

Monumental signage to front entrance of Tennessee State University,
2010, Centennial and Temple Boulevard

1951–68: Tennessee A&I Students
and the Civil Rights Movement

In the midst of fighting the Cold War against the communist Soviet Union, the American people and the federal government had tired of toying with the Jim Crow states and their nostalgic white leadership that seemed still to be fighting the Civil War and proclaiming that slavery had nothing to do with the war. On Friday, 17 May 1954, the US Supreme Court ruled in *Brown v. Board of Education of Topeka, Kansas* that "separate but equal" [*Plessy*] was unconstitutional and violated the equal protection clause of the Fourteenth Amendment. Frank G. Clement (D) defeated former Governor Gordon Browning (D), who said, "I have always favored segregation of the races."[1] The Court gave the states time to respond to *Brown* and issued *Brown II* (31 May 1955) urging the states to implement school desegregation "with all deliberate speed." Fisk University Dean George Redd wrote, "Tennessee is definitely 'Southern'. Whatever desegregation plan the state devises, leadership should come first from the colleges and universities, both public and private ... [that] are responsible for the education of teachers, principals, and superintendents.[2] *Brown* had adverse implications for the 1941 legislative mandate to make Tennessee A&I State University equal to the University of Tennessee.

A sequence of events then began to intensify the civil rights movement. In September 1956, a federal court ordered the desegregation of Clinton High School in Anderson County. Avon N. Williams, Jr., was lawyer for the plaintiffs. Word arrived on campus in December 1956 that Edgar D. Nixon, Martin Luther King, Jr., and Jo Ann Robinson, an instructor at Alabama State College, had launched a bus boycott in Montgomery, Alabama.[3] The president of Talladega College spoke in the A&I. chapel on "Nothing as real as a Dream" for the summer commencement baccalaureate. For fall 1956, the graduate program at Austin Peay State College quietly admitted Tennessee A&I graduate Wilbur N.

---

[1] "Browning and Clement," Grundy County *Herald*, 3 June 1954, 1.

[2] Bobby L. Lovett, *The Civil Rights Movement in Tennessee: A Narrative History* (Knoxville: University of Tennessee Press, 2005) 45, 46, 50, 53, 57, 186, 211; George N. Redd, "Educational Desegregation in Tennessee—One Year Afterward," *Journal of Negro Education* 24, no. 3 (Summer 1955): 333–47; *Brown v. Board of Education*, 349, US 294 USSC (31 May 1955).

[3] A&I *The Bulletin* (1955–58); Lewis V. Baldwin and Aprille V. Woodson, *Freedom is Never Free: A Biographical Portrait of E.D. Nixon Sr.* (Atlanta: A.V. Woodson, 1992).

Daniels. A leader of the Montgomery boycott, Martin Luther King, Jr., spoke in the A&I Chapel. In May 1957, Bobby L. Cain became the first Negro student to graduate from desegregated Clinton High School. He accepted a scholarship to study sociology at Tennessee A&I State University next fall. The Montgomery bus boycott ended with a federal court order against racial segregation in November 1957. Chattanooga and Nashville buses ended racially segregated seating in 1957.[4] In December 1957, Martin Luther King, Jr., Kelly Miller Smith, and others organized the Southern Christian Leadership Conference (SCLC) to spread the civil rights movement through the region. Kelly Miller Smith and others organized the Nashville Christian Leadership Council (NCLC) as an affiliate of the SCLC in January 1958. Smith was pastor of First Colored Baptist Church, where W.S. Davis served as a deacon. The Rev. Smith was a personal friend of King and a fellow Morehouse College graduate, and he served as dean of the A&I Chapel. In January 1958, young Methodist minister James M. Lawson, Jr., arrived in Nashville from graduate school at Oberlin College, Ohio, to work for the Fellowship of Reconciliation (FOR), a pacifist organization. Glenn Smiley and other FOR officials recently had met with King, Jr., and others at Morehouse College and pledged support for the Negro's civil rights movement. In March, Lawson and Smith began recruiting students from local HBCUs, American Baptist Theological Seminary, Fisk University, Meharry Medical College, and Tennessee A&I State University for Christian workshops.[5]

President Davis, staff, faculty and students focused on accreditation matters. The National Council for the Accreditation of Teacher Education (NCATE) succeeded the American Association of Colleges of Teacher Education in 1954. AACTE continued to be a national alliance of teacher education programs and remained a cooperative constituent of NCATE. Tennessee A&I remained a member of AACTE, too. The NCATE granted full accreditation to 284 member institutions but would not grandfather in the HBCUs unless they prove regional accreditation by 1 July 1960. Nearly 40 percent of the 109 HBCUs had gained approval from the North Central Association of Colleges and Schools (NCACS), Middle States Association of Colleges and Schools (MSACS), and the Southern Association of Colleges and Schools (SACS). Many HBCUs needed extra time and money to meet the new NCATE plus SACS standards. Beginning in 1956, SACS accepted eighteen (31 percent) of 59 HBCU applicants as fully accredited and equal members instead of the old Jim Crow "A" or "B" approval.

---

[4] See photograph of Martin Luther King, Jr., with President Walter S. Davis, photographs, Special Collections, TSU.

[5] Lovett, *Civil Rights Movement*, 107–55; "Wilbur N. Daniels," Bobby L. Lovett, *How It Came to Be: The Boyd Family's Contribution to African American Religious Publishing from the 19th to the 21st Century* (Nashville: Mega Publishing, 2007) v, 97, 111, 116, 127, 128, 136, 137, 153, 163.

On 25 April 1958, the NCATE informed Tennessee A&I that it would have to achieve full accreditation by SACS to gain NCATE accreditation. Tennessee A&I received the new SACS accreditation on 4 December 1958 and gained NCATE accreditation. Fewer than 20 of the 109 HBCUs simultaneously achieved that feat.

Tennessee A&I State University had 3,266 students, 244 faculty members (27 percent doctorates) and a physical plant of 41 buildings including a new dormitory for women. The dormitory costing $542,236 was named for dean of women, Edna Rose Hankal, on 30 May 1958. The university built a dormitory for men (1958) for $558,338 and later named it for Governor Frank G. Clement (D).[6] Tennessee A&I used $500,000 to build the Education Building in 1958, later naming it for R.E. Clay. During homecoming, Tennessee A&I dedicated Hankal Hall, Kean Hall, and Wilfred W. Lawson Agricultural Building. In 1959, Tennessee A&I leased pastures from the Vocational School for Negro Girls on Heiman Street. Davis got the SBOE to pressure Nashville to stop rezoning adjacent properties from residential to commercial. On 6 June, the Veterans' Dormitories were scheduled for demolition. On 13 July, Davis notified the commissioner of education that the university had a deficit of $124,358.47, partly because of costs for covering SACS standards. He had also spent $83,300 to hire eleven more doctoral faculty members. "We have developed plans to prevent this from ever happening again," said Davis.[7]

The campus stayed busy. Marian Anderson, the famous contralto and promoter of civil rights, gave a concert at Tennessee A&I on 17 January 1955, after her triumphant debut at the New York Metropolitan Opera House. Students took pictures with her, penned flowers on her dress, and helped host a reception in Goodwill Manor. She would return to Nashville. On 19 March 1955 there was "A Night at Birdland," featuring the Count Basie Orchestra, jazz singer Sarah Vaughn, the George Shearing Quintet, Stan Getz, Lester Young, and the Errol Garner Trio. For summer 1956, A&I expected 1,307 men, 1,111 women, 97 graduate students, and 42 workshops, study groups, conferences, and associations. The enrollment reached 2,800 for fall 1956. Presidents of the other local HBCUs sat on the stage for fall convocation. Some 22 new faculty members were introduced, and Davis was the main speaker.[8]

Bennie Ross "Hank" Crawford, Jr., born 1934 in Memphis, came to Tennessee State as a freshman in 1958. He majored in music, and played with the

---

[6] Dedication of new men's residence center, TN A&I University, 25 November 1964, box 80, folder 38, Frank G. Clement Papers, 1920–69, ac. no. 94–007, TSLA.

[7] Davis to Commissioner of Education, 13 July 1959, Davis Papers.

[8] A&I *The Bulletin* (1954–55), and photographs of Marian Anderson, Presidential Papers, 1912, W.S. Davis Papers, 1943–68, Special Collections, TSU; Marian Anderson Concert, 11 February 1957, program, box 4, folder 13; Ambrose A. Bennett (1884–1957) Family Papers, 1918–96, ac. no. 1999.100, TSLA.

Tennessee A&I Collegians. Crawford soon had his own band, Little Hank and the Rhythm Kings. Ray Charles, the rhythm and blues star, came to campus, met Crawford, and hired him as a saxophonist. The band members named him Hank. Crawford became the musical director of the Ray Charles Band by 1963. He recorded his own albums including *Misty*, and arranged music compositions for many other singers and bands.[9]

In the fall of 1959, the new $500,000 Student Union Building opened. Students and staff dedicated the building on October 1, allowing the university to move the cafeteria from Elliott Hall (Women's Building) and shifting the center of student activity and gatherings from the old campus on the north side of Centennial Boulevard to the new campus on the south side of that street. McKissack architects designed a large cafeteria, meeting and game rooms, recreational areas, a post office, bookstore, snack bar and grill, eight offices for Greek organizations, an office for the Student Christian Association and an office for the TSU Credit Union. The facility also included the Blue and White Room (replacement for the Crystal Ballroom), faculty lounge, a barber and beauty shop (on the basement level), even a guest apartment and offices for student affairs and related services. The Student Union Board of Governors sponsored an elaborate banquet and held an Open House and a debate on the presidential election of 1960. The Davis administration approved a $1.5 million annex. On 23 April 1982, TSU named the facility for the longtime head of student affairs Joseph A. Payne.[10]

For the opening convocation on 30 September 1959, President Davis titled his address, "Tennessee Agricultural and Industrial State University as a Mature Land-Grant Institution":

> Last August the State Board of Education granted full land grant status to this institution; and since our last convocation, the Southern Association of Colleges and Secondary Schools [SACS] has granted us *membership* as a full-fledged land-grant university. Therefore, the University offers greater opportunities for each of us, but, at the same time, we will have to assume greater responsibilities. We shall use all the wisdom and physical strength

---

[9] See profiles of individuals, *The Bulletin* and *Accent* issues in Special Collections, TSU. Five of Hank Crawford's recordings are in the TSU library. Sharon E. Hull, "Books and Recordings by TSU Alumni," in *A History of the Alumni Association*, ed. Vallie P. Pursley (Special Collections, TSU, August 1990) 36–41.

[10] Davis Papers, 1959–61; TSU presidential papers, 1912–present, consists of correspondence, newspaper clippings, programs, reports and speeches relating to the presidents of the university, Special Collections, TSU. Negroes voted overwhelmingly for John F. Kennedy (D); persons under 21 could not vote before 1971.

that God has given us, and with a prayer on our lips, we shall live up to the university's motto: "We will think; we will work; we will serve."[11]

In fall 1959, Davis's words were put to the test as some local black college students were preparing for another phase of the civil rights movement. They informally adopted the name Nashville Student Movement (NSM). In November, they began test demonstrations at downtown restaurants, sitting at the lunch counter and asking for service. When the manager refused, they said thank you, walked five blocks back to First Colored Baptist Church and briefed Smith and Lawson. Smith tried negotiations with the lunch counter operators but the merchants would not budge. The college students broke off the tests for the Christmas break.[12]

Tennessee A&I State University enrolled 3,438 students. Other HBCUs in Tennessee had 2,967 students including a few whites. In 1960, Tennessee A&I graduated 533 students. Tennessee's private HBCUs graduated 416 students.[13]

After the Christmas break, and even before the Nashville students could resume their plans for sit-in demonstrations, a few students at the HBCU North Carolina Agricultural and Technical State College began a spontaneous sit-in demonstration in Greensboro on 1 February 1960. Negro church minister Douglass Moore called James Lawson on February 10, asking for support for the Greensboro movement. Lawson agreed to call for his trained group of students, and some two hundred students met him at a Fisk University auditorium that Friday evening. They began plans to commence real demonstrations in Nashville

---

[11] Ibid.

[12] Lovett, *Civil Rights Movement*, 161–63; "Nashville Sit-ins 1960–2010," *Nashville Retrospect*, February 2010, special spread of pictures from Nashville Public Library, Nashville Room, and Nashville *Banner* files, February–May 1969, Nashville Room, Nashville Public Library, Church Street; David Halberstam, *The Children* (New York: Fawcett Books, 1998) 77, 180–81.

[13] Fred McCuistion, "The Present Status Higher Education of Negroes," *Journal of Negro Education* 2, no. 3 (Summer 1962): 347–49, table 1; Hurley H. Doddy, "The Status of the Negro Public College: A Statistical Summary," *Journal of Negro Education* 31, no. 3 (Summer 1962): 370–85; Ruth M. Powell, "The History of Negro Educational Institutions Sponsored by the Baptists of Tennessee from 1864–1934," (master's thesis) Tennessee A&I State University, 1954. Note: The Presbyterian-supported HBCU Swift Memorial College (1883–1955) in Rogersville, Tennessee, closed down in 1955. The TWI Maryville College, also of Presbyterian background, readmitted black students just after *Brown*. Besides Tennessee A&I State, there yet existed nine other HBCUs: American Baptist Theological Seminary (1924–), Fisk University (1866–), Knoxville College (1875–), Lane College (1882–), LeMoyne College (1871–), Meharry Medical College (1876–), Morristown Junior College (1881–1988), S. A. Owen Junior College (1953–1968) and Zion College (Chattanooga City College, 1949–68). Morristown merged with Knoxville College; Owen merged with LeMoyne; Chattanooga City College merged with UT-Chattanooga.

by sending a small party into the business district to count the seats at the lunch counters. They intended to send in reserves as soon as arrests removed the others from the seats. Lawson told them to dress nicely, pray, not stare at the hecklers, not fight the attackers, take books and study at the counters and not to leave the seats until a signal is given by the leader. Kelly Miller Smith was nervous because NCLC had little bail money; they decided to depend on prayers and community donations. A few white supporters like the Rev. Will D. Campbell acted as observers, watching the police action and taking notes. Campbell, a native Mississippian, arrived in Nashville just after the announcement of *Brown*. He funneled donations to the NCLC and became one of several whites to join the Rev. Smith's First Colored Baptist Church. Campbell later spoke in TSU's A-Auditorium.[14]

On Monday, 13 February 1960, the NSM launched demonstrations. Dozens of students suffered arrests, but the demonstrations continued, and they spread to Chattanooga, Knoxville, Memphis, and across the region. The police invaded First Colored Baptist Church and arrested Lawson on March 4. The publisher of the Nashville *Banner*, James G. Stahlman, applauded the police's action, and convinced fellow trustees at Vanderbilt University to force Chancellor Harvie Branscomb to expel Lawson from the Divinity School. Stahlman had promoted himself as a friend and supporter of Meharry Medical College and Tennessee A&I State University, but the heavy involvement of A&I and other black college students soured this relationship.[15]

The demonstrators continued until someone bombed the home of Z. Alexander Looby across from Meharry. Thousands gathered at Tennessee A&I, marched past the bombed home, hooked up with marchers at Fisk and Meharry, crossed James Robertson Parkway near the state capitol building and stopped at the mayor's office. Mayor Ben West came to the steps to face the crowd. NSM leader Diane Nash a Fisk student pressured him to admit "Segregation is wrong." West said, yes. He formed a biracial committee and began talks with business leaders and the NCLC.[16]

Limited to one four-year term, moderate Gov. Frank Clement (D) had left office. His political ally Buford Ellington (D), a self-professed segregationist born in Mississippi, became Tennessee governor in 1959. On 8 April 1960, the director of the State Board of Education (SBOE) sent a letter to Walter Davis and other public college presidents in Tennessee:

---

[14] Will D. Campbell, *Brother to a Dragonfly* (New York: Continuum Publishing, 1977); W.D. Campbell, *Forty Acres and a Goat* (San Francisco: Harper and Row, 1988); Frye Gaillard, "Will Davis Campbell (1924–)," *The Tennessee Encyclopedia of History and Culture*, ed. C. Van West (Nashville: Rutledge Hill Press, 1998) 120–21.

[15] Lovett, *Civil Rights Movement*, 157–200.

[16] Ibid.

As chairman of the SBOE and acting on behalf of the Board, I am instructing you to dismiss promptly any student enrolled in the institution of which your are president who shall, in the future, be arrested and convicted on charges involving personal conduct.[17]

President Davis called a mass assembly to inform the students about the dangers of expulsion. Some of the faculty members said in the classrooms, "I am not going to mark you absent from my class, but if your name and picture appear in the newspaper there is little I can do to help you."[18]

James Stahlman and the *Banner*, other newspaper reporters and photographers acted as the vanguard of white supremacy, taking photographs, listing names, occupations, and sometimes addresses of the student demonstrators who could lose their jobs and suffer harassment from police and state authorities. The Negro press usually—but not always—photographed the students as heroes. The Nashville student movement gained some national press and this helped the Nashville sit-in demonstrations to spread north and south.

The recently formed SCLC under Martin Luther King, Jr., feared that the spread of the student movement would provoke violence from white race radicals. But Ella Baker at SCLC in Atlanta and Septima Clark at the Highlander Folk School in Monteagle, Tennessee, sought to help the students preserve their independence during the movement. Baker and Clark called a meeting of student activists from the HBCUs, including sending a letter to the NCLC, Kelly Miller Smith, and others. The letter asked them to sponsor a student delegation, which was to meet 15–17 April 1960, in Raleigh, North Carolina, at Shaw University during the college spring break. King, Glenn Smiley and Lawson of the FOR, and others attended the meeting. The students refused to join existing civil rights organizations but allowed young Lawson to compose the aims, principles, and beliefs of the new Student Nonviolent Coordinating Committee (SNCC). King and others promised to help with SNCC's fundraising. Diane Nash became coordinator of activist programs for SNCC.[19]

The pressure and negotiations with the NCLC by Mayor West's committee and the student movement forced Nashville city leaders to decide to begin the first voluntary desegregation of public facilities in the South. On 10 May 1960, Diane Nash and a few NSM members walked up to a once-segregated Nashville lunch counter and ate an afternoon snack. Faculty and students at Tennessee A&I raised thousands of dollars to help rebuild the Looby home.

Meanwhile, in 1960, Tennessee resisted desegregation, but racial separation in public higher education came to an end anyway, and, as a result, Tennessee

---

[17] Commissioner of education to college presidents, Nashville, 8 April 1960, Davis Papers.

[18] Lovett, *Civil Rights Movement*, 177–200.

[19] Lovett, *Civil Rights Movement*, 209–13.

A&I lost the argument that it needed extra money to become comparable to UT. The resistance took place despite the admission of one black graduate student at TWI Austin Peay State College in 1956. In 1954 until the fall of 1959, TWI Memphis State University (MSU) refused to admit a few undergraduate students until a federal court order forced the admission of six black students. MSU, however, did not lift the on-campus segregation regulations until 1961—after persistent protests by the students and the Memphis branch of the NAACP. According to a 1962 report by Will Ed Turner to the SBOE, Tennessee seemed proud that it had spent $1,086,585.71 on out-of-state scholarships for Negro students in the years since 1937. After this program ended, this money was not shifted to Tennessee A&I's budget, even though the original out-of-state scholarship money was taken from W.J. Hale's A&I budget. It seemed that, up until 1944, that Tennessee A&I was punished financially because Negroes—including two A&I graduates—had dared to sue Jim Crow Tennessee.

State officials did not look kindly upon the heavy involvement of Tennessee A&I students in the 1960–61 phase of the civil rights movement. After the Civil Rights Act of 1964 forced the state's TWIs, both private and public, to desegregate, Tennessee A&I State University became less important to Tennessee officials in regard to legally maintaining a Jim Crow higher education system. Beginning in 1968, then, the institution's presidents had to beg for funds to improve and expand the facilities, and state officials restricted A&I's out-of-state black enrollment, which severely constrained its budget. By 1985, despite Governor Jim N. McCord's 1940s arrangement with Meharry Medical College, Governor Lamar Alexander argued that Meharry no longer needed special funding from the state because blacks could enroll in the state's public medical programs at TWIs.[20]

The 48th summer commencement was held in Kean Hall on August 14. Leo Branton, Jr., a noted civil rights leader was the speaker. Despite the turmoil of 1960, Coach Edward S. Temple and the Tennessee A&I State University women's track team, the Tigerbelles, left for Emporia, Kansas, to practice, then traveled to New York and then on to the Olympics in Rome, Italy. Mrs. Charlie B. Temple and four-year-old daughter Edwina helped pack things for the team's needs because black college students could not use certain hotels and restaurants in America. The team was hoping simply to place high on the American team but

---

[20] George W. Brooks, *History of the Tennessee Education Congress, 1923–1967* (Washington DC: National Education Association, 1975) 28, 62, 120; Tennessee A&I State *College Alumni Directory, 1924–37, The Bulletin* (February 1938) from the library of Lois C. McDougald; Lois C. McDougald, *Alumni Directory of History Majors*, Department of History and Geography, 1982, Special Collections, TSU, 1–21; Lovett, *The Civil Rights Movement in Tennessee*, 311–13.

they were about to stun the world by winning nine Olympic gold medals. The world was watching Tennessee A&I students.[21]

In the meantime, Negroes in west Tennessee, where 70 percent of the state's black population resided, especially in predominantly black Fayette County and Haywood County, began organizing to register to vote and increase their political participation. Former A&I journalism graduate Theodore Roosevelt Poston arrived and wrote influential civil rights stories for the New York *Post*, exposing the sad story to the outside world. The Fayette County *Falcon* (4 August 1960) said regretfully, "The eyes of the Nation were on Fayette County."[22] That December, landowners evicted those black families who had dared to participate in the voter registration drives in Haywood and Fayette counties. Students from Tennessee A&I State University and SNCC members ferried supplies on weekends from Nashville to sustain the black families who had been evicted.

Tennessee A&I graduate Cordell Hull Sloan led the civil rights movement in Lebanon, Tennessee. He was born in 1931 in Nashville, attended public schools, and graduated from the Tennessee School for the Blind (Colored Division) after a brain tumor destroyed his eyesight. Sloan completed bachelor's and master's degrees at Tennessee A&I, and attended Vanderbilt University's divinity school with J.M. Lawson and two other black students. In 1960, the Presbyterian Church assigned Sloan to organize a congregation in Lebanon. One day, when passing the white school, Cordell's son asked his father why he could not attend "that school." In spring, 1961 Sloan and his neighbor, Cathy White, took their children to McClain Elementary School to enroll, but the officials turned them away. On 23 August 1961, they turned away several other Negro students from segregated Lebanon High School. Roy Bailey, Jessie L. Bender, Ephraim Sweatt, Acie McFarland, and others mortgaged homes and land to finance a lawsuit. Avon Williams, Jr., and Z.A. Looby became attorneys for plaintiffs, and the federal court ordered desegregation of the schools in *Sloan et al. vs. the Tenth School District of Wilson County, Tennessee* US 406 F.2d 1191 (1961). Later, 150 college students, including ones from Tennessee A&I State University, demonstrated against segregated businesses, forcing the city of Lebanon to desegregate other public facilities.[23]

---

[21] "Register to vote," *The Broadcaster* (April–May 1960); news, 1960, Special Collections, TSU; Lovett, *America's Historically Black Colleges and Universities,* 355–56.

[22] Lovett, *Civil Rights Movement,* vii, 71–72, 275, 278, 295, 297, 448.

[23] Ibid., vii, 157-58, 182, 438; Wali Rashash Kharif and William L. Montel, *Reminisces and Reflections: African Americans in the Kentucky-Tennessee Upper Cumberland since the Civil War* (London KY: Janze Publications, 2005) 212–36; Richard A. Couto, *Lifting the Veil: A Political History of Struggles for Emancipation* (Knoxville: University of Tennessee Press, 1993) 202–07.

At the 1960 fall convocation, Dean Carl M. Hill announced that a faculty committee had adopted new standards to improve the students' writing skills. They had been working on this problem since instituting the senior project in 1944. President Davis told students and faculty, "To acquire a head full of knowledge, to develop a loving heart, to train your hands to work and vote, to maintain a good head, and get a pocket full of money and the world can't do you any harm."[24] The Chemistry Building was completed in 1961 at a cost of $500,000 and dedicated on 16 November 1962. In 1963, another $5 million building plan was announced that would include a home economics building, $1.92 million for a women's dormitory, $886,000 for another six-story men's dormitory, $2 million for two more dormitories, more renovations of Harned Hall biological sciences facility, business education facilities, the A-Building, and Goodwill Manor, and $500,000 for a physics-mathematics building. Goodwill Manor (1912) suffered a lot of use in the days of Jim Crow when A&I had to house its visiting dignitaries there. Students did some work on the facility as part of a class project. Davis wanted to extend the back of the A-Building to cover the outdoor pool. These plans would be financed by bonds.[25]

The Department of Speech and Drama also requested improved facilities. They offered AB, BS, MA, and MS degrees in drama and theatre, speech and drama, speech and hearing, and teacher certification. The department included Theta Alpha Phi Honor Society, the Players Guild, Experimental Theatre, and plans for a Civic University Theatre. Since 1925, the Children's Theatre had included elementary and secondary youngsters from the community who were trained to understand, appreciate, and enjoy good drama. However, the theater program was making do in the old A-Building (1934) auditorium, which had about 800 floor seats and a stage originally designed for basketball and general programs, and which was later used by music students who practiced on the huge built-in pipe organ. Testing programs and the Clay Sunday School also used the auditorium. The department directed E. James Fisher to complete his master's thesis on "The Improvement of Speech and Drama Facilities in Negro Colleges and Universities from 1952–1962" (August 1963). His study demonstrated that A&I's 22-year old program was the most productive among HBCUs in producing plays. Tennessee A&I received that honor from the eighteen-member Collegiate Dramatic Association from 1930 to 1951. By 1961, graduates included W.V. Harper, who served as costume and scene designer for

---

[24] "New Writing Standards," *The Meter*, December 1960, 1; "Homecoming," *The Bulletin* (November 1960): 1; A&I, *The Faculty Manual of Rights, Duties, Obligations and Procedures for Faculty Members at Tennessee A&I State University* (May 1961) 1–10.

[25] News, facilities documents, 1960s, Special Collections, TSU.

national television in Copenhagen, Denmark.[26] President Davis set aside $100,000 to renovate the A-Auditorium. Technical theater professor William D. Cox directed the work. He ordered continental seats and new electrical equipment for the back stage area, repair of spotlights and new lights, and added dressing rooms and offices to replace the old gym space. Workers removed the windows behind the stage and filled in the space with bricks and plaster to improve the acoustics. Negro architect Quincy Jackson did the work.[27]

Freedom Rides and Other Challenges

Despite court rulings that began the process of integration, other efforts to modernize Nashville after World War II instead dislocated downtown Negro neighborhoods, whose history extended back to slavery, Civil War and Reconstruction years. Nashville used federal, local, and state funds to begin clearing the downtown slums including Black Bottom and Hell's Half Acre.[28] Thus, all but one of eight historic black churches extending back from 1833 to 1901 moved out of the downtown area. Mount Olive Missionary Baptist Church and St. Andrews Presbyterian Church rebuilt on the south border of the Tennessee A&I campus across Albion Street. A housing development for many Negro professionals and middle-class families surrounded the two churches. Ivanetta and Walter Davis would settle there in a fine home after his retirement. President Davis again pressed city officials to stop commercial development near the campus. The overall Nashville-Davidson County black population percentage fell from about 40 percent to 24 percent after the 1962 city-county consolidation incorporated many of the small, mostly white towns into Nashville-Davidson County government. With Z.A. Looby serving on the consolidation city-county commission, Negroes managed to retain the two city council seats they had held since 1951.[29]

The Nashville Chamber of Commerce, which barred Negro members, began developing plans to expand the city economy and attract big business. In the 1960s, they formally invited University of Tennessee to build a downtown

---

[26] See the Thomas Edward Collection Papers, 1907–, manuscripts, plays, newspaper clippings, correspondence, photographs, scrapbooks, etc., Special Collections, TSU.

[27] Ibid., box 1, folder 1, folder 18, "The Negro in the American Theatre from 1925–1950," 1–24, "The Rise of Negro Professional Theatres from 1897 to 1943," 1–15, newspaper clippings about Poag, 1960–1975, box 5, folder 11, photographs, box 6, folders 1–51.

[28] Bobby L. Lovett, *The African American History of Nashville, Tennessee, 1780–1930: Elites and Dilemmas* (Fayetteville: University of Arkansas Press, 1999) 1–314; Don H. Doyle, *Nashville in the New South, 1880–1930* (Knoxville: University of Tennessee Press, 1985) 117–42. Note: TSU named the R. E. Clay Chapel for Thomas E. Poag, and renovated this 800-seat auditorium in 2000.

[29] See Davis Papers.

campus, which became Nashville's premier institution of higher education. But the black youngsters' daily marches, protests, the heavy police presence and desegregation of lunch counters caused white shoppers to shy away from downtown Nashville. After the CORE Freedom Rides failed in the 1940s, *Boynton v. Virginia,* 364 US 454 (1960), the federal court said racial segregation even in a privately operated restaurant in an interstate bus terminal violated the Interstate Commerce Act (1887).[30] Thus, in February 1961, James Farmer became president of the Congress of Racial Equality. He wanted CORE to dramatize the recent Supreme Court decisions, and demonstrate to the federal government the need for the Executive Branch to support US Supreme Court decisions. On April 15, Farmer announced the Freedom Rides would start from CORE's headquarters on May 4, ending at New Orleans on the May 17 anniversary of *Brown v. Board of Education.* The NAACP advised CORE not to try such dangerous demonstrations, but the interracial pairs paying fares on a couple of buses made it down the East Coast and through part of the upper South. A student leader in the Nashville SNCC John Lewis, and James Farmer were among the 18 black and white Freedom Riders arriving in Atlanta. But on May 14, at Anniston, Alabama, some white men surrounded and burned one of the two buses on the highway. Anniston's mayor denounced the KKK attack. Alabama's governor refused to help the riders. The Rev. Fred Shuttlesworth, product of the HBCUs and a leader in the Birmingham SCLC, led a caravan to rescue the demonstrators. Farmer, on May 17, announced the end of the rides.[31]

But Diane Nash reached Farmer by telephone from Nashville and informed him that the SNCC was continuing the Freedom Rides. A stunned James Farmer objected, but Diane Nash argued that if a group of Alabama racists stopped the rides, the civil rights movement was doomed. Diane Nash met with Kelly Miller Smith and other NCLC officers, who were shocked that the students had taken on such a project. NCLC gave in after long hours of discussion and donated money to the Freedom Ride project. Early that morning, SNCC selected an integrated group of Nashville sit-in veterans: William Barbee, Paul Brooks, Catherine Burks, Charles Butler, Allen Cason, Lucretia R. Collins, William Harbour, John Lewis, Salynn McCollum, and Jim Zwerg. Six of them were Tennessee A&I State University students. McCollum was from the TWI George Peabody College for Teachers. Zwerg was a white Wisconsin student on exchange at Fisk.[32]

---

[30] Alfred H. Kelly and Winfred A. Harbison, *The American Constitution: Its Origins and Development* (New York: Norton and Co., 1963) 885–1011.

[31] Lovett, *Civil Rights Movement,* 122, 140–81; Andrew M. Manis, *A Fire You Can't Put Our: The Civil Rights Life of Birmingham's Reverend Fred Shuttlesworth* (Tuscaloosa: University of Alabama Press, 1999) xvii.

[32] Ibid., 160, 161.

The ten students left Nashville, made it to Birmingham and boarded a bus. Local police stopped the bus and arrested them, placing the white students under protective custody. The police packed the black students into three cars, carried them 150 miles to the Alabama-Tennessee border near Ardmore and told them to "cross the state line and save Alabama and yourself a lot of trouble." Catherine Burks, an A&I senior, smiled and said (in a sweet tone) to Birmingham Police Commissioner Theophilus "Bull" Eugene Connor, "We'll be back."[33]

In the darkness, the students made their way to some homes they figured had black families, like the "safe houses" on the Underground Railroad. The families hid the students. Tennessee A&I student William Harbour telephoned Diane, who told them stay put. Leo E. (Kwame) Lillard, a graduating A&I senior, volunteered to drive a car SNCC had borrowed that was large enough to squeeze everyone in. When asked how he found the students, Lillard said, "I chose the oldest house, and knocked on the door. That was the right house!"[34] The students came out of hiding, crammed into the automobile and rode back to Birmingham. Shuttlesworth remained afraid of more white violence, but he found secret lodging for the students. That morning, he took them and other volunteers to the bus station. Authorities arrested Shuttlesworth. But via cars and trains there arrived more riders, including Joseph Carter, Carl Bush, Rudolph Graham, Susan Hermann, Bernard Lafayette, Frederick Leonard, William B. Mitchell, Ruby Doris Smith, Etta Simpson, Henry Thomas, Susan Wilbur, and Clarence Wright.[35] Again, most of them were students from Tennessee A&I.

On May 19, to prevent bloodshed, a nervous John F. Kennedy administration used an emissary to negotiate the release of the bus in Birmingham. Law officers escorted the bus to the outskirts of the next city—Montgomery—but abruptly turned around, leaving the Freedom Riders on their own. The bus terminal looked quiet until a mob emerged and began shouting "Git dem' Niggers; Git dem' Niggers." A&I's William Harbour suffered a gash on the head. Others lay bleeding with black eyes, while the local police claimed the ambulance companies' cars were all broken down. The federal emissary John Seigenthaler was attacked as he helped some girls into cabs.[36]

---

[33] Lovett, *Civil Rights Movement*, 157, 160, 161, 174.
[34] Ibid., 144, 160, 161, 174, 177.
[35] Ibid.
[36] Vanderbilt University, "John Seigenthaler," http://johnseigenthaler.com/pages/2/page 2.html?refresh=1112205880859, 1–2 [accessed 11 September 2011]. Note: John L. Seigenthaler, Sr., was born in Nashville, worked for the Kennedy administration, and became editor of the Nashville *Tennessean*. Upon retirement, he founded the First Amendment Center in 1991 and moved it to the Vanderbilt University campus in 1993. Vanderbilt celebrated Mr. Seigenthaler on his 75th birthday, naming the building in his

The Freedom Riders scattered about in private homes, went on a hunger strike, and refused to leave Montgomery except in an integrated bus. Farmer, King, Diane Nash, and others rushed to Montgomery. Alabama's governor John Patterson opposed President Kennedy for not standing up to the Negroes. Then, Patterson turned to his quail-hunting partner Governor Buford Ellington of Tennessee and asked him to do something. The Alabama Secretary of State sent a copy of a May 24 Alabama General Assembly resolution to Ellington on 26 May 1961 condemning the Freedom Rides as outside conspiracies against the "sovereign state of Alabama."[37]

Back in Nashville, some of the college students picketed downtown Greyhound and Trailways bus stations. Kelly Miller Smith called the executive council of the NCLC into session and sent Mitz Rollins to Alabama to check on the students.[38] The NCLC called a mass community meeting at St. John AME Church. James Bevel a student at ABTS criticized Ellington's threats against the students: "Disciplinary action about what, and for what? Taking a bus ride as a citizen to New Orleans?" Davis showed up late, sat with other Negro college presidents and said he did not intend to expel any students.[39]

James Farmer, Diane Nash, and King announced on May 23 that the Freedom Rides would continue. Lawson recruited Nashville students and ministers, held a nonviolence workshop, and headed to Alabama. Kennedy wanted SNCC to end the demonstrations, but Diane Nash and SNCC threatened to bring demonstrators to Washington, DC. Kennedy asked J. Edgar Hoover and the FBI to help protect the students, but Hoover—a racial conservative— passionately disliked Martin Luther King, Jr., and other civil rights leaders. Hoover claimed the civil rights movement was Communist-inspired, and that the FBI should not interfere with local law enforcement. FBI agents stood by taking notes when mobs surrounded the black church where a mass meeting was taking place. King came outside to look around, but the whites threw missiles and called him "Nigger King." Some leaders went out the back way, while King, Ralph Abernathy, and others stayed with the frightened audience. Kennedy ordered 600 heavily armed federal marshals to Alabama. They held back the Klansman-like mob with tear gas. Kennedy convinced the governor to send state guardsmen and trucks to transport the church people to their homes.[40]

---

honor. Seigenthaler, Vanderbilt University, and the Freedom Forum established the Seigenthaler Scholars program for students of color. He remained notable in America as a civil rights leader and advocate. He spoke to the students, staff, and faculty members at Tennessee State University on several occasions.

[37] Lovett, *Civil Rights Movement*, 162–63, 169, 170, 172, 373.
[38] Ibid.
[39] Ibid.
[40] Lovett, *Civil Rights Movement*, 178, 182–85.

When the original Freedom Riders returned to Nashville, they appeared bruised, battered, and quite shaken. Tennessee A&I student Curtis Murphy said to anxious news reporters that the Freedom Rides would continue. The student movement increased the pressure on city leaders to help the injured Freedom Riders, and even Stahlman's Nashville *Banner* staff reportedly gave a few dollars to the fund. Telephoned bomb threats arrived at SNCC headquarters at 1905 Jefferson Street, but some students from A&I went over to Peabody College to recruit more white students. Other students engaged in downtown demonstrations in support of the Freedom Riders. For blocking exits while conducting "stand-in" demonstrations at downtown theaters, Nashville police arrested 26 students including Tennessee A&I State University students Leroy Shaw, Carl H. Bush, Frederick Leonard, Lester G. McKinney, Leo E. Lillard, and Allen Cason.[41]

The Kennedy administration negotiated the release of the buses, secured volunteer drivers, and allowed the riders to proceed under federal protection. John Lewis and others wrote the names of their next of kin on pieces of paper and handed them to persons in the crowd just before the bus left Montgomery and headed toward Mississippi. When they arrived in Jackson, Mississippi, the authorities arrested the students. The May 28 ride from Nashville to Memphis to Jackson was composed of nearly 100 percent Tennessee A&I students, including Catherine Burks, William E. Harbour, Frederick Leonard, Lester G. McKinny, William B. Mitchell Jr., Etta Simpson, Mary Jean Smith, Frances L. Wilson, and Clarence M. Wright. Another bus from Nashville to Montgomery to Jackson carried A&I students Allen Cason, Jr., Franklin W. Hunt, Larry Fred Hunter, and Pauline Knight, among others.[42]

Some of the Freedom Riders recalled their experiences on 18–22 February 2009 when Tennessee State University hosted the 55th Annual Conference of the National Association of Student Affairs Professionals, attended by representatives from many HBCUs. On Friday, February 20, they held a session on "TSU Civil Rights and Freedom Riders" at Nashville's Radisson Hotel at Opryland. Jean Smith recalled the authorities kept her in an infirmary because they did not want reporters to see the overcrowded jail conditions. Allen Cason recalled he converted hostile white prisoners by convincing them they all were brothers in the struggle, after officers placed him there, hoping they would kill

---

[41] Note: For the stand-in demonstrations, the students purchased tickets at the movie theaters and stood in line to go into the white section of seating. Owners had them arrested for "obstructing commerce."

[42] Lovett, "Let Nobody Turn Me Around: Sit-ins and Public Demonstrations Continue to Spread," *Civil Rights Movement*, 158–200.

him. Failing at that tactic, officers tried to break Cason's will by placing him on bread and water for 30 days. He survived to tell his story.[43]

SNCC learned that the Kennedy administration had appeased Mississippi officials, who did not want a repeat of federal marshals on their soil as was done next door in Alabama. The compromise allowed Mississippi to arrest the students based on state segregation laws. The local judge turned his back on the hearings, turned around at the end of the arguments and exclaimed, "Guilty." Buses and trains of Freedom Riders continued arriving in Jackson. Mississippi emptied the over-crowed jail and sent the prisoners to Parchman Prison Farm to do hard time, eat bread and water, endure cells too crowded to sleep, and suffer being cut off from their families. The students were angry at the Kennedy administration. The NAACP, CORE, SNCC, and the NCLC had to bear the burden of raising thousands of dollars to pay fines and bonds.[44]

Several A&I students remained in Mississippi in jails: Lester G. McKinney, William Mitchell, Allen Cason, and Larry Hunter along with Albert Dunn and William Barbee. Others rushed back to Nashville to take final examinations and graduate. Most faculty members graciously gave late examinations and make-up work. Lucretia R. Collins, Carl Bush, Rudolph Graham, Charles Butler and others had exams. Collins's family posted $500 bond, flew her to Memphis, where she traveled by bus to Nashville. Ellington refused to allow any Freedom Riders to graduate. Students and faculty members stood outside Kean Hall and refused to march unless *all* eligible students participated. Davis convinced Ellington he could not legally refuse to give a diploma to a student who completed all requirements in the catalog. When word arrived to march, a loud cheer rent the air. Theodore R. Poston served as commencement speaker on May 29.[45]

Following the Freedom Rides, Tennessee A&I State University became a target of racial hatred. Some segregationists and others were busy writing letters of protest to Governor Buford Ellington. One woman, in a letter to Ellington dated 6 June 1961, said, "I am a member of [Tennessee Federation of] Citizens for Constitutional Government." The TFCCG was formed in 1956 to oppose federal court-ordered school desegregation. Whitmore Stokes, Jr., of Nashville demanded the governor enforce rules and regulations about class attendance and punish Tennessee A&I students who had participated in the "assault on Alabama." On 24 May 1961, Richard Wright wrote, "A large number of the students at Tennessee A. & I. seem to be more interested in their radical activities than in a concentrated pursuit of the education for which they are enrolled"—

---

[43] The author was present to record notes on the participating freedom riders at the 55th Annual Conference of the National Association of Student Affairs Professionals, Nashville, 18–22 February 2009.

[44] Lovett, *Civil Rights Movement*, 160, 161, 179.

[45] Ibid., 169, 170–71.

they should be "sent home (Michigan and California), for example." Curtis McPherson of Memphis (6 June 1961) wrote, "I am protesting against these so called Freedom Riders going all over the South stirring up trouble." Frank W. Prescott, a member of the Tennessee Constitutional Convention (22 May 1961) penned: "The authorities at A. & I. must have given the green light *sub silento* to the troublemakers who invaded a sister state." Prescott asked for an investigation. Marvin B. Norfleet of Memphis (22 May 1961) wrote: "Such indoctrinated young [Northern] 'carpetbaggers' and racial agitators have no place in any of the student bodies in Tennessee and should be finally removed from there as enemies of our beloved state and heritage … [It is] an offense to 'white' taxpayers to support these students who comfort Communism and the NAACP." S.B. Rivers wrote (5 June 1961): "Being a tax payer, I am very much against the Nigger Freedom 'Raiders' being allowed to attend the A. & I. State institution that is supported by the Tax Payer money. I am for expelling the Niggers taking part in the agitation." Commissioner Joe Morgan (9 June 1961) assured the writers that the SBOE had policies to deal with these students.[46]

Decherd T. Wolcott, a member of the SBOE, in a letter to Commissioner Joe Morgan (22 July 1961) and Ellington (22 May 1961): "These policies [SBOE, 8 April 1960) were used as excuses to punish some Negro students, and frighten others from exercising their [constitutional] privileges as American citizens on an equal basis with white people." James B. Thornton of Nashville wrote (22 May 1961): "Is it a crime for anyone to demand their rights?" Another man asked the governor not to expel the students and identify Tennessee with the "bad elements" in Alabama. A member of a CORE chapter in Ohio wrote to Morgan, saying that the suspension of Freedom Riders for their beliefs was morally wrong: "Some of us northerners dislike the racial views of some mountain boys who come here to take jobs away from our people, but we prefer to educate them to have better racial attitudes than punish them."[47]

On 1 June 1961, the Davis staff convened the Disciplinary Committee, all of them administrators: Alger Boswell (chairman), Joseph A. Payne, Mable B. Crooks, Lewis R. Holland, Robert N. Murrell, Fred Bright, and M.L. Claiborne. They sent a letter to the students' homes:

---

[46] Joe Morgan, commissioner of education, 1959–63, 2, RG 92; letters of complaints, to B. Ellington, "The Freedom Rides" mf 108, folder 9, file, 1961, RG 92; out-of-state correspondence, Alabama, 1958–63, box 25, folders 1–2, Governor Buford Ellington Papers (first term), 1959–63, GP 48; freedom riders, 1961, box 149, folder 2, freedom riders, lawsuits, 1961, box 149, folder 3, RG 273, TSLA.

[47] Letters, "The Freedom Rides" mf 108, folder 9, file, 1961, SBOE, RG 92, TSLA; out-of-state correspondence, Alabama, 1958–63, box 25, folder 1–2, Gov. Buford Ellington Papers (first term), 1959–63, GP 48, TSLA.

In view of the fact that you have been arrested and convicted for violating a Mississippi law and are now in litigation to prove or disprove the validity of that arrest and conviction, and in light of the policy of the State Board of Education that provides for the dismissal of a student from a college or university under its jurisdiction, when such student is arrested and convicted of charges involving misconduct, you have been placed on probation and will be denied the privilege of continuing your education at the Tennessee A. & I. State University.

On 26 June 1961, President Davis sent Joe Morgan a five-page letter that included a list of students with 10 quarters and a minimum scholarship standard grade point average below 2.0/4.0. These students were barred from re-enrolling at Tennessee A&I State University. The list noted fourteen students jailed in Mississippi. Boswell attached a list of thirteen of the expelled students from *out-of-state*. They dismissed Charles Butler, Catherine Burks, Allen Cason, William Harbour, Larry Hunter, Pauline Knight, Frederick Leonard, Lester McKinney, William Mitchell, Ernest Patton, Etta Simpson, Mary Jean Smith, Frances Wilson, and Clarence Wright. On campus, the student supporters demonstrated until Davis gave an explanation for the school's actions. The NCLC, along with 200 persons from Fisk, A&I, and local high schools marched on the State Capitol. A committee composed of Leo Lillard and Kelly Miller Smith tried to meet with Morgan and Ellington to demand rescinding the dismissal order. They never got a meeting with Ellington. Joe Morgan was just as resistant. SNCC called for a boycott of Tennessee A&I athletics. On June 3, the NCLC voted to consult an attorney. The NCLC agreed to reimburse students, including William Harbour, for loss of property in Alabama and to pay medical expenses for Jim Zwerg, who suffered severe damage to his face and head. Harbour accepted invitations to conduct SNCC workshops at TWIs and recruit volunteers at the University of Minnesota. SNCC leaders met in Washington, DC, with US Attorney General Robert Kennedy and demanded the Kennedy administration speak out against racial discrimination. In July 1961, President Kennedy made a major pro-civil rights speech on national radio and television. He issued *Executive Order 11063* to forbid discrimination in federal agencies, and he placed Vice President Lyndon B. Johnson over the Committee on Equal Employment Opportunities.[48]

Carl T. Rowan, the Deputy Assistant Secretary of State for Public Affairs under Kennedy, rejected the invitation to speak at the 13 August 1961 Tennessee A&I State University commencement: "There is no secret about it—we all know they expelled fourteen Tennessee State students for participating in the Freedom

---

[48] "Freedom riders," Memphis *World*, 20 May, 22 July 1961; "CORE," Nashville *Commentator*, 15 April 1961; "NAACP convention," Nashville *Commentator*, 20 June 1961; Darlene Clark Hine, William C. Hine, and Stanley Harrold, *The African-American Odyssey* (Upper Saddle River NJ: Prentice-Hall, 2000) 514–15.

Rides. I attended school there for one year, but I disagree with their policy. My views are known—I felt no useful purpose could be served at such a time by a speech, which would have embarrassed the administration."[49] Instead, George W. Brooks of the Negro Teachers Association spoke on "If I were a Graduate in a Day like This."[50]

A few A&I students participated in the Freedom Rides over the summer. Carolyn Y. Reed (Bush), then employed at Meharry, participated in the June 2 Freedom Ride. Charles Butler and Meryle Joy Reagon rode on a Trailways bus from Montgomery to Jackson. Cordell Reagon rode with seven other Freedom Riders on another bus from Montgomery to Jackson.[51] Upon their return from Mississippi in August, SNCC leaders held a strategy conference at Highlander Folk Center near Knoxville and discussed a new tactic of concentrating on voter registration projects in Mississippi. The Kennedy administration agreed to back the Voters Education Project (VEP), as a result of talks with SNCC leaders the previous July 16.

In August 1961, some business owners still refused to desegregate their Nashville stores. Some were outright racist about it; others claimed that their fellow whites would, as they were doing in Memphis, boycott their business if they served Negroes. Diane Nash and others headed to downtown Nashville to carry out more demonstrations. They suffered arrests after the owners called the police.[52] On September 1, Tennessee State students Charles Butler, Larry Fred Hunter, and Frederick Leonard were among 17 Freedom Riders in North Carolina. Among the 3,903 students on campus, hundreds began demonstrations by congregating outside President Davis's office each day. They camped by the iron gates on Centennial Boulevard; local newspapers took their pictures. The students sang "Take me to jail, I shall not be removed," holding signs that read: "Faculty do you Support Segregation? Tennessee A&I; which side you on?"[53]

The NCLC hired Avon N. Williams, Jr., and Z. Alexander Looby to file a federal suit against Davis, Ellington, Morgan, and SBOE members. Morgan assured them the State Attorney General would defend them against *Pauline E. Knight, et al. v. State Board of Education for the State of Tennessee, et al.* US (1961). At the October 17 hearing, the brash 39-year-old Williams knew how to get

---

[49] Lovett, *Civil Rights Movement*, 36, 73, 176–200, 235, "Freedom riders," Nashville *Commentator*, 12 August, 16, 30 September, 28 October 1961, 1–2; "Freedom riders," Nashville, *Tennessean*, 2, 3, 5, 10, 13 June 1961, 1–2; Carl T. Rowan, *Breaking Barriers: a Memoir* (New York: Little, Brown, 1991) 1–250.

[50] "Commencement," A&I, *The Bulletin*, 1961, 1–10, Special Collections, TSU.

[51] Raymond Arsenault, *Freedom Riders: 1961 and the Struggle for Racial Justice* (New York: Oxford University Press, 2006) 301, 538, 546–47.

[52] Lovett, *Civil Rights Movement*, 171–74.

[53] Ibid.

Southern lawyers off-focus by accusing them of racism. The defendants' lawyers claimed the dismissals had *nothing* to do with "race!" Williams, Jr., who eventually filed 85 civil rights cases during his career, seemed amused.[54] During a break outside the federal courtroom on Broad Street, Tennessee A&I State University students chanted civil rights slogans. Federal district Judge William E. Miller ordered the state to allow the students to enroll because the disciplinary committee had not observed the right to due process of the law:

> It is undeniable ... that the plaintiffs in being suspended, although they were given the conditional right to be reinstated if and when their Mississippi convictions should be reversed, were deprived of a valuable right or interest ... to continue their training at a university of their choice.... It requires no argument to demonstrate that education is vital and, indeed, basic to civilized society. The Court is of the opinion that the due process clause of the Fourteenth Amendment, as construed by the Supreme Court, requires in the case of a state college or university notice to the student and an opportunity to be heard before the penalty of dismissal is inflicted.[55]

The federal court recognized in *Knight* (1961) that Davis and the administrators at Tennessee A&I University remained "presumably sympathetic to the general aims and purposes of such movements and activities [such] as the sit-in demonstrations and the freedom rides. They deny any intent or purpose to penalize or punish the plaintiffs for their participation therein."[56]

Pauline Knight graduated in 1962, attended medical technology school in Indiana, taught laboratory techniques at Howard University, worked in US Environmental Protection Agency labs, and taught environmental health courses at Clark Atlanta University. She settled down in Georgia. The returning students included Catherine Burks (Brooks), Frederick Leonard, Ernest Patton, Clarence Wright, and Charles Butler. Two students remained on academic probation.

---

[54] *Pauline F. Knight et al. v. State Board of Education et al. U.S.* (1961) Civil Action No 3129, 16 December 1961, federal district court of middle Tennessee, copy by Assistant Professor Elizabeth McClain to Professor Lovett, Lovett Papers, Special Collections, TSU; Joe Morgan, commissioner of education, 1959–63, 2, RG 92; letters of complaints, to B. Ellington, "The Freedom Rides" mf 108, folder 9, file, 1961, RG 92; out-of-state correspondence, Alabama, 1958–63, box 25, folders 1–2; Governor Buford Ellington Papers (first term), 1959–63, GP 48; freedom riders, 1961, box 149, folder 2, freedom riders, lawsuits, 1961, box 149, folder 3, RG 273.

[55] Ibid., 2–3.

[56] Ibid., 156–57; Joe Morgan, Commissioner of Education, 1959–63, 2, RG 92; letters of complaints, to B. Ellington, "The Freedom Rides"; out-of-state correspondence, Alabama, 1958–1963; Governor Buford Ellington Papers; freedom riders, 1961, box 149, folder 2, freedom riders, lawsuits, 1961, box 149, folder 3, RG 273, TSLA.

Lester McKinney, Mary Jean Smith, Etta Simpson, and Frances Wilson chose not to return.[57]

Tennessee A&I State University supplied the largest number of Freedom Riders, followed by Howard University, Fisk University, American Baptist Theological Seminary, Central State University, Johnson C. Smith College, Virginia Union College, Tougaloo College, Claflin College, Southern University, Morehouse College, Dillard University, Morris College, Spelman College, Alabama State University, Florida A&M University, and a few white colleges and other organizations. In November 1961, the Interstate Commerce Commission declared Jim Crow state laws on interstate travel as illegal. A&I's Cordell Reagon and two other Freedom Riders completed one more demonstration on a railroad train from Atlanta to Albany, Georgia, on November 1. The last Freedom Ride took place on 10 December 1961.[58]

In February 1962, the NCLC, SNCC, NSM, and others held sleep-ins at segregated Nashville hotel lobbies. They launched an economic boycott against downtown establishments that persisted in racial segregation and job discrimination practices. A&I students suffered arrests for trying to enter the Tic Toc Restaurant, where an employee met them at the door: "We don't serve niggers here, and you aren't going to get inside." They locked the door; the students sat down on the sidewalk. Jimmy Stahlman's Nashville *Banner* was blocking out this news.[59]

President Davis announced that four thousand students would be enrolled by the fifty-year celebration scheduled for October 1961 through November 1962. Nearly 1,800 freshmen stood on the lawn of Memorial Library and lit candles during induction into the A&I family. Davis told them to study hard. On September 28, President Davis gave the convocation speech. He announced more "African Studies courses" to satisfy student demand, plans for new facilities, and dropping 500 students who made the academic suspension list per SBOE rules. Dean Carl M. Hill said this had not hurt enrollment at all; it helped raise the university's academic standing, and the huge freshman class made up the difference in enrollment. The Alumni Association started the W.J. Hale Scholarship Fund. Public relations said, "In our first fifty years, we have established a heritage, which we must and can uphold. Our history, though short, is one we can look upon with pride. By giving our individual attention to

---

[57] "Freedom Riders," *The Meter*, November 1961, 1–2.

[58] "CORE," Nashville *Commentator*, 28 October 1961, 1–2; Lovett, *Civil Rights Movement*, 138, 159–79; Arsenault, *Freedom Riders*, list of riders, 533–87.

[59] Lovett, *Civil Rights Movement*, 138, 159–76; discussions of the students' movement in Nashville in Highlander Folk School Audio Collection, 1953–63, II-A-2-4v (III-D-2-4v), TSLA; "Biography," 1–4, John Holland to B.L. Lovett, Shelbyville, 10 May 2002, Lovett Papers.

the task now at hand, we can extend this pride into the years ahead, knowing as we go that our accomplishments of the past and our diligence in the present are our touchstones for the future. What will the next fifty years bring?"[60] Meanwhile, there were threats to close black colleges. In Oklahoma, black citizens met and petitioned the state to continue to "operate Langston University [now with a few white students] as an important and integral part of the Oklahoma State System of Higher Education."[61]

In response to massive white resistance to school and public desegregation, as late as spring quarter 1963, students from Pearl High School, Tennessee A&I, and others were gathering at 8:30 every morning at First Colored Baptist Church on Eighth Avenue North to meet, pray, and then march on still-segregated Nashville stores. But the local demonstrations were a little less disciplined after John Lewis moved to Atlanta to head the SNCC; Diane Nash and other SNCC leaders stayed with the Mississippi voters' project; the Methodists sent James Lawson to pastor a church in Memphis; Kelly Miller Smith accepted the pastorship of a church in Ohio. Lester G. McKinney of Tennessee A&I State University now headed the local SNCC and sat as the student representative on the NCLC executive board.[62]

The precedent-setting US Supreme Court case of *Baker v. Carr* 369 US 186 (1962) had ordered reapportionment of legislative districts in Tennessee according to a "one-man-one-vote concept." The first Negro elected to the Tennessee General Assembly since 1896 would gain a seat in 1964. In December 1962, President John F. Kennedy issued an *Executive Order* proclaiming the 100th Anniversary of the Emancipation Proclamation (1 January 1863). Some 40 blacks served in the Kennedy administration. The *Report of the U.S. Commission on Civil Rights* (1963) recommended removal of all vestiges of racial discrimination and called for the adoption of affirmative action programs. On February 28, Kennedy said to Congress, "Our Constitution is color blind and neither knows nor tolerates classes among citizens…. At this time in our history, we must fulfill the promise of America to all this country's citizens, or give up our best hope for national greatness." Kennedy convened a conference of Negro leaders, including Clarence B. Robinson, head of the Chattanooga teachers union, at the White House to discuss what to do next to improve American race relations. Kennedy requested of Congress a comprehensive civil rights bill. The NAACP and other

---

[60] See Davis Papers, 1962, issues of *The Meter*, 1962, and *The Bulletin*, 1962–1971, Special Collections, TSU; "4,500 enrolled at Tennessee A. & I.," Nashville *Banner*, 25 September 1962, 4.

[61] F.D. Moon, "The Negro Public College in Kentucky and Oklahoma," *Journal of Negro Education* 31, no. 3 (Summer 1962): 322–39.

[62] Lovett, *Civil Rights Movement*, 174, 189; "Negroes enrolled in schools," *Banner*, 11 November 1961, 2.

civil rights organizations planned a March on Washington the following August to support him.[63]

Conservative Gov. Buford Ellington was ineligible for reelection, and moderate Frank Clement returned as governor. Clement, who wanted to be a Democratic vice president nominee, would not develop the hard anti-civil rights attitude as Ellington had done. Tennessee HBCUs had 6,796 students, with nearly two-thirds of them at Tennessee A&I. Only 243 Negroes attended Tennessee TWIs, and some 20 white students enrolled in Tennessee HBCUs. The University of Tennessee admitted no black undergraduates but received 57.6 percent of all state appropriations for higher education and had a budget increase of 653.7 percent since 1952. Tennessee A&I State University received a 10.3 percent budget increase from 1952 to 1962.[64] Accreditation visits were scheduled at Tennessee A&I State University for the Engineer Council for Professional Development (May 10–11), National Association of Schools of Music (May 14–15), NCATE (April 1963), and Professional Committee of the American Chemical Society (April 1963). On 13 August 1963, NCATE proposed provisional accreditation for the undergraduate program and discontinuance of the graduate program in education. TSU gained time to strengthen the program.

At the August commencement, Levi Watkins, Sr., former president of S.A. Owens Junior College and now president of Alabama State College, served as speaker. A&I had 234 graduates including 83 masters. SBOE Commissioner J. Howard Warf helped President Walter Davis present the diplomas. For fall 1963, there were 23 new faculty members, and five faculty members returned from academic leave-of-absence, studying for the doctorate. White faculty included Edward N. Cullum, Martin Chanin, Patrick J. Gilpin, Robert L. Holzmer, Gilda M. Greenberg, Prem S. Kahlon, Edna C. Masouka, Jack O'Neill, and Samuel H. Shannon.[65]

On 28 August 1963, national civil rights leaders, headed by A. Philip Randolph and Roy Wilkins, held the March on Washington (MOW) to pressure Congress to pass President Kennedy's civil rights bill. Buses left Memphis, Nashville, Chattanooga, traveled to Knoxville and then onto Washington, DC. Two dozen speakers addressed hundreds of thousands of people. The last of the speakers, Martin L. King, Jr., presented his "I Have a Dream" speech. Roy Wilkins, head of the NAACP, asked the crowd to give a moment of silence after

---

[63] William A. DeGregorio, *The Complete Book of U.S. Presidents from George Washington to George Bush* (New York: Barricade Books, 1991) 545–79.

[64] THEC reports, 1969–2010, state budgets, 1962–65, TSLA, and A&I budgets, 1952–63, Special Collections, TSU; aerial view of A&I, 7 February 1962, photo no. 9842, box 18, file no. 37, Photographs Series—Colleges and Universities, TSLA.

[65] See Tennessee A&I State University, catalogs for 1961–1964, Special Collections, TSU.

the news arrived that the 95-year-old W.E.B. Du Bois ("the old man") had died the previous morning at his home in Ghana. His wife was Shirley Graham, a former Tennessee A&I State Teachers College faculty member.[66]

The Commissioner of Education had received an anonymous "A. & I. Summary Report," claiming the reason Tennessee A&I had failed to maintain desirable growth was due to lack of the citizens' confidence in its leadership, Davis's failure to delegate duties and responsibilities, his favoritism and nepotism in hiring practices, and desire for personal gain. The writer claimed the following: that Davis gave jobs to persons from his native Mississippi; that he decided which quarterback would start a football game; and that hundreds of students returned home rather than deal with the messy registration process. He claimed the Alumni Association had taken $7,500 from the Hale Scholarship Fund and given it to the president as a savings bond. Others expressed their anger in letters to the editor about Davis airing differences with a coach in the newspapers: "Get rid of that man from Mississippi." Carl Crutchfield wrote on 10 January 1962, "It is true that I have been approached by certain parties as a successor to you. I advise you to curb the power plays made by certain of your employees or lose control of the institution."[67]

Tennessee State enrolled 4,689 students in 1964–65. Charles E. Boddie president of American Baptist Theological Seminary served as convocation speaker. The School of Engineering started a vocational education program under the federal Manpower Development Training Act to retrain men displaced by automation. Davis sent a request to Warf to raise the out-of-state fee from $55 to $75 and to raise fees for the dormitories. Davis also asked Warf to consider increasing A&I's land-grant allocation to equal that received by other Negro land-grant colleges[68] The Woodrow Wilson National Fellowship Program sponsored an Honors Program organized by visiting white instructors Patrick Gilpin and Jack O'Neill. Honors students Dorothy Granberry, Connie Swanson, and Rosie Flagg headed the opening ceremony. Davis agreed to designate an Honors Dormitory. Granberry received her PhD in psychology, returned to TSU as a faculty member, and retired in 2003. McDonald Williams became the first black director of Tennessee State's Honors Program. R. Grann Lloyd served as managing editor of the *Negro Educational Review*. Frederick and Patricia McKissack (1964) became celebrated writers, publishing dozens of children's books over the next fifty years. Associate professor of mechanical engineering Yvonne Clark began research programs with her students. Three

---

[66] David L. Lewis, *W.E.B. Du Bois: the Fight for Equality and the American Century, 1919–1963* (New York: Holt, 2000) 559–60, 562, 563, 565–69, 570.

[67] "A. & I.," Nashville *Tennessean*, 10 January 1964, 1, Davis Papers; Lovett, *Civil Rights Movement*, 169–81, 346–47.

[68] Davis to Warf, Nashville, 12 October 1964, Davis Papers.

undergraduates, including Levi Watkins, won top awards in research during the April 1965 National Institutes of Science meeting in Atlanta. A six-story Women's Residence Center for freshmen and sophomore women opened in 1964, replacing Wilson Hall. The new Physics-Mathematics Building opened in 1965 (dedicated 24 May 1966). Watson Residence Center for Men opened in 1966.[69]

For the fall quarter 1965, among faculty members there were thirteen new members and four recent doctorate recipients. The enrollment reached 5,092 students, making Tennessee A&I the third largest HBCU. The alumni numbered more than 20,000 persons—including 200 former students who had earned doctorate and professional degrees. Eighty-seven percent of Negro teachers in Tennessee graduated from Tennessee A&I, as did more than 50 engineering students. At the 53rd convocation on October 5 in Kean Hall, the theme was "Priorities for an Expanding University." President Davis spoke on "Tennessee A. & I. State University—Yesterday, Today and Tomorrow." He said the university intended to maintain a relatively large student body composed largely of young men and women with superior mentality and a burning desire to learn, and dignify and glorify everyday classroom teaching.[70] Davis aimed to improve instruction, provide more research and public service, improve facilities, academic freedom for the faculty members, establish a night school, and recruit students regardless of race, while depending less on huge pools of out-of-state students.[71]

State Begins to Pressure Davis and A&I

But the *Audit Report on Books and Records of State of Tennessee, Tennessee A. & I. State University, July 1, 1959 through June 30, 1965* showed some deficiencies. Several hundred students enrolled without paying out-of-state tuition. The auditors recommended that, "All monies from the operations of the Barber Shop and Beauty Salon [in the Student Union Building] be recorded immediately." A&I also needed to account for all the milk produced on the farm, although the Farm Manager had no control over farm operations and nine individuals controlled various areas of the farm. Warf asked Davis for a report on "how much dormitory space was being taken up by out-of-state students." Davis responded with *Objectives to be Accomplished at Tennessee A. & I. State University*:

---

[69] Ibid.; R. Grann Lloyd, "Research for the Negro Teacher," *The Negro Educational Review* 3, no. 2 (April 1952): 1–10; Raymond Lloyd, *Tennessee Agricultural and Industrial State University, 1912–1962* (Nashville: Tennessee A&I, 1962); Frederick and Patricia McKissack, *Look What You've Done Now, Moses* (Elgin IL: Cook, 1984) and other books are in the TSU library. Note: On 23 March 1974, the university named the new women's dormitory for Mary L. Wilson and Watson II Hall for Henry Allen Boyd.

[70] Davis Papers, 1962–65.

[71] Ibid.

Hire an assistant business manager; establish and improve procedures for record-keeping, monitoring and safeguarding cafeteria cash flow; establish cash-control mechanisms for the bookstore and vending machines; better define research functions under Nebraska Mays, automating the registration and financial aid processes; improve data processing; hire more personnel to help Wayne Reeves in the physical plant and maintenance department; and establish a clear role for Tennessee A&I.[72]

Curly E. McGruder the head of the Nashville NAACP youth and college division called for a full investigation and that state officials to give account of their stance on civil rights in light of the Civil Rights Act of 1964.[73] At the Frontiers International convention in St. Louis, Davis received the Administrator of the Year in Education award and took the opportunity to illustrate his views on civil rights: "We know that the great decision of the U.S. Supreme Court [*Brown*, 1954] which brought an end to the 'separate but equal' doctrine can bring full citizenship for none unless it is full citizenship for all." He described Tennessee A&I State as "a land-grant university entering the early stages of integration."[74] When addressing 300 delegates for the Tennessee Education Congress (TEC) in the A-Auditorium, Davis urged continuation of "A Watchtower organization for Negro teachers until the last step of first-class citizenship has been attained. As long as there is a NAACP, there is a need for a TEC. I believe in integration. I have always felt that I was integrated. I advise you to keep this organization together."[75]

In 1966, Tennessee State used $800,000 to build a Graduate Building on the former Spring Lakes and Rock Gardens that included foreign languages, speech, history, and the social sciences. This facility allowed the university to move programs out of the A-Building to make room for all administrative functions. The four-story Graduate Building had a faculty lounge and conference room, kitchen, office suites, graduate seminar rooms, and classrooms on each floor[76]

In 1966, Edward K. Brooke (R) of Massachusetts became the first black elected to the US Senate since the 1880s. In 1966, the General Assembly approved reapportionment of legislative districts based on *Baker v. Carr* (1962). Dorothy L. Brown and M. G. Blakemore of Nashville, Robert J. Booker of Knoxville, and Russell B. Sugarmon, Jr., and J.O. Patterson, Jr., of Memphis joined A.W. Willis

---

[72] Ibid.

[73] Davis Papers.

[74] The Frontiers International speech, box 2, folder 1, Lois H. Daniel Collection Papers; Davis Papers.

[75] Ibid. Note: TEC agreed to merge with the Tennessee Education Association (TEA), which affiliated with the National Education Association that had endorsed the civil rights movement.

[76] Ibid.

(elected, 1964) in the legislature. Blakemore, a Tennessee A&I State University graduate, had degrees in dentistry and law. Brown, a physician with offices next to the campus, was the first black woman to serve in the Tennessee General Assembly.[77]

In April 1966, some 400 students protested at a meeting about the lack of effort and scholarship on the part of some professors and the lack of accreditation of engineering programs at Tennessee A&I. Some faculty members responded that too many students failed to do acceptable academic work, perhaps because of inability, previous poor training, laziness, or lack of interest. On April 8, Davis called "a fireside chat" with faculty, staff, and students. He proposed a new division to offer preparatory courses to allow students to qualify for admission to the regular university academic programs. Students who entered the college programs would have to perform with a minimum 1.5 grade point average in the first year, a 1.8 in the sophomore year, a 1.9 in the junior year, and a 2.0 for the senior year and graduation. "No institution is fully satisfied with the degree of academic excellence which the particular institution has been able to attain for itself. Therefore, true academic excellence has the habit of ascending higher and higher as its lofty position is approached," said Davis. He intended to accredit engineering and strengthen its administration, hire two new engineering faculty members, including one with a PhD from Purdue, and establish exchange programs in engineering with Purdue and Vanderbilt. Davis announced buildings for home economics, business, fine arts, and several renovation projects. Student leaders said recent projects had destroyed the beautiful landscaping left by President Hale. "You may be assured that as rapidly as complexes are completed, the scenic landscaping that we have had in the past will be restored," said Davis. He formed a Faculty-Student Forum to continue dialogue and devise means of attaining greater degrees of quality in academics.[78]

The Black Power Movement

By the mid-1960s, black militants Stokely Carmichael, Malcolm X of the Nation of Islam, and others were arguing that liberals were trying to control the Negro's intellect, including writing and interpretation of black history and the direction of the civil rights movement; they claimed liberals gave money to the blacks' civil rights movement because of white guilt, racial prejudices, and ingrained belief in Negro inferiority. Malcolm X's advocacy of self-defense helped prod other black civil rights leaders towards more radical positions. In 1966, student anti-Vietnam War demonstrations spread across America. On

---

[77] Lovett, *Civil Rights Movement*, 206, 292, 297, 300.
[78] Report and Davis remarks, Fireside Chat, 1966, in Davis Papers.

January 6, SNCC denounced the Vietnam War. A campus SNCC flyer asked, "Where is the draft for the Freedom fight in the United States?"[79]

In Atlanta, SNCC delegates elected Stokely Carmichael to replace the mild-mannered John Lewis. A SNCC organizer arrived in Nashville. Tennessee A&I's Frederick Brooks became head of the revived local SNCC chapter. A SNCC flyer circulated on campus: "White people who desire change in this country should go where that problem [of racism] is most manifest. The problem is not in the Black community. Thus, an all-Black project is needed in order for the people to free their selves. Black Power [will] emphasize color consciousness among blacks and bring the Civil Rights Movement's decision-making process to the local [neighborhood] level." SNCC campus coordinator at Tennessee A&I George Ware explained:

> To SNCC, Black Power means that Negroes must begin to develop methods of exerting influence over their own lives. The first thing which must be done is that black people begin to become unified, because we are oppressed as a group and we must oppose our oppressors as a group. There is power in numbers and we must use this power to develop political influence through which we may develop the economic power, which we do not have now. Black Power is given an erroneous definition by the white press. Whites have power, and since we are ... black, then that power would be Black Power.

Ware continued, and he denied reports SNCC put whites out of the organization:

> They left. We say to white people that instead of trying to organize the black communities, they should go into the white communities and work to remove the deeply rooted racism, which is where the problem is. We are just pro-black. Black Power is a call, perhaps, the last call, to the black middle class to come home, and make common cause with the black have-nots.[80]

Governor Clement gave his farewell legislative address on 11 January 1967. He recalled criticism against him for straddling the civil rights fence: "I did what I thought was right and in the best interest of Tennessee and Tennesseans."[81] Buford Ellington (D) again became governor.

In April 1967, Tennessee A&I State University's music program gained accreditation in the National Association of Schools of Music. Tennessee A&I

---

[79] James E. Westheider, *The African American Experience in Vietnam: Brothers in Arms* (New York: Rowman & Littlefield, 2008).

[80] "SNCC," *The Meter*, 13 December 1966, 1–2.

[81] Governor Frank G. Clement Papers, 1920–69, ac. no. 94-007, TSLA; Tennessee A&I State University, 1968–69, box 360, folder 1, RG 92. Lovett, *Civil Rights Movement*, 45, 46, 50, 53, 57, 186, 211, 231–32; board of education minutes & agenda, 1967–70, box 7, folder 1, 2, Ellington, GP 50.

completed an $80,000 outdoor recreational facility to accommodate 224 boys and 184 girls in the summer programs, and gained a Talent Search program—a federally funded academic program to locate and educationally rehabilitate potential inner city school dropouts. The National Science Foundation awarded a $366,765 grant to Andrew Bond (chemistry) and granted $441,000 for research in mathematics. The Ford Foundation awarded faculty doctoral study fellowships. Next to the new Music Building, the six-story dormitory for upper-class women opened in spring of 1967. Graduate students had first priority followed by upper-division women. The facility housed 340 students, including honors students and members of sororities on certain floors. The building had air conditioning and bathrooms between every two rooms. On 23 March 1974, the administration named the facility for Harriet H. Hale the wife of the first president. Hankal Hall (site of the Old Main) and Hale Hall next to the Women's Building became sophomore female dorms. East (1912) and Wilson (1912) halls suffered demolition to make room for new buildings.[82]

Stokely Carmichael, the new head of SNCC, arrived in Nashville on 5 April 1967. Fisk, at first, refused to allow the students to schedule a facility for Carmichael to speak. But he spoke anyway, and told the students: "You got to be one or the other: black or white." Stop trying to look "light, bright and damned near white" instead of developing black culture. He said white donors controlled Fisk. A&I's head of student affairs Joseph Payne said Carmichael would be treated like a trespasser. A defiant SGA invited him to speak *outside* the student union building and pledged a $300 SGA payment to Carmichael. Davis refused to dispense the $300, but the Alumni Association cut the check on their campus account. Carmichael had come to Nashville to speak at the Annual Vanderbilt University Impact Symposium, where Martin Luther King, Jr., US Senator Strom Thurmond, and others expressed views on current society. Tom Anderson, a graduate of Vanderbilt University who was a member of the ultra conservative John Birch Society, wrote against Carmichael, "The search for truth does not include any right to deliberately destroy the external verities upon which our civilization was founded, and by which it has prospered beyond any civilization in history."[83] The *Banner* urged Vanderbilt to cancel Carmichael's speech. The Tennessee General Assembly passed a resolution asking the federal government to deport Carmichael to his native West Indies. On April 8, despite a bomb threat, Carmichael did speak:

> I am nonviolent right now. If a white man tries to put his arm on me, I am going to break his arm. I never have been a pacifist. I will not bow down my head and let them beat me until *they* become civilized. Segregated schools and

---

[82] Files on facilities, Special Collections, TSU.
[83] Lovett, *Civil Rights Movement*, 205.

the ghetto are products not of Black Power but of the absence of a group with the power to organize their community.[84]

Martin Luther King, Jr., pleaded with the Vanderbilt audience to understand the Negro could not uplift himself "by his bootstraps" because he had no bootstraps. Thurmond, a recognized white supremacist, blamed America's troubles on liberals, blacks and civil rights agitators like King.[85]

Nashville posted police officers throughout the Fisk-Meharry-Tennessee State area. The police raided SNCC quarters on Jefferson Street. Near Fisk, students were milling about like a street party. Rocks hit policemen, students, and bystanders. Police detained some white thugs after they fired gunshots from a speeding car. In reaction to firecrackers thrown from a window, police fired into A&I dormitories. Bricks, bottles, and a firebomb flew toward the AFROTC building perhaps as part of the anti-Vietnam protests that were beginning to sweep American college campuses. Coach John S. Merritt directed his football players to put on AFROTC helmets and help calm the campus. Ellington ordered the Tennessee National Guard to occupy the campus. They raided the dormitories, searching for weapons, tearing up the student rooms but found no weapons. SGA President James Montgomery followed them, preventing the soldiers from hitting students. Montgomery said, "Last night was the darkest night in the history of this institution."[86]

When some Tennessee A&I faculty members returned to campus, they found their way blocked by tanks and troops holding automatic shotguns. The students played music in front of the ROTC building, dancing and running across Centennial Boulevard to taunt the troops. Dean Jackson stood on the outside balcony of the A-Building and spoke to jittery white faculty members, some of who wanted to protest to Gov. Ellington. Professor Jamye Williams, the SGA president and others volunteered to go the governor's office. Ellington promised to recall the troops if the students stopped the demonstrations. The standoff was resolved, but government intelligence agents had obtained a copy of a letter from President Davis to the A&I business manager: "Deposit this $300 [Alumni Association] check to the Student Activity Fund. Two alumni feel that it may be better for them to assume this cost of the speech made by Carmichael on

---

[84] Ibid., 207.

[85] Ibid. Note: Released tapes and letters of the FBI on King, SNCC, CORE, NAACP, and other civil rights individuals and groups are released on microfilm at libraries, including TSU. SNCC members remained under constant surveillance by intelligence agents. J. Edgar Hoover and the FBI were keeping files and wire taps on King, too. Reportedly, government and police agencies paid hundreds of black informants, and even enlisted white women to work as secretaries and volunteers in civil rights organizations' offices.

[86] "Riots," *The Meter*, 9 May 1967, 1.

April 7 under the sponsorship of the Student Council."[87] Jessie Stahlman had a copy of the check. Stahlman, who politically supported Ellington, wrote, "Dr. Walter S. Davis, president of A. & I. University, told Charlie Moss that he was forced by a petition of 3,000 of his 5,000 students to give Stokely Carmichael the $300 honorarium check."[88] Stahlman said Carmichael told Davis he could not understand why a black man could speak at Vanderbilt but not at the HBCUs. Stahlman obtained a list of seven Tennessee residents and twelve out-of-state A&I University students arrested during the riots and a list of persons working with SNCC.[89]

A black power leaflet titled *Voc Populi* demanded more student academic freedom, involvement in university affairs and better services and facilities. The writer(s) was afraid the authorities intended to takeover A&I or eliminate the institution altogether. SNCC lost the court case of *Frederick Brooks, et al. v. Beverly Briley, Mayor, etc., et al.* (1967), charging city officials with conspiracy to violate civil rights laws. Avon N. Williams, Jr., said to political science students:

> Such riots will continue to be a threat until the white people of this community open their eyes and begin to recognize what justice really means—and as long as they keep their eyes shut they are going to make it possible for people like Carmichael to create disturbances among decent young boys and girls. The white power structure, when it tries to create Negro puppets, plays into the hands of black power.[90]

The white authorities launched a full attack against Tennessee State, trying to get rid of radicals and diminish the out-of-state enrollment that could contain "trouble makers and outside agitators." The state comptroller sent a team of auditors to Tennessee A&I. On April 19, the comptroller wrote President Davis to say some faculty and staff members would not turn records over to the auditors unless approved by the president. Like Hale had done, Davis directed the faculty to cooperate fully. The auditors wrote that Tennessee A&I "failed to bill the out-of-state students $33,750 in fees; students were registering irregularly; there were student work-aid discrepancies, and cheap rents charged for the faculty houses seemed unnecessary."[91] One letter to the Nashville *Tennessean* (20 April 1967) said, "I am sick of the whole catalogue of weirdoes running around

---

[87] Lovett, *Civil Rights Movement*, 208, 210.

[88] Ibid.

[89] Ibid.

[90] "Avon Williams, *The Meter*, 9 May 1967, 1.

[91] Tennessee A&I State College, 1965–67,1967–68, mf 123, box 359, folders 6–7, Tennessee A&I State University, 1968–69, box 360, folder 1; Commissioner of Education Records, 1913–70, RG 92; A&I audit, 1967–1970, box 11, folder 2; task force on action to alleviate social unrest and violence, 1967, folder 3; Buford Ellington (second term) Papers, 1967–71, GP 50, TSLA.

badmouthing the United States, from the whining draft-dodgers to the [radical] finks of Berkeley ... Most of all I am sick of Stokely Carmichael and those ministers of the gospel: Adam Clayton Powell and Martin Luther King Jr." Governor Buford Ellington called a press conference on April 20 and declared "some changes" forthcoming at Tennessee State. Another "Black Power" leaflet circulated on campus:

> When Gov. Ellington suggests major changes at our university, we should question these changes. Will they benefit us as students? Will they benefit us as Black People? We must not allow them to place us into destructive retrogression by the substitution of a white administration. Let us serve notice to any white administration we will say "Hell No"!

Davis wrote on April 27 that the unrest was the result of the manifestation of acceptance by the students of "Black Power pronouncements." The SGA leader said, "I think the administration is under pressure from the people downtown."[92] He cited a lack of state support for black Tennessee A&I was the reason for the students' anger.

A 23-year old history instructor, Rita Sanders was upset that she was blocked by the disturbances from attending her classes at Vanderbilt's law school. She was appalled at how the state had neglected Tennessee A&I State University, so, through a classmate at the Vanderbilt University School of Law, Sanders contacted Attorney George Barrett and filed *Rita Sanders (Geier) et al. v, Buford Ellington et al.,* 288 F. supp. 837, US (15 May 1968). Tennessee State's officials and others were named as defendants along with the governor. It seemed everything was going wrong for an ailing President Walter S. Davis.

On 26 May 1967, Commissioner Warf reported directly to Governor Ellington: "[Paul G.] King has been forced to resign, and an acting business manager from the State Department of Education has been appointed." The *Banner* (May 26) was among the first of many state newspapers to reveal the story: "Business Manager Resigns; to get Another Job at the School." The Clarksville *Leaf-Chronicle* (May 26) said, "[Comptroller] Snodgrass Asks Ouster of King." Warf offered the job to Will Ed Turner, but he asked for $17,000 salary (nearly Davis's salary). In June, Warf offered the job to Arthur W. Danner who was employed at Alabama State College. Warf promised him a $13,500 salary and on-campus housing. Tennessee A&I alumni learned about the secret deal and approached Danner, but he wrote to tell Wharf (8 July 1967): "However, I stayed clear of making any comments." On June 6 an anonymous letter to Danner said,

> Son, I have been in Nashville all of my life and I know how cold it can be to outsiders, especially 'white folks Niggers'. If you have any kind of job there at

---

[92] Lovett, *Civil Rights Movement*, 210–12.

Alabama State, for your sake and the safety of your family, you had better stay. We will not welcome you to Nashville to be a tool of the white man. The entire town is upset about the way the Politicians have controlled the affairs at A. & I., and they will treat you like dirt. The white people may offer you protection and 'Super Tom' President Davis will help you get adjusted, but you should know his days are numbered here. Don't be a Young Uncle Tom; stay where you are if you know what is good for you and your family.

On July 22, newspapers announced the Danner appointment. He reported directly to Warf. On September 6, Danner asked Warf to hire three more persons to help in the business office, including an assistant director at $12,000 a year. In October 1967, at Danner's request, Tennessee State hired the first permanent head of campus security forces. Paul G. King resigned his new job as "property manager." A delegation of the Alumni Association led by Inman Otey met with Warf and Ellington to protest all this derogatory publicity for Tennessee A&I State University.[93]

Still, Warf placed pressure on Davis to expel students Fred Brooks, James M. Booth, and Kenneth R. Jones. Alger Boswell, the chair of the Disciplinary Committee, said, "We believe in free speech, but we cannot allow students to interfere with other students." Davis claimed that Brooks had said, "We came here to eliminate you, and tear this joint down." The school suspended Brooks for "abusive language to the faculty and administration, public drunkenness, and participating in a riot." On August 9, Joseph Payne sent a list of 79 students to the registrar: "Tuition and fees should not be *accepted*."[94] Warf wrote to Davis: "Please admit no new out-of-state students for fall quarter, 1967. Please discontinue immediately all advertising affecting the recruitment of out-of-state students the coming academic year."[95] Davis pleaded a stay because this directive would hurt recruitment for programs in athletics and music. SBOE approved the exemption for fall 1967.

Tennessee A&I raised admission requirements from an ACT score of 12 to 17, a 2.5 high school GPA, and a $5 application fee. Students presented a petition of 70 demands including "Negro history to be required for all students," separation of the history and political science programs, better cafeteria service, better registration process, unlimited class cuts, "plays about Negroes and written by Negroes," more janitors and allocations for the academic departments. State officials gave funds to Danner to pay for additional campus policemen. President Davis created the Department of Operations and

---

[93] Ibid., 212–13; and see the exchange of the letters above in the Davis Papers and RG 92.

[94] Ibid., 213.

[95] Ibid., 211–213; Davis Papers, 1967; Tennessee A&I State College, 1967–68, box 360, folder 1, and box 359, folder 6, 7, RG 92.

Maintenance under Wayne Reeves on October 14 and announced funds for renovations, repairs, new facilities, and new academic programs.

Then Walter S. Davis sent a letter to Warf saying he would take vacation from December 26 until January 1, leaving Sawyer and Boswell on call. Indeed, by January 4, Warf was preparing a new mission statement for A&I with input from handpicked persons on campus. The *Tennessean* (February 3) said, "Strange Doings at A. & I." On February 13, Warf received a letter from Davis: "I am resting here at my original family home place [Mississippi] with my sisters who are so wonderfully kind and good to me [and] to be with." Davis said he intended to return either to the president's home or to his farm in neighboring Dickson County to rest a few days before resuming the presidency. On 2 March 1968, Davis wrote to Commissioner Warf asking for more sick leave time.[96] On May 26 and 27, Warf received letters from Davis, saying, "I have been advised by my physician that it will not be wise for me to return to my position as President of Tennessee A. & I. State University." Stahlman's *Banner* (31 May 1968) said, "Best Wishes, Dr. Davis." Warf notified Ellington and members of the SBOE. Davis submitted his resignation effective 15 August 1968, but it was reset for 1 September 1968, on his twenty-fifth presidential anniversary.[97]

The battle between Tennessee State and Tennessee officials would intensify, and another president would resign after being worn down by the upcoming phase of this battle with Jim Crow over the next five years.

---

[96] Davis Papers, 1967–68.

[97] B.L. Lovett, interview with Mrs. Ivanetta Davis, 3 December 2003, Nashville, handwritten notes, 1–3, Lovett Papers; Walter S. Davis to Commissioner H. Warf, 13 February, 2 March 1968, Danner to Warf, 29 March 1969, Walter S. Davis File.

6

1968–74: Andrew P. Torrence and the Battle of *Geier*

In the fall of 1968, Tennessee A&I State University constituents worried about the presidential selection process. Plenty of self-proclaimed leaders wanted to replace Walter S. Davis; telegrams came to the desk of State Board of Education (SBOE) Commissioner J. Howard Warf. Someone sent Warf a *Who's Who in America* clipping on Andrew P. Torrence. Erskine W. Lytle, Jr., of the Alumni Association sent Warf a list of concerns including "The First rule should be to eliminate all who suggest their own names." The *Alumni Newsletter* said, "The Committee is irritated by the apparent lack of good faith in the process of selecting a university president."[1] The Alumni Association appointed an advisory committee and delivered names of potential presidential candidates to Warf.

On 7 August 1968, alumni leaders Carlton H. Petway, Inman E. Otey, and Lytle answered a summons to Warf's office. Warf simply introduced them to the designated president, Andrew P. Torrence. He was born in 1920 in Little Rock, had graduated from Tennessee A&I State College in 1948, and had received his master's and doctorate degrees in agriculture from the University of Wisconsin. He was vice president of academic affairs at Tuskegee Institute. Lytle said we "have again been made victims of a cold and brutal injustice" at the hands the white state officials.[2]

Granville M. Sawyer continued to lead the interim administrative committee at the university, which conferred the diplomas at the June and August 1968 commencements. The SBOE officially appointed Andrew P. Torrence president on August 9. Torrence traveled to Nashville to address the A&I opening convocation on September 12. He said the university had to be tolerant of student demonstrations: "We cannot be passive about their interests and cannot condemn them for rejecting outmoded methods and ideas and for

---

[1] TSU, *The Alumni Newsletter* 1, no. 1 (Fall 1968): 1. Note: J.H. Warf succeeded Joe Morgan in 1963 as Commissioner of Education until 1971.

[2] TSU, Presidential Records, 1912–, Andrew P. Torrence Papers, 1968–74, biography, speeches, correspondence, and reports; A&I, 1968–69, box 360, folder 1, Commissioner of Education Records, 1913–70, RG 92; and A&I alumni, correspondence with Gov. Ellington, 1969, box 11, folder 1; A&I audit, 1967–70, correspondence, box 11, folder 2, A&I University, Ellington correspondence, 1969, box 11, folder 1; Gov. Ellington (second term) Papers, 1967–71, GP 50, Tennessee State Library and Archives (TSLA), Nashville; Alan Spain, "Dr. Torrence named A&I's new President," Nashville *Banner*, 9 August 1968, 2.

wanting to change situations for the better. Our colleges and universities must be willing to change from the old order."[3]

His wife, Marian Salters Torrence, recalled how they had moved to Nashville in October, when she arrived to enter the two children in school and prepare a faculty cottage as their home. The President's Home Goodwill Manor needed extensive repairs. Torrence set his anniversary date at TSU as October,[4] but he really took office fulltime on November 1. On November 25, Warf assured a worried Governor Buford Ellington (D) that Torrence indeed had officially assumed his duties. During that month, Tennessee A&I State University held a banquet in honor of President Emeritus Walter S. Davis. The governor, faculty and staff members, former students and others honored and credited him for building a larger campus and a powerful athletic program.[5]

President Torrence suggested administrative reorganization, including a new committee structure with student representation, reflective of student requests during past protests and demonstrations. Torrence appointed an *ad hoc* committee of two faculty members, one student, the school deans, and five administrative officers to handle the reorganization and implemented their recommendations. The Torrence committee structure remained in effect for the next thirty years. Torrence reduced the curfew requirement for students and lowered the GPA requirement for SGA officers to 2.5. The university implemented tutoring seminars for students who failed the dreaded sophomore examination. The faculty tightened the class attendance policy and reduced the minimum GPA for scholarships from 3.25 to 3.00 to reflect requirements by other universities. They dropped the Saturday classes. They developed 18 hours of Afro-American Studies made available to "students who desire such courses."

---

[3] TSU, Presidential Papers, 1912– , correspondence, President Torrence Papers, 1968–74, Special Collections, TSU; Andrew P. Torrence Collection, 1954–80, reel 1, folder 1, biographical, Arkansas Historical Commission, Little Rock.

[4] The author interviewed Mrs. Torrence at the luncheon and took pictures, 31 October 2008, Nashville, Lovett Papers; for letters of the president to the Board of Education and vice versa, and Warf to Gov. B. Ellington, Nashville, 1 November 1968, see RG 245; Tennessee Board of Education, Minutes, Tennessee A&I State University, 1968–69, box 360, folder 1, 1907–83, minutes 1968–74, for TSU and Torrence and SBOE Regulations, folder 1; A&I State College, 1958–62, correspondence, box 72, folder 2; Gov. Ellington Papers (first term), 1959–63, GP 48. SBOE minutes and agenda, box 7, folders 1–2, 1967–70; correspondence A&I alumni, 1969, box 11, folder 1; A&I audit, 1969–70; A&I University, 1968, box 11, folders 2–3; University of Tennessee, Nashville Extension 1969, box 14 correspondence, folder 2; task force on action to alleviate riot insurance, 1970–, box 91, folder 11; riots, 1968, box 91, folder 12; task force on social unrest and violence, box 98, folder 3, Ellington Papers, GP 50, TSLA.

[5] "Ivan Davis, son of emeritus W.S. Davis," Memphis, *Tri–State Defender*, 6 June 1974, 2.

An Ad Hoc Committee on Problems and Concerns began to look at ways to improve the dreadful registration process.[6]

The academic organization included a graduate school, school of agriculture and home economics, school of arts and sciences, school of education, school of engineering, department of aerospace studies, and a division of agriculture and home economics. The institution was a member of SACS, NCATE, Teachers College Association of Extension and Field Services, American Association of Land-Grant Colleges and State Universities, and the National Association of Schools of Music. Torrence approved a Cluster Committee for closer working relationships with major industrial and business companies and to enhance advice, financial assistance, equipment gifts, and placement of students in co-operative and internship experiences. He hired Peat, Marwick, Mitchell and Company to do a study to improve efficiency, effectiveness and quality of programs and operations. Torrence also announced some open presidential office hours. He appointed faculty to meet state legislators scheduled to visit A&I as part of their statewide tour to assess the needs of higher education. SBOE approved the name Tennessee State University on December 18, and the General Assembly passed such a bill on 8 May 1969.[7] The initials A&I denoted the Jim Crow days when, since the 1909 legislation, lawmakers distinguished the Negro State Normal School from the white state normal schools. Their intent also was to limit the Negro school's curricula. President Davis had begun working to change the name of the institution during the mid-1940s.

The TSU faculty senate was formed in 1969. Several meetings took place to determine the responsibilities of the faculty in governance of the institution. During the first year, there was "faculty involvement in decisions regarding tenure and promotion, academic programs, policies and procedures, and student evaluation of instruction," recalled chemistry professor Andrew Bond.[8]

In 1968–69, eleven blacks, including Avon N. Williams, Jr., gained election to the legislature. In 1974, they chartered the Tennessee Caucus of Black State Legislators. A&I graduate and Alumni Association president Harold Love served as a Nashville city council member, delegate to the 1964 National Democratic Party Convention, and state legislator. A&I graduate Ira H. Murphy served in

---

[6] Tennessee A&I State University, *Bulletin: Announcements for 1969–1970* 61/51–24, Special Collections, TSU.

[7] Tennessee A&I University, 1969, box 11, folder 3, A&I alumni, 1969, box 11, folder 1, A&I audit, 1969–70, box 11, folder 3; Board of Education, 1967–70, box 1, folders 1–2, Gov. Ellington Papers, GP 50.

[8] Andrew Bond, "Reflections: Faculty Senate 1969–1970," *The Senate Griot*, ed. Amiri Yasin Al-Hadid (TSU, Fall-Spring 2006–07): 1. Note: Andrew Bond, faculty member in chemistry, was founding dean of the TSU School of Allied Health Professions.

the Memphis city council and the General Assembly. Torrence introduced the black state legislators at the university's spring convocation, 31 March 1969.[9]

Andrew Torrence quickly learned that the *Rita Sanders (Geier) et al. v, Buford Ellington et al.,* 288 F. supp. 837, US (15 May 1968) higher education desegregation case required extended attention. Rita Sanders, a history instructor at TSU, along with a white instructor at TSU, and a black parent in Wilson County whose child intended to enroll at TSU filed the case in the District Court of Middle Tennessee in Nashville.[10] The initial focus of *Geier* was to stop the University of Tennessee from opening a branch campus in downtown Nashville. UT President Andrew Holt said UT did not intend to extend beyond an evening program in Nashville, but on 13 April 1969, the UT board of trustee's minutes quoted Holt as saying: "We have considered for the past several years giving this campus the same status as that of the Knoxville, Memphis, Martin, and Chattanooga [UT] campuses." The UT trustees approved Holt's recommendation of Roy S. Nicks as Chancellor of the University of Tennessee-Nashville. Since being forced in 1951 to admit six black graduate students, the UT-Knoxville campus reported the admission of 10 Negro undergraduates and 4 black graduate students for spring 1969; 36 Negroes had gained admission to the School of Medicine (Memphis) since 1961. UT had large numbers of alumni in Nashville-Davidson County/middle Tennessee, and the Chamber of Commerce, the editor of the Nashville *Tennessean,* and the city's political leaders were behind UT's intent to erect a campus and dominate higher education in the capital city. Joe Morgan at Austin Peay State University recommended that the Jim Crow University of Tennessee simply take control of TSU. John Folger, the head of the newly created Tennessee Higher Education Commission, presented the recommendation, but the federal court rejected that power play.[11]

The problem was both a racial and economic one, and allowing the HBCU Tennessee State University to be declared Nashville's public university was out of the question as far as most of the state and city leaders were concerned. The

---

[9] TSU, *Spring Convocation,* 31 March 1969, 1–3, Special Collections, TSU; Tennessee Black Caucus, 1979, series 2, box 2, folder 16, General Assembly Office of Legal Services Records, 1957–82, RG 112, TSLA.

[10] Bobby L. Lovett, *The Civil Rights Movement in Tennessee: A Narrative History* (Knoxville: University of Tennessee Press, 2005) 437; Donna Langston, "The Women of Highlander," *Women in the Civil Rights Movement: Trailblazers and Torchbearers, 1941–1965,* eds. Vicki L. Crawford, J. A. Rouse, and Barbara Woods (Brooklyn NY: Carlson, 1990) 143–68; Frank Adams and Myles Horton, *Unearthing Seeds of Fire: the Idea of Highlander* (Winston-Salem NC: John F. Blair, 1975) 89–98.

[11] Nashville *Tennessean,* "TSU & Geier," 3 February 1969; "Morgan," 10 July 1969; "Geier," 19 July, 24 December 1969, 14 December 1970, 2 April, 4 June, 14, 29 July 1971, 26 May, 10 June, August 1972, 6 March, 12, 19 April 1974; Nashville *Banner,* 29 August 1968, 4 June 1970, 17 April, 10 July 1974.

editor of the Nashville *Banner*, Jimmy Stahlman, had supported President Davis and A&I sports, and he had supported the elevation of Tennessee State to university level. Stahlman and the *Banner* had helped the local HBCU, Meharry Medical School, during some financially hard times. However, since then (1951), the sit-in and Freedom Ride demonstrations, and now the *Geier* case, changed most of the state and local white leadership's perception of TSU from being a key element in the maintenance of the old Jim Crow higher education system to being a threat to a racial system that protected white supremacy. Much of the local white leadership, including the editors of the Nashville *Tennessean* and the chamber of commerce, had been preparing since 1948 to allow UT to become the city's key public university. The state even financed UT—Tennessee's flagship public university—so it would be able to expand its dominance in higher education into the cities: UT-Martin (1967), UT-Nashville (1968), and UT-Chattanooga (1969). In no way could white leaders accept a black public university to be advertised as the city's key institution when trying to attract big business to locate in Nashville. It was a racially motivated move, but had a single aim: economic expansion.

Andrew Torrence saw the *Geier* problem for what it really was—a battle in black and white. The all-white state and UT officials had no intention of desegregating higher education on an equitable plan, and they would continue to minimize black citizens participating in the flagship, University of Tennessee-Knoxville, except mostly as student athletes and minor staff members. Torrence asked the faculty to help with the case. In April, Torrence provided them access to copies of the statements submitted to the federal court under *Rita Sanders et al. v. Buford Ellington* et al. (1969). The copies were placed in the Memorial Library. President Torrence explained he was named along with other state education officials as a defendant.[12]

Rita Sanders received her JD degree from Vanderbilt University and gained license to practice in Tennessee in 1970. She soon married and moved out of Tennessee; however, from her home in the Washington DC area, Rita continued as chief plaintiff in the *Geier* case.[13]

In 1969, the local federal court expected Tennessee and the plaintiffs to submit plans for statewide desegregation of higher education, but *Geier* defendants—UT and state officials—proposed a remedial program for under-prepared students [i.e., blacks]; a committee to mediate program allocation and avoid program duplication and cooperative programs and faculty exchanges between TSU and UTN; financial aid for disadvantaged students; and recruitment of more black students, faculty, and staff members at the TWIs. They

---

[12] *Geier*, Torrence Papers, 1969.

[13] UT, "Rita Geier to Help Lead UT Diversity Efforts," 4 September 2007, http://chancellor.utk.edu/announcement/2007090.shtml, 1 [accessed 22 November 2011].

proposed to upgrade the appearance of the TSU campus, hire additional white faculty members to help improve program quality and attract more white students to TSU. UT President Holt advised Torrence to drop some engineering programs and gain accreditation of the remaining programs to attract whites. On May 12, *Geier* plaintiffs declared the state plan unacceptable, whereas state authorities had an unwillingness to alter the structure and character of the public system of higher education.[14]

In nineteen former Jim Crow states where the 109 HBCUs existed, blacks were barred or minimized in admissions at TWIs, including UT. NAACP-supported plaintiffs filed a precedent-setting civil lawsuit *Kenneth Adams, et al. v. Elliott L. Richardson*, 28, 480 F.2d 1159, 156 (1970, 1973) in the DC federal court to force the US Secretary of Education to compel these states to obey the Civil Rights Act (1964) Title VI that forbade discrimination in higher education or suffer a loss of federal funds for education. The Court said, "the problem of integrating higher education must be dealt with on a statewide rather than a school-by-school basis."[15]

Again, the legislature had authorized UT to create its own system of campuses. In 1969, Governor Buford Ellington and the UT officials worked out a deal to take over the private University of Chattanooga campus. They also agreed to absorb the local private HBCU Chattanooga City College into the UTC organization. This little-known HBCU had begun in 1948 as Zion College in an effort by local white ministers to train Negro preachers and church workers. The founders abandoned the Zion concept upon announcement of *Brown* (1954), but blacks, including Horace Traylor—the first graduate of Zion College—took the institution and converted it into a junior college. On 1 July 1969, the state assumed the University of Chattanooga as the University of Tennessee-Chattanooga. Chattanooga City College (CCC) requested and received permission to merge into UTC. The UTC online history (2011) reads, "In 1969 the University of Chattanooga and a junior college, Chattanooga City College, merged with the University of Tennessee, one of the oldest land-grant universities in the nation, to form the UTC campus."[16] CCC President Horace

---

[14] Plans and committees, Torrence Papers, 1969; Note: Rita Geier became senior fellow at the Howard H. Baker, Jr., Center for Public Policy and Associate to the chancellor at the UT-Knoxville after retiring from the Social Security Administration as executive counselor to the commission in 2007. "Rita Sanders Geier: Senior Fellow," http://Bakercenter.utk.edu/about-us/program-fellows/rita-sanders-geier, 25 July 2001, 1. Hereafter, see Tennessee A&I State University files, box 84, folders 9–10, and Tennessee Office of Attorney General and Reporter, 1906–69, RG 241, TSLA.

[15] *Kenneth Adams, et al. v. Elliott L. Richardson*, 28, 480 F .2d 1159 156 (1970; 1973) 1–11.

[16] Bobby L. Lovett, *America's Black Colleges and Universities* (Macon, GA: Mercer University Press, 2011) 183–84; John Longwith, "University of Tennessee at Chattanooga,"

Traylor became an assistant to the president of UTC. The HBCU's few buildings and a couple of hundred students simply were immersed into the TWI at Chattanooga. Traylor eventually moved on to positions in Florida colleges.

Understandably, many blacks feared that UT intended to use its political power to take over the HBCU Tennessee State University because the white power structure in Nashville wanted UT to become the sole public university in the state capital. As demonstrated in the Chattanooga case, UT was expanding into the major four Tennessee cities, with the blessings of the governor, while adequate public funding and access to out-of-state students was being withheld from TSU. Indeed, the political situation in Tennessee made it difficult for TSU, the public HBCU, to make real progress within a complex, post-*Brown*, higher education system. In 1969, Tennessee created the Tennessee Higher Education Commission (THEC) as a coordinating and funding clearing house for the entire state college system. TSU and five former public teacher colleges remained under the SBOE, which recently had discussed the out-of-state student limitation that some state officials and the governor badly desired as a measure to stop perceived outside civil rights agitators from coming to TSU. The State Board of Education postponed a decision on 16 May 1969, but the newly formed THEC recommended activation of the 15 percent out-of-state student enrollment rule for fall of 1969. One official admitted on the record that "One objection is that the limitation will cause a harmful drop in enrollment, although the enrollment projections indicate that this will not occur anywhere but at Tennessee State [University]."[17]

While President Torrence quickly realized the continuing attack on TSU, he announced the continuing construction of buildings. The Davis administration had begun construction of the fine arts building, but it turned out to be not a fine arts building after all. The facility was just big enough to accommodate art and music. Davis had dreamed of a Fine Arts Center to be a $2.5 million project, but the final estimated cost was $734,000 for a two-story brick facility designed by black architect L. Quincy Jackson. Construction began 1 June 1968. The building was located south of the Education Building and dedicated in 1969. Music and band programs moved from Elliott Hall (Women's Building), and took over most

---

The Tennessee Encyclopedia of History and Culture, ed. C. Van West (Nashville: Rutledge Hill Press, 1998) 1012–13; Gilbert E. Govan and James W. Livingood, *The University of Chattanooga: Sixty Years* (Chattanooga TN: authors, 1947); "The University of Tennessee Chattanooga, History," http://www.utc.edu/About/History.php, 1 [accessed 14 November 2011].

[17] Ibid. Note: Tennessee later allowed public TWIs near state borders, such as Austin Peay State College next to Kentucky and Memphis State University next to Arkansas and Mississippi to have reciprocal state agreements, allowing students from the border areas to enroll as in-state students, and not count as out-of-state students under the 15 percent rule.

of the new facility, which included a band room for 160 musicians, a 226-seat recital hall, classrooms, three listening centers, piano laboratory, and choir room for 96 persons, closed circuit television, teaching studios, office studies, recording laboratory, and offices. The art faculty also managed to squeeze into the Music Building, named the Marie Brooks Strange Hall in 1972.[18]

The Torrence administration completed the Home Economics and Nursing Building (now named the Frederick S. Humphries Complex) in 1969 and occupied the facility in 1970. The building included classrooms, laboratories, offices, lecture hall, and a large suite for the nursery and kindergarten. The two-building complex, which connected in an L-shape, cost $1,431,220. On 5 May 1972, in a Kean Hall ceremony, they named this facility the Walter S. Davis Home Economics and Nursing Building. TSU also built the two-story brick Student Health Services Center in 1968 to replace the one-story frame (army barracks) hospital (1948). Prior to 1948, each dormitory reserved a room for the sick. The Health Center (1971) cost $400,000 and included 36 beds with half baths, clinic, laboratory and x-ray rooms, reception, dietary kitchen, and rooms for two physicians and a nurse. In 1972, they named the facility Queen Washington Health Center in honor of its first registered nurse and director of health services. A small brick operations building opened on the east end of campus near the agricultural complex, and served the campus until it was demolished in 1988. The university spent another $650,000 to upgrade the Mechanical Engineering Building that supplied steam and chilled water to the campus. I.C. Thompson and Associates served as architects. TSU continuously upgraded the steam plant as new buildings came on line, but the cracked pipes still emitted steam from the rock-filled ground. Torrence responded to faculty request for keys and access to buildings for after-hours research and other scholarly activities with a designated head to oversee access and security.[19]

At the opening convocation, 2 October 1969, Torrence said, "It is the task of the university to transmit what is valuable from the past while also providing optimum conditions in which human creativity may design the future. But it is not the task of the university to simply perpetuate the past." Arthur Danner remained head of business affairs, but Torrence asked the state to return control of finances to TSU as a condition for his continuing the presidency. They agreed.[20]

---

[18] *The Meter* (1968–72), renderings of buildings, Special Collections, TSU; Digital Resources, "TSU Building Programs," http://www.tnstate.edu/library/digitalresources/index.aspx.

[19] Ibid.

[20] TSU, Opening Convocation Program, 2 October 1969, Special Collections, TSU; Torrence Speech, Torrence Papers, 2 October 1969, Special Collections, TSU.

On 23 December 1969, federal district Judge Frank Gray, Jr., had ordered the *Geier* parties to present *serious* desegregation plans by 1 April 1970. On 9 February 1970, Torrence wrote to Andrew Holt, saying the UT engineering proposal to share programs with UT-Nashville was not acceptable. Torrence appointed William J. Carter, a PhD, to head the department of civil engineering and help gain accreditation. John Folger, director of THEC, scolded Torrence:

> Dear Andy: I was disappointed in your letter of February 9 to President Holt, because I feel that a greater effort could be made to work out a cooperative program in engineering. 'The fact is Negro students in Tennessee who desire an education in engineering have <u>traditionally</u> sought it here' does not mean this pattern should be continued in the future. This is not a rich state and we cannot afford the luxury of two public engineering programs in Nashville. Neither can we afford a weak, specialized program [at TSU] if it will not serve the need of the community. [I urge you to engage] a little give and take.[21]

On 24 February 1970, Torrence presented the *TSU Plan for Desegregation*. It showed TSU had 37 whites enrolled in the graduate school and 26 non-black faculty members, including 6 of 13 faculty members in history and political science and 6 of 18 in physics/mathematics.

Student unrest continued at TSU. *The Meter* (27 February 1970) said students protested, because "75 percent of the students routinely failed the organic chemistry classes. Teachers are unable to relate to us in a mature and relevant level as future college graduates and human beings. We are afraid that if this situation isn't eliminated, violence and hostilities will occur."[22]

On May 26, President Torrence selected faculty/staff representatives to meet with him, state officials, and the State Attorney General to discuss *Geier*. The TSU faculty senate issued a statement against expansion of the University of Tennessee-Nashville, saying UTN's presence deprived TSU of needed state resources and further segregated the HBCU. The faculty senate said TSU should become an Open University programmatically comparable to UT and other TWIs. They opposed setting up a school [UTN] for "white students who don't

---

[21] President Andrew P. Torrence to the TSU faculty, 26 November 1968; Torrence to the University Community, 24 March 1969; Torrence to faculty, 1 April 1969; A.P. Torrence to Holt, 27 November, John K. Folger to Torrence, 1 February, Torrence to TSU faculty, 5 February, Torrence to Andy Holt, 9 February, Torrence to Folger, 1 July, Torrence to TSU Alumni, 8 July, Folger to Torrence, 10 July, Torrence to Folger, 11 August, 9 September, Torrence to Holt, 27 November, Torrence to Folger, 9 December 1970; Torrence office memorandum, 4 February, Folger to Torrence, 3 June 1971; Torrence to TSU faculty, 30 May 1972, President A.P. Torrence Papers.

[22] "Student protests," *The Meter*, 27 February 1970, 1. Note: Low pass rates for organic and analytic chemistry remained a problem into the twenty-first century.

want to integrate, anyway."[23] *Geier* plaintiffs filed for relief on June 3, saying the state's plan was inadequate. On June 5, Holt denied any intent to establish a full UT campus in Nashville. He said he was not trying to establish a public haven for local white students. The TSU Alumni Association recommended stopping the UTN project and merging it with TSU. The UT Alumni Association was appalled at such talk. Ellington talked in a compromising tone about specific roles for TSU and UTN. But the TSU Alumni Association said, "Our alma mater can and will fulfill the state's needs and obligations in this area."[24]

TSU Denied Equitable Funding

Torrence tried to recover funds lost partly because of the out-of-state enrollment limit. This problem caused enrollment stagnation, budget constraints and difficulty in paying the debt on bonds left by the Davis building boom. On July 1, Torrence wrote to THEC about TSU getting additional funding to compensate for the high percentage of enrolled low-income students who required more remedial preparation for college work. He said, "The formula on which the State appropriation is based works to the relative disadvantage of Tennessee State University ... During the past year, TSU received only 1.1 percent of the $4.5 million dollars of federal funds which were allocated to land-grant colleges in Tennessee."[25]

Torrence and the other HBCU land-grant presidents already were pushing the land-grant issue at the federal level. The president of Alabama A&M University Richard Morrison, who served on a key government relations committee in the National Association of State Universities and Land Grant Colleges (NASULGC), led the effort for TSU and other land-grant HBCUs. They argued the HBCUs were not receiving land-grant funds for all three land-grant functions: teaching, research, and extension. Morrison requested that NASULGC form a committee composed of Morrison and two other college presidents. The delegation visited the US Secretary of Agriculture. In 1967, Congress appropriated $283,000 for each HBCU. Still, the HBCUs needed money to upgrade their facilities to carry out their research mandate; and so, the HBCU land-grant presidents kept hammering on the fact that the black institutions

---

[23] Lovett, *America's Black Colleges*, 199, 217, 230, 263, 285, 286; John Egerton, *The Public Black Colleges: Integration and Disintegration* (Nashville: Race Relations Center, 1971) 1–3; Torrence to Faculty, 26 May 1970, Torrence Papers.

[24] "UT and TSU," Nashville *Tennessean*, 14 June 1970, 1.

[25] Torrence to THEC, 1 July 1970, Nashville, Torrence Papers.

needed some research laboratories, too. Congress passed an $8.6 million appropriation for HBCU research and cooperative extension.[26]

In 1969, the black colleges formed the National Association for Equal Opportunity in Education (NAFEO) to lobby government and private agencies to further assist public *and* private HBCUs. On 20 May 1970, twelve HBCU presidents visited President Richard Nixon to discuss the needs of black colleges. On 29 June 1970, NAACP officials denounced the Nixon administration as anti-Negro. Nixon agreed to support more federal grants to the HBCUs for research, training, and community improvement projects. In 1971, HBCU land-grant institutions, including TSU, formed the Association of Research Coordinators to represent their interests before the National Experiment Station Committee on Organization and Public Policy through NASULGC. In 1972, the Congress and Nixon agreed to increase the HBCU land-grant universities from 17 to 20 institutions. President Gerald Ford (R) began a White House Initiative on HBCUs to increase federal departmental grants to these vitally important minority colleges. TSU benefitted from the HBCU land-grant movement.[27]

However, these developments on the federal level to give more aid to the HBCUs did not influence Tennessee officials to give better treatment to Tennessee State University. THEC Commissioner Folger rejected Torrence's argument for extra funding on 10 July 1970, saying, "Many students from poor families do not have learning disabilities." Torrence refused to allow Folger to dismiss so haughtily TSU's funding claims. On August 11, Torrence sent Folger a list of recent scholarly research articles to back up his arguments about racial disparities in wealth. On September 9, Folger ignored the research and rejected the TSU argument.[28]

TSU and Torrence Fight Off State Attacks

The battle between state officials and Torrence began in earnest. TSU alumni members asked Torrence what they could do to help him. He wrote a four-page letter on July 8 asking them to write to their state legislators about increasing faculty salaries, reducing teaching loads, initiating new programs, increasing library holdings to accreditation standards, and purchase of needed equipment and general supplies. On July 13 he sent the faculty a copy: "You may wish to do the same," he said. On November 27, Torrence wrote,

---

[26] *Leadership and Learning: An Interpretive History of Historically Black Land-Grant Colleges and Universities—A Centennial Study* ed. James E. Smith, et al. (Washington DC: NASULGC 1993) 1–149.

[27] Lovett, *America's Black Colleges*, 192–95.

[28] Folger to Torrence, 10 July 1970, Torrence to Folger, 11 August 1970, Folger to Torrence, 9 September 1970, Nashville, Torrence Papers, Special Collections, TSU.

Dear Andy [Holt]: I indicated in the meeting on November 25, the joint committee report is disappointing. In a period when our resources are inadequate to take care of existing needs, we cannot afford to develop two largely independent, uncoordinated academic programs a mile apart in Nashville. Campus status for UTN is incidental to the resolution of this problem. From an academic point of view, UT has had a complete program here for several years, and campus status will simply recognize a *de facto* situation. We should avoid duplication and wastefully small programs.[29]

Roy S. Nicks, the head of the UTN campus, announced he would seek cooperative programs with TSU. But Torrence wrote to Nicks on December 3 that cooperative programs between TSU and UTN really would not dismantle the dual system of higher education. In a letter to Folger on 9 December 1970, Torrence attached a five-page faculty/staff position paper, saying TSU belonged to the same accreditation associations as UT and that TSU had the personnel to serve whites. TSU conferred 403 degrees (90 masters) on August 21. Black faculty increased at UTN by 0.9 percent, but non-black faculty increased at TSU by 6.7 percent by 1970.[30] Torrence gathered additional support from TSU constituents. On December 13, Avon N. Williams, Jr., the chair of the Tennessee Voters Council (TVC) sent a telegram to constituents urging them to support the TSU faculty senate's position of May 29 to merge UTN under the auspices of TSU. Folger argued no good could come of this.[31] Torrence had launched his offensive, but Roy Nicks would become a chief adversary of TSU and its presidents.

On 4 February 1971, SBOE officials called Torrence to an executive session around 4:30 p.m. He took two administrators with him, expecting to talk about a mistake in locating a parcel of university land from previous administrations, but SBOE commissioners seemed to have something else in mind. They turned abruptly to questions about *Geier*, and asked Torrence about his dealings with Folger and THEC. They directed Commissioner E.C. Stimbert to inform THEC and UT that the SBOE was disappointed about their handling of the TSU-UTN situation. But other officials were planning to cut SBOE out of the discussion. The

---

[29] Torrence to alumni members, 8 July 1970, Torrence to faculty, 13 July 1970, Torrence to Andrew Holt, 27 November 1970, Nashville, Torrence Papers.

[30] Torrence to Roy Nicks, 3 December 1970, Torrence to J. Folger, 9 December 1970, Nashville, Torrence Papers; Dr. Roy S. Nicks, audio, 5-6-76, unrestricted audio tapes, Lee S. Greene Collection on Frank G. Clement, 1973–82, XVIII-K-6, ID-4v., TSLA.

[31] Avon Williams to TVC members, Nashville, 13 December 1970, Tennessee Voters Council Papers, and Avon N. Williams, Jr., Papers, Special Collections, TSU; note: Jamye C. Williams, telephone conversation with the author, Atlanta-Nashville, 28 October 2012, was delighted that these TUC papers were preserved by TSU.

State Board of Regents would govern TSU, and, except for the UT system, other public colleges.[32]

Seemingly in the power seat, UT published its *Desegregation Report* (14 June 1971) claiming 5.2 percent black students. But Judge Gray was not impressed, and he pushed toward an effective plan to desegregate all of Tennessee's public higher education. Gray based his decision on precedent-setting federal cases: *Missouri ex rel. Gaines v. Canada* 305 US 337 (1938), *McLaurin v. Oklahoma State Regents* 339 US 637 (1950), and *Swann v. Charlotte-Mecklenburg Board of Education* 402 US 1 (1971). The US Supreme Court had given federal district courts equity power to provide remedies to end desegregation cases. Thus, Gray pushed the parties toward the feasibility or non-feasibility of a merger or consolidation of TSU and UTN into a single institution under the aegis and control of the SBOE, the UT Board, or a combination of the two. The state kept stalling.[33]

The 1970 US Census reported 22.58 million (11.1 percent) black Americans. Most backs lived in the Southern states; they comprised 17 percent of the population of Tennessee.[34]

State Senator Avon Williams, Jr., honored an invitation from the TSU Political Science Club to address the students. Williams said UT enjoyed favoritism in the Tennessee General Assembly:

> Blacks must realize the white man has used government and money to completely enslave not only the black man but also the poor white man. We must get at these two seats of power to change the [powerless] situation we are in today. You students represent the most important people today: blacks and poor people. Black students must participate in movements today to show the white community an example of togetherness. Blacks will never attain equality as long as they are spoon-fed by whites.[35]

Senator Williams attempted to remove the UTN campus status bill off the committee calendar of the General Assembly. TSU students, supporters, and Torrence packed the senate chamber. But in 1971, the General Assembly approved UTN as a campus. On 3 February 1972, Judge Gray ordered *more* of a "white presence" at TSU and ordered UTN to discontinue graduate programs duplicative of those at Tennessee State University. He asked both sides for new plans.[36]

---

[32] SBOE meeting, Torrence and TSU officials, 4 February 1971, Nashville, Torrence Papers.

[33] Lea A. Overstreet, "Readers Reminisce about Tennessee State University," Nashville *Tennessean,* 9 February 2009, Davidson AM, 9 February 2009, 1, 4–5.

[34] See US *Census, 1970* (Washington DC: General Printing Office, 1970) Tennessee tables.

[35] Williams Papers, 1972, Special Collections, TSU.

[36] Ibid.

Nicks took off his gloves and went into attack mode. He reportedly predicted TSU would die in seven years unless it discarded its image as a black university; he reportedly bragged that TSU could not attract white students in competition with UTN. Torrence replied that detrimental statements like those, inadequate state financing, and competition in Nashville from the better-funded UT would kill TSU. Torrence denied that students and alumni wanted to keep TSU black. They wished for the institution to become the comprehensive state university for middle Tennessee. Torrence said he had no problem with recruiting more whites, but said that TSU needed proper resources to mount an effective student recruitment campaign. TSU faculty issued *Response of Tennessee State University to the Court Order of February 3, 1972*, in the *Geier vs. Governor Winfield Dunn et al.* case, saying "The merger of UTN into the TSU program is feasible as a means of dismantling" segregation.[37] This position made UT defendants angrier.

On 27 March 1972, Tennessee reported to the court, "If TSU is to be substantially desegregated, white students must *choose* TSU." The report said that for fall 1971, the University of Tennessee had 1,223 students from Nashville-Davidson County; Middle Tennessee State University (MTSU) had 2,203; the University of Tennessee-Nashville had 2,287; and Tennessee State University had 1,966. TSU had a student population that was 99.7 black, with 81 percent black faculty members. Apparently, the defendants meant to illustrate that TSU was too black, but UT and MTSU were not too white. In reality, UT had 1.2 percent black faculty and about 5 percent black students, while blacks comprised 17 percent of Tennessee's people. UT proposed reserving new faculty and staff positions at TSU for whites and reserving financial aid to *persuade* whites to attend TSU. They proposed improvement of the physical appearance of the TSU campus and transfer of the UT social work program now operating in Nashville to the TSU campus, but under UT administration. UT defendants said, "The [non-compromising] attitude of the TSU faculty is not conducive to cooperation."[38]

On 19 April 1972, a defiant Tennessee State University faculty senate reaffirmed endorsement for absorption of UTN *into* TSU. On 30 May 1972, Torrence wrote to the faculty,

> I am sure you are aware that this is a crucial time in the history of Tennessee State University. We are in the 'awkward' position of being a defendant in the Courts' mandate to dismantle the dual educational system in … Tennessee

---

[37] Response of Tennessee State University to the Court Order of 3 February 1972, in *Geier vs. Governor Winfield Dunn et al.* Case, Williams Papers, and Torrence Papers, Special Collections, TSU. Note: Gov. Ellington died in 1972, shortly after leaving office. His successor, Winfield Dunn (R), also was a native of Mississippi.

[38] Ibid., UT/Tennessee Response to Judge Gray, 27 March 1972, Nashville.

(*Geier v. Governor Winfield Dunn*). Our university faces a tremendous challenge in this matter, and we need the input of all concerned members of the Tennessee State ... community. I am sure we shall plan together the wise course for the future of our University. We have to do *something*.[39]

In July 1972, the new Governor Winfield Dunn (R) approved the request by Torrence to allow TSU to submit a position statement. But Dunn reminded Torrence that he would allow a statement only because the new State Board of Regents (SBR) had not had time to develop policy on such matters. The TSU position statement used a questionnaire administered by the graduate school. Most respondents believed the dual system of higher education should be eliminated and a merger made feasible, with UTN brought under the control and administration of TSU.[40]

Faculty Leaders Adams and Richardson

The key TSU faculty leaders, Raymond Richardson and Sterlin N. Adams, said that a predominantly black university indeed could serve blacks and whites without losing its historical [HBCU] identity. Math professor Raymond Richardson headed the Davidson County Independent Political Council, an affiliate of Williams's Tennessee Voters Council. Math professor Sterlin Adams headed the TSU faculty senate. Since the original *Geier* plaintiffs had moved out of the state, Richardson, Adams, and others formed Tennesseans for Justice in Higher Education (TJHE) and hired attorney Avon N. Williams, Jr., to prepare a plaintiff-intervenors petition to the federal district court. Through this action, the TJHE effectively broadened the case by including about 100 black Tennessee citizens and infants by their parents as complainants. Rita Sanders Geier was concerned that the opening of UT-Nashville would challenge TSU, stop the HBCU from competing effectively with other higher education institutions in Tennessee, and prevent the complete dismantling of Tennessee's *de facto* racially segregated higher education system. She wanted all Tennessee citizens to have access to quality public education. George Barrett continued to handle the case for Rita Sanders Geier plaintiffs.[41]

---

[39] A.P. Torrence to TSU faculty, 30 May 1972, Nashville, Torrence Papers, Special Collections, TSU.

[40] Graduate School survey on UTN-TSU questions, 18 July 1972, Torrence Papers.

[41] TSU, *The Geier Symposium*, Nashville, 18 April 2012, 1–22, Special Collections, TSU. Rita Geier, former SGA president Greg Carr, Raymond Richardson, Sterlin N. Adams, former TSU president Frederick S. Humphries, and some state officials who had been critical players in the *Geier* case, responded as panel members. The author served as co-moderator and took notes of the panelists' remarks, Lovett Papers, Special Collections, TSU.

Adams, Richardson, and Williams also understood that the *Geier* fight was part of a larger battle over the survival of the public HBCUs, including Tennessee State University. The 109 HBCUs comprised nearly 3 percent of the nation's higher education institutions, but they graduated 20 to 30 percent of black college graduates and produced half the nation's black doctors, engineers, military officers, and more. Yet, only 3 percent of America's faculty members were black, and a majority of them worked at HBCUs. Northern-based foundations and others were working with programs to more than double the small percentage of blacks that annually received doctorate degrees in America, but no such effort was underway in Tennessee after 107 years of Jim Crow.

Meanwhile, in *[Kenneth] Adams et al. v. Elliott Richardson et al.*, 351 F.2d 636 (1972), the federal circuit and appeals court of Washington, DC, approved the district court order for the USDOE, Office of Civil Rights (OCR) to require the Jim Crow states to submit five-year plans for fully desegregating higher education. OCR revised the criteria for the plans several times thereafter. The requirements included the disestablishment of the structure of the Jim Crow system, desegregation of student enrollment, and of faculty, administrative staffs, non-academic personnel, and governing boards. The state plans had to enhance the public HBCUs and not attempt to dismantle them. The US Justice Department later entered the *Geier* case as a friend of the court to keep an eye on Tennessee.[42]

There was fear Barrett and his plaintiffs would accept a deal with the white power structure and place TSU under the University of Tennessee. Sterlin Adams and Raymond Richardson smartly took the *Geier* case out of the hands of Barrett. Barrett later said his mission was to make the state and society realize we were one people, regardless of race and color.[43]

Adams and Richardson presented their TJHE group petition to the district federal court on 31 July 1972, asking for:

> a permanent injunction to restrain and enjoin the defendants [state of Tennessee] from continuing to operate the public institutions of higher education of the State of Tennessee on a racially dual and discriminatory basis.... The class action suit is on behalf of the intervening plaintiffs and all others similarly situated in Tennessee, including black minor children that will attend public institutions of higher education in Tennessee.... The defendants' proposals are purportedly only intended as possible temporary steps to deal with what defendants see as the problem: Tennessee State University (rather than the entire racially oriented higher education system). Their implementation will in fact largely determine the content and direction of any further steps, which defendants might propose in accordance with the

---

[42] Lovett, *America's Black Colleges*, xiv.
[43] Barrett's remarks, TSU, *The Geier Symposium*, Nashville, 18 April 2012.

order of this Court, and they almost inevitably foreshadow an unwarranted attempt to abolish Tennessee State University as a Tennessee institution by assimilation into the campus of the University of Tennessee.[44]

They asked that UTN be transferred to the immediate and full control of Tennessee State. Attorney Williams took the petition downtown to the federal district court on Broad Street.[45]

Tennesseans for Justice in Higher Education (TJHE) remade *Geier* to march in step with the national *Adams v. Richardson* (1972) case. They went beyond what they perceived as attorney Barrett's efforts to compromise with fellow local and state leaders. They used research and published works provided by black scholars to bolster their defense of HBCUs. Gray allowed the TJHE plaintiff-intervenors as part of the *Rita Geier v. Governor Dunn* case. Torrence noted the *Geier* case had taken on a new character, and he wanted to hire counsel to represent TSU. But, TSU officials were located on the defendants' side of the court, and lawyers from the State Attorney General as well as from the University of Tennessee board handled the case. Adams-Richardson plaintiffs assured Torrence that TJHE and Avon Williams, Jr., really were representing TSU's interests.[46]

Torrence, the faculty, staff, and students continued to deal with challenging matters on campus. The National Council for the Accreditation of Teacher Education (NCATE) wrote to Torrence on 18 May 1972, that TSU received approval on May 15. On 10 October 1972, the Engineers' Council for Professional Development accredited civil engineering and electrical engineering. But the mechanical engineering program needed to clear up deficiencies in basic sciences, humanities, social sciences, and marginal laboratory facilities. On 19 April 1973, the Tennessee Board of Nursing gave full approval to the nursing program, which Dorothy Coley Edmond and others had established in 1966 after Meharry Medical College had dropped its nursing program. In May, the Council of Professional Development of the Home Economic Association granted accreditation to the TSU program. TSU faculty also pointed to their most successful graduates as proof of a quality program. In line with this, on 27 April 1973, the US Justice Department argued that all students in UTN's graduate education program should be compelled to attend the program at Tennessee State University.[47]

---

[44] Petition to the federal court, 1972, 1–30, Avon N. Williams, Jr., Papers, 1922–94, Special Collections, TSU.

[45] Ibid.

[46] Ibid.

[47] NCATE to Torrence, 18 May 1972, Engineers' Council for Professional Development to A.P. Torrence, 10 October 1972; State Attorney General to A.P. Torrence, April 27, 1973, Torrence Papers. Note: Jessie E. Russell received his BS in electrical engineering in 1972, and completed an

Tennessee State had five schools: The Graduate School included curriculum and degrees in teacher education, agricultural education, plant science, animal science, art and music education, chemistry, English, history and political science, health and physical education, modern foreign languages, psychology, science education, and speech and drama; School of Education; School of Arts and Sciences; School of Engineering; and School of Agriculture & Home Economics. TSU began to shift from quarters to the semester system in 1974–75.

President Torrence developed his own *Master Plan for Campus Facility Development*. He included attractive signs for the buildings, shrubbery and trees, new paved parking, a plaza in front of the Student Union Building, and construction of a larger library. The Board of Regents approved the purchase of new parcels of land. On 21 March 1974, the SBR approved the naming of Eppse Hall, Hale Hall, Wilson Hall, and Boyd Hall. However, *Geier* demanded attention.[48]

The faculty and staff at UTN continued the plans to expand in Nashville. In January 1974, the University of Tennessee-Knoxville (UTK) had established an office of graduate studies, with a full-time director at UTN. The UTN division directors discussed the status of the pending state desegregation of higher education plan with the UTN Chancellor. A UTN committee reorganized UTN to focus on part-time students and abide by the court agreement not to initiate any new daytime programs. The April 19 federal court order terminated the graduate education program, costing UTN $400,000 out of the budget for the fiscal year 1974–75. Some division directors felt that UTN should work closely with UTK in an effort to provide all possible help to those students affected by the court's program termination. The directors discussed favorably the UT statement of objections to THEC's interim plans for continuing desegregation of Tennessee's system of higher education. The minutes from the 8 January 1974 directors' meeting included discussion of the federal department of "HEW [Health, Education, and Welfare] suing [nine] other southern states by asking plans for desegregation of all which have been disapproved by HEW." Vanderbilt was

---

MS in electrical engineering from Stanford University in 1973. In 1980, Russell, who had benefited from TSU's special programs to "polish rough diamonds" was selected by Eta Kappa Nu Electrical and Computer Engineering Honor Society as "The Most Outstanding Electrical Engineer of the Year" under age 32. For twenty years, Russell headed the effort to develop a wireless phone (cell phones) as the chief technical officer for Lucent Company's wireless business unit and chief wireless architect. Russell did as much to advance wireless technology in the world as any other Tennessean. He returned to speak to TSU students as late as 3 April 2009, as current chair and CEO of a broadband wireless communications company, focusing on new wireless communications networks and technologies. "Jessie Russell," *Blue Notes* 1, no.1 (September 1994): 2.

[48] "Regents approval of naming of buildings," Torrence to faculty, 21 April 1974; Torrence to president's council, April 1974; Torrence to TSU community, 11 February 1974, Torrence Papers.

inviting UTN students to join its naval ROTC unit. The new community colleges, Volunteer State and Columbia State were cooperating with UTN to expand the course offerings to their campuses.[49] UTN circulated reports of the *Geier* court case, perhaps to encourage protest from its constituents.[50]

When the deadline for submission of plans to the federal court approached, TSU President Torrence wrote a letter on March 25 to the faculty: "The State has the responsibility for responding to the Court Order. However, we at Tennessee State University hope to have an influence on what is proposed. Several individuals and groups at the University have been involved recently in drafting recommendations to affirm and/or substantiate the University's position taken in July 1972 and referred to above."[51] Did state officials muzzle Torrence?

Torrence Is Hurt Deeply and Resigns

Suddenly, state representative Harold N. Ford (Memphis)—a TSU alumnus—called for the firing of the president and all other administrators at TSU. Ford believed they had not effectively countered UT arguments about the quality of current TSU programs. He said TSU meant too much to Tennessee and the nation to allow it to die. Ford's emotional outburst was harmful to the TSU position on *Geier*. State senator J.O. Patterson (Memphis) blasted Ford for his reckless remarks and pledged to Torrence the support of the Tennessee Caucus of Black State Legislators. Joseph Simmons president of the TSU Alumni Association chapter in Memphis said, "If you compare the progress of TSU from 1912 to 1973, it would be likened unto a man taking brass and making gold out of it." Simmons supported Torrence. The TSU staff senate executive committee discussed Ford's inflammatory remarks and said they opposed such remarks. Torrence received support from a meeting of community, students, faculty, and staff at TSU.[52] Nonetheless, Ford's bad talk had wounded Torrence deeply. Dwight Lewis covered the story in the *Tennessean*. He reached Torrence at his home, where Torrence said, "If I should ever make a decision to resign,

---

[49] UTN, Agenda, Division Director's Meeting, 1 August 1972, 9 January, 12 June, 17 July, 14 August, 13, 27 November 1973, 22 January, 12, 26 February, 12, 26 March, 9, 23 April, 9 May, 11 June, 9, 23 July, 12, 13 August, 16 September, 21, 22 October, 12, 24 November 1974, 14, 28 January, 11 February, 1, 8 April, Lovett Papers, Special Collections, TSU.

[50] Ibid.; UTN, division directors meeting, minutes, 1 August 1972.

[51] Torrence to faculty, 25 March 1974, Torrence Papers.

[52] "Harold Ford introduced legislation to give TSU more state funds," Memphis *Tri-State Defender*, 19 January, "J. O. Patterson blasts Ford," 26 January, "Joseph Simmons defending Torrence," 26 January, "Harold Ford," Memphis, *Tri-State Defender*, 21, 28 September, 5 October, 9 November 1974, 1; "Harold Ford stuns Kuykendall," Memphis *Press Scimitar*, 6 November 1974, 1.

professionally, I owe it to my students, faculty and staff to let them be the first to know and not the news media."[53] The SBR Chancellor claimed he knew nothing about it.

On 4 April 1974, Torrence scheduled a hurried noonday staff and faculty meeting in the main auditorium. Torrence had gathered his executive council only that morning to announce his plans. In the packed auditorium, President Torrence said, "I have tendered my resignation as President of Tennessee State University, effective October 1, 1974, or at an earlier date acceptable to the Board [of Regents]. Needless to say, I do this with a great deal of regret and after much consideration of my own future and the well being of my family." He said "I set a minimum and maximum period of tenure for five to ten years, respectively. My service has been within that period."[54] Torrence noted the accomplishments at TSU during his tenure: re-accreditation by SACS; NCATE accreditation; accreditation of civil and electrical engineering; and accreditation of extension, dental hygiene, social welfare, home economics, and nursing. The percentage of doctorate-degree-holding faculty had increased from 27 percent to 35 percent; the first *Faculty Rank, Salary and Tenure Plan* was completed in 1972; some 400 companies and agencies sought to hire TSU students; the president had reduced the number of persons reporting to the president from eighteen to only four; and the faculty senate and the staff senate were created. *The Statues of Tennessee State University* (1970) outlined functions and responsibilities of faculty, officers, and committees. TSU received $4.3 million in federal grants compared to $109,000 in 1968.[55] Torrence said,

> The agreement when I accepted the presidency of Tennessee State was that we would have autonomy equal to that of any other public institution of higher education under the State Board of Education, which was our governing board at that time…. Through the years Tennessee State University's financial problems have been enormous. Although there have been some improvements, we are still plagued in this area. In the largest measure, our plight is due to the historical neglect suffered by the University— disproportionate state and federal funds, compared with other public higher education institutions and land-grant colleges, have hampered efforts to maintain a sound financial [base] under girding for our programs.[56]

The faculty at Tennessee State had declined from 333 to 280 persons since 1968 through budget cuts forced by the out-of-state limit as part of the efforts by Gov. Ellington, Commissioner Joe Morgan, and other state officials to rein in the

---

[53] Dwight Lewis, "Is Torrence going to resign?" Nashville *Tennessean*, 4 April 1979, 4.
[54] "Letter of resignation," A.P. Torrence to TSU faculty and staff, 4 April 1974, 1–4, Torrence Papers.
[55] Ibid.
[56] Ibid.

rebellious black civil rights activists at TSU. Yet, Torrence said the university had excellent audits, more grants and gifts, and better programs. "The University stands poised to render expanded services to people of all races who accept its invitation to 'Enter to Learn and Go Forth to Serve'." I want to return to "research, contemplation, and writing." He mailed a copy to the Alumni Association on April 8.[57]

Hundreds of TSU students marched on the U.S. Courthouse, chanting "Save TSU." A sign appeared in the 1974 TSU yearbook, *The Tennessean*: "TSU + UTN=TSU." One student stood next to the sign that read "The University of Tennessee at Nashville," pointing the way for hundreds of protestors marching to the courthouse.[58] The courtroom and hallways were jammed. The overflow crowd mingled and paraded in front of the federal courthouse on Broad Street. UT officials said that UTN reported 10 percent black students and MTSU enrolled more white students from Davidson County than TSU does. Andrew Torrence defiantly said that the only way to transfer programs from UTN to TSU was for Judge Gray to order it. He said the *same* national and regional associations that accredited programs at UT had accredited TSU programs. Avon Williams argued that Tennessee had been pouring money into Middle Tennessee State University (MTSU) to create a safe haven for white students and UT administrators pursued a "thinly veiled effort to disguise racial prejudice."[59] Attorney Williams knew how to get under the skin of the white lawyers.[60] Sure enough, defendants' counsel jumped to his feet! He got into an intense argument with Williams about the definition of racism. Gray quelled the disturbance. He ordered more plans. *The Meter* said, "As students at Tennessee State University, our main object . . . is to save our school from being taken over by the University of Tennessee. Our minds and bodies are worked up and we will not stop until we have the problem well under control." Sterlin N. Adams recalled, "We believed TSU *had* to be preserved."[61]

On 20 May 1974, two weeks after Julian Bond, a charter member of SNCC and now a Georgia state legislator, spoke on campus, Sterlin Adams and

---

[57] TSU, the *Yearbook*, 1974, 41; Lea A. Overstreet, "TSU preserves black history electronically: Podcasts about early leaders to be available worldwide," Nashville *Tennessean*, Davidson AM, 9 February 2007, 4.

[58] TSU, *Tennessean Yearbook*, 1974, Special Collections, TSU.

[59] Avon Williams testimony in *Geier* trial, 19 April 1974; "Geier trial," Nashville *Banner*, 6 April 1964, 1; "Save TSU," *The Meter*, 19 April 1974, 1.

[60] Between 1967 and 1975, MTSU built five new buildings, and added several doctorates of arts degree (DA) programs. The rural MTSU campus benefited from white flight of students from Davidson County.

[61] TSU, Office of Public Relations, News Release, 7 January 1974; "Save TSU," *The Meter*, 19 April 1974, 1; remarks by Sterlin N. Adams, *The Geier Symposium*, 18 April 2012.

Richardson distributed copies of Stuart's *Black Perspectives* with an open letter to the citizens, asking for their support. TJHE asked for 16.3 percent students, faculty, and staff members in the UT system and certain programs assigned exclusively to TSU.[62] On 1 August 1974, TJHE rejected all ideas for merger except "Merger of UTN under TSU!" Adams informed the campus constituents of the three plans circulated in federal court, and asked them to send comments "to TJHE." He published *Tennessee Planning for Desegregation in Public Higher Education and Black Citizen Reaction and Interaction: A Critical Review of Geier v. Blanton From A Black Perspective* (1975).[63]

In May 1974, Torrence led his last commencement exercise. State officials did not allow him to serve until his contract anniversary, 11 October 1974; his contract ended 30 June 1974, and he returned his family to Tuskegee, Alabama. In 1979, he had a coughing spell, but insisted on helping out at his family's flower shop in Little Rock, Arkansas. Back in Alabama, Torrence went to the hospital in Birmingham and learned he had colon cancer. He died on 11 June 1980. During TSU Homecoming 2008, Mrs. Torrence said, "He taught me how to live and how to die. He was from an affluent background, but Torrence was cool and laid back." The family buried Andrew P. Torrence in Little Rock, where he had been a deacon at Greenwood Missionary Baptist Church.[64]

On 1 July 1974, the Regents appointed TSU vice president of academic affairs Charles Fancher as the Acting President of Tennessee State University.[65] Fancher was a soft-spoken, gentle man and an expert in higher education matters. At the annual faculty-staff banquet on August 26, Fancher welcomed new faculty members, including 14 with doctorate degrees. Five of the returning faculty members also had recently completed their doctorates. Fancher spoke

---

[62] President W.J. Hale had asked for exclusive programs not offered by UT in 1942, but Hale was fired.

[63] Ibid; Sterlin Adams, *Tennessee Planning for Desegregation in Public Higher Education and Black Citizen Reaction and Interaction: A Critical Review of Geier v. Blanton From A Black Perspective* (Nashville: author, 1975) 1–20; Reginald Stuart, *Black Perspectives on State-Controlled Higher Education: The Tennessee Report* (New York: John Hay Whitney Foundation, November 1973) 1–24; Sterlin N. Adams, coordinator, Raymond Richardson, Chairman, Tennesseans for Justice in Higher Education, Nashville, 20 May 1974, letter to "Dear Fellow Citizens," 1–2, Nashville, Lovett Papers.

[64] A.P. Torrence to Alumni and Friends of TSU, 8 April 1974; A.P. Torrence to My Friends-Members of the Tennessee State University Community, Nashville, 4 April 1974; A.P. Torrence File, 1968–1974. Note: Mrs. Torrence retired in Little Rock. She was scheduled to visit TSU for homecoming in November 2012.

[65] Nashville *Banner*, 9 April 1970, 16 August 1974, Nashville *Tennessean*, 1 December 1974; in 2011, at First Baptist Church, Capitol Hill where he served as deacon, Charles Fancher celebrated his ninetieth birthday. His wife Evelyn Fancher also celebrated a long membership at that church.

brilliantly on "The Discovery of TSU." He said that mechanical engineering, architectural engineering, and chemistry eventually would gain accreditation, an evening program would open, and the university expected to award the first education specialist degree in spring 1975. Acting President Fancher announced that five presidential candidates would soon visit the campus.[66] On October 23, the TSU Alumni Association commended TSU "for developing higher education for the deprived classes of citizens and developing leadership and citizenship [skills] for the survival of those classes systematically deprived by the society, even resulting from official acts of government. The State of Tennessee has conspired to destroy Tennessee State University by subverting it either to the control of the erstwhile Jim Crow, the University of Tennessee, or reducing the status and function of TSU. [We call for] resistance to covert moves by the state."[67]

President Torrence had inherited an institution that was heavily in debt. When he regained control of TSU's business operations in 1969, the reserves and auxiliary income quickly earned $621,892, but this money had to support general operations and help reduce construction debts and deficits. The old East (Men's) and Wilson Hall (Women's) dormitories with 508 students were debt free, but they had to be closed and demolished. Watson II (Boyd Hall) and the GRC (Hale Hall) dormitories had opened to house 700 students, but TSU owed $11.59 million on the dormitories. The interest rate was 6 percent financed by the US Department of Housing and Urban Development. The TSU debt service was $215 per student compared to $142 at TWIs under the SBR. To raise dormitory fees would lower the occupancy rates and hurt the TSU budget. Thus the out-of-state student limit imposed by Tennessee officials achieved its aim to lower the influx of out-of-state students into TSU even if it hurt the HBCU's bottom line. TSU's percentage of out-of-state students declined from 41.4 percent to 20.8 percent in five years. Full-time enrollment reached 5,458 students in 1966–67 but did not reach a projection of 7,400 students. The state officials' attack on TSU had only begun.[68]

Tennessee officials forced the HBCU Tennessee State University into greater dependency on raising tuition and fees. Yet, the white state officials knew that since Emancipation blacks earned a lower annual income than whites and

---

[66] Bobby L. Lovett interview/conversation with Charles Fancher, Maxwell House Hotel, Nashville, 22 March 2009, 1, Lovett Papers; note: Lovett was a new faculty member at the August 1974 faculty-staff banquet in the cafeteria of the Payne Student Union building.

[67] TSU, Alumni Association statement, 23 October 1974, 1–2, Special Collections, TSU.

[68] THEC Reports, 14 May 1970, Nashville, Special Collections, TSU; TSU, *The Tennessean*, yearbook, 1987, 30.

that black Americans had a tenth of the wealth amassed by white Americans. Sixty percent of TSU's students had family incomes below $5,000, compared to Austin Peay (18.7 percent), Tennessee Tech (26.6 percent), East Tennessee State University (22.4 percent), MTSU (19.6 percent), and Memphis State (18.9 percent). Yet, state officials denied TSU any differential as requested by Davis and Torrence, and refused to apologize for the past and continuing bad effects of the white-imposed Jim Crow system. Indeed, black Tennesseans sought nothing more than equal education. Not until 1969–70 did TSU begin receiving near-equitable federal research funds from the USDA. But since 1912, "UT for white students" had received 85 percent or more of federal land-grant-related funds, with no attempts to allow TSU to recover funds lost in past decades. State officials kept the institution's reserve funds of nearly a half million dollars that they had confiscated in 1943. A THEC report (May 1970) said TSU was perhaps "the only public institution in Tennessee that did not and could not profit from the use of its reserve funds."[69]

Tennessee State University, its presidents, the students and the faculty members were also in for a 32-year battle with the *Geier* case. This dynamic and disruptive aspect of the institution's history would dominate the coming decades; and yet, Tennessee State University survived its battles with state officials and the local white community. The institution, although held back by such events, nevertheless grew and made much progress with "a Touch of Greatness," even in the next ten years, 1975–85, although the battle of *Geier* became more embittered.

---

[69] Ibid.

7

1975–85: Frederick S. Humphries: TSU-UTN Merger and Survival

Sterlin Adams, Ray Richardson, and other faculty members engaged intensive operations to find a strong president to succeed Andrew P. Torrence. The Adams-Richardson group gathered information about the Regents' deliberations and candidates but continued its own search. The board's search committee recommended three finalists and held some interviews on campus. A TSU graduate was among the three finalists, but the faculty feared state officials could manipulate him. Nevertheless, the TSU campus group had stacked the deck of candidates in their favor.

Campus constituencies seemed to prefer Frederick S. Humphries, a graduate of Florida A&M State University (FAMU) who had a PhD degree in chemistry from the University of Pittsburgh. He had formerly directed the Thirteen College Curriculum Program—a Carnegie program that included Tennessee State University. He taught chemistry at FAMU, and joined the Curriculum Resources Group of the Institute of Service to Education in Boston until 1970, becoming vice president in the Washington, DC, office. He was visiting Nashville when a TSU search committee member recommended that he apply for the position of president at Tennessee State University as he held a lot of opinions about black college presidents. Humphries had been critical of blacks leaving the education of black Americans in the hands of the white education system unless whites cast aside the last vestiges of segregation and racism: "I see the destiny of black people in the destiny of black colleges."[1]

On October 3, when Regents tried to test him with questions about the *Geier* proposals, a well-briefed Humphries responded shrewdly that a compromise desegregation plan for TSU-UTN was a good plan, but needed more specifics; and, given the divided leadership between the two universities, justice would be served if TSU became the comprehensive university in the city. He said his priorities would be to remove the uncertainty around TSU's campus and explain its role in the state university system under the jurisdiction of the State Board of Regents (SBR). He intended to bring TSU faculty pay in line with the rest of the system. He believed the public needed to develop the same sort of public confidence in TSU as exists in the expertise of the UT-Nashville. The Regents

---

[1] James W. Smith, ed., *Leadership and Learning: An Interpretative History of Historically Black Land-Grant Colleges and Universities: A Centennial Study* (Washington DC: NASULGC, 1993) 118, 119.

voted 7–4 to elect Humphries. When the telephone call came, Humphries recalled saying, "I can't believe it."[2]

White American resistance to providing blacks with real equal access to quality education remained a problem. When the Regents elected Frederick S. Humphries in 1974, the public secondary school desegregation issues were heating up even in the North. In *Milliken, Governor of Michigan, et. al.,* 418 US 717 (1974) a federal court said, "The state of Michigan through state officers and state agencies, had engaged in purposeful acts which created and aggravated segregation in the Detroit Schools."[3] But the court refused to combine Detroit and suburban school districts to achieve equity in the quality of black and white education. Like his predecessor Torrence, the last thing Humphries wanted to do was be consumed by *Geier*.

Arriving on 1 January 1975, President Humphries announced his intentions to make some changes at TSU. He quickly exhibited his style of management by moving art and music into Arts and Sciences, shifting business education from the School of Education to the School of Business, and making the AFROTC program and Aristocrat of Bands autonomous. At times he seemed to micromanage. In June, Charles Fancher became associate vice chancellor for academic affairs at the State Board of Regents, and Humphries hired Bernard Crowell to replace Fancher.[4]

But Tennessee State University was being squeezed out of the higher education market in Nashville. The University of Tennessee-Nashville (UTN)— with University of Tennessee (UT) clout, Tennessee Higher Education Commission (THEC) support, and the support of the city's Chamber of Commerce, the editor of the Nashville *Tennessean,* and the local white leadership—quietly ignored the existence of the public HBCU just one interstate exit away. Assuming that white students, too, were racially motivated, as they were, and preferred to attend institutions run by whites for whites, the leadership quietly moved full speed ahead to make UTN the public university for Nashville.[5]

University of Tennessee officials remained confident in asking state officials for money to continue to expand the previously two-year UTN into a four-year institution. They also intended to extend higher education on a more convenient basis to the working-class. UTN officials planned an associate degree called College-Within-the Walls to serve the huge state prison population that helped feed the Nashville economy. The THEC was set to approve the program by May.

---

[2] Ibid., 118.

[3] *Milliken, Governor of Michigan, et. al.,* 418 US 717 (1974) 767, 791.

[4] Smith, ed., *Leadership and Learning,* 115–19.

[5] Connie L. Lester, "Community Colleges," *The Tennessee Encyclopedia of History and Culture,* ed. C. Van West (Nashville: Rutledge Hill Press, 1998) 198–200.

UTN planned to hire a faculty member in English with a speech and drama background, and they hooked up with Cheekwood Botanical Gardens and Fine Arts Center. They contacted the local public television station about offering lectures in American civilization. They planned to expand gerontology and the center on aging, criminal justice and urban studies. They had graduate program courses up and running with the help of the University of Tennessee-Knoxville (UTK). They planned women's studies courses if the faculty and money were available. UTN tailored its classes and programs to fit evening, adult, non-traditional students, many of whom were working-class, married, already held jobs, and some had earned high school equivalency certificates. UTN classes began at 5 p.m. and lasted late into the night. Few of these non-traditional students either handled a regular load of credits (16–18 per term), or had the time to devote to intellectual and extracurricular activities like traditional college students. Faculty advisement seemed lax enough to allow the students to progress at their own, slow, pace. Unlike TSU, UTN was under few quality guidelines or direct oversight from the state. The program had no gymnasium or recreational facilities; it relied heavily on part-time faculty. The ambitious UTN faculty and staff intended to serve the area's 113,363 adults.[6]

President Frederick S. Humphries was astute and aware of national and local developments in higher education desegregation including the *Adams v. Richardson* (1972) case. State officials had not counted this into their calculations. Humphries wrote in the *Tennessean* yearbook:

> As you, the university community, know, TSU has been engaged in a historical struggle since 1968. Whether traditionally Black Colleges will be allowed to exist and continue as viable forces in education is very much rooted in that struggle. The institutions which we control and which are most responsive to our needs must not be lost. There is every indication by what we observe [*Adams v. Richardson*] on the national scene today that we should and will guard Tennessee State with jealousy, for it is one our most precious possessions. So whenever there is talk of phasing in or phasing out, merger or submerger, we must adopt the position which most effectively safeguards our individuality, our purpose … our mission. The amount of energy–emotional, physical, and psychological—which has been expended to preclude this institution from being absorbed or lost is immeasurable. As a result, much progress has been made and will continue to be made to insure the existence of Tennessee State University.[7]

Fred Humphries recalled that he and Harold M. Love, state representative and a graduate of Tennessee State, met with the new governor, Ray Blanton, in

---

[6] UT-Nashville, Arts and Sciences, *Trends and Options Status Report*, 13 May 1975, 1–2, Lovett Papers, Special Collections, TSU.

[7] TSU, "President's Message," *Tennessean, Yearbook*, 1975, 51.

January 1975, about matters pertaining to TSU. It seemed clear that the governor would prefer the University of Tennessee emerge from the *Geier* situation as the dominant institution. The fact that Humphries was really on the side of the defendant in the *Geier* case and that, through his insistence on protecting the existence of the HBCU Tennessee State University, he appeared to be playing advocate for the plaintiff, did not endear him to Governor Blanton and other state officials. McDonald Williams, professor of English and director of the university honors program at TSU, recalled being at the first meeting of the SBR where Blanton had scheduled to elect Roy S. Nicks chancellor (executive head) of the Regents. Despite resistance from the governor, Humphries spoke out prior to the decision being made, and accused Nicks of denigrating TSU. He said that TSU constituents wondered if Nicks could be an impartial SBR chancellor. Regardless, Blanton and the Regents proceeded to elect Nicks as Chancellor of the State Board of Regents. Humphries came to regret his remarks, and Blanton and Nicks would become enemies of both him and TSU. Humphries later said, "Tennessee State University, founded in 1912, deserved the respect and support of the courts and consequently the governing board and the citizens of Nashville."[8]

On 1 April 1975, President Frederick S. Humphries sent a letter to the black state legislators—some of them TSU graduates, asking them to vote against UTN's budget requests:

> Additional expansion of the UTNashville, whether it be in the area of responsibility for programs and services or physical plant will duly complicate the desegregation of higher education in Nashville. Therefore, we urge you to work against the funding of any request. We feel … representatives … should be allowed to make known its view for the Finance Ways and Means Committee of both houses.[9]

On the morning of 24 October 1975, the fourth president of Tennessee State University engaged inauguration ceremonies in Kean Hall. Vernon Jordan, head of the National Urban League (1971–81), was convocation speaker. Humphries said, "Today, you do me, my wife, my children, and my family a great honor." William J. Simmons, the university minister, offered the prayer: "We meet together to give honor and responsibility to Frederick S. Humphries, as fourth President of Tennessee State University." The faculty hosted seminars titled "Changes and Challenges of Higher Education in the Seventies," and Roy S.

---

[8] TSU, *The Geier Symposium*, 18 April 2012, 9; Hunphries remarks at the Geier Symposium, 18 April 2012; Dr. McDonald Williams, letter to B.L. Lovett, Atlanta, 12 October 2012; telephone conversation between McDonald Williams, Dr. Jayme Coleman Williams, and B.L. Lovett, 28 October 2012.

[9] Fred S. Humphries, Nashville, 1 April 1975, to Harper Brewer, Dedrick Withers, and John Ford, Humphries Files, Special Collections, TSU.

Nicks—now Chancellor of the SBR—was one of the speakers. The Department of Communication produced *A Raisin in the Sun* for inaugural activities. Humphries selected Sterlin N. Adams as presidential assistant, and the administration organized a forum to discuss the TSU role in the community.[10]

Humphries had inadvertently reopened the battle that former President Torrence had lost with Tennessee's Jim Crow officials. He, like Torrence, needed faculty support to reinforce his flanks. On 10 February 1976, Cecille E. Crump, chair of the Tennessee State faculty senate, sent a letter to Clarence B. Robinson (class of 1934) chair of the Tennessee Caucus of Black State Legislators:

> For the past eight years during the court litigation, we have been struggling against innumerable odds to maintain and develop further an institution of higher education for all people. Our deterrent has been the competition engendered by another publicly funded institution in the city. The UTN position is ... they are in need of additional physical facilities for ... evening-time operation. Their request strengthens the need for the state to merge the two institutions.[11]

In his effort to protect the legacy and existence of Tennessee State University, President Humphries risked his tenure further by openly opposing the powerful University of Tennessee and its constituents in the legislature, in Nashville, and in the governor's office. When merger seemed the inevitable decision by the federal court, the question was whether TSU would become part of the SBR or the UT system of higher education. Humphries had asked the previous chancellor of the Board of Regents for a lawyer, but Ed Boling had refused, so Humphries asked again at the Blanton board meeting, and was again told no. Both the Regents and Blanton favored UT assuming TSU, and Humphries said the UT president even visited the TSU president's office to urge merger into the University of Tennessee system. Humphries gathered key faculty members and his presidential council to help him decide what to do. Sterlin Adams, Cecile Crump, and McDonald Williams formed a committee to give input to the president about the merger decision. After a late-night session of examining and discussing the issue, they reported to the president in favor of the SBR system. The next morning at 9 a.m., President Humphries spoke to the TSU family and said he was in favor of a merger with the SBR system. He was surprised that the SBR council of presidents resolved to support TSU becoming a

---

[10] TSU, *Tennessean Yearbook*, 1976, 36, 37, 38, 39; Vernon E. Jordan, Jr., *Vernon Can Read: A Memoir* (Basic C Books, 2001) 163–62. Jordan served in Tennessee as a civil rights worker in 1963.

[11] Cecille E. Crump, Nashville, 10 February 1976, to C.B. Robinson, *Geier* Files, Special Collections, TSU. Note, Crump held a doctorate and headed the business program for many years. She attended First Baptist Church, Capitol Hill, where former president W.S. Davis and his family were members.

part of the SBR system, though Chancellor Nicks seemed to be opposed to them. Humphries was aware that this was "a landmark legal case that set the precedent for the first time a HBCU has successfully acquired a TWI in the history of the United States." Perhaps the *Geier* results had gone beyond the intent of the original plaintiffs, which, according to Rita Sanders Geier, was "to address egregious disparities in funding, curricula, facilities, and faculty at still-segregated TSU, and to eradicate statewide policies and practices that perpetuated a dual system of higher education in Tennessee, one black and one white." Attorney George E. Barrett said, "The legal theory established by *Geier* became the basis for the US Justice Department and the US Educational Department [USDOE] to promulgate rules and regulations, for these states that still have *de jure* or *de facto* systems of public higher education, as these obligations to dismantle such systems."[12]

Federal Court Merges TSU and UTN

During the *Geier* court testimony, in a matter-of-fact manner, Humphries agreed with plaintiffs' attorney Avon Williams, Jr., that Tennessee had imposed a disparate burden of desegregation on TSU while denying it the required resources. It was difficult to attract white students and others to a run-down physical plant. Sterlin Adams, Edward Isibor (engineering dean at TSU), Elias Blake, and John Barrell provided more ammunition against the state. Of 6,483 black students in public colleges, 5,084 of them attended TSU since being forced to desegregate in 1951 and 1965. The UT system had 252 black undergraduates, 55 black graduate students, 16 black students from Knoxville College in "occasional attendance," and 4 black faculty members. Judge Gray had heard enough. On 21 January 1977, he ordered merger of UTN and TSU by 1 July 1979 under the State Board of Regents. Charles E. Smith, the head of UTN, told the UT board of trustees on February 12, that, "Judge Gray's decision has produced a chilling effect on our campus." On February 22, he sent a letter to SBR legal counsel to say the merger plans seemed "a takeover rather than a merger."[13] On February 28, Gray denied the UTN faculty request for *Geier* intervener status.[14]

---

[12] Frederick S. Humphries, résumé, 2012, 1; George E. Barrett to Bruce D. Rogers, Nashville, March 27, 2012, 1–4, reflections on *Geier*, Rita Geier to Dean Bruce Rogers, response to questions about *Geier*, March 27.

[13] Charles W. Smith to Charles B. Fancher, Nashville, 8 April 1975, Fancher file, Special Collections, TSU; C.W. Smith to UT Board, Nashville, 12 February 1975; Smith to SBR legal counsel, 22 February 1975, Lovett Papers. Note: when completing his doctorate in education at UT-Knoxville, Smith wanted to find out why the majority of UTN graduates did not transfer to TSU, in his "Transferring Influencing Factors," doctoral dissertation. Graduate School Dean James Reeves responded that the quality of TSU graduate programs had attracted dozens of white students including graduates from University of Tennessee,

The US Department of Justice agreed with Gray's merger decision but felt that he should have dealt also with racial inequities in faculty salaries in the public higher education system. Notably, the Department of Justice's brief reminded everyone that Tennessee became the first state (1901) to pass criminal statues requiring racial segregation in all public *and* private colleges. Gray avoided this can of worms. He included no punitive measures on UT. Tennessee voters recently approved repeal of the segregated school and anti-interracial marriage sections of the state constitution.

In *Adams v. Richardson* (1972–77), the DC federal court ordered the Department of Health, Education, and Welfare (HEW) and its Office of Civil Rights (OCR) to develop new guidelines to gain compliance and dismantle the dual racial systems of higher education in 19 former Jim Crow states. The 1978 OCR criteria included enhancement of public HBCUs' programs comparable to those at TWIs. These guidelines would go much further after Jake Ayers, Sr., parent of a student at HBCU Jackson State University, filed *Ayers v. Fordice* US 970 F.2d 1378 (1975; 1992) and *US v. Fordice* 505 US 717 (1992, 1996, 2000, 2002) that forced Mississippi to strengthen its three public HBCUs and desegregate the TWIs.

On 11 May 1977, the State Board of Regents filed *A Plan for the Merger of Tennessee State University and the University of Tennessee-Nashville*. UTN students had the option of earning a degree from UT, subject to approval of the UT board of trustees. UTN faculty petitioned to transfer to the other UT campuses, but UTK refused their petition. UTN faculty, however, gained blanket tenure, rank, and salary protection in the merged TSU. Avon Williams filed Objections of Plaintiff-interveners to the Plan for the Merger, because there was no such protection for the current TSU president and black faculty:

> The plan was generated by the current Chancellor [Roy S. Nicks] of said State Board of Regents who has a blatant conflict of interest in his former relationships with UT and UTN; and, he has been inimical towards the legitimate interests of TSU in all his actions during the history and trial of this case, including his testimony. His adversary position is clearly reflected in the composition of said entire proposal which he prepared and submitted to the State Board of Regents for its approval and submission to this court.[15]

David Lipscomb College, Peabody College, Belmont College, Murray State University, University of Georgia, Austin Peay, MTSU, Memphis State, Vanderbilt, Trevecca College, and the University of New Mexico.

[14] Note: UTN had almost no full-time black faculty members or black administrators.

[15] *Sterlin Adams, Raymond Richardson, et al., Objections of Plaintiff Interveners to the Plan for the Merger*, federal district court of middle Tennessee, 1977, Avon N. Williams, Jr., Papers, Special Collections, TSU.

Although state officials had tried in 1968 to stop TSU student activism, the student leadership in the 1970s continued their quest to save TSU from "white control." Student Government Association President Bryan Williams met with Nicks about anti-TSU remarks that seemed to "downgrade black students that face historical disadvantages that make them and other blacks low academic achievers; but this is far from true for the majority of TSU's student body."[16]

After the Merger

President Frederick S. Humphries held a staff/faculty meeting in Kean Hall to give information about the merger, which he believed was forthright and just. Reminiscent of 1943, state officials impounded $475,000 of TSU's money. They claimed TSU had padded the enrollment figures by admitting 912 students that should have been on academic suspension. In reality, the faculty Committee on Academic Suspension annually interviewed suspended students and recommended another semester to improve their grade point averages. But rumors said the governor and SBR officials planned to fire Humphries.[17]

Sterlin Adams, Richardson, some TSU faculty members, and some members of the Tennessee Caucus of Black State Legislators organized a caravan of citizens (3–4 buses) to attend the next SBR meeting. In a crowd with Governor Ray Blanton (D), Nicks, and black legislators walked with their heads down. Blanton was a former US congressman who sharpened his political teeth among rural, white, west Tennesseans. The FBI was investigating Blanton for corruption in office. Instead, the Regents placed Humphries on probation for fiscal mismanagement and unsolved problems at TSU, giving him nine months to solve the problems.[18] He and his staff would have to prepare an extensive response report like state auditors had forced W.J. Hale and W.S. Davis to do.

---

[16] Tennessee, State Board of Regents, Nashville, 11 May 1977, *A Plan for the Merger of Tennessee State University and the University of Tennessee-Nashville*; Avon Williams, Jr., Nashville, 22 June 1977, Objections of Plaintiff-Interveners to the Plan for the Merger, filled in District Court, Middle Tennessee, Nashville, *Geier* Files. Bryan Williams, president of TSU SGA, meeting with Chancellor Nicks, in Avon N. Williams, Jr., Papers, which also contain *Geier* Files for the late senator's law office, Special Collections, TSU.

[17] Lea A. Overstreet, "Readers reminisce about Tennessee State University," Nashville *Tennessean*, Davidson AM edition, 9 February 2009, 5.

[18] TSU, *The Meter*, September 1977, 1; see mf 40, folder 7, SACS, 1977, Governor (Leonard) Ray Blanton Papers 1975–79, GP 52, TSLA; photos of the president, TSU, *Tennessean, Yearbook*, 18–19. Note: during the Blanton administration, James Earl Ray, the man convicted of killing Martin Luther King, Jr., escaped from prison but was recaptured before he could leave the country. Gov. Blanton was convicted of selling pardons to the highest bidders in the Tennessee prison system. Fred S. Rolater, "Leonard Ray Blanton (1930–96)," *Tennessee Encyclopedia of History and Culture*, 70–71.

Associates and mentors in Atlanta, Nashville and Washington, DC, who actively observed the exchange of leadership positions at the HBCUs and who knew Humphries from his Thirteen Curriculum days reportedly told Dr. Humphries to stay put and let them handle the situation. A local officer of Alpha Phi Alpha Fraternity sent a letter (8 July 1977) to Governor Blanton: "We also believe that Dr. Humphries received some bad advice on his arrival as a new person from outside the state. But we believe, after talking to him, Humphries will become a great administrator. We are asking you and the State Board of Regents to consider an extension of time for him to do the job."[19] He reminded Blanton that four state legislators and Congressman Harold E. Ford (class of 1967) were members of Alpha Phi Alpha. Blanton replied, "I know there is not a move to replace black leadership at Tennessee State with white leadership. I am personally committed to having strong black educators in our state system, and I know that Dr. Nicks and the board are equally committed." A letter addressed from the past executive secretary of the Southern Association of Colleges and Schools (SACS) asked for information on news reports that the SBR had passed a June 24 resolution relative to the effectiveness or ineffectiveness of Dr. Frederick Humphries as president of TSU. The SACS letter was copied to THEC and SBR, raising alarm that Tennessee officials' attack on TSU may jeopardize SACS accreditation. State officials rushed a letter in return with Governor Blanton's signature, saying the SBR did not place Humphries on probation, but merely advised him of their concern and their expectations on problems to be cleaned up in admissions, records and business affairs.[20]

At parties, receptions and meetings, Sterlin Adams took charge of gaining Avon Williams's political support. Adams cultivated very close ties to all members of the Tennessee Black Caucus, and Humphries became one of the most politically skilled of TSU's presidents. Humphries sent materials on the proposed health and physical education building to them so they could pressure other legislative leaders, the governor and other state officials. Adams enclosed a copy of the $10 million capital fund request to the State Building Commission. Avon Williams was very close to Lt. Governor John Wilder who chaired the Building Commission.

---

[19] Gordon W. Sweet, ex secretary of SACS, Atlanta, 6 August 1977, to Gov. Ray Blanton; Gov. Blanton to Sweet, Nashville, 11 August, 1977; E. Harper Johnson, president of Tau Lambda Chapter of Alpha Phi Alpha Fraternity to Gov. R. Blanton, 8 July 1977, Governor (Leonard) Ray Blanton Papers 1975–79, GP 52, TSLA; "Scope and content note," 1–2, and mf 40, folder 7, SACS, 1977, box 6, folder 16, State Board of Regents, 1975–76 folder 16, UTN, folder 9–10, Governor (Leonard) Ray Blanton Papers, GP 52.

[20] Ibid.; Kenneth W. Goings, "Harold Eugene Ford (1945–)," *Tennessee Encyclopedia of History and Culture*, 318–19.

The student leadership had been involved in this fight, too. Marcus Lucas president of the TSU Student Government Association (1974–75) and his officers helped by sending a letter to Senator Williams, saying the students on the TSU campus were the recipients of the discomforts, inconveniences, limitations on programming, and constraints on future potential and success. Williams requested and received a detailed state funding report on the TSU facilities.[21]

The TSU-friendly state legislators and the Black Caucus put through the funding bills for a building for the business program, new president's house, new track and field facility, new physical education and convocation building, new library, renovation of the old library, renovation of Harned Science Hall, and a new engineering building. In the summer of 1977, the Brown-Daniel Memorial Library opened on the former site of the Alumni Building. The three-story facility included carrels for faculty and graduate students, a large classroom for demonstrations, offices, a space for special collections, and space for expanded holdings. Evelyn P. Fancher, director of university libraries, worked hard on improving the conduct of the students who used the new facility, and expanding the library's holdings and special collections. The old Memorial Library was renovated and converted into the Learning Resources Center (LRC), housing the new University College, which the Humphries administration created in 1982 to more effectively administer the general education program and reduce student attrition. LRC also housed the Honors Program, the campus radio station, and the University Media Center. The Lewis Holland School of Business Building was constructed in 1977 and located on the western boundary of the campus on the south side of Centennial Boulevard. McKissack architects designed the three-story brick business building including office suites, large lecture halls, and classrooms. The facility was dedicated on 17 October 1978, and named for Lewis R. Holland the head of business programs (1949–72). The Humphries family was the first to live in the new President's Home, a one-story modern ranch style that opened in 1977 at a cost of $82,000. Goodwill Manor had sat vacant since the Torrence family moved into one of the teachers' cottages.[22]

The 400-meter, eight-lane Edward S. Temple Track facility was opened on the north campus on April 8. Harned Science Hall and McCord Hall for biology

---

[21] Marcus Lucas, SGA President, TSU, 6 May 1975, to Senator Avon N. Williams, Jr.; THEC Report on Facilities, 1975, to Senator Avon N. Williams, Jr., 1975, Williams Papers, Special Collections, TSU.

[22] Goodwill Manor was placed on the National Register of Historic Places on 25 March 1982, by the US Department of Interior, National Park Service, torn down in 1986, and a replica costing $450,000, including $80,000 in contributions from alumni and friends, was built and dedicated on 30 April 1992. Tennessee State University, *Alumni Directory, 1995*, 1–10.

programs underwent renovation. The university built the huge physical education and convocation center on the site formerly occupied by East Hall for Men and the old Men's Vocational Trade Building. Dedication of the Howard Gentry, Sr., Physical Education Center Complex took place on 2 December 1980, and included a 14,000-seat arena, indoor track named for Olympic star Wilma G. Rudolph, dance studio, and an eight-lane indoor pool named for former Tiger Sharks Coach Thomas Hughes.[23]

Meanwhile, the UTN campus was in uproar over Gray's merger decision. UTN Chancellor Smith shared US Justice Department and federal court documents with faculty/staff. The UTN dean of arts and sciences included on his agenda a "status report concerning the court case, *Geier vs. Blanton*." Smith said," because the merger was to take place by 1 July 1979, if the district court's order was reversed by the Sixth Circuit, or even the US Supreme Court, UT defendants would find themselves in the unenviable position of having a clear right to operate UTN for which it has no available faculty, no funding, no property, no students, no administrators, and no hope of unscrambling an accomplished merger." On 30 May 1977, Smith shared the April 4 transcript of the discussion of a state appeal by THEC. On June 21, Smith sent a memorandum to faculty/staff, writing that the last filing to the court made by Avon Williams in the desegregation litigation has been distributed; "if you would like to review that material, please check with your dean or director." On June 22, Smith sent another copy of the desegregation litigation by counsel for the plaintiffs with a copy of Judge Gray's response.[24]

SBR Chancellor Roy Nicks sent a memorandum to Smith on June 29, notifying him of the decision to go ahead, implement the plan, and form merger committee appointments by 7 July 1977. Smith wrote to Nicks to say that he declined to send any merger committee appointments during the UT appeal of the case. Smith continued to send copies of his letters to UTN faculty and staff members. One of the letters on August 23 announced that Judge Gray had denied the UT motion for a stay in the implementation of the merger plan. On September 13, Smith sent the faculty members a copy of UT's motion to the Sixth Circuit. UTN officials prepared a two-page statement and *Notice to UTN Students* to be read to telephone callers: "The University will continue to make every effort to have the merger decision reversed. It [UT] does feel that it is important for students to be aware of the possibilities." On 10 February 1978, a UTN dean

---

[23] History and photographs of TSU facilities and buildings, Special Collections, TSU.

[24] Copies of the letters of Chancellor Smith and other UT–Nashville administrators corresponding about Avon Williams and the unfolding *Geier* case, used in this paragraph, are in the Lovett Papers, as a result of Lovett—while Dean of the College of Arts and Sciences at TSU, 1988–2000—recovering and storing boxes of UT-Nashville correspondence left behind in Dean Zuzak's office, TSU Downtown Campus.

sent the faculty a copy of a recent WSM-TV newscast featuring the UT legal counsel's appeal. A white student at UTN, Yvonne Wood, had worked in the governor's office and attended UTN at night, graduating in 1978. She recalled spending "many hours having lively discussions about the court case with my major professor, Dr. Coleman McGinnis." He said, "When I was hired at UTN in 1972, I was aware of the lawsuit."[25]

In September 1978, SGA members conducted a march to the state Capitol, protesting bad conditions on the TSU campus. The students called President Humphries to a meeting asking him to respond personally to continuing problems in the registration process, constant breakdown of air conditioning equipment, physical condition of the dormitories, and poor service and food preparation in the cafeteria. It seemed that state officials were trying to bring the HBCU to its knees before any merger went into effect. But SGA President Winfred Jenkins (1978–79) said the president has been at the university long enough to foresee problems that may occur; the administration should use preventive maintenance to deal with potential problems and breakdowns. They said the administration had poor communications with the students. Humphries said he had scheduled regular meetings with the SGA leadership to hear student concerns. Humphries sent a letter to Nicks asking for an increase in appropriations because even with a 10 percent fee increase TSU would suffer a $600,000 deficit, forcing more cuts in services and personnel.[26]

On 15 December 1978, the FBI seized the office of Governor Blanton's chief aide T. Edward Sisk in an investigation of cash-for–clemency. These officials, and perhaps others, were carrying on with corruption that was typical in Tennessee government, but they had become arrogant in their efforts to enrich themselves. Federal prosecutors brought Sisk and Governor Blanton before a grand jury on December 23; yet, on 15 January 1979, Blanton pardoned 52 prisoners. On January 17, the state's constitutional officers agreed to force Blanton out immediately. They installed Lamar Alexander (R), who had won election the

---

[25] Ibid.; Yvonne Wood to Bruce Rogers, Lebanon, Tennessee, 18 April 2012; Coleman McGinnis, in his own words, *The Geier Symposium*, 11, 15.

[26] Note: TSU had to hire a dynasty of lower-level white state bureaucrats from state comptroller and treasury offices, and one of them was a former UTN student, with no graduate degree. They appointed him vice president of finance and business at TSU. He later received a TSU degree. Under the guise of affirmative action for whites as part of the 1984 *Geier* merger agreement, Nicks and SBR aggressively balanced administrative positions along lines of race at TSU, but less so at the TWIs, while state officials put a financial squeeze on TSU's black administration before and after the implementation of the merger.

previous November, as the new governor. Blanton was convicted in 1981, went to federal prison in 1986, served 10 years, and died in 1996.[27]

In 1979, SGA President Winfred W. Jenkins sent a letter to the new Governor: "Be assured we do not wish, nor intend at this time, to question the integrity of any officials having oversight authority for our University though we will remain vigilant."[28] Humphries held late-night meetings in the President's Home with campus activists and friends of TSU. He informed them of problems and threats from state officials. Friends took the matters to Black Caucus members, other state and federal officials. The Black Caucus members attended a meeting in Humphries's office and learned that state officials had withheld money that had been appropriated to address TSU problems. On February 17, they failed to repeal the out-of-state student limit.[29]

On 1 July 1979, the faculty and student body of the two institutions merged amicably. The 1979–81, *General Catalog, Tennessee State University,* read:

> The present-day Tennessee State University exists as a result of the merger on July 1, 1979, of the former Tennessee State University and the University of Tennessee at Nashville. The General Assembly sanctioned the UTN as a bona fide campus of UT in 1971, and the new university occupied its quarters in the then recently completed building at the corner of 10th and Charlotte … It was the erection of the above-mentioned building which gave rise to a decade-long litigation to 'dismantle the dual system' of higher education in Tennessee which culminated in the court ordered merger by Judge Frank Gray in February 1977. The missions of the two universities … were … compatible due to their historic backgrounds or connection to a land-grant institution.[30]

TSU had to continue using the UTN campus and give tenure to UTN faculty.[31]

---

[27] Rolater, "Leonard Ray Blanton," *Tennessee Encyclopedia of History and Culture,* 70–71.

[28] Winfred W. Jenkins, SGA President, TSU, to Gov. Lamar Alexander, no date, Williams Papers; legal counsel series, 55 boxes, Blanton Papers, GP 52; and see: Tennessee Commission for human development, 1976–81, box 15, folder 13, board of regents, box 26, folder 4, Lamar Alexander education proposals, 1979–81, box 100, folder 16, Tennessee State University, 1986, box 662, folder 8, correspondence, box 677, folder 3, higher education–T.S.U-U.T.N. Merger proposal, 1979, box 682, folder 12, Southern Regional Education Board, 1983–84 box 693, folder 1, University of Tennessee, 1982–85, box 695, folder 6, Martin Luther King, Jr., Tennessee Holiday Commission, 1985, box 738, folder 9, lawsuits–*Geier v. Alexander,* 1984, box 795, folder 4, Tennessee State University, 1981, box 816, folder 7, Francis Guess, photographs, series 14, box 893, folder 13, black caucus and legislation 1981–83, box 896, folder 3, Gov. Lamar Alexander Papers, 1979–87, GP 53, TSLA.

[29] See Senator Williams's bills, Williams Papers, Special Collections, TSU.

[30] *General Catalog, Tennessee State University, 1979–81,* introductory pages.

[31] TSU-UTN merger proposal, 1979, box 682, folder 12, Gov. Lamar Alexander Papers, 1979–87, GP 53.

President Emeritus Walter S. Davis died on 17 October 1979 in the Hubbard Hospital at nearby Meharry Medical College. They held the funeral at First Baptist Church, Capitol Hill, where Davis served on the board of deacons. TSU held memorial services in the auditorium on Friday, October 19, with the body on view. Humphries said, "It was under Dr. Davis's leadership that the ground work was laid for what has become known as 'A Touch of Greatness' at Tennessee State University."[32] Davis recently had taken a photograph with the late president Hale's youngest son, sitting on a rail, their backs to the Cumberland shores. Davis, perhaps like former President Hale, also died with a broken heart, feeling betrayed by Tennessee's officials.

The SGA president wrote letters to the Black Caucus again complaining about the conditions of the TSU physical facilities. In March 1980, President Humphries held a tour of the campus for Senator Avon Williams and other state legislators. Williams persuaded the mayor to make city improvements, including more streetlights and sidewalks in the TSU area, part of William's 19th State Senate District. TSU secured some capital project appropriations.[33]

Some former UTN faculty formed a formidable group of dissidents in the merged TSU. They held their meetings at the downtown campus as many of them refusing to move to the main campus. They complained about ill treatment as whites. They pooled their money and hired a lawyer and constantly fought Humphries and his vice president of academic affairs, Bernard Crowell. They used open, arrogant, and clandestine tactics, and seemingly had ready access to the Nashville *Tennessean* and Roy Nicks. At a faculty-staff forum, President Humphries was compelled to say, "Those who continue to engage in adversarial activities … at the institution will demonstrate that loyalties have not been extended to an expanded university. This cuts both ways. When there are adversarial activities, there should be an expectation of adversarial responses. The cheek, regardless of how pious the bearer, is only going to turn so often."[34]

Former governor of California Ronald Reagan took office as President of the United States on 20 January 1981. Racial and fiscal conservatives in America were giddy about the victory—which they called the Reagan Revolution—that appeared to signal a triumph over American liberalism. The Reagan revolutionaries intended to dismantle New Deal and Great Society programs and stop the civil rights revolution. They put a cooperative black man, Clarence Thomas, in charge of making ineffective the US Civil Rights Commission. They proposed reducing taxes on the wealthy classes and ending the regulatory

---

[32] W.S. Davis Memorial Services, TSU, 19 October 1979, 1–2, Special Collections, TSU; *Tennessean* yearbook, 1987, 35.

[33] Humphries File, correspondence, 1979–80, Special Collections, TSU.

[34] Humphries File, TSU Faculty-Staff Forum, President's Remarks, 24 March 1981, Special Collections, TSU.

restraints on capitalism to allow the conservatives to get as much money and political power as needed to control America. But through *Adams, Geier* and other court cases, the HBCUs continued to do battle with the former Jim Crow states and their officials.[35]

Senator Williams began to feud with Governor Lamar Alexander (R) and with THEC's director Arliss Roaden about the appearance of poor treatment for the state's HBCUs, TSU and Meharry Medical College. The THEC turned down seven TSU capital requests and gave only four of them a priority recommendation to the legislature. Alexander cut HBCU items in the state budget even though heavily white UT received a long list of set asides from state appropriations. Especially indicative of racial insensitivity was the treatment of Meharry that had helped Tennessee officials since 1941 provide Jim Crow scholarships to train black medical professionals. Though the TWIs still failed to produce enough black doctors, the governor felt Meharry did not deserve state funds.[36]

Tennessee State University acquired the old state girls' school property as surplus state property in 1982. TSU later converted the old dormitories, buildings and grounds into the Heiman Street campus to house certain services including police and security, personnel, printing and business services, and apartment housing for students. The plaza in front of the Joseph Payne Student Union Building was completed and dedicated on 16 April 1982 for alumnus Hazael E. Welton, who contributed $100,000 to the university. Senator Williams sponsored SB 289 (1983) for projects to renovate the administration building including energy conservation, improvement of the electrical distribution system, steam lines, building cattle barns, planning a new stadium, and building a general services building.[37] Despite the *Geier* battle, TSU and Humphries were moving ahead.

SBR universities had a negative racial disparity of certificates, associate, bachelors, and doctoral degrees awarded to blacks and whites; blacks received 13

---

[35] "Don't You Wish You Were White?" Bobby L. Lovett, *The Civil Rights Movement in Tennessee: A Narrative History* (Knoxville: University of Tennessee Press, 2005) 403–10.

[36] Ibid., 373–79; and see the Williams Papers.

[37] Humphries Papers, Special Collections, TSU. Note: J. Frankie Pierce, leader of the local Colored Women's Clubs, persuaded the state to open the Tennessee Vocational School for Colored Girls on 9 October 1923. The 63-acre campus at 2700 Heiman Street employed 69 workers to supervise girls 12–15 years old from across the state. The school became integrated in 1966. After Pierce's death in 1954, Mattie Coleman, Mattie Flowers, Dorothy Read, Virginia Edmondson, and Marlene Howlett served as directors until 1979. Virginia Edmondson, "J. Frankie Pierce and the Tennessee Vocational School for Colored Girls (1923–79)," Bobby L. Lovett and Linda T. Wynn, eds., *Profiles of African Americans in Tennessee* (Nashville: Local Conference on African American Culture and History, 1996) 102–03.

(4.6 percent) of 279 doctoral degrees issued by the public TWIs from 1982–83. Excluding TSU, blacks comprised a small percentage of students enrolled at public TWIs. A plan to increase the number of black doctorates and the supply of black faculty was presented to the THEC Desegregation Monitoring Committee.[38]

On 16 June 1981, Williams sent a letter to Nicks, saying "the Tennessee Voters Council fully supported TSU and its black administration and faculty, and that full and substantial and other support should be afforded to provide the highest quality of education at said institution," notwithstanding its predominantly black staff. Jamye C. Williams, the head of the department of communications at TSU, was the Tennessee Voters Council (TVC) secretary.[39]

On June 17, Williams wrote to Nicks questioning the cutting of certain TSU degree programs. Nicks said Humphries and staff had approved certain changes although the Regents had not yet accepted all recommendations. On September 12, at the TVC quarterly meeting, Williams wrote to Humphries that TVC and the Black Caucus were getting for TSU all that they possibly could from the state, based on the formula. He urged them to bring the matter up in the federal court hearing on desegregation November 22–24. TVC sent a protest to Alexander, Nicks, and the THEC. State officials allowed the duplication of TSU degree programs at TWIs Middle Tennessee State University and Austin Peay State University.[40]

President Humphries was forced to cut the budget another $1.5 million. He formed a faculty committee led by professor of business James A. Ellzy to give advice on the cuts. They recommended three phases of budget cuts, including cutting 20 percent of the personnel over three years. In a letter to a TSU supporter dated 13 March 1982, Nicks said the state treated TSU fairly and equally, according to a THEC funding formula and TSU's 6,350 FTE students.[41]

Many Davidson County college students continued the flight 30 miles to MTSU. Again, 99 percent of first-time, white freshmen refused to even consider a minority college. Avon Williams and the NAACP-Legal Defense Fund prepared a motion for further relief through the federal court. Black plaintiffs complained of the lack of progress by Tennessee in affording equal access of black students, faculty, and staff at the TWIs. The dissident faculty (mostly former UTN faculty

---

[38] THEC, "Outline of a Plan to Increase the Number of Black Doctorates and the Supply of Black Faculty for Colleges and Universities in Tennessee," 21 November 1983, 2 February 1985, 1–10, tables 5–6.

[39] Note: Upon retirement from TSU, Jayme Williams deposited the TVC Records in the Special Collections, TSU.

[40] Tennessee Voter Council Files, 1981–82, J. Coleman Williams, secretary, Special Collections, TSU.

[41] Correspondence and Documents, 1982, Humphries File, Special Collections, TSU.

members) at TSU employed a lawyer to file their own motion, claiming the merged TSU remained a predominantly black institution and TSU had an inferior education delivery system.

The Black Caucus began plans to enhance TSU. The initiatives included establishment of a research center, construction of a general services building on the campus, and full transfer of the UTN downtown campus property to the control of TSU. Caucus members helped with the problem of the unfair allocation of land-grant and federal agriculture funds. They sponsored a resolution opposing state funding of any agriculture research, extension services, or other agriculture programs at any land-grant institution unless [TSU] received an equitable amount.[42]

President Reagan endorsed the ongoing White House Initiative for Enhancing HBCUs, and though publicly expressing his reservation that Martin Luther King, Jr., was not a hero, Reagan signed the Martin Luther King, Jr., National Holiday bill in 1983. Under Governor Alexander and State Commissioner Francis Guess (TSU alumnus, BS, 1972, MBA 1974) Tennessee approved the King holiday in 1985. OCR still maintained that states may not place unfair burdens on black students and faculty, and public HBCUs could not be merged or closed without OCR review. The Justice Department had few objections, if any, to the TSU-UTN merger.[43]

Tennessee State University increasingly found itself deep in America's racial milieu. In Nashville, 85 percent of whites lived in predominantly white neighborhoods, and 72 percent of blacks lived in predominantly black neighborhoods. Nashville's wealthiest whites isolated themselves from the masses of blacks and the poor, working-, and middle-class whites. Nashville was in turmoil after plaintiffs' attorney Avon Williams convinced the Sixth Circuit Court of Appeals to overturn the 1982 revision of the Nashville-Davidson County Metro schools desegregation plan. A new plan was implemented, but this would cause more white resentment and white flight. Pearl-Cohn Public High School near TSU had 95 percent black students.[44]

The nation's TWIs began to hire small numbers of black faculty/staff members between 1969 and 1985, reaching an average of 5 percent black faculty. Tennessee HBCUs averaged 20 percent white faculty members. After the merger, black faculty declined from 71.6 percent to 51 percent at TSU. Vanderbilt

---

[42] See the Avon Williams Papers, 1982–83.

[43] Francis Guess, photographs, series 14, box 893, folder 13, Martin Luther King, Jr., Tennessee Holiday Commission, 1985, box 738, folder 9, Alexander Papers, GP 53.

[44] Lovett, "After Geier and the Merger: Desegregation of Higher Education in Tennessee Continues," *Civil Rights Movement*, 371–401; Shelby State/State Technical Merger [Memphis-Shelby County], 1978–82, box 691, folder 5, black caucus and legislation, box 896, folder 3, Gov. Alexander Papers, GP 53.

University minimized the number of black students and faculty to 3–5 percent. The University of Tennessee-Knoxville had 2.4 percent black faculty in 1981 compared to 2.7 percent in 1975, and at UTK fewer than 6 percent of the students enrolled were black, but there were plenty of black athletes and no black coaches. Memphis State University increased its black faculty from 3.2 percent in 1975 to 3.5 percent by 1981. Whites comprised nearly 30 percent of the students at TSU. Chancellor Nicks said that the small-town locations of many TWIs were a barrier to the recruitment and retention of black faculty: "I am not satisfied with the progress we have made in faculty recruitment. I think that suggests ... a more affirmative stance [is needed] in regard to recruiting minority faculty."[45]

Clarence B. Robinson, head of the Black Caucus, said, "It may be that they [whites] do not know what we consider *racism*. They may be sincere in what they are doing, but they are passing up the best opportunity to contribute to integration efforts in Nashville I have seen yet."[46]

Humphries moved the TSU School of Business to the downtown campus on 1 July 1979, hoping that by offering an MBA degree program that TSU could outgrow the competing new school of business at TWI Belmont College in south Nashville. Also, white Davidson County students were driving thirty miles to heavily white MTSU instead of attending business classes on the main TSU campus in heavily black north Nashville. Some TSU students marched on President Humphries's office to prevent the School of Business moving from the main campus to the former UTN campus (where it exists today). Many felt the main campus students would be *bussed* downtown for the convenience of white students, who reportedly did not want to take classes in heavily black north Nashville. SGA President Georgette Peek believed the decision disguised another takeover attempt. Under severe pressure from both sides of *Geier*, Humphries told a student protest delegation that TSU could not continue as "solely a black institution." Roy Nicks and SBR forced TSU to drop all students who did not pay their registration fees on time. Amid these difficulties, Humphries made a plea to

---

[45] Staff, "Uneven employment: TSU Has Most Black Teachers, Officials," Nashville *The Tennessean*, 29 December 1981, 1, 4.

[46] Ibid., 378, 379; Moses Freeman, "An Interview with Clarence B. Robinson," Chattanooga, April 1983, http://www.tnstate.edu/library/digital/interview.htm, 1–5, 3 September 2004, Special Collections, TSU; Sterlin Adams, "Tennessee Planning for Desegregation in Public Higher Education and Black Citizen Reaction and Interaction: A Critical Review of *Geier vs. Blanton* from a Black Perspective," unpublished paper, Tennessee State University, Nashville, Special Collections, TSU; and see Reginald Stuart, *Black Perspectives on State-Controlled Higher Education: The Tennessee Report* (New York: John Hay Whitney Foundation, November 1973) 1–23.

Senator Williams. On 15 January 1983, Williams responded that he found the state rule being applied without regard to race but his hands were tied.[47]

Williams was still angry with Gov. Alexander for cutting state grants for Meharry, funds for TSU, and for vetoing special appropriation bills sponsored by the Black Caucus and Williams. Alexander returned letters explaining that he was leaving only monies in the appropriation bills that satisfied the stipulation of the court-ordered merger.[48]

Meanwhile, in 1983, the USDOE, Office of Civil Rights, called for a new round of five-year state higher education plans. Former Jim Crow states needed more specific plans. Again, Tennessee remained under the *Geier* case, and Tennessee officials did as little as possible to truly desegregate the state's higher education system to favor equality of education for the black citizens. The Tennessee Desegregation Monitoring Committee report (1983) recommended that the University of Tennessee and Memphis State University develop proposals to continue to desegregate graduate and professional education. Some 80 percent of Tennessee's minority faculty and administrators still were concentrated at Tennessee State University that also had 32.5 percent white administrators, 10.48 percent other race faculty, and 39.6 percent white faculty. Black administrators represented 5.3 percent of the 1,190 administrators in Tennessee's public TWIs, excluding the ones at TSU. Blacks, including persons not of African-American descent [descended from the 1865 Emancipation of slaves], numbered only 3.5 percent of the 5,755 faculty members in Tennessee's public colleges and universities. The percentage of black professional employees in Tennessee institutions had declined since 1981. Tennessee's total black graduates at all levels had declined between 1981 and 1983. Tennessee's higher education governing boards had 5.9 percent blacks (not 17 percent) on the staff and two black persons on the Desegregation Monitoring Committee. Dissidents argued that a too-black TSU was the problem.[49]

UTN Constituents Rebel Against Merged TSU

Upon the retirement of Judge Frank Gray, Jr., in 1978, Thomas A. Wiseman, a longtime Democratic state politician and former state treasurer, took charge of the *Geier* case. President Jimmy Carter (D) of Georgia had nominated Wiseman to that political patronage seat. Wiseman publicly proclaimed a dislike of alumni,

---

[47] Letters exchanged between Humphries and Williams, January–March 1983, Avon Williams Papers.

[48] Avon Williams Papers, exchange of letters between Williams and Governor Alexander, 1983.

[49] Tennessee Desegregation Monitoring Committee, 1983 Report, 1–32, Avon Williams Papers; note: boxes of yet-to-be cataloged *Geier* Papers are part of the Williams Papers.

students, and faculty members who labeled the merged TSU as an HBCU. Thus Wiseman supported his fellow Tennessee politicians. He allowed the UTN dissidents to become plaintiffs in the *Geier* case. Judge Gray had refused to do so.[50] One of the leaders of the dissident group, Coleman McGinnis, a political science faculty member, recalled "But as the actual implementation of the merger evolved, I became convinced that the State, especially TBR, was not living up to its responsibilities to ensure that the 'expanded TSU' would carry on the missions of both institutions. In fact, both the white and adult [mostly white] enrollment dropped precipitously over the next four years." In the summer of 1984, Wiseman approved a Stipulation of Settlement. TSU Student Government President Tony Spratten (1984–85) led a protest march to the federal courthouse. He said, "We have got to have faith and have a dream." TSU student Rossi Turner said, "TSU is being singled out." Part of the *Settlement* apparently was written by white dissidents: "SBR will within 180 days develop at TSU an Institute of Government, funded through the normal budgetary process." Even the US Attorney complained of the obvious racial bias against the HBCU, TSU:

> Item K, the establishment of an Institute of Government relates itself to none of the five objectives and should be eliminated. Further, it would have the effect of weakening a department, which needs to be strengthened; namely, Government and Public Affairs—the department to be designated as the home of the Ph.D. program in Public Administration and a projected Ph.D. program in Political Science. This item is simply out of place in a document, which aims to correct segregation woes in the entire state by pinpointing one program in one institution, Tennessee State University.... There is no *Race Relations Institute* for MTSU, Memphis State, UT, or any of the white institutions. The true test of the validity of the remedies proposed is whether they fit or are related to the purposes and objectives.[51]

Sam Ingram, president of MTSU, objected to transferring black and white teachers between MTSU and TSU to achieve a better racial balance. Some teachers at MTSU wanted to relocate to TSU in the big city of Nashville. Black professors did not want to move to MTSU in small-town Murfreesboro. MTSU had nine full-time black faculty members and 859 black students out of 11,369 total students. TSU had 34 percent white enrollment. Still, Ingram seemed to

---

[50] Cassandra Spratling, "Proud Heritage on Hold: Black Colleges Defining a New Role," *Detroit Free Press*, 8, 9, 10 May 1983, A1-8A; McGinnis remarks, *The Geier Symposium*, 18 April 2012, 11.

[51] Academic Deans Executive Council, Tennessee State University, Nashville, 8 August 1984, to Nathaniel Douglass, Attorney for Plaintiff Intervenors, USA, Civil Rights Division, Department of Justice, Washington, DC, 1–4, Lovett Papers; Beth Clayton, "SGA President Tony Spratten led protest march to federal Courthouse," *Nashville Banner*, 28 August 1984.

want to keep things the way they were. He insensitively said, "If our students need additional graduate programs, it bothers me that they will have to be denied. And just going to TSU may not help."[52]

On July 26, Humphries had complained to Senator Williams that THEC officials had not approved the TSU proposal for a master's degree in nursing. They claimed Nashville did not need another nursing degree as Vanderbilt University had such a program.[53] MTSU was allowed to continue to duplicate TSU graduate programs.

About a week after Wiseman's approval of the *Settlement*, Chancellor Nicks gave SBR directives to the campus presidents. Each president would continue to be held accountable for progress, or the lack thereof, toward achievement of all desegregation goals, which included: making recruiting visits to other race high schools; encouraging, employing, and involving persons of other races in all programs and activities; increasing efforts to attract and employ other race faculty and administrators; and including progress in affirmative action as a factor in the review of department heads, deans, and vice presidents. Nicks took time to write a strong letter (5 October 1984) to President Humphries. He would have to begin immediately to implement the stipulations. Rumors swirled that Humphries was leaving and had told his confidantes that he had done all he could do at Tennessee State and that it was time for him to move on. Besides, instead of continuing to battle in Tennessee, Humphries had an opportunity to serve perhaps as president of Florida A&M University, his alma mater.[54]

The TSU Council of Deans blasted the *Settlement* as biased against Tennessee State University, especially the placement of TSU's administrative appointments under the domain of Roy Nicks and the SBR, which would ensure hiring fewer blacks that were equally or better qualified compared to average and mediocre non-black candidates. The TSU deans argued that the *Settlement* "omits reference to the poor desegregation record of other state institutions of higher education in Tennessee such as MSU, which is located in a service area [Memphis] that exceeds 40 percent African American population." Memphis State University had no black department heads among 45 positions, had a large

---

[52]"MTSU-TSU faculty swapping," Nashville *Banner*, 8, 29 August 1984, 3; *Rita Sanders Geier, et al, Plaintiffs, USA, Plaintiff-Intervener, Raymond Richardson Jr., et al., Plaintiff-Interveners, H. Coleman McGinnis, et al., Plaintiff-Interveners v. Lamar Alexander, et al. Defendants*, in US District Court for the Middle Tennessee District, Nashville, 1–8, 25 September 1984, Lovett Papers.

[53] Humphries to Williams, July 26, 1984, Nashville, Williams Papers; Jewell Winn, "The Geier Consent Decree Year: Fulfilled or Unfulfilled Promises?" (PhD diss., TSU, 2008) 1–242.

[54] Roy S. Nicks, Nashville, 4 October 1984, to all university presidents, Nicks to President F.S. Humphries, 5 October 1984, Nashville, Lovett Papers.

number of faculty members who appeared opposed to hiring black heads, and, later, suffered a racial discrimination lawsuit related to this problem. Avon Williams claimed MTSU was a haven for whites who simply did not want to attend predominantly black TSU. The TSU Deans' Council said the proposal that TSU cooperate with MTSU and Austin Peay State University to eliminate program duplication was hypocritical. SBR and THEC officials seemed to encourage the TWIs to compete *with* TSU's academic programming: The *Stipulation* "allows selfish, personal interests to be rewarded by providing for a specific program to be established at TSU that is the design of a particular group of plaintiff-interveners who stand to personally benefit from the establishment of such an autonomous [Institute of Government]."[55]

On August 24, the Interdenominational Ministers Fellowship of Nashville, "Concerned TSU Staff and Students and Concerned Citizens of the Greater Nashville Community" wrote,

> *Geier v. Alexander* was originally filed in 1968 to halt the continued expansion of the former UTN at the expense of Tennessee State University. It was never the goal of the earlier court actions to open the door for the eventual dismantling of TSU. However, much to our shock and disappointment, the door has been opened wide for the dismantling of TSU. The proposition before Judge Wiseman's court that TSU has become re-segregated is both false and ridiculous. The proposed *Stipulation* ... makes TSU, the victim of segregation, and a scapegoat in order to draw the attention ... away from the real issue in higher education in ... Tennessee: the hypocritical and token nature of desegregation that has taken place at the state's historically white institutions.   As a community, we say, 'stop picking on TSU,' and put the spotlight on [them] that continue to move at a snail's pace toward desegregation.[56]

The *Settlement* said, "SBR shall immediately establish a 1993 interim objective for Tennessee State University of 50 percent white full-time equivalent enrollment." TSU must have 50 percent white recruiters. The TWIs had to "utilize a black for recruiting other-race students." The state's public schools of veterinary medicine, dentistry, and pharmacy had to make special efforts to enroll and graduate black students. The *Settlement* seemed to place the burden of desegregation on the longtime victims of Jim Crow, but Wiseman stepped in and said, "The ultimate goal is *not* any ideal ratio of mix of black and white students

---

[55] Academic Deans Executive Council, TSU, Nashville, 8 August 1984, to Nathaniel Douglass, Attorney for Plaintiff-Intervenors, USA, Civil Rights Division, Department of Justice, 1–4, Lovett Papers.

[56] Interdenominational Ministers Fellowship of Nashville Concerned TSU Staff and Students, and Concerned Citizens of the Greater Nashville Community, 24 August 1984, 1–4, Lovett Papers.

or faculty. The goal is a system of higher education in ... [public] colleges and universities in which race is irrelevant, in which equal protection and equal application of the law is a reality."[57] It was a rhetorical statement, seemingly to please the public.

When the State Board of Regents made its report on 29 January 1985, the chancellor and TBR general counsel claimed that many of TSU's facilities were equal or better than those at many of the white universities. Some state officials inspected TSU campus facilities and used elaborate charts and square footage formula to claim TSU suffered "space under-utilization." TBR reports recommended some minor repairs and renovations for less than $4 million. The report included reports on program duplication and barriers to enhancing TSU and the plan for realignment of certain specified programs. TWIs continued to duplicate TSU degrees.[58]

Some, mostly white, faculty dissidents organized a Caucus for Excellence and Integrity in Higher Education and held a meeting on the old UTN campus on 18 April 1985. They invited a few blacks to integrate the caucus. They produced a "Position Paper: Issue: TSU in Crisis, Caucus for Excellence and Academic Integrity at TSU:"[59] "There is an enrollment crisis; there is a budget crisis; there is a crisis in the classroom; there is a crisis in university management ... [We need] an interim chief executive with a mandate, moral soundness, and academic integrity." However, SGA president-elect (1985–86) Augusto Macedo wrote a letter to the chair of this Caucus:

> I was nominated to serve on your Executive Committee, which I declined. I was deeply disturbed and highly dissatisfied with your organization, which is composed of Neo-Nazis. Your only goals are to condemn [TSU] and return

---

[57] *Rita Sanders Geier, et al., plaintiffs, United States of America, Plaintiff-Intervener, Raymond Richardson, Jr., et al., Plaintiff-Interveners, H. Coleman McGinnis, et al., Plaintiff-Interveners, vs. Lamar Alexander, et al., Defendants, No. 5077, Stipulation of Settlement,* 1984, district court middle Tennessee, 1–34, Special Collections, TSU. Bert C. Bach, vice chancellor for academic affairs, SBR, Nashville, to university presidents, 27 November 1984, Lovett Papers; Dr. Mary W. Burger to President Frederick S. Humphries, "Implementation Measures to Achieve Current Desegregation Objectives," 5 November 1984, 1–3, Special Collections, TSU; Bobby L. Lovett, "The TSU desegregation order," *Banner,* Opinions, 23 May 1985, A-22.

[58] Susan C. Short, General Counsel and Secretary, State Board of Regents, Nashville, 29 January 1985, to Attorneys George E. Barrett, Avon N. Williams, Jr., Richard Dinkins, John Norris, Nathaniel Douglas, et al.; Mary W. Burger, vice president of academic affairs, TSU, Nashville, to Bert C. Bach, vice chancellor for academic affairs, SBR, 10 December 1984, Lovett Papers.

[59] Caucus for Excellence and Academic Integrity at TSU, "Position Paper: Issue: TSU in Crisis, Caucus for Excellence and Academic Integrity at TSU," April 1985, 1–13 including appendices, Lovett Papers.

society to the 'Good Old Days' of white supremacy. I submit to you that, we the students of TSU will not allow your organization of educated Klansmen to direct or distort the future of Black Americans.[60]

The chair attached Macedo's letter to his letter, and sent it to Roy Nicks: "May I suggest that this letter makes Mr. Macedo's participation in selecting TSU's next president of dubious value."[61]

But on May 9, the Clarksville and Nashville branch NAACP officers addressed a letter "to whom addresses to whom this goes: "We come to you out of both humanitarian concern for the sense of justice and a sense of desperation in appeal to help us turn the tide of what we believe to be gross injustice to both a people and a historically landmark of Black Cultural Heritage."[62]

The Humphries Legacy at TSU

Phase I of the new Andrew P. Torrence Engineering Building opened on 29 April 1984. Governor Lamar Alexander attended the opening ceremony. No state funds arrived to help build Phase II for engineering after Torrence Hall opened. The old engineering building, McCord Hall (1950–), underwent renovation to accommodate undergraduate biology programs in the College of Arts and Sciences. Harned Hall (1927–) continued to house biology's research laboratories, classrooms, and graduate programs. Engineering retained some programs on the ground floor of the Industrial Arts Building (1933–) while the School of Allied Health Professions occupied top floors.

Humphries ended his TSU tenure on 30 June 1985. He left behind a good legacy: SACS re-accreditation, the accreditation of specific degree programs, new buildings for business, physical education, library, engineering, president's home, outdoor track facility, and other campus improvements, including renovations for Memorial Library, Harned Hall, and McCord Hall. He raised scholarship monies to counter student enrollment declines caused by state policies, awarded TSU's first doctorate degree in 1983, and expanded other degree programs. There was a new PhD program in public administration under an Institute of Government, an MS degree in mathematical sciences, a BS/BA degree in interdisciplinary studies, a new Cooperative Agricultural Research building, new computer centers for academics, administration, and social

---

[60] Augusto Macedo to Dr. John W. Cooke, TSU, 22 April 1986, Lovett Papers.

[61] J.W. Cooke, Chairman Caucus for Excellence and Academic Integrity to Dr. Roy Nicks, Chancellor, Board of Regents, 25 April 1986, Lovett Papers.

[62] James E. Yeary, Sr., and Charles L. Townshend, Jr., Clarksville and Nashville NAACP, 9 May 1990, to All Addresses to Whom This Goes, Nashville Branch Office NAACP, Lovett Papers.

sciences, and a new respiratory therapy program in the School of Allied Health Professions. Humphries recalled, "I went down [to Nashville] with the notion, hell: I want to have an opportunity to build a great institution. We never got judged on what we did; we got judged on what we took in."[63]

---

[63] Frederick S. Humphries, "Reflections," in James W. Smith, ed., *Leadership and Learning*, 115–120; Marjorie Caldwell, "Raising the window of accountability at FAMU," University *Faculty Voice* 5, no. 10 (June 2001): 1, 8. Note: Dr. Humphries remained skeptical about HBCU survival. "I don't meet many people who are willing to give black colleges a million dollars, or believe in what we're doing to the extent that they're willing to give us a million dollars."

8

1985–90: Roy P. Peterson and Otis L. Floyd: Readjustment

Tennessee State students—even if not all of them—protected some presidents but rose up against the ones that threatened the heritage of TSU, the HBCU. Whenever faculty and staff members remained silent, students launched protests, marches, loud opinions in *The Meter*, and held sit-in demonstrations. They were highly disciplined, peaceful, nonviolent, and endowed with the best among student leadership in the whole country. Tennessee State University owes a great deal to them.

In July 1985, rumors abounded on the Tennessee State campus that state authorities had selected Roy P. Peterson, a black official in the Kentucky regents system, to be the next president of TSU.[1] Black leaders in Nashville suspected his civil rights credentials and doubted Peterson's ability to understand their fight against Thomas Wiseman's *Geier* settlement. The student leaders remained as a vanguard against what many local blacks saw as not a settlement but an attack on the institution's HBCU legacy. White officials and dissidents refused to recognize any good in any institution—even a merged one—that was predominantly black.

In Kentucky, from where Peterson had arrived, Negro slaves once comprised a fourth of the population, and 26 percent of Kentuckians had owned slaves. The Kentucky slavocracy was the most reluctant among the 15 slave states to free the blacks at the end of the Civil War. After the Emancipation, and especially during the black northern migration (1890–1970), blacks rapidly migrated out of the impoverished state of Kentucky, so that by 1985, only 7.8 percent of the population was African American. Tennessee had a 26 percent black population in 1860 and 17 percent by 1985.[2]

Jim Crow and white supremacy still reigned in both states. Under the US Department of Education (USDOE) Office of Civil Rights, as a result of *Adams vs. Richardson*, Kentucky was cited as maintaining a racially dual (Jim Crow) system

---

[1] The Alexander Papers give little insight to this controversy; George Barrett, 1985, box 644, folder 2, board of regents, 1984–85, box 645, folder 10, Governor Lamar Alexander Papers, 1979–87, GP 53, TSLA; but, see Avon N. Williams, Jr., Papers, 1922–94, and issues of the TSU student newspaper, *The Meter*, 1984–86, Special Collections, TSU; James C. Klotter, "Promise, Pessimism, and Perseverance: An Overview of Higher Education History in Kentucky," *Ohio Valley History* 6, no. 1 (Spring 2006): 45–60.

[2] Almanac Issue 2011–12, *The Chronicle of Higher Education* 53, no. 1 (August 26, 2011) 70–71.

of higher education and had to develop an acceptable five-year plan titled *Enhancement of Kentucky's Historically Black University* (1983). The plan sought to strengthen the state's only HBCU, Kentucky State University, by providing a state appropriation amounting to a minimum number of dollars for special enhancements, including new academic programs in transportation management and microcomputers, more faculty, revisions of curriculum, improvement of library and research facilities, improved or additional equipment, a graduate center, enhancement of land-grant activities, and development of cooperative programs with other state institutions/agencies. KSU would become predominantly white.[3] Local black leaders and the student leaders at TSU believed Peterson had played no visible role in saving KSU.

TSU student leaders believed the federal judge that presided over *Geier* and the *Geier* dissidents were biased against TSU; *Geier Settlement* (1984) proved it. TSU students marched to the federal courthouse with signs that read: "Fight Today to Save Tomorrow" and "Wiseman, I love TSU; Wise up!"[4]

Soon after Roy Peterson came aboard the TSU ship on 1 July 1985, he barely realized that he had entered turbulent waters in north Nashville on the "shores of the Cumberland." The leading members of the student body immediately pressured him about positions on *Geier v. Alexander*, and many of them expected Peterson to support *their* position on *Geier*. Peterson reportedly said he did not believe that any institution that was historically black could look to a future when it would be predominately black. Peterson did not know it, but clannish black Nashville was already forming a coalition against him.

When Peterson spoke at the National Hook-Up of Black Women's meeting at First Baptist Church, Capitol Hill, members of the audience questioned him about student dissatisfaction at the university. Peterson undiplomatically blurted out that the students were whispering lies, half-truths, and unfounded rumors. He perhaps did not recognize soon enough that these elite-class women were members of the same sororities and clubs, and many of them were graduates of Fisk University, Meharry Medical College, and Tennessee State University. They had first-hand information that a meeting between Peterson and the Student Government Association (SGA) on 26 September 1985 had deteriorated into an intense argument. Peterson had allegedly called the student leaders a bunch of silly children. The students also claimed he made threats against them. It perhaps would've been better if Peterson had met with the students peaceably, but he

---

[3] Bobby L. Lovett, *America's Historically Black Colleges and Universities: A Narrative History from 1837 to 2010* (Macon GA: Mercer University Press, 2011) 240–42. Note: By 2004, Kentucky State University had 35 percent blacks among 130 full-time faculty members. Mostly local white students in the state capital comprised more than half the KSU student enrollment of 2,300.

[4] TSU, *The Tennessean 1985* Yearbook, 14–15.

mistakenly ignored the situation. First Baptist Church had a deep civil rights legacy.

The new Student Government Association (SGA) President Augusto Macedo (1985–86), a political science major, published a blistering letter in *The Meter* (10 October 1985) to President Peterson:

> I was deeply disturbed … that you would allow yourself to pursue a course of action that can only be described as reactionary, since you choose to engage in name-calling, verbal abuse and threats. We consider it a gross contradiction for one to support excellence and quality in higher education while simultaneously threatening to expel those whose positions are not in accordance with your own. We gladly accept your invitation for a fight since without one there can be no victory, and especially since constitutional rights such as freedom of speech, are at stake.[5]

John Arthur, the white faculty leader of the campus dissidents, jumped into the fray, saying, "It is incredible that this administration should be attacked because of its being a 'pawn of the Board of Regents.' There are a few people at this institution, which would rather see TSU die than desegregate. Most TSU faculty, administrators and students are not racists of any color."[6]

This made matters worse because Arthur was suspected of believing in black inferiority. On numerous occasions, Arthur, a philosophy professor, had expressed the paternalistic view that the undergraduate students (overwhelmingly black) were poor learners and said they should be made to learn. Most Southern whites, too, refused to consider the legacies of slavery, Jim Crow, and the continuing *de facto* racial discrimination as some of the reasons young blacks had poor high school education, less academic preparation for college, and sometimes less motivation to excel in academics. Some TSU student leaders, such as Tina L. Fox, tried to calm the heated situation:

> We at Tennessee State University are having too many conflicts with each other. The interim president, Roy Peterson, the Student Government Association, and the student body seem to be working against one another. Why? We are having too many problems dealing with the [*Geier*] desegregation act and the choosing of the upcoming president to be fighting against each other. We need to work together as a family first, so we can fight for what we believe is right as one.[7]

Another student government activist, David C. Mills, distributed *The Committee to Save Tennessee State University* (17 November 1985) a newsletter. "If a

---

[5] SGA President Gus Macedo, "To Dr. Roy P. Peterson, Interim President," *The Meter*, 10 October 1985, 5.

[6] Ibid., 5.

[7] Tina Fox, letter to editor, *The Meter*, 10 October 1985, 5.

man has not found something he will die for he is not fit to live—Martin Luther King, Jr."[8] Mills had transferred from the University of Tennessee-Knoxville. There he had written a paper on desegregation in Tennessee, and engaged the black students' fight against open racism practiced against UT's black students. Mills believed the white officials meant to kill TSU.[9]

The TSU student leaders called for Roy Peterson's resignation. He seemed surprised that black community leaders turned against him so quickly. Peterson lost the support of the Tennessee Caucus of Black State Legislators. The Black Caucus had fought to get an $8.1 million dollar appropriation for TSU meant to help the Humphries administration, but Roy Peterson had not objected to state authorities awarding the money to allegedly bogus young (white) construction firms. Roy Peterson was a good person, but he was naïve; he perhaps should have known that Tennessee officials—including a past governor now headed to prison—reportedly conspired with their cohorts to create bogus companies and contracts that yielded "kickbacks." Reportedly, it was not uncommon for 10–20 percent or more of state construction contracts to wind up into their pockets. Many persons believed some of the public HBCUs sometimes involuntarily served as the conduits for this kind of Southern graft. Students, visitors, faculty members, and other persons noticed the low quality of patchwork repairs performed on the buildings and the quick disappearance of TSU's capital appropriations. They suspected the vice president of finance and business—a former UTN student who had prior connections to state officials before gaining his suspicious appointment at TSU—of misappropriating funds.[10]

The State Board of Regents Chancellor Roy Nicks seemed to have quieted down once Humphries exited TSU. Nicks had commissioned outside consultants to do an "administrative study" of Tennessee State. The report confirmed that TSU was not the only problem. The author Roy L. Lassiter, Jr. wrote,

---

[8] David C. Mills, "Press Release: The Committee to Save Tennessee State University," 17 November 1985, 1, Special Collections, TSU; Memorandum to selected faculty members by David C. Mills, chairman, The Committee to Save Tennessee State University, 17 September 1985; David C. Mills, "The Desegregation of Public Higher Education in Tennessee," Lovett Papers (unpublished undergraduate paper, University of Tennessee, n.d.).

[9] David C. Mills, "Press Release: The Committee to Save Tennessee State University," 17 November 1985, 1, Special Collections, TSU; Memorandum to selected faculty members by David C. Mills, chairman, the Committee to Save Tennessee State University, 17 September 1985.

[10] Editor, "TSU officials risk and lose University Funds," *The Meter*, 16 January 1987, 1, including a photograph of the TSU vice president for finance in dark glasses and looking suspicious.

Some potential under-staffing exists because the formula utilized by the THEC does not recognize that duplicated services and support are required when separate major campuses are operated.... It is doubtful that the institution can meet its court-ordered desegregation in the face of perceptions which hinder the recruitment of students generally, and white students in particular. More specifically, the institution cannot be governed in the media [i.e., *Tennessean* and *Banner*] and on the street. Finally, polarization exists among the faculty and staff of [TSU] on the basis of race. Again, institutional leadership is required to pull the diverse elements together and to deal with problems in a spirit of collegiality and common purpose.[11]

On 29 April 1986, a mortified Peterson came to the home of Senator Avon N. Williams, Jr., who lived on the edge of the Fisk campus. Williams had distributed a stinging letter about the possibility of state graft at TSU and the weak leadership of Peterson. Peterson tried to explain that William's letter of April 24 was inaccurate about TSU offering McKissack & Thompson Architects less work than it offered white architectural firms.[12] But community leaders believed Nashville's white power structure was trying to deny work to McKissack & Thompson, and if Peterson, a black man, had participated with whites to shut out a black firm from doing business on the HBCU campus, it would have been the ultimate insult to all black Tennesseans. Williams replied to Roy Peterson's unannounced visit with a harsh letter on April 30:

I am for, and have fought for, racial integration. However, black people, after having endured so long the rigors and inequality of human slavery and segregation at the hands of white America, should not and must not be required, at the hands of either black or white people, to suffer greater losses or bear more onerous burdens than white people in the desegregation process. It is more difficult to continue fighting racial discrimination by white people against black people when black persons in positions of power and authority not only fail to show awareness of the fight in their behalf, but also participate in and/or encourage such discrimination. Perhaps you did not believe a *black* man [Senator Williams] could grant your [capital budget] request. In view of your impending 30 June 1986 separation as President, you still get the intended point of my letter.[13]

---

[11] Roy L. Lassiter, Jr., consultant, *Administrative Study of Tennessee State University: A Report Submitted to Dr. Roy S. Nicks, Chancellor, State University and Community College System of Tennessee* (Nashville: TBR, 1985).

[12] The McKissack & McKissack firm had bid on jobs on campus since 1911. They were among the first registered architects in Tennessee in 1921. They had been shut out of most large jobs at A&I campus from 1912–40s. But they designed several of the local Negro public schools and churches since 1927.

[13] Senator Avon N. Williams, Jr., to Roy Peterson, Nashville, 30 April 1986, Avon N. Williams Papers, Special Collections, TSU.

Williams copied the letter to Black Caucus members, state education heads, SGA president at TSU and the chairman of the TSU faculty senate. Peterson was isolated and the state officials could not save him. But Peterson tried to placate McKissack & Thompson by saying they would get other contracts of $500,000 or so. This minority firm received some jobs on the campus, including the renovation of Crouch Hall. Still, white firms walked away with multi-million dollar contracts, leaving behind shoddy work that almost criminal. The SBR terminated Peterson at TSU, effective 30 June 1986.

Avon N. Williams, Jr., who achieved the chairmanship of the education committee in the Tennessee senate, had continued to pursue the issue of discrimination against TSU. He was angry when he received from the director of THEC a generic response to his inquiries. In April 1986, Senator Williams wrote to Tennessee Higher Education director Arliss L. Roaden: "I appreciate your gracious boilerplate invitation to contact you if you can be of further assistance. Although your assistance thus far has not been notable, I look forward to continue calling upon you as a paid state official and employee upon matters within the scope of your employment and legal responsibility."[14] Williams copied this letter to officers of the General Assembly and other members of the Black Caucus.

Levi Jones of the sociology department, Raymond Richardson, and other faculty members met as a group in various places, including the campus offices of the Institute for African Affairs, to plan strategies to defeat perceived attempts of the state power brokers to fix the presidential search process. Jones headed the Institute of African Affairs, which was funded through a state appropriation with the Tennessee Caucus of Black State Legislators. He had a close alliance with the Black Caucus members who relied on certain TSU faculty members such as professor of political science Holt King to complete the Black Caucus Annual Retreat Report. The activist group under Levi Jones attempted to develop a list and contact unbeatable presidential candidates, but some of the potential candidates candidly said they heard the Board of Regents would bring in their choice as interim and later appoint him as permanent president. Nicks seemed to launch a decoy by saying that Peterson could apply for the presidency. Some local newspapers printed favorable stories on Peterson. Williams squashed this rumor.

Senator Williams was doing all he could in the state legislature to help TSU loyalists, but he was distracted by a progressive muscle illness and by his fight with Governor Alexander. Williams wrote a scolding letter that chastised Alexander for his support of freedom of choice in public school desegregation at a time when black Nashvillians had filed a federal law suit to further desegregate

---

[14] Avon N. Williams, Jr., to A. Roaden, THEC, Nashville, 17 April 1986, Williams Papers.

the public schools by using busing. Alexander and President Reagan's Republican Party supported freedom of choice, but many blacks knew this device could weaken school desegregation and avoid busing white children to black neighborhoods. Williams wrote to Alexander:

> On May 17, 1954, when you were 13 years of age, the U.S. Supreme Court struck down *de jure* racial segregation in the public schools of our nation, including Tennessee. Probably due to your youth and racially segregated environment at the time, you may not have been aware of much of the foregoing. I am asking you to consequently withdraw and disavow said freedom-of-choice objective, which you are seeking to impose as principle and practice of public education.[15]

Gov. Alexander was taken aback. He responded to Williams, "I had expected to be opposed by suburban whites who did not want their school districts disturbed, but I had not expected to be opposed by you."[16]

Also on 17 July 1986, the US Sixth Circuit Court heard Attorney Williams's appeal of the *Geier Settlement* (1984) consent decree. On September 5, the appeals court overruled any objections to the *Stipulation of Settlement,* saying it was a *consent decree* by which parties settle their disputes without having to bear the financial and other costs of litigating; and, it had never been supposed that one party—whether an original party, a party that was joined later, or an intervener—could preclude other parties from settling their own disputes and thereby withdrawing from litigation. Reagan's US Department of Justice objected to the *Settlement's* preferential treatment [affirmative action] for blacks. But the appeals court said the use of racial quotas to prefer minority students as provided in the consent decree to aid in eliminating residual effects of *de jure* segregation in Tennessee's higher education system did not deprive non-minority students of equal protection under the Fourteenth Amendment.[17]

Paradoxically, the Reagan administration agreed with many whites who argued to their judges that slavery, the effects of Jim Crow laws, white racial policies, and practices of the last hundred years against the black Americans should *not* be taken into account for present remedies such as affirmative action to help the blacks equal the whites because affirmative action would punish today's whites who had nothing to do with past racial oppression. The Reagan people discounted the fact that in every aspect of American society today's whites were beneficiaries of the legacies of slavery, Jim Crow, past and

---

[15] Avon N. Williams, Jr., to Gov. Lamar Alexander, Nashville, 4 April 1985, Williams Papers.
[16] Ibid., Gov. Lamar Alexander to Avon N. Williams, Jr., Nashville, 17 April 1986, Williams Papers.
[17] Bobby L. Lovett, *The Civil Rights Movement in Tennessee: A Narrative History* (Knoxville: University of Tennessee Press, 2005) 387–88.

continuing racial discrimination. They respected *Plessy v. Ferguson*'s (1896) separate but equal principle more than they supported *Brown* (1954) that promoted racial integration. Congress and Reagan gave $100 million for HBCUs in Part B of Title III of the Higher Education Act of 1986, and each HBCU— including TSU—received $350,000. Additionally, the USDOE completed a useful study of the HBCUs, Susan T. Hill, *The Traditionally Black Institutions of Higher Education, 1860–1982* (1985) with input from the United Negro College Fund, National Association of State Universities and Land Grant Colleges (NASULGC), and the National Association for Equal Opportunity in Education (NAFEO). Tennessee State University belonged to NASULGC and NAFEO. Years later, former TSU President Humphries would head NAFEO.[18]

Otis L. Floyd Succeeds Peterson

The Tennessee State Board of Regents announced Otis L. Floyd (the lone black vice president at Middle Tennessee State University) as interim president at TSU, effective 1 July 1986. He had worked as an assistant director in the Tennessee Department of Education under the current president of MTSU, and for a brief period had served as acting head of the State Department of Education. The incoming governor Ned R. McWherter (D), who often was referred to as a good ol' country boy from west Tennessee, felt comfortable with a fellow country boy (as Floyd referred to himself). A native of McNairy County, Floyd graduated from Lane College, received his master's at Tennessee State University and earned a doctorate in education at Memphis State University. He and wife, Mildred M. Moore, had four children.[19] Otis Floyd was a politically connected gentleman.[20] Student leaders believed he was another Peterson.

In the summer of 1986, the new SGA president Greg Carr announced: "The excitement is back!" SGA members planned a march to the state capitol to protest Tennessee's assault on TSU's black identity. Civil rights leader Jesse Jackson of Chicago was called to speak. Carr granted interviews on radio and television to show that TSU's black heritage was a tradition and "some traditions are forever":

> No longer would students stand being labeled substandard and 'non-racially identifiable.' No longer would we listen to blacks who dared tell us to be quiet and suffer the indignities that were so easy to succumb to. We would dare to dream.... We knew that the racist legal minds that wanted TSU to 'lose its black identity' wanted the same for all public black institutions. We were the test case, the first battleground, the lead domino. If we lost then Grambling,

---

[18] Lovett, *America's Black Colleges*, 193, 194, 195, 199, 202, 245, 267. Note: Frederick S. Humphries became a president of NAFEO after serving as president at Florida A&M University.

[19] President Otis L. Floyd, Jr., File, 1986–1990, Special Collections, TSU.

[20] Ibid.

Southern—all would die a quicker death.... We marched by the hundreds to protest our victimization. We entered alliances with ministers, politicians and alumni and educated them as we sent them to help fight our battle. Our images and ideas were flung across the country via the leading television shows, radio programs and newspapers as we took our plight to the media.... Every event became political whether it was a basketball game where we protested the prostitution of the black athlete at predominately white schools or a pep rally where we chastised 'Uncle Tom' black faculty for their help in giving our school away. We dared to publicly endorse a candidate for Governor, and we discussed our concerns in his office regularly after we won.[21]

The 19-year-old Carr became the most fearless student leader at Tennessee State since the 1960s. After receiving his undergraduate degree at TSU, he completed a PhD degree in African American studies at Temple University, received an MA and JD from Ohio State University, and became chairman of the department of Afro-American Studies at Howard University. He used the experiences as a legal basis for teaching his classes. "Thank you, *Geier*; you remind us that our struggle is far from over." He also said, "I protested the Stipulation of Settlement and went to talk to Governor Ned R. McWherter, and told him we [TSU] need money, and leave us alone. We believed that TSU could provide an equal quality education with proper resources." Carr knew this would be a long battle over the issues of race and education.[22]

Interim President Floyd continued with plans to name the downtown (former UTN) building for Avon N. Williams, Jr. The ceremony took place on September 26. On October 21, the 64-year-old Williams, then confined to a wheelchair by muscular disease and unable to give a speech wrote:

I hope [the copy of my speech] will be put permanently some place where all students, faculty and staff, present and future, are likely to read it. However, I shall not feel truly honored unless and until all state officials, staff, faculty and students understand and always remember the historic tragedy of racial discrimination and the lessons it teaches us. 'Whites' will never get it, until they learn that white persons can and sometimes must play a subordinate or minority role in our multi-racial society, as they must play in the future of a multi-racial World.[23]

---

[21] TSU, *The Tennessean 1987* Yearbook, 88–89, 99, 161.

[22] Greg Carr, in his own words, *The Geier Symposium* 18 April 2012, 5.

[23] Dedication of the Avon N. Williams Downtown Campus, Nashville, 26 September 1986, Avon N. Williams to Otis Floyd, Nashville, 21 October 1986, Avon N. Williams Papers; "A Man of Courage, Conviction and Conscience for TSU, Nashville, for the Nation, for the World: Tennessee State University remembers Avon N. Williams, Jr., 1921–94," TSU, *Accent* 24, no.3, Alumni Focus issue (30 September 1994): 1.

The Board of Regents and THEC allowed the main TSU campus to fall nearly into ruins. The so-called young, white architectural firms that needed experience left behind the worst of shoddy work; the buildings were leaking and crumbling. The Student Government Association (SGA) president complained,

> Are we merely human cows or are we men? At Tennessee State, we have been brainwashed into thinking that we are human 'cows'. We sleep in cold dormitories and teach in cold classrooms—in fact, I am writing this in a cold SGA office. We stand in unbearably long lines to register but we bear them. We eat food that we do not like even though we pay for it, but who cares? Over the years, we have been told that we are racially non-identifiable, even though we are obviously predominantly Black; ... told that we need permanent leadership, while we have been given two interim presidents. We have been told that the [all-white] OVC [Ohio Valley Conference] did us a favor by letting us in their [athletic] conference, even though we made over $600,000 during our 1986 football season and no OVC school made over $70,000.... We must continue to educate ourselves and protest cold dormitories, bad food, unfair treatment, and social injustices. We must continue to say that 'this is our school and you won't turn it into a cow factory.'[24]

The student leaders also complained that Floyd had forced Howard C. Gentry—a remnant of the Humphries administration—to resign as athletic director, effective 31 December 1986.[25] Humphries had inexplicably named the new physical education and convocation center for Gentry instead of honoring some of the great coaches like E.S. Temple, John Merritt, or John McLendon. Humphries had brought Gentry out of retirement to handle TSU's successful application for membership in the all-white Ohio Valley Conference, but many TSU constituents believed state officials had forced TSU into the OVC to help make the institution drop some of the HBCU teams from the schedule and make TSU appear less black. Floyd named the football coach Bill Thomas as athletic director *and* football coach. Next, *The Meter* editor Jerry Ingram criticized Floyd for tolerating so many interim deans' positions.[26] Ingram, journalism major, had

---

[24] Greg Carr, SGA president, "Are we merely human cows or are we men?" *The Meter*, 16 January 1987, 5.

[25] Usually, it seems, when an interim president is hired, the state officials may take the opportunity to tell them what is needed at the university, including personnel changes, and in a desire to get the job, it is assumed, the black candidate usually agrees to his/her white bosses' desires—even if it hurts the HBCU short-term or long-term; Carrie M. Gentry, *A Life Worth Living: A Biography of Howard C. Gentry, Sr.* (Nashville: R.H. Boyd Publishing Co., 2010) 82, 83, 91, 104.

[26] *The Radical—A Timely Publication*, 20 June 1989, 1–4, Lovett Papers; "TSU officials risk and lose University funds," David Charles Mills, "Living the Dream: 'Let Freedom ring!'" Greg Carr, SGA President, "Are we merely human cows or are we men," Jerry

grown up in a large family in Haynes Park just north of TSU and he was conditioned to jump into a fight and hold on with bulldog tenacity.

Roy Nicks retired and the new TBR Chancellor Thomas Garland, a recent state senator from east Tennessee, did not have a graduate degree. Perhaps because he strictly was a political appointee with the backing of his fellow legislators, Garland arrogantly meddled in TSU's internal operations. He froze TSU's 1986–87 tenure/promotion process. This unprecedented and inexplicable decision impeded the tenure/promotion progress of current candidates, caused some young faculty members to leave for other jobs, and made it difficult if not near impossible for TSU department heads and deans to attract high-quality candidates. Non-black candidates with average credentials gained favored status in this new hiring process. The TWIs had the chance to gain advantage over TSU in the competition to build a quality research and teaching faculty, and Garland's decision impeded qualified blacks' access to TSU's job openings.[27] Some persons believed Garland and McWherter would make Floyd the permanent president.

Avon Williams, who had handled affirmative lawsuits in Tennessee including 85 civil rights lawsuits, issued "A Resolution by the Tennessee Voters Council concerning Tennessee State University":[28]

> We are deeply concerned over Chancellor Thomas Garland's unprofessional actions during this [presidential] selection process. We find his conduct of the search totally irresponsible and unacceptable … It appears to us to be discriminatory and disrespectful toward the one historically black institution in the Board of Regents system. Chancellor Garland's halt of the search, the change of the rules, and announcement of his preference before the interviews say plainly that he intends to treat Tennessee State University in a paternalistic way…. He seems to be following a prearranged agenda in his handling of this situation…. We appreciate the governor's effort to carry out his campaign promise relative to securing a permanent president for Tennessee State. We, however, wish to urge him to ensure that the selection of that person be carried out in a fair and objective way…. We ask the governor, as chairman of the Board of Regents, to examine carefully the qualifications of each candidate and ensure that the one who is recommended and named is indeed the one whose credentials merit the position.[29]

Ingram, editor, "Gentry deserved better from President Floyd," Jerry Ingram, "Gentry leaves, but retains love for TSU; Thomas named in 24 hrs., Carey overlooked," *The Meter*, 16 January 1987, 1–6.

[27] Lovett, *America's Black Colleges*, see Tennessee A&I State University, 171–72, 173; Lovett, *Civil Rights Movement*, 293, 354, 391, 371–401.

[28] Lovett, *Civil Rights Movement*, 195–96, 289, 305–6.

[29] Ibid.

On 23 March 1987, the Board of Regents accepted Thomas Garland's recommendation and unanimously appointed Otis L. Floyd as the permanent president of Tennessee State University.

President Floyd presided over the May Commencement in 1987, when the highlight of the event was the keynote address scheduled by alumna Oprah Winfrey. The university had secured the services of Oprah Winfrey through her family in Nashville and contact Jamye C. Williams, who had taught and nurtured Winfrey. Oprah had arrived in Nashville in 1967 at age thirteen to live with her father after her mother sent her south to escape the troubles of inner city Milwaukee. Vernon Winfrey had settled in Nashville after a tour in the army, started a barbering business, and later became a Nashville city council member. In the working-class neighborhood of East Nashville, Oprah settled down to normal family life and grew up as a competitive teenager. She graduated from the recently integrated East High School before enrolling at Tennessee State University. However, Oprah Winfrey was not comfortable with the militant civil rights activities among some of the TSU students, who pestered fellow students for not joining the demonstrations and campus militancy. Winfrey instead set out to prove she was somebody with superior knowledge and skills. She became active in the speech and drama clubs, the Miss Black America pageants (winning one of them), working as an intern at WVOL Radio and Channel 5 Television, and landing a co-anchor job at the latter station. She left college to work in the television markets in Baltimore, Boston, and then Chicago where she became anchor for the "A. M. Chicago Show." In 1986, Oprah Winfrey turned this program into the syndicated *Oprah Winfrey Show*.

Professor Williams and the Department of Communications faculty arranged for Winfrey to complete her senior project and submit graduation papers in April 1987. The College of Arts and Sciences and the University approved her, along with hundreds of other students for the May 1987 commencement. However, someone circulated a magazine article in which Winfrey had expressed resentment of her TSU experience during the undergraduate years. A few student leaders suggested a walkout to protest against Winfrey. However, Yvonne Hodges, staff member in the TSU Public Relations Office, was close to Oprah's cousin, Carla Winfrey, who was working as a reporter for a local television station. Together with Jamye Williams, they convinced Oprah's father that everything would work out fine. Oprah arrived, received her degree, gave the speech, and disarmed the opposition by announcing at the graduation ceremony that she would fund the Vernon Winfrey Scholarships, beginning with $100,000 plus $50,000 a year, totaling $250,000 over the next few years. She said, "Every single one of us here has the power of greatness because greatness is determined by service, service to you and to others." The audience of over 14,000 gave her a standing ovation. She won many awards including the NAACP Image Award (1990) and the Hope Award (1990). Her financial assets reportedly reach a billion dollars by 2011.[30]

The federal judge in Washington DC ended *Adams v. Richardson* (1977). However, the USDOE Office of Civil Rights (OCR)—as initially ordered by the court—continued to demand five-year statewide desegregation plans in former Jim Crow states. Texas, for example, developed its second plan for OCR titled *Texas Educational Opportunity Plan for Public Higher Education* (1989) and submitted to OCR two additional five-year plans that infused more than $300 million into its two public HBCUs: Prairie View A&M University and Texas Southern University.[31] Such national developments seemed encouraging to TSU. However, some local blacks still worried about former state treasurer Tom Wiseman supervising the *Geier* case.

The Tennessee Caucus of Black State Legislators commissioned an African-American scholar in education statistics Michael T. Nettles to analyze the *Geier Stipulation of Settlement* and the statistical mechanisms used by the Tennessee Desegregating Monitoring Committee. The Nettles report concluded that defendants were failing to comply with the stipulation. The Nettles report said the methodology used by Tennessee meant that the long-term interests of black citizens of the State of Tennessee were not well represented. The Tennessee Desegregation Monitoring Committee first used the percentage of citizens by race in a given area to assign quotas and goals to the institutions; however, this method would have meant a radical change for Memphis State University because Memphis's population was now mostly black. The Monitoring Committee changed the method to reflect the actual percentage of high school graduates by race in a given "service-mix area," and this new method favored Memphis State University to remain predominantly white. The revised methodology gave TWIs lower goals and quotas and maintained higher ones for predominantly black TSU. The TWIs increased their admissions standards above the average blacks' ACT score, but not enough to hurt most white Tennesseans that routinely scored below the national average. "[They did this] without weighing the impact on desegregating higher education in Tennessee.... The suggestion that a reduction of black students [at TSU] will result in higher black

---

[30] Bobby L. Lovett, "Oprah Winfrey (1954–)," *The Tennessee Encyclopedia of History and Culture*, ed. C. Van West (Nashville: Rutledge Hill Press, 1998) 1068–69; Lovett, *Civil Rights Movement*, 347; Kevin Nance, "Welcome to Winfrey's," Nashville, *Tennessean*, 27 April 2003, 7–9; TSU, *The Tennessean 1996* Yearbook, 68–69; Susan Thomas, "Oprah returns to TSU in triumph," Nashville *Tennessean*, 3 May 1987, 1A, 2A.

[31] Wendolyn Y. Bell, Dean of the College of Arts and Sciences, to heads, TSU, 29 October 1987, 1–10, Request for report of steps taken to implement provisions of the Stipulation of Settlement in the Statewide desegregation case, Annie W. Neal, vice president for academic affairs, TSU, 26 October 1987, Lovett Papers.

enrollments at other state universities is a hypothesis for which no data have been advanced to support," said the Nettles report.[32] Apparently, the Wiseman court ignored the findings.

In a THEC report dated 29 January 1988, a confident Arliss Roaden devoted only a few paragraphs to "Black Participation in Education." Roaden listed $5 million devoted to statewide desegregation efforts, plans to increase the supply of black teachers, and a cumulative $15 million spent for capital projects at TSU, even though the institution needed ten times that amount. Tennessee public college and university deans planned to "increase Black (sic) presence" in public graduate schools. Senator Williams responded,

> One of the major problems we face at TSU is enrollment stunting both operations and development because of formula-generated financing. The UTN-TSU merger experience seems to indicate a clear relation between said under enrollment and racial prejudice. If the foregoing is true, it seems to me that we ought to be partially addressing the problems by direct education at all levels designed to reduce or eliminate racial prejudice ... [Your recent report] did not show that you are doing so at any level.[33]

Williams sent a letter to Garland and UT officers requesting a list of all capital projects in public institutions, names of architects, engineers, contracts, and the fees paid to them.[34] After the University of Tennessee released its desegregation report, black leaders were even more upset. The percentage of black faculty and students at UT's main campus remained low. There were reports of black students harassed by some cowardly white students shouting racist names from UTK dormitory windows. They and others at UT depended heavily upon black athletes to help them win regional and national sports competitions that they otherwise felt they could not win. On March 29, the Tennessee Caucus of Black State Legislators cleverly invited Roaden to present a THEC Desegregation Progress Report in person. On April 4, Williams stopped an attempt by conservatives in the state senate to amend a Black Caucus resolution that urged increased hiring of black faculty and staff at TWIs. Williams struck the words "request" "to urge" and "make an attempt." Williams said, "To set an attempt as a goal is to send a signal to public officials that we are not really serious about the [*Geier*] matter." He called for a roll call vote to place the senators on public record and passed the unaltered resolution. On April 13, Roaden sent the *Desegregation Monitoring Report of Tennessee* (1988) to Black

---

[32] Michael Nettles, *A Critique of the Methodology for Calculating Long-Range Objectives for Desegregating the Enrollments of Tennessee's Public Colleges and Universities* (Nashville: Tennessee Legislative Black Caucus, 1990) 1–30, Williams Papers.

[33] Avon N. Williams to A. Roaden, Nashville, 3 February 1988, Williams Papers.

[34] Ibid. , Avon N. Williams, Jr., to Thomas Garland and UT officials, Nashville, 24 April 1986.

Caucus members. On September 7, Williams wrote Roaden "to urge that TSU and Meharry receive the full amount of their appropriation requests." Roaden responded on September 16 that, "every consideration will be given" to these fine institutions. Williams scribbled, "Send to Otis Floyd and Dr. David Satcher [President of Meharry]." However, in *1988–1989 State Appropriation Recommendations for Higher Education,* THEC gave TSU a 1.1 percent increase. Public TWIs received 2.5 to 4.7 percent. Williams later would deal with Arliss Roaden.[35]

For now, Avon Williams continued to argue that America's criminal "injustice" system would adversely affect the HBCUs. The state's prison population was approaching 50 percent minority, whereas the state's black population was only 17 percent. White Americans committed the greatest number of crimes—including white-collar crimes and drug and alcohol violations—yet, across America, US Justice Department data showed whites did not go to jail as often or for as long as black citizens did. White Americans dominated the law profession, judgeships, juries, and access to money. Blacks constituted 12 percent of America's population, comprised 12.4 percent of drug offenses and dealers, but made up 80–90 percent of arrests for such offenses in American cities. The Tennessee Supreme Court established the Commission on Race and Ethnic Fairness in September 1994, and affiliated with the Commission on Racial and Ethnic Biases in the Court on the national level. The reports admitted "biases," but stopped short of admitting to outright racism in court sentencing. American prisons held more black men than the number of African-American men attending four-year colleges in America, and, by 2011, America would hold 25 percent of the world's prisoners. Most American prisoners were people of color. Wealthy Americans, including a governor's family, reportedly invested in stocks and bonds in the privatized prison system [Correction Corporation of America] that Tennessee granted contracts to operate the prisons, and gain continuous profits.[36]

These developments in American prison systems negatively affected Tennessee State University and other HBCUs that recruited students heavily from black and poor populations. Women soon averaged 62 percent of HBCU students, 69 percent of students at Tennessee State, and more than 72 percent at Fisk University. By 1988, the situation was urgent. Williams sent a letter (April 27) to his close friend Lt. Governor John Wilder, who wrote a letter to Roaden that reflected concern about the serious enrollment decline of black males in Tennessee's colleges and universities: "I hope that all of us will do everything we

---

[35] Correspondence between Avon N. Williams, Jr., A. Roaden, state budgets, and state senate papers in Williams Papers, 1922–94.

[36] Lovett, *The Civil Rights Movement in Tennessee,* 329.

can to turn this trend around."[37] Floyd began to push the black male issue and solutions at TSU.

On 17 November 1988, hundreds of students occupied President Floyd's office, demanding resignation of football coach Bill Thomas among other demands. The students sat on the floor inside the president's lobby, locking arms and refusing removal.[38] Local news media recorded their pictures. Al Miller (1987–88) and Fred Brown (1988–89) had followed Carr as SGA presidents.

On 7 March 1989, the attorney for the dissident plaintiffs in *Geier v. McWherter* responded to the blacks' accusations that UT and the state's TWIs were the problem. The plaintiffs' attorney notified legal counsel at the State Attorney General's office that "Judge Wiseman has made it clear that our focus should be on Tennessee State University" to become "a non-racially identifiable institution," without suggesting, "My clients are satisfied with the progress of other [TWIs] public institutions of higher education in Tennessee in eliminating the residual effects of *de jure* segregation." His clients questioned the hiring of too many blacks at TSU and the use of black language in campus publications such as *The Meter*. They objected to the hosting of the National Council for Black Studies by Tennessee State University in April 1989 and blacks publicly claiming TSU still was an "HBCU." Seemingly, they wanted to wipe TSU's black history from the history books. Dissident plaintiffs said the predominantly black administration was permitting the physical demise of the former white UTN campus and was not being serious about substantially recruiting white students.[39]

A newsletter titled *The Radical—A Timely Publication* (20 June 1989) was distributed on the TSU campus: "This paper is dedicated to the liberation of Tennessee State University, an institution for the development of black minds that is under attack at this very moment by powers that will be described in further reading." The writer seemed to accuse Ronald Dickson, the previously mentioned white vice president of business and financial affairs, of having a cozy relationship with other state officials, secretly investing the university's money and even losing some university money invested in a certificate of deposit in another state. The Nashville branch of the NAACP joined with certain TSU alumni and the Clarksville branch of the NAACP to send a letter to state

---

[37] Williams to Wilder, and Wilder to Williams, Nashville, 27 April 1988, Williams Papers.

[38] "Student protests at TSU," Nashville *The Tennessean*, 28 February 1990, 1.

[39] *Rita Sanders Geier, et al. Plaintiffs U.S.A., Plaintiff-Intervenors, Raymond Richardson Jr., et al., Plaintiffs-Intervenors, H. Coleman McGinnis, et al., Plaintiffs-Intervenors, vs. Don Sundquist, et al., Defendants*, CA 5077, U.S. District Court for the Middle District of Tennessee, 22 May 1996; John Norris in his own words, *The Geier Symposium*, 18 April 2012, 7.

authorities about the recent *Stipulation* [1984] and about Dickson's behavior: "The division of business and financial affairs of Tennessee State University under the leadership of Mr. Ron L. Dickson is practicing racial discrimination against black employees. He has given white employees higher salaries than for the black employees, selectively placed whites in strategic administrative positions in finance and computer services; and, giving jobs to four state auditors seemed suspicious." Edward Isibor, longtime dean of the School of Engineering, asked who the authorities were that collaborated with Dickson. Isibor was reassigned to teaching; this started a protracted civil court case. After his retirement from TSU in recent years, Isibor remained committed to civil rights. Before becoming dean of the School of Engineering in 1980, he had involved himself in civil rights protests, received his bachelors at Howard University, his master's at the Massachusetts Institute of Technology, and his PhD from Purdue University in 1970. In September 2011, Isibor was honored by the Nashville branch of the NAACP for his outstanding service to the engineering profession.[40]

Dissidents and newspaper reporters renewed the 1974 issue of quality of programs and black students at TSU. In 1989, they publicized that by fall of 1988 only 25 percent of TSU's students enrolled in 1982 had graduated, compared to an average 40.94 percent rate for Tennessee's public universities.[41] In fact, the whole state of Tennessee ranked so low in higher education it was embarrassing on the national level. HBCUs Spelman College and Fisk University had a higher graduation rate than any of the Tennessee Board of Regents (TBR) universities, but TSU had a mandate to equal Tennessee's SBR graduation rate. From 1978 to 1988, TSU's graduation rate exceeded those at most public HBCUs. The average ACT score at TSU increased from 18.5 to 19.4. Student majors in TSU's College of Arts and Sciences had an average 21.9 ACT score—better than the average state of Tennessee ACT score. Many TSU students in the University

---

[40] Catherine Trevision, "Jury deadlocks in TSU professor's case," Nashville *Tennessean*, 31 January 1995, 4B; Grady Wells, "Dean Edward Isibor of Tennessee State University: Helping Minorities Make it in Engineering," *US Black Engineer* 9, no. 5 (Winter 1985): 24–26, 28; *The Radical—A Timely Publication*, 20 June 1989, 1–4, Lovett Papers; "TSU officials risk and lose University funds," David Charles Mills, "Living the Dream: 'Let Freedom ring!'" Greg Carr, SGA President, "Are we merely human cows or are we men," Jerry Ingram, ed., "Gentry deserved better from President Floyd," Jerry Ingram, "Gentry leaves, but retains love for TSU; Thomas named in 24 hrs., Carey overlooked," *The Meter*, 16 January 1987, 1–6; Wanda Clay, "NAACP recognizes Dr. Edward I. Isibor," 1B, Nashville *Pride*, 18 November 2011.

[41] John L. Norris, Hollins, Wagster and Yarbrough, P.C., to Christine Modisher, 7 March 1989, Nashville, Lovett Papers; *Undergraduate Catalog 1989–91*, Tennessee State University; "TSU, Floyd," 22 January 1989 1, Sheila Wissner, "50% of Metro grads need remedial classes," 7 May 1990, 3A, A4, Sheila Wissner, "Endowments for colleges up; TSU lags," 17 April 1990, 1A, Nashville, *The Tennessean*.

Honors Program had ACT scores above the national average. From 1984 to 1988, the average scores on the National Teachers Examination rose 40 points for TSU students, and Tennessee State University began to bring its graduation rate to within 4 points of the state's average.[42]

Reporters from the local daily newspapers still pressured President Floyd to confirm the perception that black students performed poorly at TSU. Floyd, much as Humphries had done on the same ethnic question, cleverly said, "TSU accepts more non-academic achievers than any other school in the state, but probably has a higher graduation rate among that group than other [state] schools." What he meant was that the TWIs siphoned off the better-prepared black students and black athletes but the black graduation rate at the TWIs was lower than the graduation rate for black students at TSU. The *Tennessean* also featured TSU because of its low corporate donations and decline in endowment funds, but the reporters did not mention that TSU had higher research and training grant funds than any other university in the TBR system; state officials had confiscated its $337,000 reserve in 1943 and never returned the money and/or the interest. On 7 March 1989, attorney John L. Norris for the dissident plaintiffs seemed to put an end to this exchange. He filed a complaint with assistant attorney general Christine Modisher saying that in the case of *Geier v. McWherter* "our focus should be on Tennessee State University." [43]

Life went on at TSU. The institution received notification that President W.J. Hale's eldest son, "Billie Hale", Jr., had died. His daughter, Indira Hale Tucker, later recalled TSU's meager beginnings: "At my father's funeral in 1989, a lady who had been in the first graduating class of 1912 told me with great pride how much the students felt like they were participating in a great enterprise. She though it was an adventure to make one's beds and have to carry chairs from one class to another. She also expressed a feeling of unity with the faculty and staff in the enterprise, a feeling, which I cannot imagine still exists due to the size of the school. In measuring the historical impact of black institutions like Tennessee State University, she said, 'the relevant standard would seem to be against the hostility and meager resources with which black institutions [HBCUs] have [been] built into flourishing enterprises.'"[44]

TSU Begins to Move Ahead, Again

President Floyd finally received Garland-TBR permission to fill the acting administrative position. Some among the dissidents argued for a *Geier* affirmative-action appointment of whites.

---

[42] Ibid.

[43] Ibid.

[44] Indira Hale Tucker letter to B.L. Lovett, Los Angeles, 1 September 2005, 1–3, Lovett Papers.

The College of Arts and Sciences (COAS) became the battleground for this aspect of *Geier*. The COAS included eighteen majors, six master's degrees, produced more than 30 percent of the university's graduates, generated a large percentage of TSU's research and training grants, and enrolled a quarter of TSU's students. Some saw the unit as prize for control of the university, and most of the faculty members absorbed from the UTN in 1979 had been wholesale tenured in Arts and Sciences. When the merger was implemented, the UTN dean of arts and sciences reportedly refused to participate. The deanship went to TSU dean Robert Hudson. Upon Hudson's retirement in 1983, Acting Dean Wendolyn Y. Bell won the national search to succeed him. TBR ordered President Humphries to reopen the search, but Humphries maintained his acting appointments. Not one black person occupied the position as dean of arts and sciences at Tennessee's four-year public or private TWIs. W.Y. Bell's superior academic record and administrative experience, however, won the recommendation through the new search. She had been department head of Foreign Languages, a Memphis native who earned her PhD at Iowa, assistant and associate dean of arts and sciences at TSU, had scholarly publications, and had directed the 1980 SACS Self-Study and successful SACS reaffirmation for TSU. The vice president for academic affairs Annie W. Neal—a tough administrator in her own right—had endured the campus politics at University of District of Columbia after growing up black in a Southern state and learning not to back down from white intimidation. She persuaded President Floyd to present the recommendation to the Board of Regents and to "see what happens."

In December 1987, Chancellor Garland approved Bell's appointment as permanent dean. Unfortunately, she entered a local hospital and died from lung cancer in April 1988, and the appointment of a permanent dean languished. In spring 1990, Neal and Floyd took the search committee's advice and recommended the acting dean become permanent dean. Garland called the two of them out to his office and issued finger-pointing demands, warning them that no black man was going to be dean of arts and sciences. They seemed stunned. Neal was distraught and felt insulted, but she persuaded Floyd to stick to the university's decision. Garland told them *he* would talk to the black finalist. Garland called the man to a meeting at the TBR office and presented offers to serve "in a higher position" somewhere in the Regents system that needed blacks to help diversify the TWIs. Days later, the candidate called the Chancellor and said he would remain at Tennessee State University. Vice President Neal told him that they would "wait and see what happens, but Dr. Floyd and I have selected *you* to be the dean" of arts and sciences.[45]

President Floyd set out to streamline TSU's registration process. Also he further addressed the campus dissidents and the news media's attacks on TSU's

---

[45] Dean Lovett's personal notes, 1987–90, Lovett Papers.

academic and student quality. In the *1989–91 Catalog*, Tennessee State described itself as "an 1890 land-grant institution and a major urban and comprehensive university. This unique combination of characteristics—land-grant, urban, and comprehensive, differentiates the University from all others in the state and distinctively shapes its instructional, research and public service programs." "An 1890 land-grant institution" still sounded too black, too much like the phrase HBCU to the dissidents. Meanwhile, some TSU faculty members expressed concern about the state's plans to convert nearby Nashville Technical Institute to a community college. Lewis Laska, a white TSU professor of business law, wrote, "I feel the various parties to the *Geier* case should immediately ask Judge Wiseman to halt the conversion of Nashville Tech."[46]

Floyd invited the leaders of the General Assembly to tour the campus facilities. He said, "TSU should be to Nashville what UT is to Knoxville and Memphis State University is to Memphis." Jeffrey V. Carr, the brother of Greg Carr, was president of the SGA (1989–90). The student government leaders went downtown to the capitol building on Charlotte Avenue (two blocks above TSU downtown campus) and asked to see the governor. The staff told them the governor was busy, so the students sat down outside the governor's parlor, intending to stay until they told him about the dismal situation of dormitories and facilities on the TSU campus. Governor McWherter got a glimpse of the sit-in and engaged a discussion about their requests. They asked him to go with them to visit the campus, tour some of the facilities and see how TSU students had to live. That secret tour reportedly helped convince McWherter (D) to support extra capital funding for Tennessee State University. Lt. Governor John S. Wilder (D), chair of the State Building Commission and an ally of Avon Williams, gave his support. They committed to a minimum of $122 million appropriated over ten years. They gave approval to Floyd to develop a *Master Facilities Plan* (1989) to renovate and repair every building on campus, tear down some and build new facilities. The Master Plan process involved architectural and engineering firms from outside Tennessee that interviewed faculty members, department heads, and deans to assess current and future space requirements. The campus personnel submitted detailed facilities reports, and the Tennessee Black Caucus persuaded McWherter to include $24,481,000 in his fiscal year

---

[46] Lewis Laska, "An Open Forum to Discuss the Impact of the Enhanced Mission of Nashville State Technical Institute (NSTI) on Tennessee State University (TSU), Tuesday, 5 February 1991, 3 p.m., Women's Building Auditorium," 1–2; "Proposed Alteration of Vision 2000 pertaining to the Enhanced Mission of NSTI," Bert Bach, vice chancellor for academic affairs, Tennessee Board of Regents, to officials at Nashville State Tech and TSU, Nashville, 29 January 1991, 6, Special Collections, TSU.

1990–91 budget. The Black Caucus also secured money for a feasibility study on the football stadium.[47]

> The president of the SGA recalled the student protests at Tennessee State University. It was a cold evening in February and the students had just left the Administration Building after locking it down for two days. Surrounded by 100 policemen in full riot gear, we were not sure what to do next, but we knew we had to do something. So we started walking, and then marching, to the president's [Floyd] residence [about five blocks] at the far end of campus, chanting "No sell out! No compromise! I turned and looked back.... There was a sea of people.... They were moving along at a brisk pace, locked arm in arm in the middle of John A. Merritt Boulevard, from side walk to side walk, covering three traffic lanes. It changed my life, because at that moment—like never before—I understood the power of possibility. We marched again a few days later, took the downtown campus, sat in and starved, and in the end, 140 million was spent on the school. We all changed the world in a positive way in 1990.[48]

Nathaniel A. Crippens, a former state education official, said, "dormitories had asbestos problems, leaking pipes, peeling paint and even some outer brick walls [of Holland Hall] separating from inner walls," but the university had "at least three divisions pulling different ways. A small fringe group said vehemently, 'This is a black university, and Dr. Floyd must go because he is not black enough to fight to keep it this way.' On the other extreme is a small fringe group that says 'Dr. Floyd is an obstacle to TSU's becoming a white university'; it has been to court to gain its end ... In the middle is a vast majority of people who 'don't want to get involved.' Give TSU's Floyd credit for taking on the school's woes."[49]

The Black Caucus had tried to resolve the conflict. Roscoe Dixon, the chair of the Black Caucus, told the press that the organization was acting as a bridge between the SGA and the administration. Lois DeBerry, head of the Black Caucus's Annual Legislative Retreat, held talks between the two sides in her legislative office. Black Caucus leadership urged Floyd to grant the students' requests and amnesty.

---

[47] See TSU Master Plan, 1989, Special Collections, TSU.

[48] Lea A. Overstreet, "Readers reminisce about Tennessee State University," *Tennessean*, Davidson AM, 9 February 2009, 5; Greg Carr, "Notes from the New Jack Scholar," Jeff Carr, "TSU—Black to the Future?" Nashville *The Third Eye* 3, no. 5 (February 1993): 3–4.

[49] "TSU students," Nashville *Tennessean*, 28 February 1990, 1A; N.A. Crippens, "Give TSU's Floyd credit for taking on school's woes," Nashville, *The Tennessean*, 28 February 1990, 13-A; "Pressing Forward," 23 September 1990, 1.

On 23 March 1990, some 150 people met in a forum at the World Baptist Center on Whites Creek Pike to address the inadequacy of state funding for TSU. Two state building officials appeared at the meeting in North Nashville, and explained the Master Plan. "Churchwomen on Community Concerns" scheduled the meeting. Ron Smith, former president of the TSU Alumni Association, complained about "shoddy work and shoddy workmanship seems to be the common thread in the renovation of old buildings and the construction of new buildings on campuses of colleges and universities in the State of Tennessee." One state official even acknowledged, "There has been some work in the past at TSU that has been shoddy." State officials decided to establish a downtown office to supervise all capital projects at the campuses and serve as watchdog over the contractors.[50]

The SGA president continued to question the plans. Carr and other student leaders suspected the campus improvements could be part of the plan to transform TSU into a predominantly white institution. Vice President Annie P. Neal directed the Acting Dean of the College of Arts and Sciences to nominate and head a campus-wide Africana Studies Committee including student representation. They completed a curriculum proposal for a degree program and a new Department of Africana Studies. Floyd and Neal sent the documents to the State Board of Regents. Implementation took place four years later.

State Senator Avon N. Williams, Jr., remained confined to a wheelchair. A special assistant took notes and, along with his wife Joan, conveyed his speeches to others. Williams held on, still fighting Jim Crow, and continued to do so for another two years before retiring. Meanwhile, Williams had not forgotten the arrogance of THEC director Arliss Roaden and his lackluster disposition toward black higher education. When TBR Chancellor Garland announced his retirement, effective 30 June 1990, Senator Williams quickly wrote a letter (27 December 1989) to Governor Ned R. McWherter:

> It is rumored that you plan to appoint Dr. Arliss Roaden as State Board of Regents Chancellor to fill the Tom Garland vacancy. I hope you will not do so. I believe that Dr. Roaden is racially prejudiced and disposed to discriminate against black people. That belief is based upon the sworn EEOC complaint of a black woman faculty member whom I represented when he was President of TTU [Tennessee Tech University], and his lukewarm treatment of black issues as Executive Director of THEC.

---

[50] See TSU Master Plan papers, 1–120; Cindy Roland, "Forum raises questions on TSU funding," Nashville, *The Tennessean*, 24 March 1990, 3-B.

Williams urged the appointment of someone else or a black person to "render impregnable your already strong political support among black citizens across Tennessee."[51]

In June 1990, Garland signed the approval for the appointment of TSU's acting dean as the permanent Dean of the College of Arts and Sciences. Gov. McWherter appointed Floyd as Chancellor of the Tennessee Board of Regents, effective 1 July 1990.[52] Vice president of administration at TSU George W. Cox became interim president of TSU. Williams resigned his state senate seat in 1991. TSU graduate Thelma Harper (class of 1978) won the seat as the first black woman elected to the state senate.[53]

Under President Otis L. Floyd, Tennessee State University had upgraded its requirements. First-time freshmen had to have an ACT score of 19, a GPA of 2.25, and pass the Tennessee Proficiency Examination. Out-of-state students had to have a 2.50 GPA for admission. Children of TSU graduates gained admission under the same requirements (2.25 GPA) as in-state students. TSU could make exceptions for 5 percent of new students. Adult students could be admitted with a composite score on the General Education Development Test (GED), take the ACT and be admitted on a regulated admission if they failed to make the required ACT score for persons with high school diplomas. All entering freshmen had to take a writing test for placement in English composition courses in lieu of the old English Proficiency Examination. Advanced freshmen could use College Level Exemption Program (CLEP) test scores in lieu of certain college courses. Students could obtain Credit-by-Examination in certain undergraduate courses they demonstrated competence gained through previous study and/or experience. Faculty recorded daily class absences and could request Administrative Withdrawal[54] of students with excessive absences. The university requirement for a bachelor's degree increased from 128 to 132 semester hours, including a general education core of up to 45 semester hours. TSU now offered 42 bachelor's degrees (BA and BS), associate degrees in four areas—including

---

[51] A. Williams to Gov. McWherter, Nashville, 27 December 1989, Williams Papers.

[52] Otis L. Floyd served briefly in 1979 as the first African-American Commissioner of Education, and then as the first African-American chancellor of the Tennessee Board of Regents (1990–93).

[53] See Minority affairs/black caucus, 1989, box 529, folder 3, racial equality/public higher education, 1993, mf 141, folder 7, Governor Ned Ray McWherter Papers 1987–95, GP 54, TSLA; "Avon N. Williams Jr.," Tennessee *Contempora* (October/November/December 1990): 1–34. Bobby L. Lovett became permanent Dean of the COAS and served until retiring to the classroom 21 August 2000. Lovett, Bell, and Cox were natives of Memphis.

[54]

nursing—master's degrees in 26 areas, and several doctorate degrees. TSU maintained accreditation by SACS and many others.[55]

Tennessee State University had become Tennessee's most racially diversified institution, public or private. Many student activists, including Gus Macedo, Greg and Jeff Carr, Jerry Ingram, and the aforementioned other students, took the lead in protest, civil disobedience, and persistent diligence to protect Tennessee State University. They, along with faculty and staff members and alumni, did it all with a 'Touch of Greatness.'[56] Consequently, Tennessee State University continued to make progress. Indeed, presidents Hale, Davis, Torrence, Humphries, and Floyd had laid the groundwork for a stronger TSU and made it relatively easy for the next president, students, and faculty/staff members to move forward. Going forward would not be a cakewalk for Tennessee State University, but the really tough battles with Jim Crow were now behind them.

---

[55] See TSU Catalogs, 1986–1991.

[56] See Jeff Obafemi Carr, *Black Stuff: Poetry and Essays on the African-American Experience* (Nashville: Third Eye Press, 1998).

9

1991–2005: J.F. Hefner: Students Matter Most

In April 1991, James A. Hefner, the recent president of Jackson State University in Mississippi, became TSU's sixth president. Hefner, a native of North Carolina and an economist, formerly worked at Tuskegee University and Morehouse College. During the search process interviews with the Deans' Council, Hefner said he wanted to come to TSU because of the opportunity to lead an institution bigger than Jackson State. The deans knew Hefner would have a tough job increasing enrollment, maintaining diversity in the student body, implementing new academic programs, taking Tennessee State University to Carnegie classification Doctoral Level Intensive Research Institution, raising money for the institution, completing the Facility Master Plan construction projects already underway, ending the *Geier* controversy, healing racial wounds on campus, and persuading the local business and white community to accept and respect Tennessee State University as the city's public university. Additionally, Hefner had to operate an urban, comprehensive land-grant university in an effective, efficient, and progressive manner.

At the Commemorative Convocation, held Thursday, 11 April 1991, the new president gave the invocation. The University Meistersingers under Charlotte Rhodes sang "Plenty Good Room," and Stephanie Rawls (TSU, 1992) gave the historical statement. Thelma Harper, the new state senator for the 19th district, gave the address. The Concert Band, under Edward "Pop" Graves, performed in the Women's Building at 7:30 that night. A banquet commemorated the founding of the university and honored twelve retirees. [1]

TSU continued to face enrollment problems as America's racial environment got worst in the 1990s—particularly in relation to poor and minority students. Half of metro Nashville high school graduates need remedial classes upon entering Tennessee colleges. Some 47 percent of students—blacks, whites, and others—in Nashville's public school system lived in poverty. Enrollment in community colleges was outpacing enrollment at Tennessee's public four-year colleges and universities. Less than one percent of white freshmen chose HBCUs where excellent help was available. [2] The flight of whites,

---

[1] TSU, *Commemoration of the Founding of Tennessee State University: Charting Directions for the Twenty-First Century*, 11–12 April 1991, 1–8.
[2] See US Department of Education reports on remedial education, a survey of 800 institutions, http://www.ed.gov/NCES/pubs/97584.html.

and even upper middle-class blacks, to the suburbs continued the re-segregation of urban public school systems based on residential and economic patterns. Thurgood Marshall in *Milliken v. Bradley* 418 US 717 (1974) wrote, "Desegregation is not ... an easy task. Racial attitudes ingrained in our Nation's childhood and adolescence is not quickly thrown aside in its middle [school] years.... In the short run, it may seem to be the easier course to allow our great metropolitan areas to be divided up each into two cities—one white, the other black—but it is a course, I predict, our people will ultimately regret."[3]

TSU was struggling to retain white graduate students and attract more white and other non-black undergraduates. President Hefner said, "Even though white students with a C+ average would get a full scholarship to attend TSU, they just weren't interested in attending the school. At the end of every year, we had money for white students left over, and as the new campus took shape more and more black students enrolled ... The percentage of white students began to decline, which was frowned upon by the state, even though we did everything to live up to the mandate.... The same was true for white faculty." For all HBCUs, "We are faced with low endowments, low Alumni giving and low income families who cannot pay full tuition. That challenge is not new [for HBCUs]."

President James Hefner began work on the inadequacy of faculty salaries—a problem since Hale's days when Davis complained to the Board of Education in the 1950s. Hefner sought to expand faculty research and improve student scholarship. TSU faculty members had an average salary of $38,595 for all ranks, compared to $40,108 for Middle Tennessee State University (MTSU), $41,310 for Memphis State University (MSU), and $44,746 for the University of Tennessee-Knoxville (UTK). Hefner conducted a Salary Equity Study using an outside firm, and then gave salary adjustments in addition to state raises to bring faculty salaries in line with peer institutions.[4]

Hefner worked successfully toward, and involved many of the white faculty members in, bringing another national honor society—Phi Kappa Phi—to campus. In the process, he often spoke to students and faculty members about the quality of learning and teaching. Regional and national associations

---

[3] *Milliken, Governor of Michigan, et al. v. Bradley, et al,* 418 US 717 (1974, 782–802. Note: Thurgood Marshall was the first black to serve on the US Supreme Court, serving 1967–92; see *Hopwood v. Texas* US 78 F.3d 932 (1996), *Wooden et al. v. Board of Regents of the University System of Georgia* US 32 F.Supp.2d 1370 (1999), *Gratz et al. v. Bollinger et al.* 539 US 244 (2003), and *Grutter v. Bollinger et al.* 539 US 306 (2003), which made race as a single factor for admissions criteria unconstitutional. TSU students were among thousands of college students who used cars and buses to journey to Washington, DC, to hear the US Supreme Court's arguments on *Bollinger.*

[4] TSU, *Research Frontiers: Annual Report Fiscal Year 2001,* 1–4, Office of Sponsored Research, Special Collections, TSU.

accredited more than 95 percent of academic programs at Tennessee State University. Hefner addressed the delivery of better services, and advocated the building of thriving research centers. In *Accent* (August 1991) he said, "Of course, we must first focus on students."[5] Carl T. Rowan spoke at the May 1992 commencement, addressing more than 700 graduates. In 1992, establishment of the Patricia C. and Thomas F. Frist, Jr., Chair of Excellence in Business began with a $600,000 gift from the Frist family that had made its millions in medicine and healthcare. Student Lecia Rivers pleaded for students "to get involved" instead of simply criticizing the SGA as performing poorly.[6]

Some black students worried President Hefner about the continuing unfair 1984 *Geier* mandates: Many of TSU's African-American students arrived from the nation's urban *de facto* segregated neighborhoods and schools, and they seemed concerned that "whites" became designated minorities at TSU and that whites received *Geier* scholarships. Among 2,716 white students, 419 (15 percent of them) received minority tuition grants/scholarships requiring a minimum 2.5/4.0 GPA and a 19 composite score on the ACT. White enrollment represented 30 percent of headcount and 21.1 percent of the FTE enrollment. Some white students said the campus was unsafe, though national reports placed TSU crime statistics no higher than at the other colleges.[7]

In *The President's Report 1993*, Hefner focused on the university's accomplishments: 42 different accreditations for the university's programs, a budget of $64.25 million, gifts of $1.02 million, and $18.59 million in grants, scholarships, loans, awards, and support to the students. In 1991–92, Tennessee

---

[5] Editor, "Phi Kappa Phi inducts TSU members," *Tennessee Tribune*, 15–21 May 2003, 9A; "Research at TSU Reaches $41 Million," "Levi Watkins," *Accent*, 1, 9, 6 May 2003; "News Briefs," *Blue Notes* on line, 15 August 2003; TSU Campus Map, http://www.tnstate.edu/TSUMaps/Map_Campus.htm, Jan. 1, 2003; Editor, "History–making surgeon, and alumni returns to Tennessee State University: Dr. Levi Watkins Jr. gives 2003 Founders Day Convocation address," *Nashville Pride*, 17 April 2003, 1A; "Hefner," *Accent*, August 1991, 1.

[6] See Carl T. Rowan, *The Coming Race War in America: A Wake-Up Call* (Boston Little, Brown, 1996); Nadine Bewry, "Students voice concerns about the new Student Union Building," *The Meter*, 6, 20 November 1992, 1, 3.

[7] TSU, Nashville; "How a 32-year-old lawsuit finally ended," *TSU Alumni Life* 1, no. 1, (Spring 2002): 4–7; Mary S. Bell, "One-sixth Caucasian students receive minority grants," *Meter* editorial, "Educate students about Stipulation of Settlement," 4, Sandy S. Madsen, "When the majority becomes the minority," 4, Rahssan Robinson, SGA president, "Demolition of old Student Union Building provokes reflections," 5, Reginald Minter, "Tiger belles Coach Temple to retire after 43-year legendary career," 7, *The Meter*, 5 November 1993, 1; Mary S. Bell, "Phi Kappa Phi chapter established at TSU," Demetrius Jones, "SGA representative views Stipulation of Settlement in different light," 5, *The Meter*, 7 November 1993, 1.

State University ranked twelfth among the nation's top producers of African-American graduates with degrees in engineering, computer science, and math (1991–92). For the period 1987–93, THEC calculated that TSU had persistence to graduation rate of 24.52 percent compared to the 43.28 percent average rate for the state's public colleges.[8] White enrollment may or may not have helped improved the persistent and graduate rates at Tennessee State University because many students enrolled at TSU received *Geier* grants, gained a decent GPA, and then transferred to a traditionally white institution (TWI).

TSU graduates continued to shine, however. For example, Brigadier General Lloyd Newton (1966) was commander of the Holloman Air Force Base in New Mexico when he spoke at the TSU Alumni Luncheon on 19 June 1992. He was the first African-American to fly in the US Air Force's Thunderbird elite demonstration unit. Newton was the speaker for Founders' Day and Academic Awards Convocation in 1994. He told the students: "The opportunity is here to be whatever you want to be. I am proof that you can [succeed]."[9]

The Tennessee State administration unfolded plans to make the TSU campus even more secure and accessible for everyone, including handicapped persons. TSU formed committees on race relations, handicapped issues, and diversity workshops on campus. Hefner took a wheelchair ride across campus to get a feel for the needs of impaired persons and changes needed in access to buildings. History professor Samuel H. Shannon, who used a wheelchair, escorted the president. Shannon, one of TSU's early white faculty members, founded and directed the Guest Lecture Series in the department, and Hefner granted an annual budget for the program.[10]

Critics in the local community complained that white students were frightened away by black rhetoric. *The Meter* responded by saying, "We hope to work towards building better racial relations on campus and present a more positive view of life at Tennessee State University. Nevertheless, [but] we will continue to explore controversial issues that affect the student body of this university and serve as a measure of student opinion."[11]

---

[8] TSU, *President's Annual Report, 1993*, 1–20, Special Collections, TSU.

[9] TSU Alumni Luncheon Program, 19 June 1992, *The President's Report 1993*.

[10] Belmont United Methodist Church, "A Service of Celebration and Thanksgiving for the Life of Sam Boyd Smith," Nashville, 19 January 2003; Joel H. Dark, head of history, memorandum to faculty, "Sam Shannon passed last night," 16 April 2003, Nashville, Lovett Papers, Special Collections, TSU; note: Shannon and Smith were two of the early white faculty members who supported the merged TSU without complaint.

[11] Rahssan Robinson, "Treatment of black students," *The Meter,* 15 April 1994, 1–2; Nadine M. Bewru and Natasha Daniels, "Rahssan Robinson, SGA president"; Getahn M. Ward and Sonya Clarke, "Hefner says TSU cultural heritage must be maintained: 'No plan to change name of university'," *The Meter,* 3 May 1993, 1.

On the night of April 6, about 300 students marched to Hefner's place. He assured them that the university would maintain its cultural heritage and, despite rumors, there were no plans to change the name of TSU. Other rumors surfaced that alleged that the Chancellor of the Tennessee Board of Regents was under pressure to dismiss Hefner because of the declining white student population at the merged Tennessee State University.[12] But Chancellor Otis L. Floyd died after a knee operation before these rumors could be substantiated. He was memorialized in a campus service, and the September 1993 *The Meter* honored Floyd as a strong man willing to stand up for his beliefs despite the rejection and mockery he received from some TSU student leaders. Charles E. Smith, former chancellor of UTN and then a UT official, became TBR Chancellor.[13]

The College of Arts and Sciences pushed forward to create the Department of Africana Studies. Since 1927, Tennessee A&I had an established course in Negro history and had many Africana-related courses in foreign languages, history, sociology, psychology, social work, political science, education, and other disciplines. However, the institution, like all but a few HBCUs (i.e., Howard University and Lincoln University), had never placed the courses into a structured curriculum and degree program. Some TSU students had been submitting petitions since 1984, but university officials had taken no action since many such programs were low-producing and did not generate enough annual graduates according to state board guidelines. But Amiri Yasin Al-Hadid, professor of sociology, began a more focused petition. THEC and the TBR approved the Africana Studies proposal on 4 January 1994. Students were required to study one of three African languages, engage a core curriculum that includes 36 hours, and engage research and internships to apply the acquired knowledge and skills.[14]

TSU broke ground for a new agricultural research station at McMinnville, with US Senator Jim Sasser and TBR Chancellor Charles Smith at the ceremony on 21 March 1994. State legislator/civil rights pioneer Clarence B. Robinson donated his papers to the TSU library.[15]

---

[12] Ibid.

[13] TSU, Getahn M. Ward, "Floyd's contributions as educator created more opportunities for education of African Americans," Keisha Clopton, "Administrative changes reshape TSU," Getahn M. Ward, "Hefner welcomes changes to TSU campus in speech to freshmen," *The Meter*, 9 September 1993, 5; 2 March 1993, 1–8.

[14] Amiri Yasin Al-Hadid, "Africana Studies at Tennessee State University: Traditions and Diversity," Delores P. Aldridge and Carlene Young, eds., *Out of the Revolution: the Development of Africana Studies* (New York: Lexington Books, 2000) 93–114.

[15] TSU, *Accent* 23, no. 3 (March/April 1994): 1–12.

Geier Continues

Meanwhile, in August 1992 at Hilton Head in South Carolina, the National Association for Equal Opportunity in Higher Education (NAFEO) held seminars and panels on the implications for HBCUs of the precedent-setting Supreme Court Decision of *US v. Fordice*, 112 S. Ct. 2727 (1992) that caused fear that some HBCUs could be merged or closed down. The law schools at the University of District of Columbia and Howard University co-hosted a conference on "The Future of America's HBCUs Post Ayers: A Strategy for Survival and Excellence." The revised OCR federal guidelines 59 Reg. 4271 embodied the principles of *Ayers v. Fordice* (1994): Former Jim Crow states had to strengthen and enhance HBCUs to overcome the effects of past discrimination, and OCR scrutinized plans to close or merge HBCUs. In *Ayers v. Fordice*, the federal court said racial discrimination could still exist under race neutral policies for the public colleges even though Mississippi removed *de jure* segregation. The court rejected the closing of HBCU Mississippi Valley State University and a proposed merger with a nearby public TWI. *Fordice* set precedent that HBCUs had a right to exist *and* compete with the TWIs, and were not merely relics of segregation history.[16]

The Tennessee Desegregation Monitoring Committee met in the THEC boardroom in Nashville on 11 May 1994. President Joe Johnson of the University of Tennessee, Director Arliss L. Roaden of THEC, and Chancellor Charles Smith of TBR were members. A.C. Wharton and F. Oliver Hardy were the black members. Wharton was a partner in Wharton and Wharton and Associates Law Firm in Memphis, chief public defender in Shelby County, and adjunct professor of law at the University of Mississippi. Tennessee's Annual Report of Progress on racial integration said,

> Our progress toward the goals established in 1991 has generally been steady and positive. And in some cases, particularly in the administrative and faculty employment areas, there is some vacillation of percentages, but the number of African-American employees has, in fact, gone up. The trend in the African-American student enrollment is up. With the overall percentage now mirroring very closely the representation [16%] of the Tennessee population, the percentage increased very positively just this past fall again. Both the numbers and percentages of African-Americans professionals employed in education have increased and we are pleased with the progress last year in degrees earned by [blacks].[17]

---

[16] THEC, *Annual Report: The Status of Higher Education in Tennessee*, 29 January 1994, Nashville, 1–131; *U.S. v. Fordice*, 1125. Ct 2727, 120 L. Ed. 2d575 (1992); *Ayers v. Fordice*, 879 F.Supp. 1419, 1477 (1995).

[17] Tennessee Desegregation Monitoring Committee, *Annual Report of Progress*, 1994, 1–21; THEC, *Annual Report*, 1–43; THEC, 1996 Annual Report on the Goals of *Tennessee*

Wharton questioned the drop in the number of African-American undergraduates at the University of Tennessee-Knoxville. The UT official said, "I do not have anything to say about undergraduates, but there is good news when you look at progression and retention rates at Knoxville—they are up for the African-American students, we are proud of that."[18] He asked that the next year's report include more specifics than simply whole numbers of black students. Richard Rhoda, THEC staff member, responded, "We will do that." Hardy supported Wharton in questioning the effectiveness of the Tennessee Pre-Professional Program (TPP), which they designed to prepare 75 African-American students per year to enter the state's professional schools as part of the *Stipulation of Settlement*. Hardy said East Tennessee State University (ETSU) medical school was doing a better job attracting and graduating blacks than the UT Medical Center in Memphis—a city with a population that was about 50 percent black. The area around ETSU was about 10 percent black. UT officials tried to shift the focus of discussion to law students where UT seemed to be doing a better job, but the other committee members well understood where the two black committee representatives were coming from. The next question asked if there were new developments in *Geier*. A state attorney answered that there were no developments, "except that the McGinnis plaintiffs have requested a conference, and we will be talking a little bit to the Judge about the status of the case." The McGinnis interveners represent a group of predominately white faculty members at TSU. "And I expect that they are going to voice their dissatisfaction with the progress at TSU. And the State is still looking at its options at this point." Wharton asked, "What are they dissatisfied about?" Upon motion to approve the report, Wharton made a "standing objection" as displeasure about "the Tennessee State [University] situation."[19]

SGA president Rahssan Robinson (1993–94) expressed concern about the adverse effects of the *Geier Settlement*:

> The fact that African Americans at a [HBCU] cannot receive justice from their own people is appalling. From African American faculty who are denied positions in favor of less qualified white candidates, to the screening out of black students via financial aid cuts, to miserable dorm conditions, to academic racism in the classroom—they originate from the same common strand of racism and evil that permeates our society.[20]

Challenge 2000, 29 January 1997, 1–50. Note: Wharton became mayor of Shelby County, and then mayor of Memphis.

[18] Ibid.

[19] Ibid.

[20] Robinson, "Treatment of black students," 1–2; Bewru and Daniels, "Rahssan Robinson (1993–1994) SGA president"; Ward and Clarke, "Hefner says TSU cultural

Governor Ned R. McWherter (D) ended his second term in January 1995. Don Sundquist (R), a former US Congressman, became Tennessee governor. Tennessee then desired an end to *Geier*. The state argued all desegregation by law had ended; Tennessee had good mechanisms in place to prevent re-segregation, thus, *Geier* supervision by the federal court should end; circumstances and the principles of law had changed since *Brown* (1954). *Geier* plaintiffs filed objections:

> Our decisions establish that a state does not discharge its constitutional obligations until it eradicates policies and practices traceable to its prior *de jure* dual system that continue to foster segregation. Rather, the Desegregation Monitoring Committee has been little more than a repository for information.[21]

Plaintiff-intervenors remained concerned "about how to change TSU's [black] racial identity," because "full-time equivalent enrollment of white undergraduates at TSU was approximately 21% in 1995, a dramatic decline since 1979 [more than 30 percent]." "The number of black first-time freshmen at MTSU declined 45% from fall of 1993 to fall of 1994," but Plaintiff-intervenors conveniently attributed this decline to MTSU's admission score of 20 on the ACT. This set of Plaintiff-intervenors also wanted Tennessee State University to stop giving merit scholarships to black students, believing this was a sham, hire "a white recruiter," and stop TSU from using "1890 land grant institution" as a phrase on publications because the term "is a code phrase for black" and "our heritage" meaning "black." They also asked Tom Wiseman to order TSU athletic teams to stop playing "a number of HBCUs" and participating in black college "city classics."[22]

TSU Competitive Among HBCUs and Other Colleges

While Tennessee officials were attacking the state's only public HBCU, the federal government was increasing support for America's HBCUs. Wilson Riley, US Secretary of Education, spoke at commencement, 7 May 1994, to 800 graduates. President Bill Clinton's *Executive Order 12876* increased funding from federal agencies to HBCUs by 21 percent and reaffirmed the White House Initiative on HBCUs that said the HBCUs were conceived out of social need at a

---

heritage must be maintained," 1; Tara Hines, "SGA President unwraps plans for 1993–94," *The Meter*, 8 October 1993, 1.

[21] *Rita Sanders Geier, et al., Plaintiffs, USA, Raymond Richardson Jr., H. Coleman McGinnis, et al, Plaintiffs-Intervenors, vs. Don Sundquist, et al., Defendants,* Civil Action No. 5077, Judge Wiseman, in the US District Court for Middle District of Tennessee, 1–24.

[22] Ibid.

time when many blacks were denied access to educational opportunities. Five percent of money awarded by federal agencies, especially the USDOE, to colleges went to the HBCUs by 1995. Federal obligations for science and engineering to HBCUs from 1993 to 1999 increased from $232,667 to $326,427.[23] Some 71 of the 105 HBCUs, including Tennessee State University, shared in the funding.

The federal appropriations, including Title III, helped HBCUs keep tuition and fees from rising too fast. These federal funds helped renovate classrooms, build new facilities, install new technology, and upgrade equipment for teaching, learning, research, and public and community service projects. The USDOE recognized 18 HBCUs, including TSU, and six private HBCUs for making substantial contributions to legal, medical, dental, veterinary medicine, and other graduate opportunities for blacks. The USDOE declared these institutions eligible for special Title III funding. Federal agencies provided $404 million to HBCUs in the fiscal year 2001 in support of science and engineering compared to $214.2 million in 1991. Howard, Morehouse School of Medicine, Meharry Medical College, Florida A&M, Hampton, Tuskegee, North Carolina A&T, Xavier (Louisiana), Southern A&M, and Tennessee State were the top HBCU recipients.[24]

In April 1994, under Dean Tilden Curry, the TSU degree programs in business received accreditation from the Assembly of Collegiate Schools of Business. Hefner also beamed with a sense of accomplishment on 24 April 1994 when the first TSU chapter of Phi Kappa Phi was inaugurated in the campus forum. Hefner also held the second annual Kudos Awards Program to praise longtime employees and retirees. In August 1994, film and television actor Robert Guillaume spoke at the summer commencement when his granddaughter, Ava Carpenter, graduated. The TSU summer commencement yielded 300 or more graduates. Isaac N. Ukwu of Africa received TSU's first PhD degree in public administration. Avon N. Williams, Jr., passed away, and the campus publications made special mention of his contributions to TSU.[25] The university announced the Samuel P. Massie Chair of Excellence in Environmental Engineering in September 1995, funded by a US Department of

---

[23] Southern Education Foundation, *Igniting Potential: HBCUs and Science, Technology, Engineering and Mathematics* (Atlanta: SEF, 2005) 1–30.

[24] See White House Initiative on HBCU reports, TSU Library, documents; "Making a Difference for HBCUs: White House Initiative on Historically Black Colleges and Universities, Executive Order 12876," President William Jefferson Clinton, 1 November 1993, White House, Washington, DC, in a compilation of news articles on TSU, Bureau of Public Relations, TSU, *Tennessee State University Newspaper Clippings*, November 1996, 1–122.

[25] "Avon N. Williams," TSU, *Blue Notes*, 1994, TSU, office of public relations, announcements and news, 1994–95, Special Collections, TSU.

Energy grant of $1.5 million. The College of Engineering and Technology also received a $6.5 million grant from the National Aeronautics and Space Administration (NASA) to establish a Center for Automated Space Science to enable scientists to expand the nation's aerospace research base.[26] In the summer of 1996, more than 300 students received degrees. Federal district judge Curtis L. Collier (1971) addressed the crowd. He was a cadet in the AFROTC and a graduate of Duke University Law School. President Bill Clinton appointed him to the federal court in 1995.[27]

Desegregation Issues Continue in Tennessee

The debate on campus continued about how to attract more white undergraduates. Ambre S. Brown, editor of *The Meter* said: "From Where I Sit: they still haven't come. People cannot be forced to attend a college and … if someone wants to drive 45 minutes to Middle Tennessee State University, you cannot change their mind."[28] Deborah E. Moore: "Regardless of skin color, TSU offers one of the best educational opportunities in the mid-state area. If your motives are to receive a first-rate education and not to play a part in the continuing racial divide, I recommend Tennessee State University. I proudly hold a bachelor's degree from TSU and will receive my master's in May. And the color of my skin matters not one iota."[29] Annette Pilcher: "The UTN campus was built to keep the UT system white. It is ironic that some of my colleagues complain about parts of the TSU family that want to keep this university predominantly black. Tennessee State has a long and distinguished history as an institution of higher learning for African Americans, and I understand the feelings generated by the white presence. I hope at some point, Judge Wiseman will eliminate the numbers and substitute a 'reasonable effort' standard."[30]

Enrollment of blacks in Tennessee institutions had grown by almost 15 percent. Persistence to graduation for blacks was 34.7 percent in public

---

[26] TSU, Office of Public Relations, 1994–95, Special Collections. Note: TSU graduate Emmett Turner became the first African-American chief of police in Nashville on 10 January 1996.

[27] Graduation programs and university announcements, Special Collections, TSU.

[28] Amber S. Brown, "From Where I Sit: they still haven't come," *The Meter,* 12 November 1997, 4.

[29] Deborah E. Moore, "Dear Old Alma Mater," *Nashville Scene,* 13 November 1997, 4.

[30] Ibid., Annette Pilcher, "School Daze," Michael R. Busby, "TSU's Excellence Adventure," *Nashville Scene,* 13 November 1997, 4; A compilation of news articles, TSU, Bureau of Public Relations, TSU, *Tennessee State University Newspaper Clippings,* November 1996, 1–122.

universities, 15.3 percent in two-year public institutions, and 41 percent at TSU. Research expenditures doubled at TSU.[31]

The University of Tennessee had a problem holding onto top black faculty recruits. UTK had fewer than 5 percent minority faculty, and few blacks held administrative positions at the college or system's level. Black scholar Michael Nettles moved on to a prestigious Northern university and later became an executive at the Educational Testing Service (ETS) in Princeton.[32] The UT administrators routinely dismissed the racial integration issue.[33] However, to coincide with the thirty-year anniversary of *Geier*, members of the Black Faculty and Staff Association at UTK called a press conference in the law school where they presented a position on desegregation or the lack thereof at UTK. They asked members of the Tennessee Black Caucus, which held its Annual Retreat at nearby Pigeon Forge-Gatlinburg, to visit the campus, investigate claims of racial discrimination, and review financial allocations to UT in terms of diversity and equity, *vis-à-vis* compliance with the Title VI mandates of the 1964 Civil Rights Act. They made urgent the need to address racist practices, marginalization, denial of opportunity, and structured patterns of rejection visited upon African-American faculty and staff at UTK.[34]

State desegregation reports said TSU made progress that "included other-race [white] speakers during new student orientation week, at commencements and convocations, at department and college/school seminars, and at Faculty Institute."[35] And TSU made progress academically, too. TSU licensure scores for 1993 were reported as engineering (16), Associate Nursing (86.7), BSN Nursing (80), Dental Hygiene (88.9), and Medical Technology (50) in percentage of students passing the examinations. For 1996 licensure scores, the percentage of TSU students passing was as follows: Engineering (33 percent), Nursing (94

---

[31] THEC, Executive Summary Tennessee Higher Education Commissioner, 1 May 2000, 1–4, Executive Summary the Tennessee Board of Regents, 1-43, Desegregation Impact Analysis of the Proposed Community College in Southwest Tennessee [Memphis], 1–18, Executive Summary the University of Tennessee, 1–28, all in *1996 Annual Report on the Goals of Tennessee Challenge 2000* (Nashville: Tennessee Higher Education Commission, 29 January 1997); THEC, *The Status of Higher Education in Tennessee*, 17 January 2000, 1–42; TBR, Daily Fall 2003 Enrollment, 15 September 2003, 1–2; TBR, office of academic affairs, "50th Anniversary—Brown v. Board of Education, Faculty Symposium," 8 October 2004, 1.

[32] Ibid.

[33] *The University of Tennessee Highlights of Campus and Institute Five-Year Plans, FY 95–FY 99* (Knoxville: UT, 2000) 1–29.

[34] Black Faculty and Staff Association, Task Force Commission Report on Race Relations at UT-Knoxville, 5 November 1998, 1–10.

[35] THEC, Executive Summary the University of Tennessee, 1–18, Executive Summary the Tennessee Board of Regents, 3, 11, *1996 Annual Report on the Goals of Tennessee Challenge 2000*, 1–19.

percent), Dental Hygiene (91 percent), and Medical Technology (100 percent). At Tennessee Tech, Memphis State, and UTK, the percentage of engineering students passing licensure tests was 38.8, 66.1 and 68.4 percent. The average ACT admission score at the public TWIs averaged 3 to 6 points above those at TSU. Between 1991 and 1993, TSU reduced the percentage of students taking one or more remedial or developmental courses from 43.4 percent to 30.4 percent. Students taking such courses at the TWIs ranged from 21 to 24 percent in Tennessee. TSU and the TWIs continued to increase license and ACT scores. The 1998 Alumni Survey showed nearly 90 percent of TSU graduates rated the quality of its academic programs as average-exceptional.[36]

Life of Progress at TSU Continues in the 1990s

President Hefner tried to continue an era of good relations with the Black Caucus.[37] From 18–21 November 1999, politicians and citizens celebrated the 25th Anniversary Legislative Retreat and Training Conference in Nashville. The retreat intended to bring together leaders representing government, business, and education, and health, religious and civic organizations, and allow elected leaders and ordinary citizens to express their concerns and receive training in leadership and organizational skills. TSU continued to supply the retreat with a grand buffet reception and a team of researchers to record the sessions and compile the annual report. Hefner made the Friday night TSU-hosted reception even more elaborate. He employed the TSU Show Stoppers, a song-and-dance team, under director Diana Poe, to entertain the audience.

Students from Memphis-Shelby County comprised the second largest group at Tennessee State. In 1992, the enrollment at TSU reached 7,590 students, 13 percent of whom were graduate students (majority white), compared to 7,405 students in 1990. TSU student enrollment remained fourth behind MTSU, MSU, and ETSU. The TSU accreditation of programs rose to 98 percent from 77 percent in 1991. Almost 90 percent of the TSU faculty had doctorates and appropriate terminal degrees in their fields compared to none in 1912. By 1995, TSU had 9,000 students, 21 percent of whom were white and 33 percent of whom represented

---

[36] Executive Summary Tennessee Higher Education Commissioner, 1 May 2000, 1–4, Executive Summary the Tennessee Board of Regents, 1–43, Desegregation Impact Analysis of the Proposed Community College in Southwest Tennessee [Memphis], 1–18, Executive Summary the University of Tennessee, 1–18, all in *1996 Annual Report on the Goals of Tennessee Challenge 2000*.

[37] "Highlights of President James A. Hefner's report to the Tennessee Board of Regents," TSU *Accent*, September 1998, 1–2; "President Hefner's Vision and Road Map for Research, 1991–96," TSU, *Research News and Programs Report* 2, no. 1 (Winter/Spring 1997): 1–4; TSU, *Faculty Research, Publications and Grant Awards*, April 1996, 1–13; TSU, *19th Annual University-Wide Research Symposium*, 24–25 March 1997, 1–77.

Davidson County; others came from 85 of the 95 Tennessee counties, 46 US states and the District of Columbia, and from more than fifty nations. The TSU budget ending 30 July 1999 was $113,633,784.45, compared to the $96,000 budget of 1912.[38]

In 1999–2000, the faculty profile reflected 43.5 percent African Americans, 45.3 percent European Americans (whites), and 11.2 percent other ethnic and national origins. The black faculty percentage was 63.5 percent at Fisk University, 51.1 percent at Lane College, 64.1 percent at LeMoyne-Owen College, and 60.0 percent at Meharry Medical College. None of the major TWIs in Tennessee had more than 12 percent black faculty. The University of Memphis had 30 percent black enrollment; MTSU 11 percent; and TSU 77 percent. Tennessee State had a 41 percent graduation rate for African Americans, compared to a 36.8 percent average overall black graduation rate for all TBR four-year institutions. The University of Memphis graduated 3,087 students with undergraduate, graduate, and professional degrees in 2000; MTSU 2,938; and TSU 1,435. TSU had $24,212,331 in research funds, compared to $21,402,621 for the University of Memphis, and $5,423,534 for MTSU. Compared to new libraries at MSU and MTSU, the TSU library (1975–) only had capacity for 90 percent of the school's needs. Tennessee State University needed money to expand the library from 81,291 square feet to 166,291 square feet.[39]

Geier Approaching an End

The final *Geier* settlement was expected by summer of 2000. Robert Smith of the TSU Alumni Association said that TSU believed in diversity, but they did not believe that everything had to be predominantly white to be good.[40] By December, plaintiffs and the state defendants finally reached an agreement, which still had to be approved by Judge Tom Wiseman. On 4 January 2001, Wiseman approved—with great pleasure and with great hopes—the settlement of the 32-year-old *Geier* lawsuit. The settlement removed the 50 percent white quota on TSU, and all public colleges and universities received mandates [not quotas] to become "racially non-identifiable." The governor was glad the *Geier v. Sundquist* case had ended and pledged full commitment to funding the desegregation budget. Richard Dinkins, who succeeded his partner, Avon Williams, as plaintiff attorney, felt this was the best the court and the parties could do. Rita Geier, Ray Richardson, Coleman McGinnis, and other plaintiffs

---

[38] J.A. Hefner to Charles Smith, Nashville, 20 November 1998, Lovett Papers.
[39] *Geier* report, 20 November 2002, 1–10; THEC, Annual Report of the Desegregation Monitoring Committee, 1 May 2000, Nashville, Minutes from the Desegregation Monitoring Committee, Annual Meeting, THEC, 30 April 1999, Nashville, 1–150.
[40] "How a 32-year-old lawsuit finally ended," *TSU Alumni Life*, 2002, 1–7; "Final settlement," Nashville *Tennessean*, July 11, 2000, 1.

believed the settlement was a good one. Richardson said, "It was the first and only time that a court has ordered a merger of that nature. There was great bitterness." McGinnis said the 50 percent quota imposed on TSU in the 1984 *Stipulation of Settlement* "became a huge division and in the end that became the focus instead of trying to deal with the issues that we thought needed to be addressed."[41] The system president of UT, against whom the lawsuits had been directed since 1937, published a newspaper response:

> The University of Tennessee, while [in the past] not meeting every numerical objective set by a federal court in the statewide desegregation case known as the *Geier* case, has an exceptional record of commitment to minorities. The *Geier* case has recently taken a new direction with the announced mediated agreement. Recent newspaper articles and editorials have dwelt on the inability of the University to meet certain of its court-ordered desegregation goals. And it is true that the university has fallen short in several of its numerical goals. However, what has not been reported is a record of remarkable achievement by the university in meeting many of its *Geier* goals, its commitment to equity and diversity.... UT is firmly committed to a sustained proactive effort....[42]

At the August 2001 Faculty Institute, the TSU faculty received presentations on the recent *Geier* settlement, the new online computer degree programs, and "Faculty Development, Technology, and Accountability." Augustus Bankhead, vice president of academic affairs, made the presentation of the academic deans, who introduced new faculty members. The Faculty Support Center under Title III announced a Faculty Development Assignment Program, offering an academic year leave at one-half salary. In his address to the faculty, Hefner said,

> On January 4, 2001, Tennessee ended a 32-year-old lawsuit, filed on grounds of racial segregation in the state's system of higher education. The consent decree for that lawsuit, signed by U.S. District Judge Thomas A. Wiseman, has provided a unique opportunity for Tennessee State University. Hefner proceeded to explain efforts to hire a host of consultants to help improve admissions and records services, public relations, and program quality at TSU. The decree calls for a provision of $70 million to $75 million total, and Tennessee State ... is to receive the lion's share of those funds. TSU will receive up to $400,000, or up to 65 percent of the cost for an image-building campaign in the Davidson County area. TSU will receive $750,000 for scholarships for full-time and part-time non-traditional students who take

---

[41] *TSU Alumni Life*, 6, 7; "Geier," *Tennessean* (December 23, 24, 2000) 1; Eddie R. Cole Jr., " Final Geier funds set," *The Meter*, 25 September 2006, 1, 3.

[42] Note: "UT," Nashville *Tennessean*, 11 July 2000, 2 January 2001, 1; a black UTK staff member said, "There are still areas, relatively speaking, no different than it was [at UT] in the 1960s."

classes at night or on the weekend at the Avon Williams campus. The university will receive $1 million per year for ten years and one-to-one matching funds up to another $1 million per year from the state, for a total of $30 million for the TSU Endowment and Educational Excellence Fund. TSU will receive $10 million in capital funds. $5 million in start-up funding and up to $2 million in matching funds for a public law school, if they established one in middle Tennessee....[43]

Some faculty questioned the allocation of funds for a school of public affairs—similar to the controversial Institute of Government in the 1984 settlement. Not many faculty members seemed enthusiastic about TSU adding an expensive law school when existing programs were suffering the need for more space, better faculty salaries, and operational budget increases. A published legal historian, attorney, and professor in the College of Business, Lewis Laska, complained that the settlement "abolished affirmative action in Tennessee"; plaintiffs' attorneys "did not win *Geier*; they abandoned and settled the case," and asked for $10 million in fees.[44]

Legalists and civil rights advocates across the nation had followed the *Geier* case. Noted attorney William C. Bednar of Austin, Texas, read "Desegregation of Higher Education in Texas: What Does the Future Hold?" at the Eleventh Annual Texas Higher Education Law Conference:

> The present situation in Texas is significantly different in several ways from the Tennessee [*Geier*] case. Tennessee fought desegregation every step of the way.... Texas has been voluntarily desegregating for over twenty years under [4] successive plans in collaboration with OCR. The Tennessee case was pre-*Fordice*, whereas Texas is now operating under a Priority Plan designed collaboratively with OCR expressly to satisfy *Fordice*. [HBCUs] PVAMU [Prairie A&M] and TSU [Texas Southern] are in substantial[45] compliance.[46]

---

[43] TSU, Faculty and Staff Institute, 16–17 August 2001, Special Collections, TSU; *TSU Alumni Life*, 5.

[44] US Department of Justice, Civil Rights Division, Frank Brewer, "A Review of Facilities at the University of Memphis (UM), Middle Tennessee State University (MTSU) and Tennessee State University (TSU)," 20 November 2001, 1–15; THEC, Desegregation Monitoring Committee, "Desegregation Progress Reports," 5 May 1986, 22 April 1987, 6 April 1988, 5 April 1989, 4 April 1990, 3 May 1991, 8 May 1992, 7 May 1993, 11 May 1994, 14 August 1995, 2 May 1996, 1 May 1998; Tennessee Desegregation Monitoring Committee, Agenda and Minutes, 5 April 1989, 11 May 1994, 1 May 1997, 1 May 2000; TSU, The Master Plan, 1988; Lewis Laska, "Geier," in the Faculty Senate Minutes, 19 September 2001.

[45] Ibid., THEC.

[46] William C. Bednar, "Desegregation of Higher Education in Texas: What Does the Future Hold?" Eleventh Annual Texas Higher Education Law Conference, University of North Texas, 2–3 April 2007, Lovett, *America's Black Colleges*, 253–54.

TSU After Geier

In 2001, Tennessee State University decided to divide the huge May commencement into morning and afternoon programs. The morning program included the College of Arts and Sciences, which had about 35 percent of the graduates, the College of Business, the College of Education, College of Engineering and Technology, the Institute of Government, and the Graduate School. The afternoon ceremonies included School of Agriculture and Consumer Sciences, School of Allied Health, and School of Nursing. Alumnus Reginald Stuart was the speaker in the afternoon. Earl G. Graves, Sr., chair, editor and publisher of *Black Enterprise* magazine, served as morning speaker. In a letter to all students, President Hefner said "Your college experience at Tennessee State … will give you the skills, poise, and outlook that say that you have been educated here."[47] TSU had 43 bachelors, 2 associate degrees, and 26 master's degrees, as well as PhD programs in biology, agriculture, engineering, education, public administration, and psychology. In addition to the colleges and schools, there were the Aerospace Studies, Center for Excellence in Information Systems—Engineering Management, Center for Extended Education, Cooperative Agricultural Research Program (CARP), and the Office of Sponsored Research.[48]

In fall 2001 (1995 cohort), the Southern states had a six-year college graduation rate of bachelor's students of 49.2 percent compared to the national rate of 54 percent. Tennessee's universities had an average of 48 percent. TSU had a 38 percent graduation rate. The University of Memphis awarded 3,087 degrees, MTSU 2,938 degrees, and Tennessee State 1,435 degrees. University of Memphis had $21.4 million in external research grants; MTSU $5.4 million; and TSU $24.2 million.[49]

Engineering celebrated fifty years of service from 17–23 February 2002. Students and faculty members engaged poster displays, lectures, student

---

[47] See TSU, Commencement Program 2001, Special Collections, TSU; James A. Hefner, "The Greatness of Tennessee State University," letter to all TSU students, 10 September 2001, Lovett Papers.

[48] See TSU Catalogs, 1999–01, 2001–03, Special Collections, TSU; "Funding for research increases 22 percent to nearly $31 million at Tennessee State University," Office of Public Relations, *Accent* (May 2002): 1; Summer Commencement and Vintagers Celebration 2001, photos of alumnus Art Benjamin and Ola Bate, TSU *Accent*, (September 2001): 3.

[49] "Consent decree brings New Opportunities to TSU," TSU, Public Relations, *Accent* 31, no. 4 (30 November 2001): 1, 4–5; US Department of Justice, Civil Rights Division, Frank Brewer, "A Review of Facilities at the University of Memphis (UM), Middle Tennessee State University (MTSU) and Tennessee State University (TSU)," 20 November 2001, 1–15; note: many students, especially whites, seemed to enroll at TSU, improve their grades, and transfer to a TWI, which gained the student in its graduation rate.

awards, a career fair, and a dinner. The Center for Neural Engineering began in 1994, with funding from several external agencies, to relate the human brain activity in engineering systems, aid in the building of better robotic systems, and involve the research faculty in biology and other non-engineering disciplines. The College of Engineering, Technology and Computer Science included departments of architectural, civil, electrical, and mechanical, aeronautical technology, and computer science.[50]

Since performing the chief mission of Tennessee A&I State Normal School in 1912, gaining approval by the American Association of Teachers Colleges in 1933, and receiving its initial NCATE accreditation in 1958, the College of Education continuously gained accreditation reaffirmation. Under a succession of capable faculty, directors, deans, and department heads the TSU teacher education program produced more than half the Negro teachers, principals, and supervisors in the state of Tennessee before desegregation. By 2001, the TSU education program produced more than 142 teacher education graduates on an annual basis. The College had a 96–97 percent passage rate on the PRAXIS teacher exit test; the SREB averaged 93 percent passing rate on teacher education tests in 1999–2000, and the average HBCU passing rate was 79 percent.[51]

The 24th Annual University-Wide Research Symposium adopted a theme of "Environmental Sustainability through Research, Literacy and Outreach." This program helped to sharpen undergraduates and graduates for the rigors of graduate and professional schools. The College of Arts and Sciences started the Research Symposium in 1978 with Rubye P. Torrey (chemistry) as chair. Elbert Lewis Myles (biology) served as chair in 2008. Baruch S. Blumberg, the Nobel laureate credited with discovering the hepatitis B virus, spoke for the 25th University-wide Research Symposium that featured presentations by students and faculty members.[52]

Alumna Marquita Qualls served as the speaker for fall convocation on 6 September 2001. She was a researcher for a major pharmaceutical company—the first Africa-American woman to receive a PhD in organic chemistry from Purdue University (May 2001). A native of Mississippi, she transferred from Tougaloo College to complete a major in chemistry at TSU. Undergraduate students in biology, chemistry, engineering, and agriculture often spent summers in research laboratories of professors at the nation's top universities. Under biology

---

[50] Hefner transferred the Department of Computer Science from the College of Arts and Sciences without the respectful input or knowledge of the Dean of the College of Arts and Sciences. The dean appropriately resigned and reassumed his teaching, research, and public service functions at TSU in August in 2000.

[51] Lovett, *America's Black Colleges*, 267–307.

[52] TSU, *Tiger Technology* 1, no. 1 (November 2001): 1–4; "Consent decree brings New Opportunities to TSU," TSU, Public Relations, *Accent* 31, no. 4 (30 November 2001): 1, 4–5.

professor Prem Kahlon in the College of Arts and Sciences for nearly twenty years a federal funded program (MARC) prepared and sent dozens of students to summer research laboratories and PhD and professional degree programs. Under mathematics professor Jeanetta Williams Jackson in the College of Arts and Sciences, the David and Lucille Packard Summer Program prepared high school seniors to major in the sciences, matriculate at TSU, if they so chose, and go on to graduate and professional schools. In 2002, Howard Industries the largest transformer manufacturing division in the US committed to providing cooperative education assignments to TSU students. With the help of co-op director Bill Gittens, history majors frequently spent the summers doing research in national forests with the US Forestry Service. The College of Arts and Sciences also directed the International Study Program that allowed students to study in European universities, and vice versa, for a semester or two. Some departments provided summer opportunities for faculty to study in Africa along with their classes and students. Tennessee State University teamed with International Business Machines and Sun Microsystems to launch a new enterprise-wide e-business computing strategy designed to create interdisciplinary curricula focused on producing work-ready students in technology fields. "This relationship epitomizes what strategic partnerships are about," said President Hefner. The Annual Graduate and Professional School Fair held in Kean Hall attracted the top schools in the country. The HBCU Think Tank united black colleges for a historic week at TSU from February 22–24. It was sponsored by the National Association of Student Government Officers and consisted of representatives from most of the HBCUs and had than more than 1,000 people attend the meetings.[53]

On the follow-up to the *Geier Settlement*, on 22 April 2002, President Hefner addressed the campus via letter and e-mail. He announced the recent hiring of a company to do the study of the university's major services for processing current and prospective students. He wrote:

> We currently have seven separate task forces in place and each focusing on very specific service-related issues.... Each task force will present its conclusions and recommendations to me by the end of April ... In its ninety years of existence, [TSU has] continually pursued and attained excellence. Today, as we embark upon a new decade, ... we welcome this opportunity to re-examine how we operate and how we can better serve our many constituents. It is my hope that all Nashville will embrace an institution that examines itself for both strengths and weaknesses and wishes to advance itself to a level that will better serve the entire community.[54]

---

[53] Raynata Reed, "HBCU Think Tank," *The Meter*, 27 February 2002, 1, 8.

[54] "Consent decree brings New Opportunities to TSU," TSU, Public Relations, *Accent* 31, no. 4 (30 November 2001): 1, 4–5, "Coordinating Committee for the Consent Decree,"

At the May 2002 commencement, there was another record graduation class. The faculty scheduled 28 persons to receive doctorate degrees. Almost 260 persons applied for the master's degree. Nearly 500 of TSU's graduates majored in the arts and sciences, 173 in business, 103 in nursing, 99 in engineering, technology, and computer science, 90 in education, 70 in allied health professions, and 29 in agriculture and consumer science. In the afternoon exercise, the Richard H. Boyd Family Endowment Fund announced a gift to establish an endowment for TSU scholarships. T.B. Boyd III (class of 1975), head of R.H. Boyd Publishing Company, made the announcement. His great uncle, Henry Allen Boyd, and his great grandfather, R. H. Boyd, helped lead the successful State Normal School Association from 1909–11. Boyd III was chair of the local Citizens Bank, the oldest (1904–), continuously operating black bank in America. His father, his three siblings, and his wife, Yvette Duke, completed TSU. One of Boyd III's daughters completely a master's at TSU, and two of his children continued enrollment at TSU in 2011. Boyd III served on the TSU Foundation board. The August 2002 commencement featured Jim Holley (class of 1965) as speaker. After leaving TSU, he earned masters and doctorate degrees, authored more than nine books, and headed large church operations in Detroit.[55]

In the May-August commencements of 2002, two students sought commissions as second lieutenants through the AFROTC unit. Tennessee State University and 15 other HBCUs maintained officer-training programs among 350 total college military units. Between 1951 and 1959, the AFROTC at TSU became one of America's largest, most productive and revered college programs. James W. Caruth, one of the first graduates commissioned as a 2nd Lt., became a pilot at the Air Force base in Puerto Rico. The AFROTC produced about 20 commissioned officers per year by 1967. The Air Force reported not one TSU student failed flight and technical training programs. The AFROTC moved into new quarters in the new Floyd-Payne Campus Center in 1992. In 1994, the Tennessee Historical Commission posted a marker in front of the old AFROTC building, recognizing the historical significance of this unit. In 1995, Air Force assistant

---

and subcommittees, 5; S. Latham, "The Hefner Presidency: the First Ten years in review," *Nashville Pride*, 31 August 2001, 7; Tosha Jones, "TSU alumnus president of law office located in downtown Nashville," *The Meter*, 30 January 2002, 12. James A. Hefner, "The Tennessee Higher Education Desegregation Consent Decree," letter to the TSU family, 22 January 2001, Coleman McGinnis to Bobby Lovett, email copy of Consent Decree, 26 January 2001, 1–32, Raymond Richardson and Coleman McGinnis, "Progress Report to the TSU Community in Implementation of the Consent Decree," 16 April 2001, TSU, "TSU Faculty Senate Resolution in Response to the Consent Decree in *Geier v. Sundquist*," 22 March 2001, and Coleman McGinnis, "Response to State's Motion to Dismiss *Geier*," 21 August 2001, Lovett Papers.
[55] TSU Commencement Programs, 2000–02, Lovett Papers.

vice-chief of staff Lt. General Lloyd W. "Fig" Newton (1966) helped TSU secure a T-38 jet fighter plane to adorn the entrance to Kean Hall. Brigadier General Toreaser Steele (AFROTC class of 1974), the deputy chief of staff for personnel in the US Air Force at the Pentagon, served as the commencement speaker for May 2002. Former HBCU students comprised about 80 percent of America's black military officers.[56] On August 2002, a Nashville *Tennessean* editorial said,

> Many factors have held back Tennessee State University through the years, racism being among them. Also high on that list was attitude. Whether real or perceived, TSU developed the reputation through the years as being inefficient, undisciplined and unfriendly, particularly to non-minority [white] students. That reputation not only held back TSU's ability to thrive, it hurt Nashville. When people in this city, including working adults, contemplated returning to college for a degree or just for a few courses, TSU was not an inviting option. Since it is the only public four-year in Nashville, potential students who marked it off their list would have either to drive farther [to MTSU] or pay more [at local TWIs] to fulfill their educational dreams. Over the last few months, however, TSU had confronted its perception and turned it around.... Now the contagion needs to spread beyond the TSU campus. TSU's transformation into the region's premier public university will require willingness from business, political and civil leaders to see the new TSU [thrive]. If ... community leaders have avoided TSU in the past, for whatever reason, they need to change their old habits. Tennessee State already has.[57]

However, economic recessions in the first decade of the twenty-first century affected the entire nation, and problems created by the recessions trickled down to Tennessee. Economic woes aggravated the American issue of race relations. Black students and their families suffered unemployment rates twice as high as whites. The wealth of black families compared to the wealth of white families continued to become more disparate. Even more black students went into debt to attend college. TSU's enrollment held at about 9,000, but the institution showed slow growth. Tennessee State suffered budget cuts and was unable to provide more grants and scholarships.

Tennessee State University opened its doors to a new class in early August 2002 as the university sought to standardize its calendar, including a two-day fall break in line with other public colleges and universities. When the residence halls opened on August 9, many upper classmen could choose to live in the Harold and John Ford Residence Complex, complete with private gate, individual bedrooms, living room, and clubhouse. Students engaged a variety of testing on the following day. On Sunday, they met for Interdenominational

---

[56] Ibid.; Mozel Avery, "Newton urges commitment to excellence," *The Meter*,13 April 1994, 1, 5.
[57] "TSU," Editorial, Nashville *Tennessean*, 14 August 2002.

Worship Service, financial aid, the Honors Program, International Student Organization and general orientation. Under Fannie Perry, for 10 August 2002, the new students attended a program called "Unleash your inner Monster!" to help the student answer some of the initial questions about college in a new and exciting way including managing time, earning good grades, choosing extracurricular activities and making any job a stepping-stone toward a bright and successful career. At the Faculty Institute Hefner spoke:

> What I want to share with you this morning comes from my values structure, especially my core belief that in higher education, specifically at Tennessee State University, students matter most…. The best professors really know their subjects and teach them well. Their classrooms are not forums for their personal ideologies … As it relates to TSU, serving students more efficiently and effectively is what we are all about … As our student population grows, it will become more diverse in age, race and socioeconomics. I applaud you for your commitment to students and this university. Remembering that 'students matter most,' let us have a banner year.[58]

On 21 October 2002, Present Hefner sent a letter to all students, urging them to "be versatile in your speech. Dress not necessarily expensively, but appropriately, because you are a student at Tennessee University and you are training to become a leader in society. You have come to Tennessee State University to invest in your future." The Office of Student Affairs started a program called Developmental Opportunities for First-Year Students, which they designed to intervene and correct the attitudes and values of the freshmen. The program intended to counter the influence of the gang and hip-hop culture on the youngsters. Hefner asked that each department form a committee to help provide programs for proper social and cultural education of the students. The faculty senate chair Harriet Insignares obliged by sending a letter to the 430 faculty members asking for their involvement. All students were required to have a mailbox in the Campus Center, and all students, staff, and faculty members had an email address and access to a computer. The Brown-Daniel Memorial Library had rows of desktop computers, and every campus building had direct or wireless Internet access and a computer lab.

The president tackled the task of gaining local acceptance of TSU by announcing the Economic Impact Study on October 10. TSU's Office of Business and Economic Research's study showed that TSU generated $493.5 million total impact on the greater Nashville area in 2001–02. The employee payroll generated $75.7 million, and students spent $105.2 million. TSU generated $41 million in research and training grants. TSU astronomer Gregory Henry obtained the first

---

[58] James A. Hefner, "Students Matter Most," 1–3, speech, Fall Faculty Institute, 12 August 2002, Special Collections, TSU.

direct evidence of an extra-solar planet by detecting a planetary transit in the HD 209458 system, confirming the existence of planets outside our solar system. Henry was a member of TSU's Center of Excellence for Information Systems Engineering and Management. Hefner said, "The University will continue to play a pivotal role in middle Tennessee's economic growth and expansion and in increasing the quality of life for all citizens."[59]

TSU Homecoming 2002 occurred from 20–26 October, with graduate Lillian Dunn Thomas (class of 1935) as the honoree. She was much involved in community, church, sorority, civic, educational, and community affairs. Her late husband, Harold E. Thomas, was plaintiff for the civil rights case *Thomas v. Hibbits et al.* (1941). The Robert N. Murrell Oratorical Contest co-sponsored by the College of Arts and Sciences and retired TSU vice president of student affairs Barbara Murrell kicked off the week's activities that Sunday. The TSU Homecoming Parade was a community-wide event, drawing 35,000-plus people, who also visited booths and food places along the parade route.[60]

Nearly 500 graduates participated in December 2002 commencement—the first one. Jamye Coleman Williams served as speaker. In May 2003, President Hefner said to the students, "But first and foremost … you are TSU students. And as students, you are the best example of what we can accomplish. As an ambassador for TSU, you will want to put your best foot forward as you meet people who may not know the TSU story. By dressing appropriately and speaking in an articulate manner, you will show people … that you are strong of character and of mind."[61]

In 2002, HBCUs—nearly 3 percent of the colleges and universities in America—contributed 29 percent of the bachelor's degrees and 15 percent of master's degrees awarded to blacks. Between 1992 and 1997, TSU awarded degrees to 41 percent of its black students overall and 47 percent of its black athletes. TSU, for the cohort year 2002, had a retention rate of 76.79 percent, compared to all Tennessee public four-year colleges that had rates of 78.51 percent for blacks and 80.85 percent for whites. TSU awarded 1,613 degrees compared to

---

[59] TSU, *Tennessee State University Economic Impact on Greater Nashville* (Nashville: TSDU, October 2002) 1–11; "Tennessee State University releases Economic Impact Study, the *Urban Journal*, Nashville, 16 October 2002, 9; "A Celebration of the Life of Robert Nathaniel Murrell," 11 February 1995, Temple Baptist Church, Nashville, 1–4; James A. Hefner, "Remarks for Faculty Meeting," 16 December 2002, J.A. Hefner, "Helping Students Learn Effective Oral and Written Communication Skills," letter to TSU academic deans, department chairs, and faculty, 7 February 2003, 1–2, Lovett Papers.

[60] "TSU Homecoming set for next week," *Urban Journal*, Nashville, 16 October 2002, 1; TSU, "Minutes," Faculty Senate, 19 September 2002, 1–4; TSU, *Blue Notes*, 14 April, 30 June, 15 July 2003.

[61] Chris Jones, "TSU's first fall commencement gets good reviews," Nashville, *The Tennessean*, 15 December 2002, 12B.

UT-Martin (1,001), Austin Peay (1,062), UT-Chattanooga (1,578), Tennessee Tech (1,854), East Tennessee (2,123), University of Memphis (3,187), MTSU (3,359), and UTK (6,046). TSU was one of America's top ten institutions-of-origin for black doctoral students in science, math, and engineering. US institutions awarded 1.3 million bachelor's degrees, including 117,000 (9 percent) to blacks.[62]

In the August 2003 commencement, James Brandon Shaw of Louisiana became the first person to receive a PhD degree in biological sciences from TSU. In fall 2003, TSU had 9,024 students, including 7,118 undergraduate and 1,906 graduate students.[63]

Harvey Johnson, Jr., (class of 1968) won reelection as mayor of Jackson, Mississippi, in 2001. He felt he got a broader education by mingling with people "from all parts of the country gathered at TSU." After the TSU experience in the AFROTC, he served in the military and returned to Mississippi.[64] Levi Watkins, Jr., (class of 1966), professor of cardiac surgery and associate dean of the Johns Hopkins University School of Medicine, was one of six new trustees elected at Vanderbilt. Some 23 percent of the Metro Nashville-Davidson County council were TSU graduates, including vice mayor Howard Gentry, Jr., council members Sam Coleman, Brenda Gilmore, Jamie Isabel, Pamela Murray, Carolyn B. Tucker (at-large), Ludye Wallace, Edward Whitmore, and Vivian Wilhoite. The governor appointed Monte Watkins (class of 1970) to the Davidson County General Sessions Court. Jo Ann North (class of 1977) was the elected Metro Nashville-Davidson County Tax Assessor.[65]

In 2004–05, James Hefner suffered accusations of financial mismanagement.

---

[62] THEC reports, 2000–02, and TSU Commencement programs and catalogs, 1999–2003; Jill M. Constantine, "Black Colleges and Beyond: An Analysis of Labor Market Experiences of Black College Students," *Review of African American Education* 1, no. 1 (1999): 84–102; Jane Buck, "HBCU faculty salaries continue to lag," *University Faculty Voice* 3, no. 1 (September 1998) 1, 4; NSF News, "Share of Black," science and engineering statistics, http://www.nsh.gov/statistics/, 2000, 8–26 [accessed 16 September 2011]; http://www.nces.gov/fastfact, 1 [accessed 16 September 2011].

[63] TSU, "Noted attorney addresses morning graduates," *Accent*, (May 2003): 3; Faculty Institute, Business and Finance report, 11 August 2003, *TSU 2003–2004 Fees*, 1–2.

[64] Brian C. Browley, "TSU alumnus makes history in Mississippi; "Harvey Johnson," *The Meter*, 26 March 2003, 1, 9.

[65] "Monte Watkins," Nashville, *The Urban Journal*, 24 August 2003, 1; "The Celebration of Life for Gregory David Leon Ridley Jr.," funeral program, Fisk University Chapel, 16 January 2004, Lovett Papers; Editorial staff, "Know your Metro Council," Brian C. Browley, "TSU alumnus makes history in Mississippi," Nashville, *Tennessean*, 5 October 2003, 1; Michelle E. Shaw, "Gilmore 'standing on the promises' in bid for 2nd term," Nashville, *Tennessean*, 16 June 2003, 4; Harvey Johnson," *The Meter*, 26 March 2003, 1, 9. Note: the Metro Council voted Howard Gentry, Jr., to assume the vacated position of Metro Nashville–Davidson County Court Clerk in August 2011.

The TSU Foundation was reported to be $2.6 million in debt.[66] The TBR Chancellor ordered audits. Hefner retired and announced on 3 December 2004 that the Regents had granted him emeritus status, office space in TSU's College of Business, and a chair of excellence: "I look forward to continuing as president until May 31, 2005." [67]

Until the end of his fourteen-year tenure, James A. Hefner had received quite good marks for his service as president. Tennessee State University had moved forward, and the institution came close to acceptance by the Nashville business community. Still, wealthy whites stirred their millions away from HBCUs, and Tennessee State University, too, received little of their monetary support. TSU alumni were also remiss in helping the institution build an effective endowment fund. The institution's enrollment topped 9,000 students, but that was far from the 14,000 that had been projected fifteen years earlier. Even so, TSU survived. Tennessee State University tried to move ahead, but the next seven years, the university suffered stagnation and some decline. The faculty and the administrators engaged in bitter confrontations over budget and program cuts. Unlike the period 1960–1995, the students—perhaps for lack of strong leadership and decreasing interest in the Student Government Association—remained quiet and uninspired.

---

[66] S. Dorsey-Duthie, "Tennessee State prez in hot water with Board over honors program awards," *University Faculty Voice* 4, no. 2 (October 1999) 1, 3.

[67] Colby Sledge, "Hefner withdraws from Fisk interim provost consideration; he seeks to regain his Regents pay," Nashville *Tennessean*, 4 July 2008, 2B; Joyce A. Jeffries, "TSU's first lady balances university life, family: Edwina Hefner, official hostess, helps husband," Nashville *Tennessean*, 2 January 2004, 2; J.A. Hefner to TSU faculty, administrators, staff and students, "TBR Resolution," 3 December 2004, Special Collections, TSU; Ashley Northington, "In Hefner we trust, President tries to improve the quality of students at all costs," *The Meter*, 26 January 2004, 1, 2; Michael Cass, "Chancellor upbraids TSU president," Nashville *Tennessean*, 10 January 2004, 1, 2A.; James A. Hefner, "The Role of Higher Education in Forging an Inclusive (Intellectual) Community," *The Boulé Journal* (Summer 1999): 9–12; James A. Hefner, "Protecting Research from Lean Economic Times," American Council on Education, *The Presidency* (Fall 2002): 43–45; "TSU's Aristocrat of Bands sparks Titan crowd," "People: Scenes from TSU Homecoming 2003," *Nashville Pride*, 14, 21 November 2003, 4A.; "Death Notices," Mrs. Ethel James Boswell, born 29 July 1915 in Chattanooga, Tennessee, the *Tennessean*, 29 December 2003, 4B; note: Hefner was serving as Provost and Vice President of Academic Affairs at Clark Atlanta University by 1912 after helping out at Texas Southern University.

10

2005–12: Melvin N. Johnson and Portia Shields

In 2005, the presidential search process allowed students, staff, and faculty members to access the interviews via the Internet. The TBR made the decision to hire Melvin Johnson. The newly elected president was in town on 10 March 2005 for his confirmation by TBR. Tennessee State University graciously held a reception for him in Elliott Hall (Women's Building) that afternoon. On 1 June 2005, the seventh president came aboard. Johnson had served as vice president for academic affairs at Winston-Salem State University and as an officer in the US Air Force. He received his degrees in economic education from North Carolina A&T University, Ball State University, and Indiana University. On 3 August 2005, Johnson announced, "We have a momentous year ahead—one in which each of us will have many opportunities to serve our University and promote its welfare!"[1] "It is so important that we work together to share the wonderful TSU story with others."[2] Adverse factors were lurking around TSU.

The Beginning of Another Decline

The state of Tennessee was suffering a vacuum of leadership especially in the three higher education boards: The University of Tennessee Board of Trustees, Tennessee Higher Education Commission (THEC), and the Tennessee Board of Regents. The higher education system and the presidencies at the state's eleven public universities had stagnated. In Tennessee, the sixteenth-most populous American state, there seemed to be a conservative political effort to deny these struggling institutions both the capable leadership and the funding needed for them to compete nationally. The higher education reform movement of 1905–09 was dead. Even the University of Tennessee, the state's flagship, was, for decades, saddled with one weak and insufficient presidential candidate after another. Consequently, UT ranked low among America's top fifty universities. The state of Tennessee could not rise higher than a ranking of 44th among the 50-state higher education systems. Students in the Southern Regional Education Board (SREB) area were discouraged by increasingly higher tuition and fees that

---

[1] Tennessee State University, *Alumni Directory, 2006*, 4th ed. (Chesapeake, VA: Harris Connect, 2006) 601; "President Johnson," *TSU Alumni Life* (Summer 2005) 1.

[2] *TSU Alumni Life* 1, no. 1 (Summer 2005): 1–2; Tennessee State University, *The Inauguration of Dr. Melvin N. Johnson Seventh President of Tennessee State University*, 1–16, 27 October 2006, TSU Library.

forced many of them to either forego a college education or resort to attending the bottomless pit of for-profit online colleges. Minority students comprised 30 to 50 percent of the online colleges' students.[3]

Tennessee State University was a merged, racially diversified institution by the time President Melvin N. Johnson took the reins in spring 2005. The institution remained one of the largest of America's universities with an HBCU legacy. The enrollment at the 105 HBCUs comprised about 380,000 students of the 18.5 million students at the nation's 4,000-plus colleges and universities. The HBCUs, including Tennessee State University, graduated about one of every five black college graduates in America. Though the country had come a long way in desegregating its public and private higher education system, *de facto* racially segregated higher education remained in the US, which had a total of 465 minority colleges and universities, including the 105 HBCUs, enrolling 35 percent of America's minority college students including blacks, Asians, Hispanics, and Native Americans. The PBCUs (predominately black colleges/universities) unexpectedly evolved or were created after 1965 partly because of the Civil Rights Act (1964) and the phenomenon of white flight from the inner cities to the suburbs. The PBCUs and their request for public funds and gifts presented a challenge to the pre-1965 HBCUs. Tennessee State was among a few dozen HBCUs to temporarily lose federally funded Upward Bound Programs but quickly regained the program in 2008.[4] Mary Love directed the Talent Search, Upward Bound, and Special Services (TRIO) programs for many years through 2012.

Under American plutocrats, government support for public universities was waning across the land.[5] The Tennessee budget for higher education declined 6.7 percent between 2007 and 2009. Federal funding to assist the 105 HBCUs, including the 53 private HBCUs, was not expanding. TSU and other HBCUs had to raise tuition and fees to compensate for a lack of adequate endowment funds, make cuts in public and private funding, incur the higher cost in personnel and operating costs, and pay the high cost to obtain and maintain regional and national accrediting agencies' standards. But program quality at the nation's institutions of higher education, including the HBCUs, perhaps did not increase as fast as the cost of tuition/fees. TSU tuition and fees rose from $48 in 1912 to $4,038 a year by 2008. Parents were writing to the Tennessee Legislative

---

[3] Brian C. Browley, "TSU financial aid is one of a kind," Rechelle Jackson, "Students' dress warrants concern from campus leaders," *The Meter*, 18 September 2006, 5, 7.

[4] Katherine Mangan, "Popular but Troubled, Historically Black Medical School Plans Ambitious Expansion," "Growth of State Dollars for Colleges Slows and Is Likely to Stall," *The Chronicle of Higher Education*, 16 January 2009, A15, A20.

[5] Sam Dillion, "States Provide Less for Universities," Nashville *Tennessean*, 16 October 2005, 3.

Black Caucus members, TSU President Melvin N. Johnson, the governor, and others, asking about students being purged from Tennessee State University, "needing only a few hundred dollars to stay in school." Annual out-of-state tuition and housing fees cost $26,064 at TSU by 2012, compared to about $300 in 1912.[6]

The TSU administration produced *Building Bridges: Past, Present and Future—Tennessee State University, President's Annual Report, 2005–2006*. Johnson released details of the $1.5 million renovation (*Geier* settlement funds) of the 200,0000-square-foot downtown Avon N. Williams, Jr., campus. Alumna Xernona Clayton, CEO of the nationally televised Trumpet Awards, was the August commencement speaker. TSU Olympic champion Wyomia Tyus earned induction into the National Black College Alumni Hall of Fame. Some 40,000 people attended the Homecoming parade.[7]

By 2007, Tennessee State University was classified as a Doctoral Research Intensive Comprehensive Level institution. The institution had 422-person, full-time instructional faculty; issued 1,545 degrees in 2007 and had students from 43 states and 32 countries including 76.5 percent from in-state and 43 percent from Davidson County. The ACT composite score was 18.04, and the average high school GPA was 2.85/4.0 at TSU. The budget was $121,319,074. In-state tuition and fees were $2,443 per semester; out-of-state (not including housing, books, etc.) was $7,581, forcing many students to stay closer to home. Some 3,552 of the 9,065 students were age 25 and older. TSU had 1,933 graduate students, with local whites comprising a majority. The faculty was 19 percent Asian, 41 percent black, 2 percent Hispanic, and 38 percent white. Some 239 (56 percent) of 422 faculty members had tenure. On-campus crime was low compared to area colleges. Some 31,063 alumni registered with the Office of Alumni Relations under director Michelle Viera. Chinedu Nwanwoala (class of 2007) said, "TSU didn't just teach me how tough life is, but how to handle it."[8]

Under faculty senate President Amiri Yasin Al-Hadid, TSU held a faculty senate retreat at Scarritt-Bennett Center near Vanderbilt University in June 2006,

---

[6] Tennessee State University, *Fee Schedule*, 2008, 1; Gertrude D. Scruggs to Tennessee Black Caucus Members, 23 May 2007, Nashville, Celestine P. Lowe, class of 1957, to Chancellor Charles Manning, Nashville, 24 May 2007, with attachment, "Questions being asked of President Melvin Johnson," Lovett Papers, Special Collections, TSU; "Annual Tuition and Fees at Colleges and Universities, 2012–13," A39–40, "Enrollment by Racial and Ethnic Group and Gender," *The Chronicle of Higher Education* 5, no 10 (2 November 2012): section B.

[7] TSU, *Building Bridges: Past, Present and Future, 2006*, 1–18, Special Collections, TSU.

[8] TSU, *Fact Book 2007*, Office of Effectiveness, Quality, and Research, 1–60; Chinedu Nwanwoala, "TSU," http://www.tnstate.edu/profiles/profiles/profiles.2.aspx, 1 [accessed 29 August 2011].

to engage strategic planning and make specific plans for the 2006–07 year. The faculty senate asked the new Provost to review the teaching workload versus other TBR universities, and to act on the recently completed Compensation Study to continue to bring faculty salaries at TSU in line with those of its peer universities. The faculty senate recommended a new policy on "Minimum Academic Requirements" because "by raising these academic standards, students are aware that there is always an expectation from the University regarding their academic achievement. Students who fail to meet these standards can receive additional academic assistance much earlier in their academic career to pilot the student toward reaching their degree objectives in a timely fashion."[9]

Maintaining high enrollment for budget purposes and increasing graduation rates became difficult. Tennessee State University lost 700 students in 2005–06 due to academic suspensions. The average ACT scores of incoming TSU students fell to 18.9 compared to the Tennessee average of 20 and the national average of 21. This drop placed TSU in the 38th percentile of the nation and within one percent of Carnegie Level I institutions. Tennessee State's enrollment decreased 0.45 percent in 2007. The TSU graduation rate had dropped from 44.3 percent in the 1999–2005 cohort to 41.2 percent in 2000–2006. The graduation rates for the same periods increased from 35.8 percent to 37.4 at Austin Peay State University, 45.5 percent to 46.8 percent at MTSU, and declined from 37.4 percent to 37.2 percent at the University of Memphis. The TBR system had an overall 43.8 percent graduation rate for 2000–06. The national college graduation rate ranged from 54–56 percent. The SREB expected an increase in high school graduates by 2012, and more of them would be minority persons that schools failed to educate sufficiently in preparation for college. In Tennessee, 50 percent of white and minority college students needed remedial classes.[10] And, Tennessee prepared to change state funding for colleges and universities based on enrollment to funding based on graduation of students. TSU focused on a retention rate strategy to drastically improve the graduation rate. Johnson said he needed "All of us, working together, to turn things around."[11]

---

[9] TSU Faculty Senate Report, 16–17 June, 2006, 1–5; M.N. Johnson "To TSU Family," 17 September 2008, University Exchange; *The Senate Griot* 1, no 1 (Fall–Spring 2006–07): 12; TSU, Faculty/Staff Institute, fall 2006: Transforming TSU—Learning Matters, 17–18 August, 2006, 1–7; Shauntae White, "TSU alumnus, vice major stars on stage," Howard Gentry, *The Meter*, 20 April 2006, 9, 10.

[10] SREB, Texas System's Report, *Service to Texas in the New Century: A Long Range Plan for the University of Texas System*, December 2000, 1–10.

[11] TSU Faculty Institute Reports, 17–18 August 2006, 1–10; Nashville *Tennessean* (4 September 2006): 8.

Geier *Is Over*

On 12 September 2006, Governor Phillip Bredesen (D) held a ceremony that included black and white officials to announce the "end of the 38-year-old *Geier* case." The next day, President Melvin Johnson sent a letter to the "Tennessee State University family," announcing, "Thanks to once-Tennessee State professor Rita Sanders Geier [et al] we can celebrate parity in higher education in Tennessee. Over the past few years, we have seen a change in attitude toward Tennessee State University in the Nashville community. Now, we are on a more level playing field. Thank you all for what you have done to help Tennessee State University grow and diversify over the last 38 years."[12] TSU inaugurated Melvin N. Johnson on Friday morning, 27 October 2006, in Gentry Center. Johnson created the university's first Presidential Medallion, Chain of Office, University Mace, and Baton designed by art professor Carlyle Johnson.[13]

TSU Seems to Move Ahead

Tennessee State University was among five university finalists recognized for outreach initiatives for the 2008 University Community Engagement Award. The TSU Center for Service Learning and Civic Engagement, led by Sue Fuller, along with the Cooperative Extension Program, helped the university serve as a bridge for connecting the needs of the community with the resources of the university. Tennessee State University Pilot Center for Academic Excellence in Intelligence Studies developed into an attractive program for students who got opportunities to visit other countries such as China. In April 2006, Tennessee Regents approved the College of Public Service and Urban Affairs; TSU also opened a new Research and Sponsored Programs building. The university added a Women's Program and implemented plans to upgrade all buildings.[14]

At the spring 2008 commencement, the speakers were Leone Bennett, Jr., scholar, author, historian, and retired senior editor for *Ebony* magazine at the 9 a.m. session, and Harold E. Ford, Jr., former member of the US House of Representatives, at the 2 p.m. session. Faculty listed some 1,100 students to

---

[12] President M.N. Johnson letter to TSU Community, 13 September 2006, TSU; "How a 32-year-old lawsuit finally ended," *TSU Alumni Life* 1, no. 1 (Spring 2002): 4–7; Eddie R. Cole, Jr., "Final Geier funds set, TSU to receive $40 million," *The Meter*, 25 September 2006, 1; Lovett, *The Civil Rights Movement in Tennessee*, 100.

[13] *Building Bridges: Past, Present, Future: the Inauguration of Dr. Melvin Norman Johnson* (Nashville: Tennessee State University, 2006) 1–8.

[14] TSU, Office of Public Relations, "Five Universities Recognized for Outreach Initiatives Selected as Finalists for 2008 C. Peter Magrath University Community Engagement Award," 21 April 2008, 1–2; Lerone Bennett, Jr., *Before the Mayflower: A History of Black America*, 6th ed. (New York: Penguin Books, 1993) 1–713; B.L. Lovett accepted President Johnson's invitation to have breakfast with Bennett.

receive graduate and undergraduate degrees. Several persons received the Professional Degree—the online computer degree. Faculty scheduled seven persons to receive PhDs in public administration, psychology, and biological sciences. They listed 41 doctors of education and 243 master's degrees during spring commencement. TSU scheduled two more graduation exercises in August and December 2008.[15]

Freedom Riders Honored by TSU

In 2008, TSU agreed to honor fourteen Freedom Riders expelled from the university in 1961 and grant them honorary degrees. The Board of Regents, however, rejected the proposal by a vote of 7–5. There was reluctance by many Tennesseans to dig up the state's embarrassing racial past, and some TBR members argued this was too many honorary doctorates to issue at one time, which could degrade the significance of bestowing such degrees. Although some black TBR members had perhaps benefited from the accomplishments of America's civil rights activists, they, too, ignored the need to rectify a dark and sinister chapter in Tennessee history and thus voted no or were absent for the vote. A TSU Office of Public Relations media alert said, "These students, now known as the 'Freedom Riders 14', were instrumental in the elimination of Jim Crow that permeated the South during the civil rights era. The Freedom Riders from Tennessee A. & I. joined students and citizens from other higher education institutions and states to non-violently protest civil rights disparities [in America]."[16]

People across Tennessee were so outraged at the TBR members that they mounted an intense online campaign to reverse the Board's decision. The faculty senate bodies at MTSU and Austin Peay reportedly passed resolutions of support for the Freedom Riders. The Great Debate Honor Society and the TSU Young Alumni Group honored some of the fourteen Freedom Riders on 4 April 2008. The Nashville *Pride* (11 April 2008) carried the photos of Mary Jean Smith, Allen Cason, Jr., Etta Simpson, and Ernest "Rip" Patton, who lived in Nashville. The TSU Alumni Association established an online letter that allowed hundreds to flood the Board of Regents with their grievances. The TSU legal counsel, with the help of university historians, submitted a statement of facts to reply to the TBR's questions. *The Meter* featured the Freedom Riders; the African Alliance honored them. The Regents reconvened through a conference call open to the public and

---

[15] TSU, *Spring Commencement Exercise of the Ninety-Seventh Year*, 3 May 2008; M.N. Johnson, *Progress and Promise: 2007–08 President's Report, July 1, 2007–June 30, 2008* (Nashville: TSU, President's Office, 2008) 1–28.

[16] TSU, Media Alert, "Date Set for Freedom Riders to Receive Degrees," 15 September 2008; Cass F.L. Teague, Jr., "Tennessee A. & I. State 14 honored at 23rd Annual Great Debate," *Nashville Pride*, 11 April 2008, A–1.

reversed their decision by a unanimous vote. On April 25, TSU released a statement: "Today, it gives me much pleasure to report that the Tennessee Board of Regents has joined the community in support of awarding honorary Doctor of Humane Letters degrees to fourteen students, who were expelled from TSU in 1961.... They are individuals who have demonstrated extraordinary achievements, setting standards that merit distinction."[17]

On 19 August 2008, attendees at the Faculty Institute discussed among other things the stagnant TSU enrollment numbers. White enrollment showed a slight increase. Undergraduates represented 80 percent of enrollment; 33 percent were 25 years and older; 82 percent were full-time students; 81 percent were black; and 65 percent were female. Graduate enrollment was 70 percent female, 32 percent full-time, and 45 percent white. Since 1995, an unexplained statewide decline in nontraditional students had negatively affected TSU, which awarded annually about 1,100 undergraduate and 481 graduate degrees. Master's programs enrolled 62 percent of the graduate students, and the College of Arts and Sciences continued to produce about 35 percent of the graduates. Tennessee State's overall graduation rate from 2000–06 was above 42 percent. This was better than the rate for two of TBR's TWIs, but below the average TBR graduation rate of 45 percent. Faculty and staff intended to address low-producing programs and respond to accusations of uneven academic quality, competition from other universities, limited resources, and historical biases against Tennessee State.[18]

The fourteen Freedom Riders received their degrees on September 18 at fall convocation before thousands of students, robed faculty members, and visitors. The local newspapers and news media carried the story. The Rev. C.T. Vivian, a noted civil rights leader who had been part of civil rights demonstrations in Tennessee in the 1960s, served as speaker. Catherine Burks-Brooks, Charles Butler (d. 2000), Allen Cason, Jr., William E. Harbour, Larry F. Hunter, Frederick Leonard, William B. Mitchell, Jr., (d. 2004), Pauline Knight-Ofosu, Earnest Rip Patton, Etta Marie Simpson Ray, Mary Jean Smith, Frances Wilson, Clarence M. Wright (d. 1974), and El-Senzengakulu Zulu (Lester G. McKinnie) received honorary doctorates. Seminars followed on Friday, September 19. The Annual African Street Festival (19–21 September 2008, held on the TSU campus) honored local Freedom Riders, including Salynn McCollum of Peabody College who was one of the two white students on the Freedom Ride out of Nashville. She recalled

---

[17] TSU, Office of Public Relations, News Release, 25 April 2008; "Freedom Riders," Nashville *Pride*, 11 April 2008, 1; "TSU Problems," Nashville *The Tennessean*, 17 August 2008, 1.
[18] *Tennessee State University Academic Master Plan, 2008–2028*, TSU, 1–21. Personal notes and documents, TSU Faculty Institute, 19 August 2009, TSU Library, Special Collections.

how Peabody College and her parents reacted negatively to her arrest in Birmingham.[19]

Matters Worsen at TSU

President Johnson had said he had been surprised at the bad condition of TSU when he took over in 2005, but many of the problems got worse after he failed to remove incompetent personnel, hired more poor mangers, and raised their salaries. In the fall of 2008, the staff failed to process late student applications and financial aid for many of the entering students in a timely manner. A crisis resulted from the delay of student financial awards from federal and other offices. There was seemingly a lack of coordination with the Office of Admissions and Records, and these problems caused nearly 1,700 students to be unable to enroll in classes. The president appealed to faculty, alumni and friends, who raised money through the TSU Foundation to save all but about 400 students. Not only did this incident damage Tennessee State, but it also resulted in the loss of hundreds of out-of-state students—the institution's bread and butter. The president notified the university on 7 October 2008 that he had fired several administrators, including the provost/vice president for academic affairs and the financial aid director, and demoted the associate vice president for enrollment management.[20] Yet, some of them survived and remained at the university.

The American economy took a dive in September 2008. The state of Tennessee cut $43 million from public higher education, including $4.5 million for Tennessee State University. In addition, TSU suffered a $6 million shortfall because of decreased fall 2008 enrollment. The cost of higher education was rising at 6 to 9 percent a year in America and in Tennessee. Tennessee State University had to freeze master academic plans and make plans for personnel reductions and program cuts. The state of Tennessee's unemployment rate exceeded 10 percent; the black unemployment rate was nearly twice that. Nearly 80 percent of TSU's students were black, and many of them originated from the state's core cities and other economically disadvantaged black communities. Further budget cuts hit Tennessee's public colleges and universities when tax collections declined for the state. A *Tennessean* reporter wrote, "A languishing

---

[19] Author's interview/conversation with Ms. S. McCollum, Nashville, 19 September 2008, Lovett Papers; James M. Lawson, "How we lead our life influences others," Nashville *Tennessean*, 19 September 2008, 12A; "Riders Get Their Reward," Nashville *The Tennessean*, 19 September 2008, 1B, 4B; obituaries page, 4B.

[20] President's letter to TSU community," 7 October 2008, Computer Internet Exchange, Special Collections, TSU; note: the state had relaxed the 1968 out-of-state enrollment limit of 15 percent, and TSU quietly exceeded the limit to fulfill a healthy budget and to reflect its national and international mission.

economy, restricted student loans, rising tuition and poor TSU policies could potentially drop enrollment to a 20-year low."[21]

On September 4, President Melvin Johnson asked TSU constituents for help for the 1,338 students "who have fallen short financially." He also presented a list of plans, including charging "the university's development officers with finding and/or developing a pool of funds for additional financial support for out-of-state students and other students who have attempted to register but face financial shortfalls."[22] But was this enough to stop TSU's decline?

Among the great weaknesses of the HBCUs was the loss of black faculty members who traditionally had led the nurturing of many of the students that were not ready for college studies. They had taken rough coal and polished the pieces into diamonds. The *University Faculty Voice* of the HBCUs said, "HBCUs losing Black faculty."[23] Whites held 83 percent of faculty positions and 69 percent of the population in America. Fewer blacks earned PhD degrees in content areas: social sciences, hard sciences, engineering, mathematics, business, and so forth. Among blacks with PhD degrees in the content areas, many of them chose to work at the TWIs that offered higher salaries, better benefits, and lighter class-teaching loads. By 2011, TSU had 27 percent Asian/others, 37 percent white, and 36 percent black faculty members.

TSU was also weak in endowment management and expertise. More than 90 percent of the HBCUs suffered a lack of systematic fundraising, maintenance, and replenishing of endowment funds. Howard University raised its alumni-giving rate to 20 percent, with 51 alumni giving more than $1 million; thus, Howard raised more than $250 million, increasing the endowment fund to more than $700 million. TSU received less than a million dollars a year, and fewer than 5 percent of the alumni gave any money. One TSU graduate gave a million dollars or more. Former Tigerbelle and Olympic gold medalist Edith McGuire-Duvall (1966) donated $1 million to the TSU foundation for various programs and to "foster greater alumni giving." The TSU endowment stagnated at about $48 million by 2011 and had suffered a deficit under President James Hefner. TSU's $48 million was more than the endowment of most other colleges and universities in Nashville, but it was far from being enough. Vanderbilt

---

[21] Colby Sledge, "TSU plans layoffs as shortfall is expected: school may drop 1,300 who can't pay tuition," Nashville *The Tennessean*, 4 September 2008, 1.

[22] Melvin N. Johnson to Faculty and Staff, "To the TSU Family," 4 September 2008, University Exchange.

[23] Michael Reed, "HBCUs losing Black Faculty," *University Faculty Voice* 6, no. 8 (April 2002) 1, 4.

University had an endowment fund of $4–$6 billion, but that too was nowhere near Harvard University's $36-billion endowment.[24]

Increasing operational costs, inflation, and diminishing revenue caused 231 four-year America colleges and universities to close down between 1960 and 2002. Twenty (8.7 percent) of these failed institutions of higher education were HBCUs. Since *Brown* (1954), fourteen HBCUs had closed because of loss of accreditation; meeting accreditation standards was expensive. In East Tennessee, Knoxville College had lost SACS accreditation and almost all of its students by 2004. Several of Tennessee's small private HBCUs, including Fisk University and Lemoyne-Owen, struggled financially and under the threat of losing SACS accreditation. America's Catholic schools and colleges were having serious financial problems, too, by 2009. A TWI Lambuth College in Jackson, Tennessee, lost SACS accreditation and announced closure by 30 June 2011.[25] Public HBCUs Florida A&M, Grambling, and Texas Southern suffered SACS warnings or probation between 2004 and 2008. A *Tennessean* headline said, "Troubles Test TSU: The biggest danger for TSU is not that it will collapse, but that it will become irrelevant."[26]

But TSU maintained its national and international recognition over other public universities in Tennessee. Counting out-of-state and foreign student populations, the percentages were as follows: TSU, 27.2; Austin Peay State University, 15.8; East Tennessee State University, 15.6; University of Memphis, 13.4; and Middle Tennessee State University, 8.1. The average for all Tennessee public universities was 12.9 percent. The TSU average ACT score was 19.8, compared to about 22 for other TBR universities. In 2007–08, with about 9,000 students, TSU was first in total number of degrees awarded to blacks (1,073). The University of Memphis, with more than 20,000 students—including about 30 percent black in a predominantly black city—was second with 1,006 degrees awarded to blacks. With 22,000-plus students, MTSU awarded 452 degrees to blacks. For 2002–03, the MTSU graduation rate for blacks/whites was 47.1/51.5; TSU 38.6 /39.3; UM 31.4 /46.1.[27]

---

[24] "Howard U. Engages Alumni to Raise the Bar on Fund Raising," *The Chronicle of Higher Education*, 27 June 2008, A1, A14–15; B.L. Lovett, "Open Letter to the Tennessean: Concerns Regarding Tennessee State University," *The Tennessee Tribune*, 28 August–3 September 2008, 3A; TSU, *Foundation Annual Report, 2010–2011*, 8–9, Special Collections, TSU.

[25] Audrey W. June, "Southern Association Strips two Black Colleges of Accreditation," *Chronicle of Higher Education* 49, no. 17 (3 January 2003): A34; Richard Morgan, "Lambuth plans to close by June 30," Nashville *Tennessean*, 15 April 2011, 4.

[26] See Bobby L. Lovett, *America's Black Colleges and Universities* (Macon, GA: Mercer University Press, 2011) 293–302; Nashville *Tennessean*, 17 August 2008, 1A, 14A.

[27] Tennessee Higher Education Commission, *Fact Book, 2008–09* (Nashville: THEC, 2009) 1–21. Note: When the author spoke informally to former President Humphries, who

TSU outpaced the TWIs in the TBR system in research and training grant dollars. The TSU division of research and sponsored research reported $51.1 million of grant submissions and $32.9 million in awards for fiscal year 2007. The US Department of Defense awarded TSU a $1 million grant to establish core laboratory facilities to support nanoscience and biotechnology research.[28] The Center of Excellence in Information Systems and Engineering Management received a $740,525 grant from the US Army Research Office to design a measurement-based controller used for vehicles and aircraft. The Cooperative Extension Program granted funds to students to find solutions to minority health disparities. In the College of Arts and Sciences, sociology professor Bagar Husaini headed a research center for medical health disparities. The federal agencies supported 67 percent of the sponsored research at Tennessee's colleges and universities.[29]

Homecoming renewed campus spirits. WTST campus radio station, founded in 1972 as a carrier-current station by Daniel E. Owens, could now transmit on 1600AM channel 99 on the campus cable system. The week's events included the Miss TSU Reunion and Tea on 31 October 2008 at Opryland Hotel, featuring all the living wives of the presidents and former Miss TSU women. Fraternities, sororities, and other student organizations also held their events during Homecoming week. The football team won the Homecoming game. TSU dedicated the multi-million dollars renovation of the Williams, Jr., campus, and the university extended its evening/weekend college into Coffee, Dickson, Lincoln, Maury, Sumner, and Williamson counties, offering low-cost daycare services for working adults and online degrees.

TSU's fall enrollment of 9,038 represented a fall from fifth place to nearly last among the state's nine public four-year institutions. On 5 November 2008, President Johnson sent a letter "To the Members of the Tennessee State University Community," saying he had appointed a Strategic Planning Steering Committee comprised of faculty, staff, students, and administrators to develop TSU's 2010–15 strategic plan and to work on related planning initiatives at the university. TSU and some twenty other consortium schools joined the Harvard University Institute of Politics "National Campaign for Political and Civic Engagement," which also would give TSU students opportunities to discuss major public policy and political issues with their national peers. At age 100,

---

also was doing research in the TSU Library Special Collections Room, he worried those TWIs as the University of Memphis would become the top producers of black college graduates and bring more questions about continuing HBCUs. B.L. Lovett conversation with F. Humphries, 8 September 2009, 1–2, Lovett Papers.

[28] TSU, *30th Annual University-Wide Research Symposium Program*, 31 March–3 April 2008; TSU *Blue Notes*, Office of Public Relations, December 2007, 1–8.

[29] TSU Office of Public Relations, *Blue Notes*, October 2008, 1–4.

Nannie Mae Fort (class of 1933) was the oldest living TSU graduate. Nearly 250 guests at the Farrell-Westbrook Agricultural Center on campus celebrated her 100th birthday.[30]

TSU announced a Dual Admissions Partnership with Nashville State Community College to offer students a structured, guaranteed pathway for attaining baccalaureate degrees in certain areas. On 8 May 2009, Johnson announced the finalization of the *University Strategic Plan* to provide a roadmap for TSU's future. The faculty senate discussed a draft of the new *Faculty Handbook.* There was a short-term marketing campaign targeted toward raising the university's profile, increasing student and community awareness, and generating student interest in Tennessee State. SACS scheduled the accreditation visit to Tennessee State University for spring 2009.

On 25 June 2009, Johnson presented the "President's 2009 Summer Budget Update" to the faculty and staff outlining the major budget reductions of $12.7 million (11.6 percent) of the annual operating budget. On August 24, Johnson addressed the faculty/staff meeting. He outlined the university's present status. The percentage of first-time full-time freshmen returning had dropped from 77.1 percent in 2004 to 68 percent in 2008. The TBR average for that period was 80 percent. TSU had 24 percent low-producing degree programs compared to 14 percent for the TBR system, and Johnson said the faculty and staff had to look at this problem. Emerging fields evolve over time and via student/market demands, he said. With a potential $14.4 million funding gap, some low-producing programs would have to make way for newer, more in-demand programs. The good news: TSU had more than $40 million in training and research grants for 2008. However, to implement the multi-year strategic plan, the university needed $36,149,700 beyond the present budget. Faculty and staff would have to increase recruitment, retention, and graduation of students as tuition and fees still comprised the university's largest category of revenue.[31]

There was indication in September 2009 that fall enrollment would increase by 10 percent. Out-of-state students showed continued interest in Tennessee State University as an international and national institution. Still, the challenge to such a highly diversified HBCU as Tennessee State was to increase the overall

---

[30] President Melvin N. Johnson letter "To the Members of the Tennessee State University Community," 5 November 2008, Computer Exchange, Special Collections, TSU; Tennessee State University, Faculty/Staff Institute Spring 2009, Agenda, TSU Library; TSU, *Transforming Tennessee State University: Strategic Plan, 2010–2015,* Special Collections, TSU.

[31] M.N. Johnson, "President's 2009 Summer Budget Update," 25 June 2009, Special Collections, TSU; TSU, Report on Low-Producing Programs in the College of Arts and Sciences, Dean's Office, May 2009, 1–54, Lovett Papers.

graduation rate for both black and white students. TSU was awarded $8 million for mathematics instruction in President Obama's Race to the Top program.[32]

Johnson Resigns

In 2010–11, the problems at TSU had compounded. Some faculty members were trying to get the faculty senate to vote no confidence in Johnson's leadership. The faculty senate had its own problems, however, including lack of quorums to do business, and the senate was upset about the administration's unilateral actions in forging ahead with implementation of a prioritization plan that reorganized the university and cut several academic degree programs. The 2010–15 strategic plan's mission and vision statements said that, "Tennessee State University, a Historically Black College/University (HBCU), fosters scholarly inquiry and research, lifelong learning, and a commitment to service. Tennessee State University aspires to achieve national and international prominence, building on its heritage and preparing leaders for a global society."[33]

The *Tennessee Tribune* newspaper said "The Boogie Man Stalks TSU" and questioned the biased reporting on TSU by the Nashville *Tennessean* and its failure to report similar financial and auditing problems at Tennessee's TWIs. The president of SACS, Commission on Colleges, even wrote to the publisher and the editor of the Nashville *Tennessean* to give the publisher, editor, reporters, and staff members a better understanding of the reaffirmation accreditation process lest they continue to paint TSU badly in public, using erroneous information that discouraged students from attending TSU. On 17 July 2010, a TSU administrator wrote a letter of complaint to the TSU family about the *Tennessean* stories that "took the information we provided and used it to focus on the negative, while minimizing the positive data and information."[34]

---

[32] The author's conversation with Dr. Fred S. Humphries, 8 September 2009, 1–2, Lovett Papers; Kathleen McEnerney, interim vice president for academic affairs, *Tennessee State University Faculty/Staff Institute, Fall 2010, August 18–19, 2010*, 1–6, and *Faculty/Staff Institute, Spring 2011, Thursday, January 6, 2011, Kean Hall*, Theme "Change is Gonna' Come," 1–9, Special Collections, TSU.

[33] *Transforming Tennessee State University: 2010–2015 Statement Plan Goals and Expectations*, Executive Overview, Office of the President, 2010, Special Collections, TSU; TSU, Summary of Unrestricted Current Funds Available and Applied and Budget Proposals, 1–123, Special Collections, TSU; Jaime Sarrio and Brad Schrade, "Engineering, nursing schools stand out as model of TSU change," Nashville *Tennessean*, 12 July 2010, 7A.

[34] G.S. Holmes, "The Boogie Man Stalks TSU," Nashville *The Tennessee Tribune*, 25–31 March 2010, 4–5; Belle S. Wheelan, SACS, Commission on Colleges, Atlanta, to publisher and editor of the Nashville *Tennessean*, 12 March 2010; Peter O. Nwosu, Special Assistant to the President for Institutional Planning, to the TSU campus, 17 July 2010, Special

Correspondingly, some white students at the University of Tennessee-Knoxville were heaping derogatory and racist language on passing black students and their visiting parents. Someone had painted racist German swastika in UTK dormitories. These acts were meant to discourage blacks—other than athletes—from choosing UTK. UTK Chancellor Jimmy Cheek apologized for the racial slurs, the signs posted with racist language, and the swastika in dormitories.[35] Nevertheless, racial hatred remained a problem all across America.

By 2011, twice the number of white Americans received college degrees compared to African Americans. This racial disparity in education seemed to help feed racial economic disparity, where high school and college diplomas translated into higher wages and more wealth. The poverty rate in Tennessee increased from 13 percent to 17.1 percent from 2000–11. In predominantly black Memphis, 34 percent of the families lived below the poverty level. Some 21.1 percent of Tennesseans had some college but had not completed a degree. Some 6.1 percent had an associate degree, though half of the state's college students attended community and junior colleges. Among 6.3 million Tennesseans, 15.1 percent had bachelor's degrees, 5.4 percent had master's degrees, 1 percent had doctoral degrees, and 1.5 percent had professional degrees. The graduation rates at four-year institutions were 60.4 percent for Asians, 53.7 percent for whites, 53.1 percent for Hispanics, and 37.5 percent for blacks. Blacks comprised 69,274 students, Hispanics 8,422 students, Asians 6,707, and whites and others made up the rest of the 332,918 college students in Tennessee. The average ACT score was 19.5 (17 for blacks). Tennessee expected to have 7 percent growth in the number of high school graduates from 2011–21, with minorities expected to have the greatest increase in college enrollments in the South.[36] Truly, although TSU had entered a new era wherein race should gradually cease to matter, the recent UT racial incidents indicated otherwise.

Collections, TSU; "TSU Responds to the Tennessean," *Tennessee Tribune*, 22–28 July 2010, 11A, "We are at a crossroads," Professor Asson-Batres (biology) to faculty members, 28 July 2010, 1–3,"Actions Don't Match Words," Raymond Richardson [professor of mathematics], to faculty members, 31 January 2010, 1–4, Special Collections.

[35] C.W. Kennedy, "UT Chancellor 'will not tolerate' [racial] intolerance," Nashville *The Tennessean*, 27 March 2010, 8B; Jaime Sarrio and Brad Schrade, "TSU navigates rocky road to becoming reaccredited," 6A, "Brad Schrade and Jaime Sarrio, "Support for Johnson may have faded," 6A, "Schrade and Sarrio, 'Gang of 4' faculty led revolt to oust Johnson as president," 6,7A, Nashville, *The Tennessean*, 12 July 2010.

[36] Almanac Issue 2011–12, *Chronicle of Higher Education* 53, no. 1 (26 August 2011): 43, 48, 85.

In 2010, out-of-state tuition was $19,498 and in-state tuition was $6,346 a year at TSU; $25,538/$8,396 at UT; and $55,000 at Vanderbilt.[37] The White House Initiative on HBCUs canceled the 2011 HBCU Technical Conference scheduled the following April at Alabama A&M University.[38]

President Melvin N. Johnson resigned effective 31 December 2010.[39] He had sent a letter to students and faculty staff members dated 7 July 2010 to that effect. Johnson looked forward to joining the faculty as a tenured professor in the College of Business. He conducted the December 2010 commencement exercise as one of his last official acts. President emeritus Frederick S. Humphries was presented the honorary Doctor of Humane Letters. He had served as TSU president (1975–85), as president of Florida A&M University (1985–2001), as president and CEO of NAFEO until 2004, and was on the White House Advisory Committee on HBCUs (1994–2010). Commencement ended with the audience standing and singing the TSU Alma Mater.[40]

The new TBR chancellor contacted an employment search agency, the Registry for College and University Presidents—a for-profit agency that assists colleges and universities in finding retired and other former administrators to help out during transition periods. He selected Portia H. Shields, who had served at Concordia College in Alabama, presiding over about 500 students for two years, and she had served for nine years as president of Albany State University with nearly 3,000 students. Shields also had been dean of the school of education at Howard University. She had earned bachelors, masters, and PhD degrees in education. The Tennessee Board of Regents appointed Shields as Interim President of Tennessee State University effective 2 January 2011. The news release said, "With Shields as interim president, the TBR can proceed carefully and thoughtfully to advertise and fill the TSU president's position at the

---

[37] Juan Williams and Dwayne Ashley "Tennessee State University," *I'll Find a Way or Make One: A Tribute to Historically Black Colleges and Universities* (New York: HarperCollins, 2004) 1–453; Chloe W. Kennedy, "UT chancellor 'will not tolerate' intolerance," Nashville *Tennessean*, 27 March 2010, 8B; Julie Hubbard, "America's illegal children face adulthood as outsiders: College dream hinges on act of Congress," Nashville, *Tennessean*, 7 August 2011, 1A, 7A.

[38] "The Serious Racial Disparity in College Retention Rates," "HBCUs are producing a Smaller Share of all Bachelor's Degrees Awarded to African Americans," "White House Cancel Conference at Historically Black Alabama A & M," *The Journal of Blacks in Higher Education*, 31 March 2011, 1–3.

[39] Brad Schrade and Jaime Sarrio, "Johnson says he'll resign as TSU president," Nashville *Tennessean*, 8 July 2010, 1A, 11A; Brad Schrade and Jaime Sarrio, "A University Challenged, second of two parts, Leadership at Crossroads," Nashville *Tennessean*, 8 July 2010, 1A, 7A.

[40] Tennessee State University, Fall Commencement Exercise, 18 December 2010, 5, 1–28, Howard C. Gentry Center Complex, Nashville, Special Collections.

appropriate time." Because TSU was on warning from SACS for its failure to document a standard concerning evaluation and feedback procedures on such evaluation, the TBR chancellor announced that Shields was the best person to get TSU on the right track to reaffirm accreditation. On January 7, Acting President Shields invited faculty and staff to "a meet and greet session" in Kean Hall. On March 10, she announced a freeze on travel and hiring: "An increase in productivity will allow us to maintain or improve our level of resources."[41]

Several other HBCUs were in financial trouble and had suffered SACS sanctions since 2002.[42] Budget cuts in the Southern Regional Education Board (SREB) territory threatened a significant decrease in the number of blacks who could afford to enroll in college. Some 84 percent of black college students (half of them assigned to junior and community colleges and online, for-profit colleges) attended TWIs, though the attrition rate was high and the graduation rate was low.[43] Most of the 105 HBCUs, including TSU, existed in the SREB and SACS territory.

On March 15, Chancellor J. G. Morgan presented to the TBR the governor's fiscal year 2011–12 budget recommendations. The TBR claimed to be the nation's sixth largest higher education system, governing 45 post-secondary education institutions, including six universities, 13 two-year colleges, 27 technology centers, and providing programs in 90 of Tennessee's 95 counties to more than 200,000 students. The chancellor said TSU was important to our state and nation.[44]

On 31 April 2011, Acting President Portia Shields announced the Academic Program Prioritization and Reorganization of Academic Programs and Colleges/Schools that discontinued eight academic programs deemed not productive or mission essential; reorganized or consolidated marginally

---

[41] "Portia Shields to serve as TSU interim president," TBR *News Release*, University Exchange, 16 December 2010, Special Collections, TSU; Jennifer Brooks, "New TSU president promises change, Accreditation, bureaucracy are problem areas," Nashville *Tennessean*, 17 January 2011, 1A, 8A.

[42] Eric Kelderman, "Troubled Barber–Scotia College Seeks Revival, Historically black college faces long odds to get back in good standing," *The Chronicle of Higher Education* 61, no. 9 (23 October 2009): A1, A20; "Mary Holmes College campus sold," *Journal of Blacks in Higher Education*, 10 June 2010, 1.

[43] Portia H. Shields to the members of the TSU family, 10 March 2011; J.G. Morgan to the members of the TBR, Nashville, 15 March 2011, Special Collections, TSU; Jennifer Brooks, "TSU, Fisk try to get back in good standing: Schools got warnings from Commission," Nashville *Tennessean*, 14, 15 April 2011, 1B, 8B; "A College Education Does Nothing to Close the Racial Unemployment Gap," *The Journal of Blacks in Higher Education*, 1 April 2010.

[44] Portia H. Shields to the members of the TSU family, 10 March 2011; J. G. Morgan to the members of the TBR, Nashville, 15 March 2011, 1–5.

productive but mission-essential academic programs; realigned some academic programs and colleges/schools; and transformed the low-producing School of Agriculture and Consumer Sciences into the College of Agriculture and Bio-Environmental Sciences by stripping the College of Arts and Sciences of its productive biological sciences program. Departments of chemistry and mathematics were stripped from the College of Arts and Sciences and attached to the low-producing College of Engineering, a unit that had struggled during its sixty-year existence. The College of Arts and Sciences' undergraduate and graduate degree programs in Social Work were moved to the low-producing College of Public and Urban Affairs. The reorganization plan terminated several low-producing academic degree programs such as the BS foreign languages, BS physics; MA English, MS music education, MS mathematical sciences, and BS Africana Studies.

The African Studies faculty argued to keep the program because "it is a unique and critically important field that is essential to the University's commitment to address the ... omission of any formal study of the culture, history, and languages of an entire continent [Africa] and its Diasporas.... For any university, and especially a HBCU, African Studies is mission essential."[45] The Department of Africana Studies had graduated its first student Desha Foster in August 1997. TSU was among eleven HBCUs that offered degree-granting African-American Studies programs. Tennessee State University's African Studies produced 23 graduates between 2004 and 2009, instead of twice that number as the state minimum formula required. The program counted 15 majors and many minors in 2009 that could graduate within the next five years. [46]

Some faculty members distrusted Portia Shields. The quick decisions that seemed to reflect a lack of in-depth knowledge about higher education curriculum and had the potential to weaken TSU's hundred-year struggle to compete with the TWIs. The Academic Program Prioritization and Reorganization of Academic Programs and Colleges/Schools seemed to

---

[45] TSU, Report on Low Producing Programs in the College of Arts and Sciences, Dean's Office, May 2009, 10, 14, Lovett Papers.

[46] "TSU graduates first Africana Studies major," TSU, college of arts and Sciences, *Highlights: College of Arts and Sciences,* 1–2; "McWherter Scholars are prepared to excel: Recipients hail from all areas of the state," *The TSU Scholar,* 27 March 1998, 1–4; Getahn M. Ward, "Africana studies program awaits Board of Regents approval," *The Meter,* 5 February 1993, 1; *Third Annual Africana Studies Conference: "Africana Studies: Education, Research and Community Engagement,"* 1–3 February 2007, Floyd-Payne Campus Center, TSU, 1–17; TSU, Report on Low Producing Programs in the College of Arts and Sciences, Dean's Office, May 2009, 10, 14, Lovett Papers.

downgrade TSU from maintaining a comprehensive, research Level I university, but the Regents approved the proposal on 29 June 2011, effective 1 July 2011.[47]

On 14 September 2011, Tennessee State University kicked off a year's celebration of the institution's Centennial Celebration at the fall convocation. Gerald Durley (class of 1964) was the major speaker. Acting President Shields and Nashville Mayor Karl Dean gave remarks at this celebration. TSU 2015 listed 430 full-time faculty members, approximately 200 part-time faculty members, and an average of 8,684 students for 2010–11. The institution projected 10,000 to 12,000 students by 2015. On September 26, *A Resolution Concerning the Threat to Tennessee State University* was circulated by the state convention of the NAACP charging that, "the heart of the dual system of higher education was and still is land-grant inequality between TSU and UT." The document had several other concerns about Tennessee State and its adversarial relationship with state officials. The document called for a financial statement of TSU by an *outside* firm, and that the presidential search for TSU's new president should follow the democratic model used in the search by East Tennessee State University when they recently were looking for a new president. In November, the TSU faculty senate echoed these concerns and demands.

Homecoming 2011 was expected, as usual, to lift the spirit on the campus when an estimated 40,000 alumni, friends and supporters arrived for the celebration. Barbara C. Murrell and NFL Hall of Fame inductee Richard L. Dent were the Homecoming Grand Marshals. However, the football team lost the game, only 19,000 or so spectators came to the event, and the controversies on campus were perplexing and unpleasant to alumni.[48] The future of Tennessee

---

[47] Portia H. Shields to "TSU Family," Nashville, 13 April 2011; Save TSU Community Coalition to Chancellor John Morgan, 17 May 2011, Nashville, 1–2. Special Collections, TSU; John G. Morgan, Chancellor, TBR, to Mary Asson-Batres, biology professor at TSU, Nashville, 26 April 2011; "Academic Program Prioritization," Office of the Provost, University Memorandum, TSU, Nashville, 12 April, 6 July 2011, University Communications; THEC, *The Public Agenda for Tennessee Higher Education, 2010–2015* (Nashville: THEC, 2011) 1–9, 1–31.

[48] Almanac Issue 2011–2012, *Chronicle of Higher Education* 53, no. 1 (26 August 2011): 43, 48, 85; Nicole Young, "'Exciting adventure' awaits TSU in its second century," Nashville *The Tennessean*, 15 September 2011, 1B–2B; To Cordia McCutcheon, secretary for HGPS faculty, Elizabeth Dachowski, "Recap of the Most Recent Faculty Senate Meeting" (15 September 2011), 1, Lovett Papers; Raymond Richardson to TSU personnel, attached Resolution adopted by the State Convention of the NAACP, 24 September 2001, 1–5, Lovett Papers; *TSU 2015, Transforming Tennessee State University: 2010–2015 Strategic Plan Goals and Expectations* (Nashville: TSU Office of Institutional Planning and Assessment, 2011) 1–10; Cassandra Teague, "TSU celebrates '99 Years of Academic Excellence and Achievements at Homecoming," *Nashville Pride*, 4 November 2011, 1B; Almanac, 2012–13, *The Chronicle of Higher Education* 51, no. 1 (31 August 2012): 31–32, 91–92.

State University is promising even though many questions remain that will have to be answered in future chapters on the TSU story.

The TBR announced on-campus interviews for the four presidential finalists, scheduled for 29 October–1 November 2012. They selected Glenda B. Glover (1974) as TSU's eighth president, effective January 2013. Since 1912, Tennessee A&I State Normal School has evolved into a college, then a university, and finally a research doctoral institution. The student body has documented during the school's one-hundred-year history that Tennessee State University is an institution of undeniable quality, contrary to the claims of local detractors and despite its long and arduous battles against great odds and adverse conditions. Students, alumni, faculty and staff members, parents, and presidents have literally carried the institution on their backs. The institution has admirers both nationally and internationally that outnumber the local detractors and who have allowed Tennessee State University to retain its self-esteem and maintain that Big Blue ego. The institution's presidents, students leaders, and others have devoted their careers to etch these extraordinary characteristics into the limestone buildings and the very fabric of a peculiar institution—Tennessee State University (1912–2012).

11

TSU Diamonds: TSU Student
Athletes, Coaches, and Sports Legends

The history of modern American sports is tied to the schools, colleges, and universities. When America began the transformation from an agricultural economy to an industrial one, and from a rural society to an urban society, people had more leisure time and began to engage more in the arts, humanities, science, and sports. Some players organized the National Association of Baseball Players in 1858, while the National League of Baseball Clubs began in 1876. The American Baseball League began in 1899, and the World Series began in 1903. The popular tune, "Take Me Out to the Ball Game," took hold in 1908. Football became so popular—and deadly—that the president of the United States Theodore Roosevelt called a conference to discuss how to solve the problem. In 1906, sixty-two TWIs formed the Intercollegiate Athletic Association that became the National Collegiate Athletic Association (NCAA) in 1910.[1]

Only four historically black colleges and universities (HBCUs) existed before 1865, and none of them offered four-year college degrees. By 1910, there were at least 240 freedmen's schools, historically black colleges, and universities, but only a dozen or so truly were baccalaureate institutions. There were few Negro high schools, especially in the South where 90 percent of black Americans lived, but where almost all of the HBCUs were located. The first of the Negro land-grant schools, Alcorn State College (1871–), fielded a baseball team in 1875, but it was not yet offering four-year degrees. Fisk University (1866) graduated its first college class in 1874, and built its first gymnasium in 1888 to help develop "sound, vigorous, and evenly balanced, strong, and graceful bodies."[2] Biddle University (Johnson C. Smith University) and Livingston College played the first intercollegiate HBCU football game on 27 December 1892. Fisk University students organized a football team in 1893–94. Black colleges in Atlanta formed a collegiate baseball league in 1896. Howard University played Harvard

---

[1] Bobby L. Lovett, *America's Historically Black Colleges and Universities: A Narrative History from 1837 to 2010* (Macon GA: Mercer University Press, 2011) 1–324; "TSU Athletics building on its past," *TSU Alumni Life* 1, no. 1 (Spring 2002) 10–11.

[2] Lovett, *America's Black Colleges,* 348–64; Joe M. Richardson, *A History of Fisk University, 1865–1946* (Tuscaloosa: University of Alabama Press, 1980) 155–60; William A. Degregorio, "Theodore Roosevelt: 26th President," *The Complete Book of U.S. Presidents* (New York: Barricade Books, 1991) 373–91.

University in football, and played Yale University's baseball team in 1898. Florida A&M State Normal College placed intramural sports under faculty supervision in 1899 and soon began its intercollegiate athletic program in baseball and football. West Virginia State College fielded its first football team in 1903, the same year that Florida A&M began tennis and basketball competition. Fisk University organized basketball in 1903. In 1906, Florida A&M engaged in varsity competition with Alabama State College and Tuskegee Institute, and Fisk University expanded extracurricular sports and engaged in competition with other schools. By 1912, student newspapers and local Negro newspapers began to cover sports competition.[3] Negro colleges, however, were not invited to be members of the NCAA.

Hampton, Howard, Virginia Union University, and Shaw University formed the Central Intercollegiate Athletic Association (CIAA) in 1912. Morehouse, Fisk, Florida A&M, and Tuskegee formed the Southeastern Conference in 1913. Prairie View A&M State College, Bishop College, Paul Quinn College, Wiley College, and Sam Houston College formed the Southwestern Athletic Conference (SWAC) in 1920–21. Several HBCUs formed the Mid-Eastern Athletic Conference, and other HBCU sports conferences followed. Cleve Abbott started the Tuskegee Relays in track and field in 1927. S.E. Brady at Fisk University headed this HBCU athletic association. Tennessee A&I State Normal Teachers College began joining the black college conferences by 1930.[4]

President William Jasper Hale had begun the athletic tradition at Tennessee State in 1912. He saw the value of intercollegiate sport competition and the prestige and publicity it could bring to this infant normal school. Students engaged recess time in front of Old Main, where they participated in games and group exercises. Students and faculty then organized the Athletic Association in 1912 to promote participation in intramural football, baseball, tennis, handball, center ball, and croquet. A fee was required for membership. Girls engaged in all sports but football. Basketball was played mostly outdoors until 1923, when the students completed a well-lit gymnasium on the top floor of the Men's Trades Building. The girls organized a competitive basketball team. A football stadium was erected in a field just east of East Hall Men's dormitory in 1931. During the 1930s, the federal Works Progress Administration (WPA) provided labor and funds to improve the stadium, including adding more seating and a cinder track. In November 1953, the college named the facility the W.J. Hale Stadium. The new Administration, Physical Education and Health Building was completed in 1934, and included a gymnasium on the stage in the present auditorium. At the far backside (south) of the stage, a row of temporary bleachers serviced spectators of basketball games, physical education classes, and intramural sports events.

---

[3] Ibid.; Richardson, *A History of Fisk University*, 155–160.
[4] Ibid.

Spectators also could sit in the auditorium seats and look up at the games. Tennessee A&I's physical training program consisted of courses to "promote the physical development and secure ease and grace of carriage, general development of shoulders, chest and body."[5]

Swimming—Tiger Sharks

From 1945 to 1968, Tennessee A&I State University developed a credible swimming team under Coach Thomas H. Hughes. The swimming pool was located in the basement underneath the stage of the Administration, Physical Education and Health Building. WPA funds, in 1941, helped build an outside swimming pool alongside of the south windows of the inside pool. From 1950 to 1954, the Tiger Sharks won five Central Intercollegiate Athletic Association Championships, including an interracial meet. Donald E. Jackson captained the team. His five children later attended Tennessee State. Leroy Jones broke the 50-yard dash record. They lost to Southern Illinois University 49–35 in February 1956. Hughes became the first Negro member of the College Swimming Coaches Association. By 1967–68, the Tiger Sharks had eight swim meets scheduled through March. The Tiger Sharks won the Alabama State University Invitational Meet (1971) and the Dillard University Invitational Meet (1973).

On 2 December 1980, Tennessee State dedicated the T.H. Hughes Aquatic Center in Gentry Center Complex. The two pools at the A-Building fell into disrepair and were closed, which included filling in the outside pool with dirt. With the new pool, Tennessee State hosted the HBCU National Collegiate Swimming and Diving Championships. Donald Moody broke three meet records and took first-place honors. The team included James Adams, Tony Bable, Charles Clemmon, Fred Cochran, Michael Dowdy, Marvin Drummond, Anthony Hodges, Lester Ingram, Nate James, Allen Linton, Alfie Stallworth, and Anthony Wright. James I. Bass was the coach. The schedule included Vanderbilt, Eastern Kentucky State, University of Louisville, Georgia State, Georgia Institute of Technology, Albany State Invitational, Hampton, Western Kentucky, Johnson C. Smith, Alabama A&M, and University of Evansville. TSU won the HBCU swim meet in 1983. Since 1950, TSU had won eight championships, and some 173 lettermen participated on the teams.[6]

---

[5] A&I *The Bulletin*, 1912, 1–4.

[6] *A History of the Alumni Association*, ed. Vallie P. Pursley (Special Collections, TSU, August 1990) 1–65; Dwight Lewis and Susan Thomas, *A Will to Win* (Nashville: Cumberland Press, 1983) 357–59.

Tennis

By 1917, the Tennessee A&I tennis teams competed against Fisk University, Walden University, and Meharry Medical College. The campus had six outdoor tennis courts and "spots for track and a basketball field"—all built by students. In the 1930s, Tennessee A&I State College used federal Works Progress Administration (WPA) money to develop a series of regulation outdoor recreational facilities including tennis courts. There were tennis courts in the city of Nashville, but not for use by Negro citizens until the mid-1950s. A Tennessee A&I tennis team under Coach Tom Harris began competition in 1946. In 1951, Earl Woods and Walter Simpson won the Mid-Western Conference doubles match. The A&I team, including Wilbert Davis, Ted Grizzle, Robert Ryland, Wilbert Ryland, and Melvin Watson, traveled to Notre Dame for some tennis matches in May 1955. Some 500 people watched this integrated competition. From 1946–79, the coaches included Tom Harris, James Lawson, Ronald Harris, and Michael Payton.[7]

Boxing

Boxing teams remained popular through the 1950s among Negroes because of the exploits of champions George Dixon, Jack Johnson, Joe Louis, and Sugar Ray Robinson. Dixon became world featherweight champion in 1892. Jack Johnson remained heavyweight champion of the world from 1902 until 1915. In 1937, Joe Louis of Detroit (born of Alabama sharecroppers) became the only Negro since Jack Johnson to hold the Heavyweight Championship of the World title. The Tennessee A&I boxing team won the Mid-Western Boxing Tournament in 1941. Boxing declined by late 1944, when Sergeant Joe Louis Barrow and his boxing team were touring in the Pacific. His mother, Lily Barrow, visited the Tennessee A&I State College campus to promote war bonds. Boxing resumed after World War II, and Tennessee A&I won three titles, including the 1947 Mid-Western Conference Boxing Tournament. In 1961, the NCAA and others discontinued collegiate boxing.[8]

Baseball

Baseball required open fields but little equipment, and Negro communities quickly embraced the sport. There were sandlot teams in almost every neighborhood, and baseball games were a part of the annual picnics after slavery. Five professional Negro baseball teams existed by 1900. Eight professional teams formed the Negro Baseball League in 1920, and Negro

---

[7] Lewis and Thomas, *A Will to Win*, 366.

[8] Lewis and Thomas, *A Will to Win*, 364; Donald Spivey, "The Black Athlete in Big-Time Intercollegiate Sports, 1941–1968," *Phylon* 44, no. 2 (Second Quarter 1983): 116–25.

baseball teams were good enough to win more than 60 percent of games played against white teams. Professional Negro baseball teams recruited players from the HBCUs' college and high school departments.[9] By the 1920s, Nashville had minor league Negro baseball teams, including the Elite Giants. In Memphis, the Red Sox were the community's idols. The Negro press regularly covered Negro baseball, and the editors criticized any spectators for drinking, foul language, gambling, and dressing "naked to the waist." They expected patrons to display proper etiquette. Women dressed up and flocked to local baseball games, and thus men spectators dressed up too. The baseball prowess of the HBCUs increased after thousands of World War II veterans hit the campuses. After the white national baseball leagues began to hire black players such as Jackie Robinson in 1947–48, Negro baseball teams and stadiums such as Martin Baseball Stadium in Memphis died a slow death. Baseball competition among the HBCUs continued, however.

The students at Tennessee A&I State Normal School first formed a baseball team with the married men against the single men on 4 July 1912, at Greenwood Park. *The Bulletin* (1914–15) pictured Tennessee A&I's first intercollegiate baseball team; they had a 4–1 record that year. By 1926, the A&I State Normal Teachers College baseball team had 18 members. They participated in the formation of a Nashville City League, including Roger Williams University, Walden College, and Fisk University. A&I won the league championship, and A&I graduates went on to teach and coach baseball at schools across Tennessee, the South, and the nation.

Most men's collegiate sports were suspended during WWII; however, after the war baseball was revived on campus and became competitive within a few years. Under Lawrence E. Simmons, the Tennessee A&I State University team posted 12–2 and 12–3 seasons in 1952 and 1953 before Samuel Whitmon took over the team. Fifteen of Whitmon's twenty players were freshmen. Hylon Adams was the coach from 1969 to 1973, followed by others such as Jacob Robinson and Allen Robinson. By 1981, TSU had a large baseball team consisting of 28 members, including Curtis Burke, Terry Blocker, and Reggie Robinson. By 1983, four Tennessee State players—George Altman, Sam Bowens, Roy Johnson, and Fred Valentine—later played for professional baseball leagues. In 1983, these

---

[9] Howard Bryant, *Shut Out: A Story of Race and Baseball in Boston* (Boston: Beacon Press, 2002); Don Rogosin, *Invisible Men: Life in Baseball's Negro Leagues* (New York: Kodansha International, 1983) 55, 145–46, 273; Joe Formichella, *Here's to You, Jackie Robinson: The Legend of the Prichard Mohawks* (San Francisco: McAdam/Cage, 2009); Bruce Adelson, *Brushing Back Jim Crow: the Integration of Minor-League Baseball in the American South* (Charlottesville: University of Virginia Press, 1999).

same four baseball athletes were among the first 53 individuals inducted into the TSU Hall of Fame.[10]

The traditionally white institutions (TWIs) recruited away the better black baseball players after passage of the 1964 Civil Rights Act. The Little League teams in the Negro community declined in number, although some neighborhood organizations tried to keep baseball alive in the black communities. In Nashville, Kappa Alpha Psi Fraternity Alumni Chapter sponsored the Kappa Kittens, but most of the new generation of African-American youngsters no longer understood the game of baseball. Professional baseball teams turned to recruiting Latinos instead. The number of black American baseball players declined from almost 30 percent to less than 10 percent of the team members by 2008. Baseball was dying in black culture.

At Tennessee State University, baseball suffered such decline of spectator interest that the university had no choice but to discontinue the program by the early 1990s. On September 25 1993, Willie Stargell, former star for the Pittsburgh Pirates, and Bill White the president of the National Baseball League, headed a reception and fundraiser at a Nashville hotel to help revive baseball at TSU. Former Negro League baseball player Clinton "Butch McCord," a TSU alumnus who played baseball while on a Tennessee A&I football scholarship in 1944, enlisted their help. McCord learned to play ball in Nashville sandlot teams. In 1947, he signed with Tom Wilson, the proprietor of one of Nashville's few black-owned Negro ballparks. McCord's career in the Negro leagues included playing for teams in the military service, the Nashville Cubs, Nashville Black Vols, Baltimore Elite Giants, and the Chicago American Giants. He returned to Nashville and worked for the US Postal Service until his retirement in 1988. He died in 2011. Meanwhile, the gallant effort by McCord, White, and Stargell unfortunately did not revive baseball at Tennessee State University.[11]

Track and Field: World Acclaim

Track and field competition became popular at the HBCUs. This sport, like baseball, required little equipment. Black Americans had been racing each other and against horses since slavery times, and after Jessie Owens won the Olympics in Nazi Germany in 1936, America placed greater emphasis on track and field events. Owens became a favorite speaker across America. He raced against a horse at a Negro Baseball League game in Nashville's Sulphur Dell Stadium in

---

[10] Lewis and Thomas, *A Will to Win*, 257, 361–62.

[11] TSU, "Baseball is back!" *Accent* 22, no. 4 (Fall 1993): 1; James A. Riley, *The Biographical Encyclopedia of the Negro Baseball Leagues* (New York: Carroll & Graf, 1994); "Clinton 'Butch' McCord," Negro Leagues Baseball Museum, http://coe.ksu.edu/nbe-museum/history/players/mccord.html, 1–2, 11/19/2011; the author interviewed McCord in his Nashville home, 30 August 2000, Lovett Papers, Special Collections, TSU.

April 1940. Negro youngsters now wanted to gain attention, fortune, and fame by running and jumping, and Tennessee A&I State Normal Teachers College now had women and men students on the track and field teams.

Women's track and field began its era of greatness under President Walter S. Davis, who, after taking control of the institution in September 1943 and gaining accreditation from the Southern Association of Colleges and Schools (SACS) in 1946, moved full speed ahead to meet the General Assembly's mandate to make Tennessee A&I State College "equivalent to University of Tennessee for white students."[12] Davis included sports in the school's purpose.

Leon Farbes served as men's track coach from 1943 to 1946, followed by Tom Harris a former coach at Wilberforce University. Harris became A&I's men and women's track coach in fall 1946. He hailed some dump trucks on Centennial Boulevard and unloaded some of their dirt to help build up the old horseshoe-shaped cinder path around Hale Stadium. Harris then recruited star trackmen such as Leroy Craig and Edward S. Temple. At the annual HBCU track and field championships at Tuskegee, A&I men and women placed third in the events.

In 1959, A&I men's track came into its own with Ralph ("Hawk eye") Boston, Edward Adams, John Moon, and Melvin Clipper on the team. Boston and Moon led the team in capturing the third successive Midwestern Field and Track Competition title. Boston captured first places in the high jump, pole vault, broad jump, javelin, and the 120-yard high hurdles, breaking the record with 14.3 seconds.[13] The "slim runners from A. & I." successfully defended their crown at Tennessee State on 8–9 May 1959, went on to the NCAA Mid-East Track Meet at the University of Chicago at the end of May, and to the NAIA nationals in Sioux City, South Dakota, on 5–6 June 1959. Ralph Boston won five events at the NCAA Mid-East; Moon won two events. The four-man team finished second. Boston and Moon then went to the NCAA meet in Lincoln, Nebraska, and to the National AAU in Boulder, Colorado, the following week. Boston entered the broad jump and won with a leap of 25.3 feet. Moon ran in the 100- and the 220-yard dash. Coach Ray H. Kemp became a member of the NAIA track and field committee in May 1959. The team won Mid-Western Athletic Conference Championships in 1954, 1955, 1956, 1957, and 1962.

Ralph Boston was among the few American men who won three medals (gold, silver, and bronze) in Olympic events, 1960–68. He gained induction into the TSU Sports Hall of Fame in 1983. Boston won the NCAA Silver for the

---

[12] Lois C. McDougald, *A Time-Line Chronology of the Tennessee A. & I. State College Campus 1909–1951* (Nashville: Tennessee State University, January 1981) 160–68; Tennessee, Annual Statistical Report of the Commissioner of Education, Year Ending June 1947, SBOE, 1–23; A&I *The Bulletin* 36, no. 5 (1948): 1–45.

[13] Lewis and Thomas, *A Will to Win*, 176–82, 295–97.

Olympic Hall of Fame and National Black College Alumni Hall of Fame. TSU named its Sports Hall of Fame Room in the Floyd-Payne Campus Center in 1996 for Ralph Boston. He served as director of customer relations for Ericsson, Inc., consultant to the US Olympic Team, and sportscaster on national television. In 2002, he gained induction into another Hall of Fame in Modesto, California. By 2003, the Annual Ralph Boston Golf Tournament highlighted the Homecoming Week festivities at Tennessee State.[14]

Leon Farbes, Richard Mack, Raymond H. Kemp, and Willie Stevens coached the men through 1966. The program disbanded in 1967. In 1978, David Boyd took over the team. Robert Cooper, Arthur Perry, Jerome Ward, Tommy Wakefield, Tony Wakefield, and Ervin Ward composed the cross-country team by 1980. Hezekiah Foreman succeeded as men's coach. In 2012, Chandra Cheeseborough-Guice coached the small men's team.

Jessie Abbott, who received degrees from Tuskegee and the University of Wisconsin, served as Tennessee A&I State College's first women's track and basketball coach. Mamie Brown, Dorothy Davidson, Belle Doughtrey, Elizabeth Hurd, Flora Jordon, and Grace Prater answered Abbott's fall 1943 announcement of the formation of a women's track team. In spring 1944, the Tennessee A&I State College women's track team dressed in their homespun white shorts and shirts and participated in the Tuskegee meet. Abbott had nothing but an open field for practice. In 1945, Lula Bartley succeeded Abbott after Abbott returned to classroom teaching. Student athletes, including Audrey Patterson, Mickey Reed, and Jean Patton along with Coach Thomas Harris, began Tennessee A&I's winning tradition. In September 1948, the campus honored A&I's first Olympic contenders, who placed in the 100- and 200-meter races at the Olympics in London: Audrey "Mickey" Patterson and Emma Reed of Memphis (formerly the National AAU junior high jump champion). Audrey Patterson won Tennessee A&I College's first Olympic medal—a bronze medallion for taking third place in the 200-meter dash. She considered Jessie Owens her inspiration.[15]

That year, nine of America's women Olympic contenders in track were Negroes. In 1948, the US placed first among participating nations with 38 gold, 27 silver, and 19 bronze Olympic medals.[16] The London Olympic Games were the first to be shown on home television, and A&I celebrated with a parade on Centennial Boulevard.

---

[14] Ibid., 12, 142–47, 255, 295–303; Carroll Van West, "Ralph Boston (1939–)," *The Tennessee Encyclopedia of History and Culture* (Nashville: Rutledge Hill Press, 1998) 79.

[15] "Olympic Medal Winners," www.olympic.org/uk/athletes/results/search_r_uk.asp, 1 [accessed 7 August 2008].

[16] "National Olympic Committee, London 1948, Games of the XIV Olympiad," www.olympic.org/uk/games/past/index_uk.asp?OLGT=1&OLGY=1948, 1–2 [accessed 7 August 2008].

Nell Jackson was national AAU 200-meter champion in 1950. The Tennessee A&I team had now increased from three members to nine team members. Jean Patton won the silver medal in the 100-meter dash; Patton also won two gold medals in the 4x100-meter and 200-meter races in the inaugural Pan American Games in Buenos Aires in 1951. She enjoyed a welcome party at the Nashville Airport after returning from Los Angeles, where she defeated Australia's champion in the 100-meter dash at 11.1 seconds. Crowds greeted her, too, in a parade down Centennial Boulevard. Shortly after, Coach Harris decided to leave the institution for a higher paying college job, and the athletic business manager Clyde Kincaid took over the track team.[17]

In August 1951, Tennessee A&I State College became a university, and a modern physical education facility opened on Centennial Boulevard. President Walter S. Davis called recent A&I graduate Edward S. Temple over to the A-Building office and offered him the opportunity to work on his master's degree, earn $150 a month working in the campus post office, and help Coach Kincaid by coaching the women's part of the track team. Temple had spent the summer working as a construction worker on the new gymnasium (Kean Hall) while waiting to get a teaching job. Although the A&I track field was a rough, semi-circular path around the football field and near a trash dump, Temple imposed strict discipline, requiring neat clothes, hair in place, promptness, and completion of coursework with passing grades. Temple completed his master's degree in 1952 and became the head of the women's team in 1953–54.[18]

Temple had neither A&I scholarships nor a salary comparable to a university track coach. When there was bad weather, the Tigerbelles would run through the hallways of Kean Hall, careful to hit the steel double-doors at the end of the corridor without hurting themselves. In 1955, the A&I women won their first national track and field championship. Temple was on cloud nine; it was the first time a black school had ever won a national championship. Before the advent of desegregation, the Tennessee A&I women's team was filled with star athletes. Coach Temple knew how to recruit, retain, and graduate the best of female athletes.[19]

---

[17] Lewis and Thomas, *A Will to Win*, 111.

[18] Bobby L. Lovett, "Edward S. Temple (1927–)," *The Tennessee Encyclopedia of History and Culture* (Nashville: Rutledge Press, 1998) 915–16; Edward S. Temple, "A Historical Study of the Recreational Facilities for Negroes in Nashville, Tennessee, from 1943 to 1953," (MS thesis, Tennessee A&I State University, 1953).

[19] Sharon Hull, *TSU: An Olympic Tradition*, 1–4, Brown-Daniel Library Special Collections; TSU office of public relations, "The Olympic Torch is coming to TSU: an official celebration site for the Olympic Flame as it makes its way from Atlanta," Special Collections, TSU; "Countdown 100: TSU Olympic Medal Recipients," 1–3, Special Collections, TSU.

Mae Faggs of Bayside, New York, competed in the 1948 Olympics as a high school student and again in the 1952 Olympics. She held AAU records in the 220- and 200-meter events. She came to TSU as a 21-year old freshman in fall 1952 and set new records in the sprints at the AAU meet in 1953. Along with Cynthia Thompson, Patricia Monsanto (Bayside, New York) Faggs helped to strengthen the A&I team. Former coach Harris had recruited Cynthia Thompson from Jamaica to run the 100-meters, and she participated on the US Olympic team that set two world's records in 1952. At the 1954 Annual Evening Star Games in Washington, DC, Faggs took first place in the 100-yard dash. Faggs, Thompson, Ravoyda Fuller, and Margaret Davis won first in the 660-yard relay. When the university could only afford a train ticket for Faggs to compete in a meet, Temple telephoned ahead for the opposing coaches to look after Mae Faggs and send her home safely. Through 1955, Faggs and teammates continued their winning ways. They trained hard and always believed they were the best in the nation. Mae Faggs won races in Tuskegee, Montgomery, Oklahoma, and at the Pan American Games in Mexico City. Faggs helped Isabelle Daniels, Barbara Jones, Martha Hudson, and Lucinda Williams to develop their skills and win races. Hudson set a Pan American Games record in Mexico City in the 75-yard dash. Daniels was a member of the 400-meter and 800-meter relay teams in 1952 and 1956.[20]

In October 1955, the US Olympic Committee hosted a preview meet in Madison Square Garden in New York, and Temple took his team to the match. Isabelle Daniels, Charlesette Rederick, Mae Faggs, and Ella Rea Turner won first place in the four-lap, 660-yard relay. The A&I team also won the AAU Women's Championship. The team participated in the National Amateur Athletic Union races in Philadelphia, where Wilma Rudolph won all her races. In 1956, Rudolph returned to Temple's summer camp, and in October, she accompanied Temple, Daniels, Faggs, Margaret Matthews, Willye White, and Lucinda Williams to the qualifying events for the US Olympic Team in Washington, DC. The US included Faggs on a ten-member Goodwill Tour team to travel through Africa in 1956.[21] The Tigerbelles used automobiles, packed sack lunches from the college cafeteria, and avoided Jim Crow restaurants and hotels. They had to unload from cramped car seats and perform against college teams that had scholarships, hot food, and first-rate travel and housing.

---

[20] Hull, *TSU: An Olympic Tradition*, 1–4; TSU office of public relations, "The Olympic Torch is coming to TSU."

[21] Anne E. Schraff, *William Rudolph, The Greatest Woman Sprinter in History* (Berkeley Heights OH: Enslow Publishers, 2004); Linda Jacobs, *Wilma Rudolph: Run for Glory* (St. Paul MN: EMC Co., 1975); Edward S. Temple and B'Lou Carter, *Only the Pure in Heart Survive* (Nashville: Broadman Press, 1980); *A History of the Alumni Association*, ed. Vallie P. Pursley, 48, 57.

The team made it to the 1956 Olympics in Melbourne, Australia, where Tennessee A&I State University became the first school or club to have six members qualify for competition. For the first time, all four members of the American women's relay team originated from the same organization. The Tigerbelles won four bronze medals and one silver medal—all of the medals won by the US women's Olympic team. Willye B. White, a high school student in 1956, won silver in the long jump. She entered A&I as a freshman in 1959. The American 4x100-meter relay team—Isabelle Daniels (Holston), Mae Faggs (Starr), Margaret Matthews (Wilburn), and Wilma Rudolph—received bronze. The campus gave the team a triumphant welcome. In 1957, the women's team won its second AAU crown. Cuba invited the 15-member team to compete there on October 10. Daniels set a new 220-yard record with a time of 0:24.7. The Tigerbelles participated in a two-day meet between the US and Russia in Moscow on 27–28 July 1958 and engaged track meets in Poland, Hungary, and Greece. In the fall, Rudolph became a student at Tennessee A&I State University. Margaret Matthews won the world record in the 100-yard dash during a meet in Hungary. Rudolph won the 100-meter dash at Cleveland, Ohio, and again at the A&I track meet in 1959. In summer, the Tigerbelles won the relays at the Pan American games in Chicago, winning 12 first places, including three gold medals by Lucinda Williams.

When the time approached for the 1960 Olympics, the sit-in demonstrations against downtown Jim Crow establishments had begun, but Temple did not allow his Tigerbelles to become distracted. The Tennessee A&I State University team participated in the National AAU Meet in Corpus Christi, Texas, in 1960, and won the 100- and 200-meter races, thereby qualifying for the 400-meter relay in the Olympic trials at Texas Christian University weeks later. The promising but high-strung Willye White suffered expulsion from the team because she continued to break Temple's rules. White joined a youth program in Chicago and won a silver medal in the 400-meter relay in the 1964 Olympics. The Tigerbelles left for Kansas to practice, traveled to New York and on to Rome. They were not expected to be among America's top winners.

However, at the 1960 Olympics in Rome, the Tigerbelles won with raw guts and determination. They gained world fame. Tigerbelles comprised nearly a third of the members on the American team. Barbara Jones (Slater) won the bronze medal. Lucinda Williams (Adams) won the gold medal. Martha Hudson (Pennyman) won the gold medal. Hudson had been named a 1959 AAU All-American in the sprints. Wilma G. Rudolph won three gold medals for the 100-meter, 200-meter dash, and 400-meter relay, and became such a celebrity she couldn't leave the American housing compound without creating a mob scene.[22] The team visited the Pope at the Vatican. Temple then took them to the British Empire Games in London, where Rudolph won all her events, then on to Germany, Holland, and other places in Europe, where they received acclaim from the crowds. They also received a royal welcome at home. Anna Lois Smith, Wilma Rudolph, Coach Temple, Barbara Jones, Ralph Boston, Jo Ann Terry, Shirley Crowder, Lucinda Williams, and Martha Hudson took a group photo in front of campus buildings.[23]

Back in Clarksville, Tennessee, Blanche and Eddie Rudolph beamed with pride when the citizens sponsored a parade and a banquet for 1,100 persons at the Armory to welcome Wilma home. Rudolph traveled to Chicago, Philadelphia, and Atlanta, and to the NAACP banquet in New York City (27 November 1960) and other cities that honored her achievement. She met with President John F. Kennedy, whose friendly gesture countered the racial taboos of Southern Jim Crow. Barbara Curry (Murrell), a graduate student and Miss Tennessee State (1959–60), chaperoned Wilma. Rudolph received honors from the Tennessee governor, the Nashville *Banner*, and *Sports Magazine*.

Wilma G. Rudolph (1940–94) was born to Eddie B. and Blanche P. Rudolph on 23 June 1940 in St. Bethlehem, near Clarksville, Tennessee. Wilma was born an underweight child and suffered many childhood diseases including pneumonia, scarlet fever, and polio. Blanche Rudolph and her daughter Wilma rode the segregated Greyhound bus fifty miles between Clarksville and Nashville to receive polio treatments at George W. Hubbard Hospital. Until age eight, she had to wear leg braces before deciding to try to walk. Blanche Rudolph and the children took turns massaging Wilma's crippled legs, and she received therapy until age twelve. Despite the damage done to her by polio, Wilma participated in basketball and track at Burt High School. At age 13, tall, and weighing only 89 pounds, she won all her races including the 50-, 75-, 100-, and 200-meter. She also scored more than 800 points as a basketball player. Wilma's teachers forced her to excel in life without any excuses. Wilma recalled how the black history course at the school illustrated black heroes to the students and taught them the facts of segregated life. She said, "The object of it all was to give us black kids somebody to be proud of, not to tell us we were still oppressed."[24] In 1954, basketball

---

[22] "Track Stars Win," *The Meter*, October 1960, 1; Nashville *News Star*, 14 August 1960; *A History of the Alumni Association*, ed. Vallie P. Pursley, 53; "100 Moments: Martha Hudson", TSU Athletic Department, 1, Special Collections, TSU.

[23] Ibid. See the Temple Papers, Special Collections, TSU.

[24] Bobby L. Lovett, "Wilma Glodean Rudolph," *Scribner Encyclopedia of American Lives: Notable Americans Who Died Between 1994 and 1996*, vol. 4 (New York: Scribner's, 2001) 469–71; Bobby L. Lovett, "Wilma Rudolph (1940–1994)," *Tennessee Encyclopedia of History and Culture*, 813–14.

referee Ed Temple took a closer look at the skinny-legged youngster, and her parents agreed to allow Wilma to attend Temple's summer track camp. Rudolph was excited to go to the university and train with college women. Temple ran the girls five miles per day on farm roads to build endurance and confidence. Temple took the 14-year-old with the team to Tuskegee. Mae Faggs (barely five feet tall) helped develop and chaperone the tall and skinny teenager Wilma Rudolph.[25]

In 1961—the year her father died—Rudolph won the Sullivan Award as top amateur athlete in America, and gained induction into the Helms Hall of Fame, which included A&I's Johnny McLendon (basketball), George Altman (baseball), and Henry A. Kean (football). They voted Rudolph AAU All-American for 1960, 1961, and 1962. She became Female Athlete of the Year and the first woman invited to run in the New York Athletic Club Track Meet. She accepted invitations for the Melrose Games, *Los Angeles Times* Games, Penn Relays, and Drake Relays. She ran against the Russians, and made goodwill tours of Africa and other places. Cassius M. Clay (Muhammad Ali), who won the gold medal on the US boxing team in Rome in 1960, visited the campus, eying Wilma, but Temple shooed him away. Ali became Heavyweight Boxing Champion of the World in 1964, had his title stripped in 1967 for refusing the military draft, won the case in the US Supreme Court in 1970, and regained his title in 1974. On one visit to Tennessee A&I State University, Ali posed with Temple in front of the Memorial Library.[26]

While attending Tennessee A&I, Wilma Rudolph joined Delta Sigma Theta Sorority. She received a bachelor's degree in elementary education on 27 May 1962. Rudolph took a teaching job in Clarksville and married Robert Eldridge, a star basketball player at A&I. They moved the family to Evansville, Indiana, where she became director of a community center. The couple had two daughters and two sons: Yolanda (1958), Djuana (1964), Robert, Jr., (1965), and Xurry (1971). Rudolph became involved in the Job Corps in Boston and in Maine. By 1967, she was working with the White House to develop Operation Champion for inner-city children. In 1967, she was inducted into the Tennessee Sports Hall of Fame, and by 1972 Rudolph was covering news of the Olympics. On 14 March 1974, she gained membership in the Black Athletes Hall of Fame. On 2 December 1980, TSU named its indoor track for Wilma Rudolph. On 10 January 1993, a section of US Highway 79 in Clarksville was renamed Wilma Rudolph Boulevard.[27]

---

[25] Ibid.

[26] "Muhammad Ali, Temple, and Students," in front of the Memorial Library, The Photographs Collection, Special Collections, TSU.

[27] Ibid.

The students were betting on 19-year-old Edith McGuire to fill Wilma's shoes.[28] Temple was counting on Wyomia Tyus, Flossie Fletcher, and Vivian Brown. In the 1964 Olympics in Tokyo, Ralph Boston won silver, Tyus won two gold medals; McGuire (Duvall) won gold and two silver medals. Temple expected to have a much stronger, deeper team by 1965.[29]

In August 1967, Temple became coach for the combined women and men's track and field team. He meant to get the men's track program moving again and to get as many Tigerbelles on the 1968 US Olympic team as possible. The Tigerbelles placed four members on the 1968 US Olympic team scheduled for Mexico City. The 23-year-old Wyomia Tyus qualified for the 100- and 200-meter and won two gold medals. Madeline Manning (Mims) won a gold medal in the 800-meter race. Manning was a member of Olympic track teams also in 1972, 1976, and 1980. Tyus, Barbara Ferrell, M. Bailes, and M. Netter won gold in the 4x100 relay. Eleanor Montgomery and Martha Watson also participated in the 1968 Olympics.[30]

John Carlos and Tommie Smith, who won gold and silver in the 200-meter relay, refused to look upon the American flag while the national anthem played. As planned, they instead raised their clenched fists in a Black Power salute to protest against the depth of racism and continuing racial discrimination across America. Blacks were angry about the assassination of Martin Luther King, Jr., on 4 April 1968. Temple and his wife, Charlie B., counseled the Tennessee A&I State University team to avoid the intense politics at the 1968 Olympics.

The Tigerbelles returned home to win their fifth consecutive AAU Women's Track indoor championship. They defended their Southeastern AAU Championship at Hale Stadium (May 1969), won the National AAU Outdoor Women's Track and Field meet in Ohio in July, and competed in the All-Europe Games in August. At this time, Temple decided to take a job offer with the Peace Corps. Temple resented that all the schools in Tennessee together could not come close to Tennessee A&I in Olympic competition; yet, Tennessee State endured lack of quality track facilities despite their world records. However, the sports editor at the *Banner* interceded and got Temple an audience with Governor Buford Ellington. The governor, a friend of Jimmy Stahlman, who was the editor of the *Banner* that promoted TSU sports, agreed to give the university money for track scholarships and a new rubberized track around the football field.

---

[28] "Who will fill Wilma's Shoes?" *The Meter*, October 1963, 1.

[29] Ibid.

[30] TSU, "The rest of the Temple Story: Mrs. Temple," "President's Corner," "Edward S. Temple Seminars Honor a Legacy," 7, *Accent*, 22/4, fall 1993, 2, 3; Tommie Morton-Young, *Nashville Tennessee* (Charleston SC: Arcadia Publishing, 2000) 51,58,64,65,66,123, photos pertaining to A&I persons.

In 1971, Mamie Rallins entered Tennessee State after she found track competition to be the only way out of the economically depressed south side of Chicago. Iris Davis, who was listed among the USA top ten in the 60-yard dash and was undefeated in outdoor and indoor competition, captained the Tigerbelles team and won the 60-yard dash at the USA-USR international meet. Rallins joined stars Iris Davis and Madeline Manning on the 1972 Olympic team. Rallins won the 100-meter hurdles, and Manning won the silver for the 400-meter US relay team. Chandra Cheeseborough, a high school student in Temple's summer programs, won two gold medals in the 1975 Pan American Games. Cheeseborough, Kathy McMillan, and Brenda Morehead made the 1976 Olympics team but did not qualify for their favored races. Cheeseborough finished sixth in the 100 meters. McMillan won a silver medal at the 1976 Montreal Olympic Games in Canada.

The 1977 Tigerbelles consisted of manager Edwina Temple, Brenda Moorehead, Devorah Oliver, Brenda Fuller, Yolanda Eldridge (Rudolph's daughter), Mary Williams, Teresa Baugh, Kathy McMillan, and Deborah Jones (representing Bermuda in the 1976 and 1980 Olympics). Moorehead, Cheeseborough, and McMillan toured Europe with the US team in the summer of 1977. Moorehead, Ernestine Davis, Cheeseborough, and Debbie Jones set a world record in the 880-yard relay. The Black Athlete's Hall of Fame inducted Temple in June 1977. The Tigerbelles won first place in the 1978 National Indoor Track and Field Meet in Madison Square Garden. In 1978, the community contributed sufficient money to fix the TSU track. A special luncheon for Nashville leaders at Third National Bank acknowledged Temple. By this time, the Tigerbelles had accumulated 18 Olympic medals and 26 Pan American Games gold medals in the years since 1948. On April 7, TSU dedicated the $500,000 Edward S. Temple Track on the north campus. Rudolph signed autographs for the fans. Cheeseborough enrolled at TSU in 1979 and became its first female athletic scholarship holder. Cheeseborough, McMillan, and Morehead made the 1980 Olympic team, but President Jimmy Carter boycotted the Moscow games as part of Cold War politics.[31]

Temple continued to sharpen the skills of his team, looking toward the next Olympics, and further developing the team's star, Chandra Cheeseborough. The Tigerbelles became the 4x1,100 relay champions in the Pennsylvania Relays, and 1981 National Indoor Champions. They named Cheeseborough Female Athlete of the Meet. The Tigerbelles team won their fifth straight indoor championship meet in February 1982 at Madison Square Garden. Cheeseborough set a world indoor record there in the 200- meter with a time of 23.4 seconds. In the 1984

---

[31] TSU Sports, Nashville *Tennessean*, 5 June 1976, 1; Jessica Hopp, "TSU coach sprints back to Olympics," and "Ex TSU Coach Temple led first U.S. team to China in '75," Nashville *Tennessean*, 4 July 2008, C1, C3.

Olympics, Cheeseborough won gold medals in the 400-meter relay and the 1600-meter relay—the first woman to do so; she received a silver medal in the 400 meters.[32]

On 17 October 1993, Edward S. Temple retired from TSU. *The Meter*, dated 5 November 1993 said, "Tigerbelles Coach Temple to retire after 43-year legendary career." Temple described his stay at TSU as like "climbing the rough side of the mountain, but it was worth it." He had received honors from across the world, including appointment as head coach for the American teams in two Olympics. He coached TSU teams to 34 national titles. Upon Temple's advice, the TSU president selected Cheeseborough as Tigerbelles coach. In 1994, the Department of Social Work and Sociology and the College of Arts and Sciences together organized the Edward S. Temple Seminars in Society and Sports to honor him and build upon TSU's rich athletic legacy. Rudolph was the speaker at the Wilma Rudolph Luncheon. The city of Nashville named a portion of 28th Avenue North as Edward S. Temple Boulevard. Charlie B. Temple had already retired on 30 September 1993, but she graciously served on the planning committee for the Temple Seminars, helping to get Rudolph and other former Olympic stars to participate.

Charlie B. Temple had prepared the team's nutritious sack lunches for their travels to the track meets, served as mother to the young women, washed the uniforms and counseled the young women about their personal problems. Ed Temple volunteered in the TSU campus Post Office, helping postmistress Charlie B. to sort the day's mail. They were an inseparable team, Ed and Charlie B., having met in a psychology class at Tennessee State. Charlie B. had wanted to leave the university, where she had been since she was a student, but, instead, she stayed and supported her husband.[33]

In 1994, the National Woman's Hall of Fame inducted Wilma G. Rudolph. She received two honorary degrees. The Nashville *Tennessean* in May 1994 announced the death of her mother Blanche Pettus Rudolph at age 85 from heart disease. Then, Wilma Rudolph discovered she had brain and lung cancer. She often made quiet and personal walks around the TSU track with retired Coach Temple talking about various things. These walks ended after Rudolph entered the hospital with blood clots. She died quietly on 12 November 1994, in her Brentwood home. Four thousands mourners filled Kean Hall for the memorial service on November 17. The following day, the family held the funeral at

---

[32] Martha W. Plowden, *Olympic Black Women* (Gretna LA: Pelican Publishing, 1996); TSU, "Countdown to 100: TSU Olympic Medal Recipients," 1–3, Special Collections, TSU.

[33] Mrs. Charlie B. Temple (1950) died in 2008. It was awkward for some young faculty members and department heads, such as me, to walk into the university post office to gather the mail and there sat world famous Coach Temple, sorting mail. We admired and deeply respected Mr. and Mrs. Temple.

Clarksville's First Baptist Church. The governor had the state flag lowered across Tennessee. In 1995, Clarksville held a breakfast in her name. On 11 August 1995, TSU named its newest women's residence hall in her honor. The Wilma Rudolph Memorial Commission placed a marble marker at her grave in Clarksville's Foster Memorial Garden Cemetery. A Wilma Rudolph Track Club under the Police Athletic League for city youth soon operated in Nashville. The man hurt most by the loss of Wilma was Edward S. Temple who had many outstanding memories of her. The achievements and life story of Wilma Rudolph appeared in newspapers, magazines, film, and books.[34]

The TSU Tigerbelles brought 31 Olympic gold, silver, and bronze medals back to campus, and dozens of medals they won at other track and field events, including the Pan American Games. The Tigerbelles team totaled 16 national track championships on their record. Temple often bragged proudly that "only one" of his girls failed to graduate from college. Few other colleges in the nation had a better record in recruiting, retaining, training, educating, and graduating women track and field athletes. Other coaches tried to "pick his brain" for techniques of training, sports philosophy, and discipline.

Wilma Rudolph was the first woman to win three gold medals in a single Olympiad, the first to receive the Sullivan Award, and the first to receive the NCAA Silver Anniversary Award. Margaret Matthews Wilburn was the first American woman to leap a record twenty feet in the broad jump. Chandra Cheeseborough was the first woman to win gold medals as a member of both the 100-meter and 400-meter relay teams in the same Olympiad (1984). Wyomia Tyus was the first athlete male or female to defend the sprint title in subsequent Olympiads (1964, 1968). Barbara Jones Slater was the youngest female (at age 15) to win a gold medal in track and field. Madeline Manning Mims was the only American woman to win an Olympic gold medal in the 800-meter event (1968). Willye B. White was the first female track athlete to represent the US in five Olympiads: 1956, 1960, 1964, 1968, and 1972. TSU Coach Cheeseborough gained induction into the USA Track and Field Hall Fame in 2000 and Tennessee Sports Hall of Fame in 2002, was selected as Assistant Women's Track Coach at the 2008 Olympics in China, and was designated Head Women's Team Coach for the USA in the World Championships in Athens, Greece, 2009.[35] The National Track and Field Hall of Fame included Ralph Boston (1974), Mae Faggs Starr (1976), Edith McGuire DuVall (1979), Madeline Manning Mims (1984), Wilma G. Rudolph (1974), Edward S. Temple (1989), Wyomia Tyus (1980), Martha Watson (1987), and Willye White (1981). By 2012, no other institution in Tennessee had come

---

[34] Plowden, *Olympic Black Women*, 121.

[35] TSU, "History Makers at Tennessee State University: Legendary Tiger Belle puts TSU on the map," TSU Exchange, www.tnstate.edu, 1 [accessed 4 February 2008].

close to matching these achievements. The Tigerbelle alumni held a reunion in 2002, with Temple and Cheeseborough leading the activities.

With "A Touch of Greatness," student athletes won local, state, regional, national and international sports competitions, including 17 gold medals in the worldwide Olympics: Wilma Rudolph (3), Wyomia Tyus (3), Chandra Cheeseborough (2), Barbara Jones (2), Ralph Boston (1), Mae Faggs (1), Ryan Fann (1), Martha Hudson (1), Madeline Manning (1), Edith McGuire (1), and Lucinda Williams (1). TSU student athletes won eight silver Olympic medals: Edith McGuire (2), Ralph Boston (1), Chandra Cheeseborough (1), Madeline Manning (1), Kathy McMillan (1), Willye B. White (1), and Wyomia Tyus (1).[36] TSU student-athletes won seven bronze Olympic medals: Ralph Boston (1), Isabelle Daniels (1), Mae Faggs (1), Ryan Fann (1), Martha Matthews (1), Audrey Patterson (1), and Wilma Rudolph (1). Other TSU Olympic participants included Estelle Baskerville, Vivian Brown, Shirley Crowder, Iris Davis, Eleanor Montgomery, Brenda Morehead, Mamie Rallins, Emma Reed, Anna Lois Smith, JoAnn Terry, and Martha Watson. Six TSU student athletes represented Bermuda, Jamaica, and Panama in the Olympics: Helen Blake, Marcella Daniels, Lorraine Dunn, Debra Jones, Una Morris, and Cynthia Thompson. TSU won three consecutive NAIA National Basketball Championships, and graced NCAA tournaments.[37] In 2003–04, TSU completed construction of an Olympic Plaza with a 45-feet tall centerpiece sculpture named The Olympian as a witness to the institution's world-class student athletes.[38]

Basketball Champions

Basketball became a popular sport at Tennessee A&I after the students outfitted their own arena above the boys' shops in 1923–24. J.H. Alston coached the men's basketball team in 1925–26. The team had seven members and three weeks of practice before competition began. Members included Lawrence D. Blackburn, Cleveland Harris, Alex Hopson, Alton Jackson (captain), Samuel E. Jones, R.E. Johnson, Theodore Poston, and Elbert Purdy. John Riley coached the A&I girl's team that had 11 members: Pearl Baines, Earline Brown, Ella Henry, Ruth Herrod, Beulah Gibson, Annie L. Johnson, Cordelia McElioth, Clara Mimms, Elizabeth Perkins, Helen Stubblefield, and Emma Whiteside. Tennessee

---

[36] David J. Elitle and Tamela M. Elitle, "Races, Cultural Capital, and the Effects of Participation in Sports," *Sociology of Education* 75, no. 2 (April 2002): 123–46; Gary A. Sailes, "The Myth of Black Sports Supremacy," *Journal of Black Studies* 21, no. 4 (June 1991): 480–87.

[37] TSU Office of Alumni Affairs, *Tennessee State University Alumni Directory 2006* (Chesapeake VA: Harris Connect, 2006) xvi–xxiii.

[38] See Edward S. Temple Papers & Collections; TSU, "Countdown," 3; Wynn, "Tennessee State University's Championship History," 7B.

State and other colleges and universities did not equally finance, promote, and schedule women's collegiate sports until after the 1964 Civil Rights Act.

Men's basketball continued to advance. In 1930–31, the men's basketball team had a record of 14–2, including playing on-campus fraternities as opponents. Fletcher "Nick" Turner and T.D. Upshaw coached the team at one time. In 1944–45, the men's basketball team at Tennessee A&I had a record of 13–9; 26–2 in 1945–46; 22–3 in 1946–47. The 1947–48 team, which included Joshua Grider and John Hilliard, won the Mid-Western Conference Championship.

President Walter S. Davis and athletic director Arthur Kean conceived the first Negro boy's high school basketball tournament on campus. This allowed them to get a close look at the opposition and recruit assistant coaches and players. On 21–23 March 1946, the National High School Tournament took place on campus, with sixteen top teams from twelve states. Cushing High School of Oklahoma won the tournament. Out of that tournament, A&I recruited Nathaniel Taylor from Oklahoma to play basketball and football (1945–49). Vernon E. McCain, Taylor's high school coach from Oklahoma, became the new basketball coach and assistant football coach at Tennessee State. They moved the basketball practice to Pearl High School on 17th Avenue North and Jo Johnston Avenue because the A&I stage of the A-Auditorium housed the returning World War II veterans. In 1948, Shelton Matthews succeeded McCain as head of the basketball program. His first team was undefeated, averaging 72.1 points per game and holding opponents to an average of 40.9 points. Seniors included Joshua Grider, John Holland, Frank Lewis, Nathaniel Taylor, and Clarence Wilson. Four players joined the Harlem Globetrotters show team. A&I won the black college national championships in 1948–49 and 1949–50, and again in 1952–53 and 1953–54. They became the first of the HBCUs invited to the NAIA basketball tournaments at Kansas City, Missouri, on 10 March 1953, winning two of their three games.[39] Coach Clarence Cash resigned in July 1954. Davis demanded perfection.

President Walter S. Davis recruited coach John McLendon, a notable tactician who did not see basketball in black and white. Davis told McLendon that A&I had the athletes and the backing of the state, and that he was to gain the national spotlight. McLendon left Hampton Institute and the Central Intercollegiate Athletic Association (CIAA). He believed he could continue to advance integrated basketball by coming to Tennessee A&I State.[40]

---

[39] TSU, "TSU's Dick Barnett and John McLendon tabbed for Induction into National Collegiate Basketball Hall of Fame," news release, TSU Athletics, Public Relations, 1–2, 5 April 2007.

[40] Jacqueline I. Bryant, "Basketball Coach John B. McLendon, the Noble Revolutionary of U.S. Sport," *Journal of Black Studies* 30, no. 5 (2000): 720–34—transcript of an interview with McLendon

John B. McLendon studied at the University of Kansas, where he studied under James Naismith, who reportedly invented basketball. When Naismith demanded the integration of campus swimming, McLendon got the other 60 black students among the university's 4,000 or so students to support the demand. McLendon then attended the University of Iowa to study for his master's degree in physical education. As coach from 1940 to 1952 at North Carolina College for Negroes, McLendon's basketball team won the CIAA championship twice. In 1944, his team played a secret, integrated game with neighboring Duke University. McLendon was part of the integration of the National Association of Intercollegiate Basketball in 1953. McLendon had begun this racial integration effort with the formation of the National Athletic Steering Committee (NASC) with black colleges. Some 36 HBCUs joined the National Association of Intercollegiate Athletics (NAIA).[41]

Davis and Arthur Kean told McLendon that the Tennessee A&I State University basketball team, with a record of 13–5 in the last season, should be ready to compete on the national level. McLendon recruited six-foot Ronald Hamilton of Kansas City. They ran three miles a day in less than 20 minutes for 21 days in a row so that no other team with better conditioning would enter a game with A&I. Whereas many teams played slow ball half court, McLendon teams played fast break, rushing to the other half of the court and scoring right away. McLendon was a master at teaching the mechanics and strategies of the basketball game. McLendon warned them to never lose a game at home. Ron Hamilton said, "When I got down to Tennessee State, we trained hard, practiced hard, and played hard. We wanted to live up to the school's winning tradition."[42] In 1955–56, the Tennessee A&I State University team had a 24–9 record, including participation in the NAIA tournament. No one expected this team to go as far as they did, but a superbly conditioned team with superb shooting ability was hard to stop.

In 1956–57, the Tennessee A&I State University basketball team won the NAIA championship at Kansas City, Missouri, with a history-making 92–73 score. President Davis was jubilant.[43] Without Davis's knowledge, McLendon had insisted the team be allowed to spend the tournament week in a nice

---

[41] Milton D. Katz, *Breaking Through: John B. McLendon, Basketball Legend and Civil Rights Pioneer* (Fayetteville: University of Arkansas Press, 2007) 73, 74–110, 149, 203; Jacqueline I. Bryant, "Basketball Coach John B. McLendon, the Noble Revolutionary of U.S. Sport," *Journal of Black Studies* 30, no. 5 (2000): 720–34—transcript of an interview with McLendon; "The Game of his Life: John B. McLendon (1915–1999) and the Evolution of Modern Basketball, Program," University of Memphis, 23 March 2006.

[42] Katz, *Breaking Through*, 74–110, 149, 203; Bryant, "Basketball Coach John B. McLendon, the Noble Revolutionary of U.S. Sport," 720–34.

[43] Katz, *Breaking Through*, 78–83.

downtown hotel instead of the rundown places assigned to blacks. Team members were Dick Barnett, John Barnhill, Joe Buckhalter, Henry Carlton, Albert Cook, Marshall Hurst, Remus Nesbitt, Rubin Perry, James Satterwhite, and Nurlin Tarrant. The HBCU Texas Southern University that beat A&I had come close in 1956 but lost in the NAIA finals 60–55 to McNesse State. McLendon recruited Dick "Skull" Barnett from a large Gary, Indiana, family but decided to send the undisciplined Barnett home in the first year. Davis went to the bus station and brought the young man back to campus. Barnett shot basketballs every day, climbing through the windows when Kean Hall was closed. The left-handed Barnett hit 32 points in one game at Kansas City. The Tennessee A&I State University team had a 26–4 season in 1956–57.[44]

Tennessee State repeated the NAIA championship in 1957–58, beating Western Illinois 85–73, at Kansas City and again winning the coveted James A. Naismith Trophy. McLendon played the entire championship game without a substitute. The A&I team killed the other teams with the fast break and the press. Barnett was most valuable player, and local whites increasingly came out to the A&I campus see Barnett and the team play. Davis reportedly had to reserve seats to abide by state segregation laws and gain white support for the A&I program. The team played in the Georgia Invitational, Tennessee Holiday, NAIA Eastern and NAIA Midwest tournaments, winning the consolation trophy and beating all but one team. The Tigers beat Knoxville College 150–85 but A&I no longer belonged in the small college category. The Tigers' record in 1957–58 was 31–3, including a 62–81 win over East Texas State.[45]

The National High School Athletic Association (NHSAA) tournament remained at Tennessee A&I State University. In 1958, Pearl High School won the national championship in "Tennessee A. & I. State University's 'Little Kean Garden,'" said the Pittsburgh *Courier* (29 March 1958). The 6'4" Ronnie Lawson, bound for UCLA, led the scoring. The Champions received the Henry Arthur Kean Memorial Trophy. The last NHSAA game was held on the A&I campus in 1964, and on 16 June 1968, they dissolved the NHSAA and joined the integrated state high school leagues, which played the games at the TWI campuses. Tennessee A&I hosted Blue Ribbon Clinics to help sharpen the skills of Negro athletes.[46]

McLendon and Davis saw athletics as a way to further the Negro's effort to gain equal rights. They believed in their call for first-class citizenship that Negro

---

[44] Ibid., 91.

[45] Lewis and Thomas, *A Will to Win*, 222–23, 308–09; Katz, *Breaking Through*, 109.

[46] Ron Lawson faxed materials to B.L. Lovett, 20 March 2003: Bill Traughber, "Pearl High achieved national mark," Nashville *Tennessean* sports clipping, and copy of Charles H. Thompson, "The History of the National Basketball Tournaments for Black High Schools," (PhD diss., Louisiana State University, 23 April 1980).

Americans must demonstrate their worthiness with first-class performance. When preparing to return to the NAIA tournament, McLendon said, "The boys can get jittery there, since we'll be going for our third [championship] in a row."[47] The team won all their games but one in 1958–59. The schedule included 17 traditionally white institutions (TWIs), many of whom were eager to post a win over the two-time national champions. Davis wanted major university class competition status and nothing less. The Tennessee A&I State University Tigers Basketball Team won its third consecutive NAIA basketball title in 1958–59. This NAIA record has never been broken.

McLendon won election to the Memorial Basketball Hall of Fame and the NAIA Hall of Fame. Dick Barnett became a three-time All-American and was named NAIA Basketball Championship most valuable player in 1958 and 1959. He was a top draft choice in the National Basketball Association, played on two NBA championship teams until 1973 (scoring more than 15,000 points), and, along with McLendon (d. 1999), was inducted into the National Collegiate Basketball Hall of Fame in 2007. McLendon, "the father of black basketball," left A&I and became a professional basketball coach. He felt that he had complained about the lack of a black coach in the professional league and so had to accept the new coaching position. He left his two children to complete their studies at A&I. Barnett and many of the original team members returned to TSU for an exhibition reunion on 27 October 1984. TSU named the basketball court for McLendon in 1995.[48]

Harold "Hal" Hunter, the assistant coach since 1957 and former National Basketball Association player, succeeded McLendon, but Hunter seemed to miss the quality of players like Barnett, "Big Diamond" Jim, and other star shooters. In 1960, the Tennessee A&I team won the South Central NAIA Tournament and the Mid-West Conference Championship and took third place honors in the NAIA finals. They placed Bert Merriweather, Ben Warley, and Gene Wert on the NAIA Tournament Team. The National Invitational Tournament (NIT) turned down Tennessee State, although A&I ranked second in the nation. The NAACP chapter in New York City, where the tournament played, believed racial prejudice caused the rejection. NIT officials claimed Tennessee A&I was too small a team to compete effectively in the NIT tournament. President Davis agonized over the treatment by the NIT.[49]

Tennessee authorities began placing pressure on public colleges to make athletic programs pay their own way. Davis had been dipping into the academic budget to fund the athletic program. Business manager Paul King said, "Our

---

[47] Katz, *Breaking Through*, 110–12.

[48] Ibid; "100 Moments: McLendon's Court," TSU Athletic Department, Special Collections, TSU. McLendon died 8 October 1999; Katz, *Breaking Through*, 210.

[49] Lewis and Thomas, *A Will to Win*.

athletic programs must operate within its state-supported budget or gain new revenue. From now on, all athletes must make what the university considers normal progress toward a degree." Hunter had requested four-year athletic scholarships instead of traditional one-year aid, but Tennessee State had no budget surplus.

In 1961–62, the team still showed plenty of speed; they had a record of 16–9. The next season included games against NIT basketball powers such as St. Bonaventure. The team played games in the states of Washington and Hawaii. They were trying to dispel the NIT's notion that Tennessee A&I was "too small." The A&I team's record improved to 24–5. However, in the age of segregation of higher education, the smaller HBCUs, such as Tennessee A&I, were unable to compete with the larger, richer TWIs to recruit the best black athletes. It became harder for Tennessee State to win national championships by beating white colleges.

Unfortunately, Davis and Hunter fell out with each other. The crisis came to a head when two star basketball players drew suspension for poor academic performance. SGA president Gerald Durley and other students began protest against President Davis's interference with the basketball program. Hunter's teams still posted winning seasons for the next few years, and Robert Eldridge helped the team beat Southern Illinois 65–61 in 1966. With a 19–7 record, A&I met defeat in the first round of the 1966–67 South Central NCAA College Division Tournament held in Indiana.[50] Davis and Hunter—both men frustrated by losing that competitive edge on the nation level—would not patch up their differences about how to win.

By April 1967, state officials retaliated against Tennessee A&I State University and its students who were active in the civil rights movement by implementing a rule to place a 15 percent cap on the number of out-of-state students enrolled. Davis pleaded such a cap would devastate the recruitment of athletes and marching band members. State officials stayed the new rule for fall 1967 for the band and the athletic teams only. Tennessee A&I State University began to suffer enrollment stagnation and budget deficits. President Davis took sick leave in December 1967. Governor Buford Ellington, a conservative Democrat, already had told the news media that there were going to be some changes because of the riots by college students in the Fisk-Tennessee State Jefferson Street corridor in April 1967. In January 1968, while Davis remained on sick leave in his Mississippi family home, Hunter wrote a letter to Ellington complaining about poor treatment he and the basketball team had received at Tennessee A&I.

---

[50] "Dr. Davis—Coach Hunter end Feud," *The Meter*, January 1964, 1; "100 Moments: McLendon's Court," 1–2.

Davis had written to the Board of Education that he had to remain on sick leave a while longer and a university committee would operate the institution. Things got worse on 4 April 1968 when civil rights leader Martin Luther King, Jr., was murdered in Memphis by a white assassin. Again, for the first time since the April 1967 student riots, state troops blocked off Tennessee A&I State University. Some blacks were fed up with the way the state was treating the HBCU Tennessee A&I State University. Thus on 15 May 1968, A&I history instructor Rita Sanders and others initiated *Rita Sanders (Geier) v. Gov. B. Ellington* (1968) lawsuit to force desegregation of higher education in Tennessee and gain better treatment and more finances for TSU.[51]

President Davis was ailing. The change of events and the stress was too much for him to continue trying to build a greater university. Davis submitted his letter of resignation in May 1968, effective September 1. However, before leaving the office he fired Hunter. An angry Hal Hunter said, "I was dismissed while I was still in Russia. They hired Ed Martin on June 1 and my dismissal did not come out in the newspaper until July 8. It separated me from what I consider scum bums."[52] His A&I teams had won 155 games out of 208.

Edward Martin arrived after Howard Gentry, Sr., the athletic director contacted him and offered him the job. Gentry had agreed with Davis, and criticized Coach Hunter for not playing more NCAA-caliber teams. Gentry had coached Martin in college. Martin's South Carolina State College team had defeated Hunter's team in the 1967 NCAA South Central Regional. Martin said, "When I first came here, Tennessee State was every coach's dream. Every coach I knew wanted to work for President Davis. We had heard over the years that Davis was a man who supported his coaches financially and in every other way. He was the big league. He was way ahead of his time."[53] The 43-year-old Martin assumed control of the team with star player Theodore "Ted" McClain. But Martin's basketball team—the first to play on Kean Hall's brand new floor—ended the 1968–69 season at 14–12. Luckily for Martin, Andrew P. Torrence, who succeeded Davis as president in October 1968 did not have fits about athletics. Martin survived.[54]

One of A&I's great players was Leonard "Truck" Robinson, who amassed 2,249 points during his TSU career and joined professional basketball. Ted McClain led the team to the Division II National Championship game in 1970, but they lost. McClain was drafted in the NBA in 1971. The team entered NCAA tournament play six times through 1975 with a record of 19–9 including making

[51] Lovett, *America's Historically Black Colleges*, 175.

[52] Lewis and Thomas, *A Will to Win*, 239, 242.

[53] Ibid., 242–43.

[54] "100 Moments: Coach Ed Martin's Legacy Lives On," TSU Athletic Department, Special Collections, 1.

it to quarterfinals and semifinals. The team was invited to the Vanderbilt University Invitational Tournament in 1973–74, beating Middle Tennessee State University 63 to 59 in the first round and losing to Vanderbilt in the second round. They won the South Regional in 1970–73 and again in 1975. The season in 1975–76 ended with an overall record of 19–7–0. Martin compiled a TSU record of 301–143 and an overall record of 501–175, making him one of the 89 coaches to win more than 500 college basketball games.[55] From 1962 to 1975, Tennessee State appeared in eight NCAA Division II basketball tournaments. No team repeated John McLendon's team records. Beginning with Joe Buckhalter in 1958, some 22 Tennessee State players were drafted by the NBA by 1994.

And so, there were lingering memories of Tennessee A&I's dominance in basketball—the days when championship banners hung from the rafters, fluttering in the air, rent with the smell of popcorn, while thousands of voices rose and fell with endless cheers within the warmth of "Kean's Little Garden." A new generation of TSU Tigers tried to restart the old winning ways.

Attempts to Recapture the "Good Ole Days" in TSU Sports

In 1980, Howard Gentry, Sr., Center (1980) included a regulation swimming pool, aquatic center and a 10,000-seat basketball arena. President Frederick S. Humphries selected the name of the building, though many persons felt that TSU's more nationally known coaches deserved the honor. The Tiger Gems women's basketball team posted a winning record in 1979–80 under Coach Edna Overall and assistant Maxine Merritt. Dick Barnett served as spokesman in 1983 when the members of the 1956–1959 NAIA Championship Basketball Team received induction into the TSU Sports Hall of Fame.

Under President James A. Hefner (1991–2005), TSU sports attempted a comeback. The men's basketball team won the Ohio Valley Conference (OVC) Championship in 1993. They entered the NCAA tournament but did not survive into the finals. Barnett was the Grand Marshal for the 1993 TSU Homecoming Parade. In 1994, Teresa Lawrence Phillips coached the women's basketball team to a 20–9 season, where they finished first in the OVC season, capturing the OVC tournament title, and making it to the first round of the NCAA tournament. Edward Martin gained induction into the Tennessee Hall of Fame on 4 February 1994.[56]

---

[55] Ibid., 233–37, 242–50; "100 Moments: Remembering Ted McClain," TSU Athletic Department, Special Collections, 1.

[56] Marlin D. Jones, "Inheriting a Legacy: Tennessee State University from 1937 to 1996," *The Meter*, 15, 29 November 1996, 5–8; Evelyn P. Fancher, "Tennessee State University, 1912–1974: A History of an Institution," (PhD diss., George Peabody College, 1975). Martin died in February 2002.

TSU Football

Football became the favorite spectator sport at the HBCUs. In 1912, President W.J. Hale hired a physical education teacher, Howard N. Robinson, who began building competitive intercollegiate sports teams. Robinson arranged a football game against Roger Williams University, which only recently (1909–29) had relocated on Whites Creek Pike (present site of the World Baptist Center). The first football team consisted of 13 members: John Anderson, Theophilus B. Boyd, Herman Davis, McKinley Downs, Billy Hickson, Albert Howell (captain), R.E. Jones, Oscar Rodgers, Baxter Scruggs, Henry J. Stockard, Oscar Tolliver, James Vaughn, and Dan McWherter (reserve). They practiced on the East Campus behind the L-shaped men's dormitory, dressed in a small room next door above the Men's Trades Building, and paid for their own equipment. The 1912–13 football teams allowed only three points and no touchdowns. The State Normal boys beat Burrell Academy of Florence, Alabama, 26 to 0. The *Nashville Globe* (28 September 1913) described the game played in Nashville's Athletic Park. Burrell had beaten Alabama State Normal School, which had beaten Fisk University. The Nashville *Globe* said, "There will be hot times in Nashville tonight! Everyone out on the hill near the river is expected to join in the wigwam dance."[57] A banquet was prepared for the football team. The *Globe's* editor Henry Allen Boyd had a younger brother, T.B. Boyd, on the State Normal team.

In 1913–14, students eagerly anticipated the November 8, afternoon football game with Roger Williams University at Athletic Park. Roger Williams University stunned State Normal 3–0. T.B. Boyd, "a fantastic runner," led the football team. Roger Williams "held that line." In 1914–15, A&I fans feared the news that Fisk beat Alabama A&M State College 46 to 0. State Normal tied that game and ended with a 3–1–0 record in football.

Tennessee State's football team beat Knoxville College in 1923 and 1924. By 1925, the schedule included Lincoln University, Missouri, the Elks Club in Chattanooga, Morris Brown College, Philander Smith College, Walden College, and Simmons University. In 1925, Tennessee State Normal was the state champions. They played five games, winning four games and tied in one game; on November 1, they beat Rust College in Memphis 61–0, and they traveled to Atlanta on November 15 to beat Morris Brown College 10–0. In 1926, the 18-member football team beat four of five opponents, except that Knoxville College beat Tennessee A&I. In 1927, A&I beat Knoxville College in two games: 26–18 and 27–13. They played the game with Rust College in Memphis on 29 October 1927. Memphis had a great park system, including parks for Negroes. A rough

---

[57] "State Normal Game," Nashville *Globe*, 28 September 1913, 1; Patrick Hester, "Twenty Seniors to play their last Homecoming, "Tennessee State University's first football team, 1912–1913," *The Meter*, 9 October 1987, 10.

football stadium at Tennessee A&I was ready for 1927. C. Randolph Taylor (BS, Tufts College) served as A&I coach and science teacher.

Homecoming always occurred on Thanksgiving Day, until 1971. The cafeteria served an elaborate Thanksgiving Dinner attended by faculty members, their families, staff members, and students. In 1927, Meredith G. Ferguson president of the Alumni Association made all the community welcome "to join our happy family in the celebration of our first Homecoming Day." Laura V. Patterson of Memphis was Miss A&I. A fan said, "The terrible Tennesseans of A. & I. State College completely outplayed the Fisk University Bulldogs in their scoreless game on Thanksgiving Day." Fisk beat State Normal 20–0 in the 1929 season.

Tad D. Upshaw, a 1928 all-Southern guard, became the new football coach. TSU beat Kentucky State by a score of 6–0. Kentucky State got a new coach named Henry Arthur Kean. The football schedule for 1929 included Miles Memorial College, Morris Brown College, and Lincoln University. Fisk University remained the great rivalry for Thanksgiving Day. Guy E. Holloman, a 1926 A&I graduate, became the football coach in 1929. In 1930, Tennessee A&I State College became a member of the Southeastern Athletic Association.

In 1931, President Hale hired recent A&I graduate Walter S. Davis at $65 a month to replace Able Lewis in the agricultural program. Davis also had to teach in the high school department and coach the football team. Walter Davis was a keen student of football; he attended various football clinics across the country, learning the game in-depth. The team posted a 5–1–1 record in 1933. Tiger football gained membership in the Midwestern Athletic Association on 4 January 1934. Davis left to pursue his master's degree. Reubin A. Mundy coached the football team. In 1934, the Tigers defeated Lane College 8–0 and defeated the "national Negro football champions" Wilberforce University. Forrest Strange became A&I's first All-American. In 1937, the record was 3–2. In 1938, it was 6–0. Lawrence Simmons (class of 1937) coached the team in 1939 with a 3–7 record, ending with a 0–0 tie against LeMoyne College in Memphis. In January 1940, the college honored the football team at the Annual Athletic Banquet. The team lost twelve seniors and All-American Chaney Humphreys. Hale said, "The fundamental principles of football underlie life and living—honesty, loyalty, abiding faith, determination, and hard work."[58]

Tennessee A&I State College suspended football from 1940–44, as did Fisk. In Memphis, the town's only HBCU, Lemoyne College, dropped football in 1941; World War II really caused a great absence of able-bodied men. High school football picked up the slack. Memphis's Booker T. Washington High School and

---

[58] "Tennessee 'Tigers' Outscore Opponents during 1929 Season," *Ayeni* (1930): 90; *Ayeni* (1931): 98.

its North Memphis rival Manassas High School faced each other for the championship in the Elks Blues Bowl in 1943. Washington beat Manassas 26–0.[59]

In 1943, the students at Tennessee A&I State College demanded football return to the campus or they would boycott class. Acting President Davis met with the lead protestors and promised to restart the football program. In December, S.E. Brady the head of the SIAC and other conference officials convened in New Orleans to reset HBCU schedules for football, basketball, and track. Davis contacted Henry Arthur ("Snake") Kean, the coach at Kentucky State College, a former player at Fisk, a producer of All-Americans, and winner of several football championships. Davis offered Kean the job as head of A&I's physical education department. Davis said he expected to enroll at least 1,080 students and at least 40 of them would join the football team. Kean had his picture taken with new faculty in fall 1944.[60]

The 1944 A&I State Tigers played a total of 11 games against Langston University (twice), Clark College (twice), Wilberforce University (twice), Florida A&M College (twice), Lincoln University, Arkansas AM&N State College, and Tuskegee Institute. A&I won the Mid-West SIAC title, beating Tuskegee 13–0 in the Fourth Annual Vulcan Bowl in Birmingham before 8,500 spectators. A&I Tigers had a record of 8–2–1.

Davis and Coach Kean committed to bringing the annual Tennessee A&I football game back to Memphis. Memphis-Shelby County was home to nearly 40 percent of black Tennesseans. The head of the Universal Life Insurance Company, J. E. Walker, headed the arrangements committee. Walker was a native Mississippian like Davis. A graduate of Meharry Medical College, Dr. Walker founded a bank and an insurance company in Mississippi before migrating to Memphis in 1923. He opened the Universal Life Insurance Company in Memphis. In 1936, he formed the Negro Democrats Club in Memphis-Shelby County though most blacks were Republicans. During the Great Depression, he used students at LeMoyne College to do surveys on the economic conditions in Negro neighborhoods. Walker served as head of the National Negro Business League in the mid-1940s, edited the *Memphis Negro Business Directory*, and often visited A&I to help promote the business education program and uplift Negro Americans.[61]

---

[59] Bobby L. Lovett, *The Civil Rights Movement in Tennessee: A Narrative History* (Knoxville: University of Tennessee Press, 2005) 237–53; G. Wayne Dowdy, *Crusades for Freedom: Memphis and the Political Transformation of the American South* (Jackson: University Press of Mississippi, 2010).

[60] "A. & I. new faculty," Nashville *Globe*, 6 October 1944, 1.

[61] Lovett, *Civil Rights Movement*, 193, 194, 265, 268, 279, 285; Robert A. Sigafoos, *Cotton Row to Beale Street: A Business History of Memphis* (Memphis: Memphis State University Press, 1979) 309, 332–33; Roberta Church and Ronald Walter, *Nineteenth Century*

President Davis traveled to Memphis to help Dr. Walker with arrangements. Davis spoke for the War Bond Drive on March 30 at the Mississippi Boulevard Christian Church. The church was pastured by Blair T. Hunt, who earned his master's degree at A&I during summers, and who often headed train cars filled with west Tennessee teachers headed to the summer sessions at Tennessee State. Hunt had also served as principal of Booker T. Washington High School since 1931. By the 1940s he was chief Negro spokesperson for the fearful Boss E.H. Crump machine. Hunt operated Booker T. Washington High School with an iron fist: no teachers, students or parents dared challenge him; and, the Crump city machine gave the school all the facilities and equipment Hunt asked for. Additionally, the efforts by Walker and Davis did not intend to rival those by Lt. George W. Lee's Annual High School Blues Bowl. Until he fell out of grace with the Crump machine in 1940, Lee, along with fellow black Republican millionaire Robert R. Church, Jr., ruled black Memphis politics. Lee stayed out of old man Crump's way and engaged in the High School Blues Bowl that was graced by the presence of William C. Handy, "the father of the blues" who Crump once used in his mayoral campaigns. But Lee quietly used some of the game's proceeds for food for the poor and money for Negroes to buy poll tax receipts for voting.

Coach Kean and President Davis made it known to the Crump machine and everybody else that they were in Memphis simply to play football and they intended to win in a decisive way the game with the black and gold Lions of Arkansas AM&N State College scheduled for 9 December 1944. They were not there to support Lee's Negro Republicans, Walker's black Democrats, or bother the Crump machine. On December 6, Booker T. Washington High School, the Mid-South Champion, was to face Sumner High School, the Mid-West Champions, in the Sixth Annual Elk's Blues Bowl game. Washington H.S. had defeated Nashville's Pearl High School for the state championship. Coach "Rip" Boone's undefeated Washington Warriors football team won the national championship game 7–0 and placed eleven players on the Memphis all-city team. Memphis was ready for the Tennessee A&I Tigers. Kean told the Nashville *Globe* and the Memphis *World* that the two college teams were ready as could be considering World War II conditions. Kean prepared his teams through constant practice. The game took place on Saturday at 2 p.m. in the Washington H.S. stadium with 2,000 spectators. Kean impressed the crowd by making substitutions on every play. Raymond Whitmon performed as Tigers'

Memphis Families of Color 1850–1900 (Memphis TN: Murdock Printing, 1987) 16–19, 20–25; Bobby L. Lovett, "Beale Street," Van West ed., *Tennessee Encyclopedia*, 53–4; Kenneth Fieth, "Edward Hull Crump (1874–1954)," *Tennessee Encyclopedia*, 220–222.

quarterback; the Tigers' defense was led by Shannon Little. The Tennessee A&I State College Tigers won the 1944 Memphis Classic 50–19.[62]

In 1945, the Tigers beat Philander Smith College 87–0. The Memphis *World* said, "Tennessee State Tigers Topple Southern (Baton Rouge) 33–0."[63] The game took place on a muddy field in a cold, driving rain. Robert "Bulldog" Drummond (a tackle) set up a Tennessee State score by blocking a punt on the 23-yard line. Davis left almost everything up to Kean, who had extensive knowledge of the game after further training by the great football coaches in Indiana and Michigan.

After seeing the high-stepping marching bands on the football fields at Indiana University and Michigan University, Davis hired a director to build a dazzling marching band to grace the games by fall 1946. Kean recruited additional great players when more Negro high schools came on line in the South. Tennessee A&I State College won the black college national championship in 1946. The 1947 Tigers football team went undefeated and won the black college national football championship. They played the 29 September 1950, game against Langston University at night in Nashville's Sulphur Dell Baseball Park.

Tennessee A&I produced 11 All-Americans by 1951 and began sending players to the National Football League (NFL) in 1952. In 1954, the Tigers won the black college national championship. Kean earned the Lucius L.L. Jones Memorial Award for Coach of the Year, presented on 28 January 1955. Kean died from a heart attack on 12 December 1955. He had a record of 162–30–5. Kean's teams held three National Black Football Championships. The gym was named Kean Hall.

When Howard Gentry, Sr., became interim head coach, Tennessee A&I State University already was a notable football power and Kean had left a good team in place. After coaching at other colleges, Gentry joined Kean on the A&I coaching staff in 1949. The schedules included North Carolina A&T, Morris Brown, Grambling, South Carolina State, Central State, Southern, Lincoln, Prairie View, Kentucky State, and Jackson State. The Tigers won their fourth national black college football championship in 1956. Shannon D. Little, J. C. "Buddy" Coffee, Raymond Whitmon, Forrest Strange, Cornelius Jones, and Howard Green assisted Gentry. Their football teams had records of 7–2–0, 10–0–0, 5–0–1, 4–4–0, 9–1–0, and 7–3–0. Coach Gentry was overjoyed. However, President Davis was

---

[62] "Tennessee A. & I.," *Memphis World*, 1 December 1943, 3 March, 24, 28 November, 1, 12 December 1944, 20 November 1945, 1–3.

[63] "A. & I.," *Memphis World*, 20 November 1945, 1.

impatient. He diplomatically transferred Raymond Kemp to the faculty and placed Gentry in Kemp's athletic director job.[64]

Lawrence Simmons became coach in 1961. Like Davis, Simmons had played at A&I and coached the team in the 1930s. Simmons was an assistant coach at Tennessee State (1946–51), head coach at South Carolina State College (1951–53), returning to Tennessee State as offensive coordinator (1953–55), and coached at a high school in Illinois (1956–61). Davis and Simmons set about the job of getting the football team back into competitive shape "within four to five years." Tennessee A&I State University had records of 7–3 (1960), 4–4–1 (1961), and 1–7–1 (1962). They lost to John Merritt's Jackson State Tigers. Coach Simmons resigned. President Davis reportedly took over the duties of head coach for the rest of the year.

In April 1963, Davis sent his assistants Homer Wheaton and two other graduates to drive to Mississippi to talk to the dynamic young coach that beat Tennessee State. Davis hired John A. Merritt at a salary of $10,000, free on-campus housing, and a five-year guarantee. Merritt earned less than $7,000 at Jackson State, and his assistants earned even less money. On May 21, Merritt and his assistant Joe Gilliam, Sr., officially became coach and assistant coach. Alvin Coleman, another Merritt assistant, was hired to round out a coaching team the envy of all.[65]

Under "Big John" Merritt, Tennessee State returned to its winning tradition of the Arthur Kean years. In 1963–64, the team won six and lost three games. Merritt posted records of 8–2–0, 9–0–1, 10–0–0, 6–3–0, and 6–2–1. John Ayers Merritt was born in 1926 in Falmouth, Kentucky, completed high school in Louisville, joined the US Navy, played football at Kentucky State College, married Maxine Owens in 1947, and entered graduate school in 1950. He was a high school coach before taking the job at Jackson State. Merritt's teams maintained winning ways: 1968, 6–2–1; 1969, 8–1–0 (lost to Southern); 1970, 11–0–0; 1971, 9–1–0 (lost to Texas Southern); 1972, 11–1–0 (loss to Grambling); 1973, 10–0–0; 1974, 8–2–0. In 1973, TSU began playing nearby Middle Tennessee State University, beating that TWI 23–0. MTSU avenged the lost in 1974 by a score of 20–10. TSU beat MTSU in 1975 by 21–14, and 26–17 and 27–0 the following two years. The Tiger defense had a NCAA record of holding opponents to negative yardage.

---

[64] Carrie M. Gentry, *A Life Worth Living: A Biography of Howard C. Gentry, Sr.* (Nashville: R.H. Boyd, 2010) 53–60; Reginald A. McDonald, "Instrumental Music at Tennessee State University: The Early Years, 1912–1946," *The Journal of Tennessee State University* 1, no. 1 (April 2012): 33–56.

[65] "John Merritt," Nashville *Capitol City Defender*, 11 April, 22 May, 12 June 1963, 1; "100 Moments: John Merritt," TSU Athletic Department, Special Collections, 1–2; Lovett, *America's Historically Black Colleges and Universities*, 348–58.

In 1978, with 5,240 students, TSU was qualified to join a larger conference but Merritt felt the Tigers were not welcomed in the TWI conferences even though the conference members now relied heavily on black players. Merritt felt it was one thing for a TWI to lose to another TWI team using black players, but it was an insult for TWI coaches to lose to an HBCU using all black players *and* all black coaches. TSU had an 84 percent winning football record as opposed to 60 percent for UT, 42 percent for UT-Chattanooga, 39 percent for East Tennessee State, 58 percent for Memphis State, and 36 percent for Vanderbilt. Tennessee State already was playing some top NCAA football teams including Ball State University, San Diego State University, and UT-Chattanooga. TSU had won more NCAA basketball games than Vanderbilt, Memphis State, East Tennessee State, Austin Peay, and Tennessee Tech since 1967. TSU had 47 players drafted into the National Football League compared to 43 for the University of Florida and 42 for UT. TSU produced 93 football All-Americans including Ed "Too Tall" Jones and "Jefferson Street" Joe Gilliam Jr. In 1974, Jones and Waymond Bryant were the first and fourth players picked in the NFL draft. In 1979, State Senator Avon N. Williams, Jr., sponsored state senate bill 350 to require other Tennessee public colleges to play TSU in sports but the bill was defeated.

After the federal court merged UT-Nashville and TSU in July 1979, there was pressure to include a more integrated athletic schedule for the merged institution. TSU applied for membership in the all-white Ohio Valley Conference (OVC) against much student and alumni opposition that felt the OVC schedule would cut down on playing the more exciting games with other HBCUs. Student leaders felt state officials were readying TSU to become mostly white. President Humphries brought Howard Gentry out of retirement to handle this tricky political process. Merritt's teams encountered the first two OVC opponents in 1982, beating Eastern Illinois (20–19) and losing to Eastern Kentucky (7–13). President Emeritus Walter S. Davis died in fall 1979.

John Merritt became notable for staying politically connected to support for the football team. Merritt called on local politicians when he needed financial help and when one of "my boys" got in trouble. Local politicians wanted appearances with "Big John" Merritt. Even after the university stopped the practice of giving free admission to Hale Stadium for faculty members and their immediate family, he continued to cultivate good relations with them. He phoned favorite professors on Saturday mornings: "How many tickets you need for the game today? Ok, pick them up at the 'Will Call Window'." He visited the professors to see "how my boys are doing in your class." The professors kept him informed any time a football player missed too many classes, failed to study for tests, and did not turn in written assignments. Merritt always made certain the delinquents soon came to see the professor and brought their completed assignments with them. He managed a one-man academic advisement program, saying to parents "I will see that your boy gets a good college education, and graduates if you let him play for me."[66] In the summers, during the Merritt years, one could see huge pro football players (Merritt's former players) walking the campus, attending classes, and completing the courses needed to graduate.

Ed "Too Tall" Jones (lineman) gained induction into the Tennessee Hall of Fame on 4 February 1994. Jones lettered in TSU football (1970–73), played for the Dallas Cowboys, and spent 15 years in the NFL. Several TSU players went on to coaching careers, among them Ken Pettiford. The Jersey City native joined the TSU football team in 1970. As a quarterback, Pettiford waited in the wings behind two excellent quarterbacks. The Tigers went 11–1 under Pettiford, won the Pioneer Bowl, and gained rank by the Associated Press and the United Press International. He threw for 1,748 yards (49.6 percent completed passes) and 22 touchdowns. Pettiford became an assistant coach at TSU and then a coach at Fisk after leaving the NFL in 1976. In 2002, he became head football coach at Savannah State University.

In 1980, the President of the United States called to congratulate Merritt for his 200th win. The schedule in 1981–82 included Jackson, Southern (twice), Texas Southern, Alabama State, Grambling, University of Louisville, Nicholls State, Central State, UT-Chattanooga, and North Carolina A&T. In 1982, the city named a portion of Centennial Boulevard John A. Merritt Boulevard, with the governor, mayor, and the district congressman present.

Failing health caused Merritt to retire from TSU in 1983. In October, fifty-three persons gained induction into the first class of the TSU Sports Hall of Fame for students, coaches, and administrators in TSU sports. Walter S. Davis was the top inductee. John Merritt died 15 December 1983. Merritt had compiled a record of 172–33–7 at TSU and 232–65–11 overall, ranking him ninth on the all-time victory list. He won 46 of 47 games in the Hole after losing his first two games there. The football records for 1969–1982: 8–1–0, 11–0–0, 10–0–0, 8–2–0, 5–4–0, 7–2–1, 8–1–1, 8–3–0, 8–3–0, 9–1–0, 8–3–0, and 10–1–1. TSU won black college national championships in 1966, 1970, 1971, 1973, 1979, and 1982. The team made the NCAA Division I-AA playoffs in 1981 and 1982. Merritt's teams trained 75 All-Americans. He became the first black football coach named to the National Football Sports Hall of Fame, Helms Sports Hall of Fame, College Football Hall of Fame, and Sheridan Coach of the Year. He compiled 30 straight wins, using the pro-football-type T formation with multiple sets, a wide-open style. He depended heavily on Gilliam and Coleman. Merritt was outspoken, humble and deeply rooted in psychology and TSU sports history. Merritt said:

> A black kid doesn't understand how to win just for the sake of winning. He has to have a reason to win. The same damn thing holds true here at Tennessee State University.... This [Hale Stadium] is holy ground. We made

---

[66] "B.H. Lovett, "Notes on Merritt," 1–5, Lovett Papers.

this ball field out of a cornfield, but some of the greatest football players in America were once right here. And the memory of all those guys is still right here in every clod of dirt you pick up and in every blade of grass you see.[67]

Merritt was elected to the Football Hall of Fame on 6 December 1994.

After Frederick S. Humphries resigned on 30 June 1985, interim President Roy Peterson served the university from 1 July 1985 until 30 June 1986. Student leaders, the black community leaders, and members of the Tennessee Caucus of Black State Legislators persuaded the TBR and the governor to release Peterson. Acting President Otis L. Floyd came aboard on July 1. Student leaders assailed Floyd about campus conditions and his lackluster civil-rights credentials. The students assailed Floyd in the student newspaper, *The Meter*, and occupied his office suite. They accused him of disrespectfully dismissing Gentry, Sr., in favor of football coach Bill Thomas, who became coach *and* athletic director. The football program entered the NCAA Division I-AA playoffs in 1986. Floyd became permanent president in March 1987. But TSU's sports program and the quality of its coaching abilities began to decline. Some 200 students marched on Floyd's office in 1990 and demanded that Thomas be fired. He quietly left the university to become football coach at Texas Southern University. Floyd, too, left on 30 June 1990 after state officials secured him the position of Chancellor of the Tennessee Board of Regents. TSU vice president for administration George Cox served as Acting President.

After a heated president's position at Jackson State University, James A. Hefner hurriedly exited Mississippi and took over TSU in mid-April 1991. President Hefner smartly promised "strong athletics *and* sound academics." By 2002, TSU boasted of a graduation rate of 63 percent for athletes—the highest in the TBR system and won the OVC Academic Banner. In 1993, the Tigers played their 40th football season in "the Hole"—W.J. Hale Stadium in which the team had a record of 72–5–1. Tiger Football had an overall record of 120–18–2 since 1953. However, large football games had to be moved to a 45,000-seat stadium at Vanderbilt University. TSU begged the state for a new or expanded stadium. Members of the Tennessee Caucus of Black State Legislators secured money for feasibility studies but that is as far as the movement went. TSU alumni and other supporters of the athletic program either did not have the financial ability or were not willing to raise millions of dollars needed for a new stadium. TSU was not UTK where the sports community raised money to build a 105,000-seat football stadium. TSU also suffered because the OVC away-games drew dismal crowds. More TSU "Big Blue" fans showed up than home fans. When the TWIs came to Nashville they brought no marching band and only a busload of

---

[67] See Lewis and Thomas, *A Will to Win*, on details of the Merritt years; Ron Wynn, "Tennessee State University's Championship History," *Tennessee Tribune*, 27 September–3 October 2012, 2B, 9B.

spectators. TSU had to stay on the road, playing money-making "Classics" with other HBCUs and attracting crowds of 50,000 to 60,000 in large cities such as Atlanta, Las Vegas, and Memphis. TSU reportedly earned more money than all OVC football programs combined.

The Tennessee State University football team claimed the OVC championship by beating Murray State University on 14 November 1998 after more than 3,000 fans had shown up for the pep rally at the Amphitheater. The last football game at Hale Stadium saw the defeat of Texas Southern University by a score of 28–14 on 21 November 1998. The Tigers had a seven-game winning streak under Coach L.C. Cole, who had a three-year record of 16–16 at TSU. The team gained its second OVC title in 1999 along with No. 1 ranking in NCAA Division I-AA. TSU lost the playoffs, and Cole left for Alabama State.

When the Houston Oilers National Football League team moved to Nashville, they renamed themselves the Tennessee Titans. The city built a 68,000-seat football stadium, and TSU became a co-tenant in 2000. Hale Stadium was abandoned. The attendance began to decline until some games drew at most 35,000 people, and on average less than 6,000 spectators, sitting in a 68,000-seat professional football stadium. TSU athletic officials created the John Merritt Classic to open each season and generate bigger crowds in the new Titans' stadium.

But there were sober reminders of TSU's past glory. Eldridge Dickey, three-time All-American quarterback (1965–68) died on 22 May 2000. He led TSU to undefeated seasons and bowl berths in 1965 and 1966, played with the Oakland Raiders, 1968–71, and then became a minister. The funeral for Joe Gilliam was held on 28 December 2000, in Kean Hall. In 1970, "Jefferson Street" Joe Gilliam, Jr., had led the TSU Tigers to an 11–0 season, followed by a 7–1 season. He also had 9–1 and 11–1 seasons at TSU. In 1972, Gilliam was drafted by the Pittsburgh Steelers, and in 1974 he became the first black quarterback to start a regular National Football League season game. Doug Williams, a graduate of Grambling University, quarterback for the Super Bowl XXII Washington Redskins in 1986, and current head coach at Grambling, said, "I am here because I owe so much for what Joe Gilliam [Jr.] did for the NFL."[68]

James Reese, an alumnus and a member of the TSU football staff since 1991, became football coach in 2000. The Big Blue Tigers finished the 2001 football season ranked No. 25 nationally in the I-AA. The 2002 football schedule was particularly tiresome including Prairie View, South Carolina State, Jackson State, Grambling State, Florida A&M, Alabama A&M, UT-Martin, Eastern Illinois, Murray State, and Eastern Kentucky. By October 10, TSU had lost all but one game (Prairie View State University). The John Merritt Classic (7 September 2002) honored Samuel Whitmon an inductee into the TSU Sports Hall of Fame. In

---

[68] "TSU Remembers Joe Gilliam Jr.," *Accent* (March 2001): 6.

2002–03, the football team lost all but two of its games. The team won the Merritt Classic.[69]

In September 2003, TSU won the Memphis Classic. Alumnus "Too Tall" Ed Jones, who had business offices in Memphis and Dallas, was there, cheering for "The Big Blue" and heading the two-day Ed Jones Gold Tournament as part of the Annual Memphis Classic weekend activities. The football game drew 52,000 fans in Memphis and pumped millions of dollars into the economy. There were dances, barbecues, tailgate parties, nights out at the nearby casinos, concerts featuring top national entertainers, "Battle of the Bands" events, college recruitment nights at local hotels, and food and merchandise booths and more tailgate parties that surrounded the stadium one- and two-blocks deep. On 20 September 2003, the road-weary TSU Tigers faced Florida A&M in the Atlanta Classic before more than 62,000 fans. The Tigers lost the game but won the next game of the season, the opening OVC contest. Coach Reese resigned in November 2004.

Tennessee State University hired an outside consulting group to conduct a full evaluation of the athletic program. Athletics were extremely expensive, especially the Aristocrat of Bands whose expenses cost $40,000 or more to perform in an out-of-town football game. Again, TSU's athletic programs, its supporters and the alumni could not raise large amounts of private funds in the same way that UT did. Since slavery ended in 1865, black American families still had only one-eleventh of the wealth of the average white family. In September 2006, TSU and Vanderbilt University football teams met for the first time. Vanderbilt won 38–9. Reportedly, President Davis had wanted this game to happen long ago.[70]

TSU's men basketball team won the OVC Championship in 1993 and made it to the first round of the NCAA tournament. In 2002, the TSU men's basketball team finished seventh in the nine-team Ohio Valley Conference. On 15 April 2003, the university hired Cy Alexander, III, after firing Nolan Richardson on 9 January 2003 for poor conduct (making threats with a pistol) and mismanagement that caused the basketball program to suffer NCAA sanctions. The TSU Tennis Team received new indoor tennis courts. In softball, the Lady Tigers won several games, and in volleyball, the Lady Tigers finished 4–22 in the 2001 season. The 2002–03 Lady Tigers basketball teams had gone through a

---

[69] *Alumni Life* (Spring 2002) 1–2.

[70] LaVonte Young, "Vandy storms to win on Tiger turnovers," *The Meter*, 25 September 2006, 1; David Climer, "After long history apart, TSU, Vandy finally to play," Nashville *Tennessean*, 22 September 2006, 1, 14A.

rebuilding program, finishing with a 3–22 record, although senior forward LaRissa Thomas joined the first-team All-OVC, averaging 18.3 points per game.[71]

In 2004-04, the TSU women's softball team, under coach Joyce Maudie, won its OVC opener against UT-Martin. The cross-country team finished fifth in the Georgia Invitational. The Lady Tigers Volleyball Team ranked 20th in the nation in service aces in 2003–04, winning the OVC Championship. The Tigers Ladies Golf Team competed in the Tennessee Tech Lady Classic, finishing eighth. The Men's Golf Team took the Gulf Coast Collegiate Classic championship. Robert Dinwiddie won All-OVC for the second straight year, with a 70.5 per round. The Golf Team, under Coach Catana Starks, continued to win tournaments, and the golf teams won titles as late as 2005.[72] Women's track coach, Cheeseborough, gained induction into the Tennessee Sports Hall of Fame, the National Track and Field Hall of Fame and became OVC Track Coach of the Year in 2002. The Tigerbelles claimed the 2002 Ohio Valley Conference indoor and outdoor titles. In the OVC indoor tournament, the men's track team finished fifth. Ryan Fann, a sophomore, became a member of the US High Performance Paralympic team for the 2004 games in Greece. In 2005 football, the Tigers lost almost every game including Homecoming and the last game (47–0). TSU now competes in Division I of the NCAA.[73]

The student athletes, coaches and staff developed a great legacy in sports competition. The TSU football program placed at least 62 players into National Football Leagues. TSU football player Rodgers-Cromartie was drafted by the Cardinals with the 16th pick in the first round of the 2008 NFL draft and selected to the 2010 NFL Pro Bowl. In August 2011, former TSU football player Richard Dent gained induction into the NFL Hall of Fame. At 6'5" and 265 pounds, the 55-year-old Dent received his Hall of Fame ring before a cheering crowd on 25

[71] Sam Latham, "TSU hires Cy Alexander to revive men's basketball," *The Urban Journal*, Nashville, 6 April 2003, 1, 15.

[72] TSU, "History Makers at Tennessee State University," TSU Exchange, 4 February 2008, 1.

[73] See University publications, *Meter, Accent*, and so on, 2000–05, Special Collections, TSU.

September 2011 at a Chicago Bears' game. Dent played for several NFL teams but made his mark on the Bears' defense in the 1980s. He was one of the honorees for the 2011 Tennessee State University Homecoming festivities.[74]

---

[74] Sports page, "TSU's Rodgers-Cromartie selected to 2010 NFL Pro Bowl," Nashville *Pride*, 8 January 8 2010, 7B; "Richard Dent," http://www.nfl.com/player/richarddent/2503721/profile, 1 [accessed 25 November 2011].

Conclusion

One theme that emerges clearly is student activism and power evolved at Tennessee State, and this insurgency of the students profoundly influenced the history and the development of the institution. Students initiated the athletic programs in 1912. They built their own gymnasium in 1924. The summer session students supported President W.J. Hale when he got in trouble in 1915 and 1922. In lockstep with the unfolding civil rights movement, students and the NAACP pressured President Hale and the state from 1935 to 1942 to start a graduate program. Students, alumni, and friends tried to help save Hale in 1943. In 1943, students threatened to boycott classes unless the new president Walter Davis reinstitutes the football program. Their demands gave Davis a reason to begin a winning athletic program at Tennessee A&I State College. Students brought world recognition to Tennessee A&I by bringing home dozens of Olympic medals as well as other track and field championships in North America, Europe, and the Pan American Games. Students brought three consecutive national basketball championships home from 1957–59, won six national football championships, regional, conference, and national titles in volleyball, boxing, swimming, and other sports.

In 1960–63, students used sit-ins, public marches and protests, Freedom Rides and uprisings to help defeat Jim Crow. Students marched on the federal courthouse in downtown Nashville, chanting "UTN+TSU=TSU" during the *Geier* court trials in the mid-1970s, perhaps influencing the federal court to order a merger in 1977. Students took over the president's office, marched on the state capitol, and insisted the governor come with them to see the appalling conditions on campus. These actions perhaps influenced the governor and other political leaders to grant TSU a $122 million master plan to transform the campus into something entirely new in 1990–2001. Students protected some presidents and opposed the ones that threatened the heritage of TSU.[1]

Another theme in the history of Tennessee State—one that perhaps also haunted other HBCUs—was the long periods of instability in leadership. Starting in 1985, there began 27 years of less-than-stellar governance. TSU stagnated, grew, and then began to decline. Tennessee State University became more vulnerable to dictates from its governing board, state education bureaucrats, and outside forces intent on transforming the institution into what they perceived the HBCU should become. The faculty joined the president in 1968–74 to fight state officials that seemed to undermine the institution in favor of the University of

---

[1] Tennessee State University, *75th Anniversary, Tennessee State University, 1912–1987: Some Traditions are Forever* (Nashville: TSU, 1987) 1–28.

Tennessee. Several of the presidents—Hale, Davis, Torrence, and Humphries—had fought courageous battles with state officials and Jim Crow to protect the institution, demand its equality with the white colleges and universities, and make some institutional progress.

But TSU entered a racially intense era. In 1954, resistance to *Brown* reached its apex, and white flight to the suburbs helped with re-segregation of urban public school systems based on residential and economic patterns. By 2000, some 47 percent of students, blacks, whites and others in Nashville's public school system suffered poverty. America became segregated by economics. People of color—Native Americans, African Americans, Hispanic, and Latino Americans—often suffered the most. The affirmative-action policies that were designed to help the minorities catch up to the whites after the hundred-year-plus brutal system of Jim Crow came under attack in the local, state, and federal courts. America became more segregated, *de facto*. Thurgood Marshall's dissenting opinion in *Milliken v. Bradley* US (1974) had warned of these developments. *Hopwood v. Texas* US (1992), *Wooden et al. v. Board of Regents of the University System of Georgia* US (1999), *Gratz et al. v. Bollinger et al.* US (2003), and *Grutter v. Bollinger et al.* US (2003) made race as a single factor for admissions criteria unconstitutional. Tennessee State University students were among thousands of college students who used cars and buses to journey to Washington, DC, to hear the US Supreme Court's arguments and protest anti-affirmative-action decisions. Two busloads of TSU students and constituents journey to Washington, DC, to witness the dedication of the new Martin Luther King, Jr., National Monument in fall 2011.

In this intense racial milieu, Tennessee State University struggled to retain white students and increase the enrollment of all students by 2011–12. Nevertheless, Tennessee State University had nearly 9,600 students in fall 2011. The institution was undergoing reorganization in efforts to react to the twenty-first-century budget realities. The winning sports tradition in basketball, football, track, and field seemed long ago, and the most vocal and most active alumni were aging fast. TSU alumni such as Ada Jackson and Gwen Vincent, who worked tirelessly in alumni association activities, were not being replaced as rapidly in Nashville. Local TWIs were sprinting ahead of TSU. The online for-profit colleges and universities were the choices of minority students by a ratio of 6:1. Some 84 percent of black college students no longer attended the HBCUs. Tennessee State University held its fall convocation in September 2011 to open the Centennial Celebration. The institution has been in a struggle of survival like the one of 1912; yet, with "A Touch of Greatness," Tennessee State University—the descendant of Tennessee Agricultural and Industrial Normal School and the merger with University of Tennessee at Nashville—was poised for another hundred years of greatness.

Selected Bibliography

Allen, Walter R. and J. O. Jewell, "A Backward Glance Forward: Past, Present, and Future Perspectives on Historically Black Colleges and Universities," *The Review of Higher Education*, 25 (2002): 241-261.

Allen, W. R., E. G. Epps, and N. Z. Hanffreds. *College in Black and White: African American Students in Predominantly White and Historically Black Public Universities*. Albany, NY: University of New York Press, 1991.

Arsenault, Raymond. *Freedom Riders: 1961 and the Struggle for Racial Justice*. New York: Oxford University Press, 2006.

Atwood, R. B. "The Origins of the Negro Public College." *Journal of Negro Education* 31/1 (1962): 241-242.

Bell, Derrick. *Silent Covenants: Brown v. Board of Education and the Unfulfilled Hopes for Racial Reform*. New York: Oxford University Press, 2004.

Bergeron, Paul H., Stephen V. Ash, and J. Keith, *Tennesseans and Their History*. Knoxville, TN: University of Tennessee Press, 1999.

Bergon, Carol, Christopher L. Miller, Robert W. Cherny, and James L. Gormly. *Making America: a History of the United States*. Boston: Houghton Mifflin Company, 1995. Blackwell, James E. *Desegregation of State Systems of Higher Education: An Assessment*. Atlanta, GA: Southern Education Foundation, 1984.

Bond, Horace Mann. "Why a Negro College?" *Journal of Negro Education* 17/1 (1948): 234.

Booker, Robert J. *And There Was Light! The 120-Year History of Knoxville College, 1875-1995*. Virginia Beach, VA: Donning Company Publishers, 1994.

Boyd, Henry T. "A follow-up Study of the Graduates of the Department of Business Education at Tennessee A. & I. State College with Implications for Evaluating the Curriculum and Guidance Program." M.S. Thesis, Tennessee A. & I. State College, 1951.

Brinkley, Velma H. and M. H. Malone, *Images of America: African American Life in Sumner County*. Dover, NH: Arcadia Publishing Co., 1998.

Brooks, George W. *History of the Tennessee Education Congress, 1923-1967*. Washington, DC: National Educational Association, 1975.

Brown, M. Christopher, and K. Freeman, edited. *Black Colleges: New Perspectives on Policy and Practice*. Westport, CT: Praeger Publishers, 2003.

Brown, M. Christopher II. *The Quest to Define Collegiate Desegregation: Black Colleges, Title VI Compliance, and the Post-Adams Litigation*. Westport, CT: Bergin and Garrey, 1999.

Brown, Ina C. *National Survey of Higher Education of Negroes: Socio-Economic Approach to Education Problems*. Washington, DC: U.S. Bureau of Education, 1942.

Bullock, Henry A. *A History of Negro Education in the South from 1619 to the Present*. Cambridge, MA: Harvard University Press, 1967.

Carson, Clayborne. *In Struggle: SNCC and the Black Awakening of the 1960s*. Cambridge, MA: Harvard University Press, 1981.

Christian, Charles M. *Black Saga: The African American Experience, A Chronology*. New York: Houghton Mifflin Co., 1995.

Clemons, Fatino M. "A History of the Women's Varsity Track Team at Tennessee State University." M.S. Thesis, Tennessee State University, 1975.

Cooke, A. L. *Lane College: Its Heritage and Outreach, 1882-1982.* Jackson, TN: Lane College, 1987.

Crowell, Christopher. "History of the Sanders v. Ellington Case Leading to the Implementation of the University of Tennessee Nashville." Ed.D. Dissertation, Tennessee State University, 1996.

Drewry, Henry N. and Humphrey Doermann, *Stand and Prosper: Private Black Colleges and Their Students.* Princeton, NJ: Princeton University Press, 2001.

Du Bois, William E. B. *The Souls of Black Folk.* New York: Bantam Books, 1903, 1989.

Egerton, John. *Speak Now Against the Day: the Generation before the Civil Rights Movement in the South.* New York: Knopf, Inc., 1994.

Egerton, John. "Suit Unresolved on Dual Colleges." *Race Relations Reporter,* May 3, 1971, 2-4.

Embree, E. R. and J. Waxman. *Investment in People: The Story of the Julius Rosenwald Fund.* New York: Harper and Brothers Company, 1949.

Engs, Robert F. *Educating the Disfranchised and Disinherited: Samuel Chapman Armstrong and Hampton Institute, 1839-1893.* Knoxville, TN: University of Tennessee Press, 1999.

Fishel Jr., L. H. and Benjamin Quarles, edited. The Negro American: a Documentary History. Glenview, IL: Scott, Foresman and Company, 1967.

Fisher, J. E. *The John F. Slater Fund: A Nineteenth Century Affirmative Action for Negro Education.* Lanham, MD: University Press of America, 1986.

Fleming, Cynthia G. "A Survey of the Beginnings of Tennessee's Black Colleges and Universities, 1865-1920." *Tennessee Historical Quarterly* 39/1 (1980): 195-207.

Franklin, John Hope and Alfred A. Moss Jr. *From Slavery to Freedom: A History of African Americans.* 7th edition. New York: McGraw-Hill, Inc., 1994.

Garibaldi, Antoine M. *The Revitalization of Teacher Education Programs at Historically Black Colleges: Four Case Studies.* Atlanta GA: Southern Education Foundation, 1989.

Goldfield, David. *Still Fighting the Civil War: The American South and Southern History.* Baton Rouge: Louisiana State University Press, 2002.

Goldman, Roger. *Thurgood Marshall: Justice for All.* New York: Carroll and Graf Publishers, Inc., 1992.

Guterl, Matthew P. *The Color of Race in America, 1900-1910.* Cambridge, MA: Harvard University Press, 2002.

Halberstam, David. *The Children.* New York: Fawcett Books, 1998.

Harlan, Louis R. edited, *The Booker T. Washington Paper*s. Urbana: University of Illinois Press, 1972-1985.

Hartshorn, W. Newton and George W. Penniman, editors. *An Era of Progress and Promise, 1863-1910: The Religious, Moral and Educational Development of the American Negro Since Emancipation.* Boston, MA: the Priscilla Company, 1910.

Harris, Leonard. *The Philosophy of Alain Locke: Harlem Renaissance and Beyond.* Philadelphia, PA: Temple University Press, 1989.

Hauke, Kathleen A. edited, *Ted Poston: A First Draft.* Atlanta, GA: University of Georgia Press, 2002.

Hawkins, Hugh edited, *Booker T. Washington and His Critics: Black Leadership in Crisis.* Lexington, MA: D. C. Heath and Company, 1974.

Hine, Darlene Clark, William C. Hine, and Stanley Harrold, *The African-American Odyssey* combined volume. Upper Saddle River, NJ: Prentice Hall, 2000.

Jackson, Cynthia L. and E. F. Nunn, *Historically Black Colleges and Universities: A Reference Handbook.* Santa Barbara, CA: ABC-CLIO, 2003.

Jenkins, Earnestine. "The Voice of Memphis: WDIA, Nat D. Williams, and Black Radio Culture in the Early Civil Rights Era." *Tennessee Historical Quarterly*, 65/1 (2006): 254-267.

Jenkins, Martin D. "The Participation of Negro Land-Grant Colleges in Permanent Federal Education Funds," *Journal of Negro Education* 7/1 (1938): 282-291.

Johnson Sr., Charles W. *The Spirit of a Place Called Meharry: The Strength of Its Past to Shape the Future.* Franklin, TN: Hillsboro Press, 2000.

Jones, Lance G. E. *The Jeanes Teacher in the United States, 1908-1933.* Chapel Hill, NC: University of North Carolina Press, 1937.

Lamon, Lester C. "The Tennessee Agricultural and Industrial Normal School: Public Education for Black Tennesseans," *Tennessee Historical Quarterly* 32/1 (1973): 42-58.

Lewis, David L. *W. E. B. Du Bois, Biography of a Race, 1868-1919.* New York: Henry Holt & Company, 1993.

Lewis, Dwight and Susan Thomas. *A Will to Win.* Nashville, TN: Cumberland Press, 1983.

Lockett, Patricia W. and M. McHollin, edited, *In Their Own Voices: An Account of the Presence of African Americans in Wilson County.* Lebanon, TN: authors, 1999.

Lloyd, Raymond Grann. *Tennessee Agricultural and Industrial State University, 1912-1962: Fifty Years of Leadership through Excellence.* Nashville: Tenn. A. & I. State University, 1962.

Lovett, Bobby L. *The African American History of Nashville, Tennessee, 1780-1930.* Fayetteville, AR: University of Arkansas Press, 1999.

Lovett, Bobby L. "Tennessee State University," *The Tennessee Encyclopedia of History and Culture*, C. Van West, edited. Nashville: Tennessee Historical Society, Rutledge Hill Press, 1998.

Lovett, Bobby L. and W. T. Wynn, edited. *Profiles of African Americans in Tennessee.* Nashville: Local Conference on Afro-American Culture and History, 1996.

Lovett, Bobby L. "James Carroll Napier (1845-1940): From Plantation to City," Randy Finley and Thomas. A. DeBlack, editors, *The Southern Elite and Social Change.* Fayetteville, AR: University of Arkansas Press, 2002.

Lovett, Bobby L. *A Black Man's Dream: The Story of R. H. Boyd and the National Baptist Publishing Board.* Nashville, TN: Mega Publishing Company, 1993.

Lovett, Bobby L. "Wilma Glodean Rudolph," *The Scribner Encyclopedia of American Lives*, vol. 4. New York: Charles Scribner Sons, 2001.

Lovett, Bobby L. *The Civil Rights Movement in Tennessee: A Narrative History.* Knoxville: University of Tennessee Press, 2005.

Martin, M. D. "Enrollment in Negro Colleges and Universities, 1937-1938," *Journal of Negro Education* 7/1 (January 1938): 118-123.

McDougald, Lois C. *A Time-Line Study of the Tennessee A. & I. State University, 1909-1951.* Nashville: Tennessee State University Printing, 1981.

Mims, Edwin. *History of Vanderbilt University.* Nashville: Vanderbilt University Press, 1946.

Morrison, Richard D. *Walking in the Wilderness, An Autobiography of Richard David Morrison.* Huntsville, AL: author, 1993.

Neufeldt, Harvey and C. Dickinson, *The Search for Identity: A History of Tennessee Technological University 1915-1986.* Memphis, TN: Memphis State University Press, 1991.

Nettles, Michael T., and Katherine Millett. *Preparing HBCUs to Address the Crisis of African American Education through Higher Standards in Teacher Education.* Atlanta, GA: United Negro College Fund, 2002.

Nettles, Michael T. and L. W. Perna, eds. *African American Education Data Book*. 3 volumes. Atlanta: Frederick D. Patterson Research Institute United Negro College Fund, 1997.

Osborne, W. P., C. L. Osborn, and Luie Hargraves, edited. *Contributions of Blacks in Hamblen County, 1796 to 1996*. Morristown, TN: Progressive Business Association, 1995.

Preer, Jean L. *Lawyers vs. Educators: Black Colleges and Desegregation in Public Higher Education*. Westport, CT: Greenwood Press, 1982.

Posey, Josephine M. *Against Great Odds: The History of Alcorn State University*. Jackson: University Press of Mississippi, 1994.

Richardson, Joe M. *A History of Fisk University, 1865-1946*. University, AL: University of Alabama Press, 1980.

Rosgin, Don. *Invisible Men: Life in Baseball's Negro Leagues*. New York: Kodansha International, 1983, 1995.

Rowan, Carl T. *South of Freedom*. New York: Knopf, Inc., 1952, 1980.

Samuel, Albert L. *Is Separate Unequal? Black Colleges and the Challenge to Desegregation*. Dubuque, IA: W. C. Brown, 1968.

Shannon, Samuel H. "Land-Grant College Education and Black Tennesseans: A Case Study in the Politics of Education," *History of Education Quarterly* 22/1 (1982): 139-157.

Shannon, Samuel H. "Agricultural and Industrial Education of Tennessee State University during The Normal School Phase, 1912-1922," Ph.D. dissertation, George Peabody College, 1974.

Smith, James W., edited. *Leadership and Learning: An Interpretive History of Historically Black Land-Grant Colleges and Universities—A Centennial Study*. Washington, DC: The National Association of State Universities and Land-Grant Colleges, 1993.

Southern Education Foundation. *Unintended Consequences: Perspectives on Teacher Testing and Historically Black Colleges and Universities*. Atlanta, GA: SEF, 2003.

Southern Education Foundation. *Ending Discrimination in Higher Education: A Report from Ten States, 1974*. Atlanta, GA: SEF, 1974.

Strickland, Arvarh E. edited. *Selling Black History for Carter G. Woodson: A Diary, 1930-1933, Lorenzo J. Greene*. Columbia, MO: University of Missouri Press, 1996.

Taylor, Carmelia G. "A History of Graduate Studies at Tennessee State University from 1935 to 1986." Ph.D. dissertation, Tennessee State University, 1995.

The Marcus Garvey and Universal Negro Improvement Association. Berkeley, CA: University of California Press, 1983-1989.

Thompson, Charles H. "The History of the National Basketball Tournaments for Black High Schools." Ph.D. dissertation, Louisiana State University, 1980.

Tushnet, Mark V. *The NAACP's Legal Strategy against Segregated Education, 1925-1950*. Chapel Hill, NC: University of North Carolina Press, 1987.

UT, The University of Tennessee Sesqui-centennial, 1794-1944. Knoxville: University of Tennessee Press, 1945.

Waller, James. "The History of Intercollegiate Basketball at Tennessee State University from 1925 to 1978," M.A. thesis, Tennessee State University, 1975.

Watson, Griff. "a Profile of World War I Casualties from Nashville and Davidson County, Tennessee." Tennessee State University Library, Special Collection, 1983.

Wells, Jovita. *A School for Freedom: Morristown College and Five Generations of Education for Blacks, 1868-1985*. Morristown, TN: Morristown College, 1986.

White, James H. *Up from a Cotton Patch: J. H. White and the Development of Mississippi Valley State College.* Itta Bena, MS: J. H. White, 1979.

Williams, Frank B. *East Tennessee State University: A University's Story, 1911-1980.* Johnson City, TN: East Tennessee State University, 1991.

Williams, Juan and D. Ashley, *I'll Find a Way or Make One: A Tribute to Historically Black Colleges and Universities.* New York: HarperCollins, 2004.

Williams, Juan. *Thurgood Marshall: American Revolutionary.* New York: Random House, 1998.

Woodson, Carter G. *The Mis-Education of the Negro.* Washington, DC: Association for the Study of Negro Life and History, 1933.

Yerby, Frank G. "The Little Theatre in the Negro College." M.A., Thesis, Fisk University, 1938.

Government Documents

Southern Education Foundation Records, 1882-1979, Atlanta University Center, Robert W. Woodruff Library, Atlanta, Georgia.

Record Group 51, Tennessee, Department of Education Records, 1873-1978, RG 51, Tennessee State Library and Archives, Nashville.

Record Group 92, State Department of Education and Board of Education Records and Papers, 1873-1978. Tennessee State Library and Archives, Nashville.

Record Group 273, State Board of Education Record and Minutes, 1874-1984, Tennessee State Library and Archives, Nashville.

Tennessee, Governors' Papers, Tennessee State Library and Archives, Nashville, www.tennessee.gov/tsla.

Tennessee, *Messages of the Governors of Tennessee.* Nashville: the Tennessee Historical Commission, 1972, 1990.

Tennessee, *Senate and House Journals.* Nashville, TN: state printer, 1865-2008.

Tennessee Higher Education Commission, *Annual Desegregation Monitoring Reports*, 1985- 1998, Nashville.

Tennessee Department of Education. *Report Card 2002: a Summary of Tennessee's Public School Systems.* Nashville: Department of Education, 2002.

Tennessee Caucus of Black State Legislators. *Report of Findings of the 125th Anniversary Legislative Retreat and Training Conference: "Securing Prosperity for our Children in the 21st Century."* Nashville, TN: The Office of Minority Affairs, 1999.

U.S. Bureau of Education, *Survey of Negro Colleges and Universities, Bulletin No. 7.* Washington, DC: Government Printing Office, 1928.

U.S. Bureau of Education, *National Survey of the Higher Education of Negroes.* Washington: General Printing Office, 1942.

U.S. Department of Education, National Center for Education Statistics. Washington, D.C. www.nces.gov

U.S. *Report on Economic Conditions of the South.* Washington, DC: National Emergency Council, 1938.

U.S. Commission on Civil Rights. *The Black/White Colleges: Dismantling the Dual System of Higher Education.* Publication No. 66. Washington, DC: Civil Rights Commission, 1981. www.usccr.gov.

U.S. Department of Interior. Historic Preservation: Cost to Restore Historic Properties at Historically Black Colleges and Universities. Washington, DC: General Accounting Office, 1998. www.doi.gov/diversity.

U.S. Department of Education. *Historically Black Colleges and Universities, 1976-2001* Washington, DC: USDOE, National Center for Education Statistics, 2004.

U.S. House of Representative, Subcommittee on Select Education, Committee on Education and the Workforce. *Distance Education: Challenges for Minority Serving Institutions and Implications for Federal Education Policy.* Washington, DC: House of Representatives, October 6, 2003.

U.S. Census Bureau. *Quick Facts.* Decennial Census, 1910-2010. Washington, DC: GPO, 2010.

Special Collections, Correspondence, and Personal Papers

Davis, Walter S. President of Tennessee A. & I. State University, 1943-1968. Special Collections, Tennessee State University.

Floyd, Otis L. President of Tennessee State University, 1986-1990. Special Collections, Tennessee State University.

Hale, William J. President of Tennessee A. & I. State College, 1911-1943. Special Collections, Tennessee State University Library.

Hefner, James A. President of Tennessee State University 1991-2005. The TSULSC reported that J. A. Hefner removed boxes of his papers from Tennessee State University Library, Special Collections soon after the financial controversy and his resignation, 2005.

Humphries, Frederick S. President of Tennessee State University, 1975-1986, Special Collections, Tennessee State University Library.

Torrence, Andrew J. President of Tennessee State University, 1968-1975. Special Collections, Tennessee State University Library.

Looby, Z. Alexander. Papers, 1900-1972. Fisk University Library, Special Collections.

Lovett, Bobby L. Collection, 1973-1984. Tennessee State University Library, Special Collections.

Robinson, Clarence B. Papers, 1934-1985. Tennessee State University Library, Special Collections.

Robinson, Walter C. Papers, 1927-1962. Tennessee State University, Special Collections.

Smith, Kelly Miller, Papers, 1921-1984. Vanderbilt University, Special Collections. See SNCC newsletters,

Temple, Edward S. Papers and Collections, 1950- . Tennessee State University Library, Special Collections.

Tennessee Caucus of Black State Legislators, *Report of the Annual Retreat.* Nashville: Tennessee State University, 1982-1998. Tennessee State University Library, Special Collections.

Shannon, Samuel H. Oral History Collection. Tennessee State University Library, Special Collections.

Williams, Avon N. Jr. Papers, 1922-1994. Tennessee State University Library, Special Collections.

www.tnstate.edu/library. Special Collections

Index